D1566463

DOOLALLY SAHIB AND THE BLACK ZAMINDAR

DOOLALLY SAHIB AND THE BLACK ZAMINDAR

Racism and Revenge in the British Raj

M.J. AKBAR

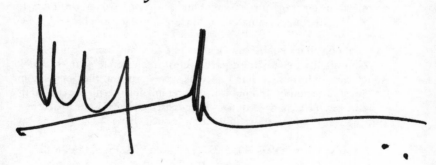

BLOOMSBURY

NEW DELHI • LONDON • OXFORD • NEW YORK • SYDNEY

BLOOMSBURY INDIA
Bloomsbury Publishing India Pvt. Ltd
Second Floor, LSC Building No. 4, DDA Complex, Pocket C – 6 & 7,
Vasant Kunj, New Delhi 110070

BLOOMSBURY, BLOOMSBURY INDIA and the Diana logo are
trademarks of Bloomsbury Publishing Plc

First published in India 2022
This edition published 2022

ISBN: HB: 978-93-54355-27-1; e-Book: 978-93-54355-28-8
2 4 6 8 10 9 7 5 3 1

Printed and bound in India by Thomson Press India Ltd.

MIX
Paper from
responsible sources
FSC® C010615

To find out more about our authors and books, visit
www.bloomsbury.com and sign up for our newsletters

For Gazala and Lokesh Sharma,
my sister and brother-in-law,
with more love than words can express

Praise for M.J. Akbar's
Gandhi's Hinduism the Struggle Against Jinnah's Islam

'This is a masterly book, with fresh insights and sound conclusions. It is judgmental in a very sophisticated way. Finally, no similar book has ever been written.'

K. Natwar Singh, author and former Minister for External Affairs, in *Hindustan Times*

'The book intricately explains the events leading to partition between 1940 and 1947, by conducting a thorough investigation from archives and original sources.

By doing this it also contrasts the ideological belief of Gandhi (who believed in faith, civilizational harmony) and Jinnah (who believed in a nation based on religion). I am enjoying reading your book.'

Sharad Pawar, former Chief Minister of Maharashtra, Union Minister for Defence and eminent national leader

'The book tells history as if it were a story. The heavy underpinning of information from various archives and primary sources makes the reader familiar with facts that are frequently ignored by professional historians in their writings on the events of the Partition of India.'

The Tribune

'... M.J. Akbar's book is a labour of love suffused with enviable erudition.'

Ishtiaq Ahmed, Professor Emeritus of Political Science, Stockholm University, *Daily Times*

'M.J. Akbar's latest book, *Gandhi's Hinduism the Struggle Against Jinnah's Islam*, offers a unique perspective, laced with interesting anecdotes, of a largely familiar narrative, by juxtaposing the contrasting roles of Gandhi and Mohammed Ali Jinnah in...'

Deccan Herald

'The book analyses both the ideology and the personality of those who shaped the fate of the region, and spells out the blunders, lapses and conscious chicanery that permeated the politics of seven explosive years between 1940 and 1947.'

India Today

'In this tale, there are no heroes; only villains. The British justification for Partition was that pre-Partition Indian leadership could not agree among themselves. That, in essence, was why it happened. Akbar breaks idols and shreds received wisdom in this authoritative book.'

The Statesman

'...Akbar tells this story with his usual diligence about facts and facets and his customary lucidity.'

Business Standard

'Akbar's latest book, *Gandhi's Hinduism the Struggle Against Jinnah's Islam* is a brilliant read and offers some of the most interesting, exclusive details of events leading to India's independence.'

Sunday Guardian

Contents

Acknowledgements   xi

Preface   xiii

1. The Wise Fly   1

2. The Punch and Vindaloo Show   29

3. English Intoxication, Indian Hallucination   61

4. Beef, Beer, Ham and Baboo Hurry Mohan   86

5. Love, Doolaly and the Coloured Races   117

6. Gifts of Fortune in a Land of Regrets   147

7. I Don't Care a *Damree*!   175

8. Service with a Wile   204

9. Justice Pulbandi and the Black Zamindar   234

10. Charpoy Cobra: Life After War   267

11. The Englishman in India Has No Home and
    Leaves No Memory   298

Notes   329

Index   353

Acknowledgements

The pandemic of the last two years has been shadowed by a constant ache: Mallika and I have been unable to meet our delightful and loving grandsons Julian and Kayan, our beautiful (if occasionally stern) daughter Mukulika and her husband Carl Nordenberg who has become such a good friend over many a spirited evening. They live in Singapore. Technology has elided across time and space, but, paradoxically, the net effect is also a reminder of the warmth we have missed because of distance. Hopefully, 2022 will release us from the fetters of contagion.

The great enchantment of these years was watching our third grandson, Agastya, turn from an infant into a child whose innate intelligence began to filter into observation, perspectives, and conversation, while his emotions matured into love for his Papa, Prayaag, his Mama, Shanta, his 'Didi' Pushpa, and for his grandparents. Is there any phase of life more exciting than the transition from 18 to 42 months? For Mallika and me, being with Agastya, Shanta and Prayaag at our home in Goa was a joy. It helped hugely in the making of this book as well.

All through the painful pleasure of the writing process, Mallika was a continuous reference point. When she did not like a passage she was candid with her softly spoken and sharply effective remarks. Mallika is the anchor of love which sustains our family in an embrace which includes my beloved elder sisters Sajda Baji in Patna, Wajda Baji and Saadat Baji in Kolkata, and Mallika's brother Dr Madhu John in California.

I cannot sufficiently thank Paul Vijay Kumar of Bloomsbury for his quiet persistence and assistance in the evolution of this book;

and am beholden to Rajiv Beri, who heads Bloomsbury in India, and the gracious Prabir Bambhal, for their trust and encouragement. Ravi Mishra gave invaluable help from one of the finest libraries in Delhi.

I am deeply grateful to my sagacious elders Ajit Doval and Nripendra Mishra for their affection and their advice. This has meant more to me than perhaps they realise. Each of my regular conversations with Kunwar Natwar Singh, who has always indulged me with a benevolent and affectionate eye, left me with greater knowledge and more understanding. Thank you, sirs.

Friends are the nurture of life, and one feels blessed that—covid notwithstanding—the circle has grown: Habib Rehman, Sunil and Geeta Gujral, Tapan Chaki, Rani Mitra, S. Prasannarajan, Tony Jesudasan, Arif Vazirally, Y.S. Chowdary, Kiran Vadodaria, Subhash Chandra, Rajeev Shukla, Chuti Ray, Rajni and Vidya Gupta, Devesh Kumar, Manjushri and S.M. Basu, Mohandas Pai, Suman Bhattacharya, Freddy Svagne, Gopal Hosur, Naresh Gujral, Satpal Malik, Satish Gupta, Ranjan Bhattacharya, Jamshed Zaidi, Anil Bhasin, Veenu Sandal, Ranjan Mukherjee, Anil Shetty, Tariq Mansoor, Bilahari Kausikan, K.P. Nayar, Preet Malik, Ashok Swarup, Praveen Saini, Rajinder Chaudhury, Manoj Arora, Darren Rickards, Lakshman Menon, Rahul Bhatia, Gautam Kapoor, Prof. Dheeraj Sharma, Jawid Laiq, Pankaj Mehra, Partha Mitra, Shashi Shrivastava, Apurba Jasraj, Omer Haider, Alok Banerjee, Abdul Khaliq, Virendra Kapoor, Surya Prakash, Majeed Memon, Tayyab Khan, Joyeeta Basu. There are so many friends to whom I owe a particular debt, and each will know why: Shobhana Bhartiya, Raian Karanjawala, Rajiv Nayar, Sanjiv Goenka, Geeta Luthra, Sandeep Kapur, Ram Madhav, Rajiv Kapoor, Tejinder Singh, Naem Nizam, Akash Chopra, Awanish Dwivedi, Vishveswar Bhat.

There are two names missing. You will find them in the dedication. Thank you, everyone.

Preface

As the Bishop Told His Wife

The voice of high church in 19th-century England was often the voice of a humane conscience. Few British accounts of their remarkable Indian experience are more observant, rational and sympathetic than the journals of the second Anglican bishop of British India. If this Oxford scholar had been appointed governor-general during the 1820s, the British Raj might have evolved a less provocative and prejudiced culture. But Bishop Heber was merely a viceroy of God, not plenipotentiary of a multinational.

On Monday, 16 June 1823, the Right Rev. Reginald Heber, Lord Bishop of Calcutta, his wife Amelia and young daughter Emily, accompanied by friends and relatives, went by the Ramsgate steamboat to board the *Thomas Grenville* at Lower Hope. Two evenings later, the winds turned favourable, and the *Grenville* sailed for India.

The bishop's reading list for the 15-week trip to Bengal was eclectic, ranging from Walter Scott's 'amusing' *Quentin Durward* to the instructive *Gilchrist's Hindoostanee Guide*, which included a translation of an Urdu ghazal by Nawab Asaf [Asif] ud-Daula, a former ruler of Awadh. Heber conceded that the Urdu refrain '*ruhe ruhe*' was untranslatable but was charmed by the wistful lines on the evanescent nature of love and life. It was a glimpse into Indian sensibility:

In the world mayest thou, beloved!
Live exempt from grief and pain

On my lips the breath is fleeting,—can it,
will it long remain.[1]

They anchored at the coastal island of 'Sauger', or Sagar, at the point where the river Hooghly decants into the Bay of Bengal, at daybreak on 4 October after a night of thunder and lightning. Almost the first thing Bishop Heber saw under a 'hot and copper sky' was a more prosaic view of India, a human corpse floating down the 'coffee-coloured water'. At noon villagers came aboard to sell fresh fish and fruit. The bishop, in contrast to his countrymen, found that the 'deep bronze tint is more naturally agreeable to the human eye than the fair skins of Europe'. The most interesting visitor, 'a man dressed in muslin, who spoke good English, and said he was Sircar, came down in quest of employment, if any of the officers on board would intrust their investments to him, or if any body chose to borrow money at 12 per cent'.[2]

India had arrived. Business had begun.

Bishop Heber saw Arab and Maldivian trading ships heading upriver and heard Brahmins prophesy that the Hooghly would rise 'fourteen cubits higher, and drown all Calcutta'[3]. Heber commented, archly, that such a phenomenon would drown half of Bengal as well, but the soothsayers seemed interested only in the fate of British Calcutta. He noted that Indians liked potatoes, introduced by the Portuguese, the 'best thing which the country has ever received from its European masters', but sat for dinner with their knees drawn up, 'like monkeys'[4]. When they stopped at a riverbank, the priest found that Hindus would not allow him into their homes.[5]

He was beginning to discover what the books did not tell him.

Calcutta was more welcoming. On 10 October, a parade of servants paid obeisance as the prelate entered his official residence: *sirdar bearer* (head of waiters), *chobdars* (macebearers), *sataburdars*, *hurkuras* (messengers and those who carried silver sticks before a

---

[1] Reginald Heber, *Narrative of a Journey Through the Upper Provinces of India from Calcutta to Bombay, 1824–1825* (Philadelphia, 1829), 30.

[2] Ibid., 42–43.

[3] Ibid., 47.

[4] Ibid., 47.

[5] Ibid., 50.

person of rank), *khansamas* (stewards), *abdars* (who cooled the water), *sharabdars* (who brought alcohol), *khitmutgars* (footmen). Emily was assigned an ayah, a bearer, a footman, a silver stick and a cook. A *sircar* (financial agent) was soon present with an offer to manage transactions. A Bengali newspaper editor appeared 'with a large silken and embroidered purse full of silver coins', but this was a pretend-gift 'in order that we might go through the form of receiving it, and replacing it in his hands', a relic of the old custom of never 'approaching a superior without a present'. Duty done, the editor wanted the money back.[6]

The bishop and the Bengali were exploring in early manoeuvres the space between substance and shadow.

The servants were obedient, but not quite what they seemed. Though slavery had been abolished in British territories, Heber wrote, the language and gestures of servants were redolent of a past age: 'I am thy slave' or 'Thy slave hath no knowledge'. He entered a caveat: 'In general, however, I do not think that the Bengalee servants are more submissive or respectful to their masters than those of Europe.' The phrases represented polite if ornate custom, not servitude. The hands folded 'in an attitude of prayer' or bare feet trotting across the house were merely akin to removing one's hat or bowing in England.[7]

On 20 November, during a visit to Calcutta's newly created Botanical Garden in the company of Lady Amherst, the bishop made a startling observation without being unduly startled by it.

Such public spaces

> used to be all cultivated by the convicts in chains... In the Botanic Garden their labour is now supplied by peasants hired by the day or week, and the exchange is found cheap, as well as otherwise advantageous and agreeable: the labour of freemen here, as elsewhere, being infinitely cheaper than that of slaves.[8]

Within five weeks of reaching Calcutta, the bishop had learnt a central truth about British colonialism without fully grasping its implications.

---

[6] Ibid., 54.
[7] Ibid., 59–60.
[8] Ibid, 70.

Hiring peasants was 'infinitely cheaper' than the cost of using chained convicts or slave labour. This was not an accident of market forces. This was a consequence of conscious policy. Wages were suppressed to subsistence level from the onset of empire.

In 1759, or within two years of winning the battle of Plassey in 1757 and becoming masters of Bengal, the East India Company passed an order placing a cap on salaries, adding that it would withdraw its protection from any employer who violated this regulation. Astonishingly, wages for Indians remained the same for more than a century and did not rise to any great extent even after a hundred years. This was why even a modestly paid official could keep a domestic retinue beyond the imagination of an equal in Britain. Even Bishop Heber was surprised by the number of servants at his residence.

Low wages and punitive taxes left the impoverished with no surplus to survive a crisis such as drought, leading directly to the death of millions by mass starvation during horrific famines through two centuries of British rule. The callous Company compounded such crime by total indifference towards any form of famine relief. The starving were left to their own devices.

In March 1824, Bishop Heber met a 'Brahmin from Madras, now in Calcutta soliciting subscriptions for the sufferers of famine on the Coromandel coast'. The conscientious Bishop felt duty-bound 'to subscribe, if it were only to show them that in such undertakings Christians would gladly co-operate with them, and even intrust their money to their distribution'.[9] Bishop Heber's generosity towards Indians was so unusual that it became famous through the country. One Indian told this man of God and goodwill 'that my fame had gone through all the country, and that I was considered as the only great man who had come from foreign parts to Lucknow, with less disposition to take than to give money. "Most of them," he said, "come to strip us poor people"'.[10]

The Indian was right. The East India Company stripped the poor.

From one informed, descriptive and objective journal the tense, multi-faceted tapestry of the British Raj begins to take shape.

---

[9] Ibid., 94.
[10] Ibid., 362.

The bishop got his first elephant ride in 'Barrackpoor', in the company of Lord Amherst; the governor-general's splendid ten-foot-high mount was a gift from the 'king of Oude' (Awadh). During this visit to the cantonment town outside Calcutta from 28 October, the bishop also encountered his first cobra, which was sighted and killed.[11] Over the next fortnight, Bishop Heber witnessed a different kind of poison, racism, in the appalling British attitude towards their own 'half-caste' children, because half their blood had come from an Indian mother. 'I have never met,' writes Bishop Heber, 'with any public man connected with India, who did not lament the increase of the half-caste population, as a great source of present mischief and future danger to the tranquillity of the colony.'[12]

In an astonishing mind-warp, the British were convinced that their mixed-breed children, then called 'Eurasian' and now 'Anglo-Indian', had inherited the worst of both genes. Living evidence that this was an utter fabrication did nothing to change minds suffused with the doctrine of white supremacy. The finest, most exceptional example of Anglo-Indian brilliance was born in Calcutta in 1778, only five years before Reginald Heber was born in England.

James Skinner was denied a commission in the Company army because while his father Hercules, a lieutenant-colonel, was a Scotsman, his mother Jeany was a Rajput. The government had banned recruitment of Anglo-Indians to its forces when Lord Cornwallis was governor-general. James, deeply disappointed but determined to emulate his father, joined the cavalry of the ruler of Gwalior, Maharajdhiraj Daulat Rao Scindia. Skinner's talent came to the notice of General Gerard Lake, commander of British forces in the wars with the Marathas. Unable to induct him directly, Lord Lake asked James Skinner to raise his own cavalry unit, so that they could fight alongside the British. First Skinner's Horse was raised on 23 February 1803; the Second Skinner's Horse in 1814, with the inspirational motto *Himmat-e-mardan, maddad-e-Khuda!* (The courage of man, and the help of God!). In an astounding display of hypocrisy, the British were happy to use an Anglo-Indian as an ally but never ready to give their own flesh and blood equality.

---

[11] Ibid., 61, 63.
[12] Ibid., 64.

Paradoxically, the East India Company displayed no such hesitation about recruiting Indians—the sepoys who fought at Plassey or Buxar or Seringapatnam or Alwaye or Delhi were mainly from Bihar and Awadh. For reasons which the sahib expressed but never explained, Bengalis were kept out of army ranks. Bishop Heber was clearly a bit puzzled and sought the reason: 'I have, indeed, understood from many quarters, that the Bengalees are regarded as the greatest cowards in India; and that partly owing to this reputation, and partly to their inferior size, Sepoy regiments are always recruited from Bahar [Bihar] and the upper provinces.'[13]

The British were not alone—the Portuguese were as vehemently prejudiced and contradictory. On the one hand, Fray Sebastien Manrique was in awe of Dhaka merchants with such wealth that they weighed their money rather than counted it. He admired the skill and industry of Bengali craftspeople: 'The inhabitants [of Bengal], both men and women, are wondrously adroit in all manufactures, such as cotton cloth and silks, and in needlework, such as embroideries, which are worked so skilfully, down to the smallest stitches, that nothing prettier is to be seen anywhere.'[14]

Thirty pages later, however, Bengalis turned into

a languid race and pusillanimous, given up, as most Asiatic peoples are, to self-interest. The Bengalas are, therefore, mean-spirited and cowardly, more apt to serve than to command, and hence they easily accustom themselves to captivity and slavery. To be well and successfully served by them they should be treated rather with harshness than mildness; indeed this is so true that they have a very common saying, *Mare Tacur, na maare Cucur* [Strike and become a Thakur; don't strike and remain a dog].[15]

Manrique was influential in creating European notions about 'exotic' India:

---

[13] Ibid., 88.

[14] Sebastien Manrique, *Travels of Fray Sebastien Manrique 1629–1643*, Vol. 1, trans. C. Eckford Luard with H. Hosten, (Routledge, 2016), 34.

[15] Ibid., 64.

The [Bengali] men are not, generally speaking, naturally much addicted to sexual intercourse, but the women surpass them in this, and in order to secure their services employ various charms and drinks which they give to the men. These sometimes cause their death, or at any rate make them mad or ill for life.[16]

Such expertise extended to making an aphrodisiac from poppy seeds, a variation of *posto*, which increased potency for two or three years but left you rather limp subsequently, quite defeating its own purpose.[17]

As the first subjects of British rule, Bengalis created a particular niche in Indo-Anglian anthropology. At the top of the 'native' hierarchy was the Bengali 'Baboo' who acquired wealth as a business agent or partner of the British. He added Indian glitter to Calcutta society by hosting parties with English fare and Indian entertainment like the enticing nautch, or dance. Bishop Heber writes on 18 November 1824 that he kept away from a 'large' puja party given by Baboo Rouplal Mullick, because a Christian priest's presence might be construed as sanction to idolatry. Such scruples did not inhibit his pregnant wife (their second daughter was born in Calcutta in January 1825). When the music stopped, Amelia Heber could not comprehend why so much fuss was being made over nautch, although she was impressed by the low, sweet voice of a famous singer called Vikki, 'the Catalani of the east'.[18]

Bishop Heber, remarkably, was the first British dignitary to reach out to influential Indians as social equals, and he did so with grace. On 21 April 1825 he hosted a dinner party to mark his 42nd birthday. Lord and Lady Amherst were present. To everyone's shock, the guest list included 'several of the wealthy natives', for

no European of high station in Calcutta had previously paid [attention] to any of them... I introduced these Baboos to the Chief-justice, which pleased them much, though perhaps they were still better pleased with my wife herself presenting them

---

[16] Ibid., 66.
[17] Ibid., 59.
[18] Heber, 66–67.

XX

Preface

pawn [paan, or betel leaf], rose-water, and attar of rose before they went, after the native custom.[19]

This graciousness won Indian hearts.

That no sahib had ever invited Indians to such a social occasion nearly seven decades after the British conquest of Bengal, let alone introduced them to a chief justice, speaks for itself.

Bishop Heber went further and sought a meeting of minds. On the morning of 8 March 1825, he conversed with the wealthy, generous, convivial and well-educated Radhacant Deb. 'He is a young man of pleasing countenance and manners,' records the Bishop, 'speaks English well, and has read many of our popular authors, particularly historical and geographical. He lives a good deal with Europeans....'[20] Deb defended his faith and traditions, claiming that many aspects of Hinduism, like caste, had been misrepresented, and even attempted to justify *sati*. He admitted the beauty of Christian morality but was shocked by European indulgence in wine and beef and argued that it would not suit the people of India. Heber enjoyed the conversation, which included a passage on the intriguing sect of Freemasons, and they parted with 'mutual expressions of anxiety to meet again'.[21]

The bishop left Calcutta in June, with Dhaka as his first destination, to understand India and Indians. He found 'suttee' abundant in places like 'Ghazeepour'. The district magistrate, a Mr Melville, claimed he was helpless. The British had promulgated an ordinance 'commanding all persons celebrating a suttee to send in notice of their intention to the nearest police officer', but no punishment had been prescribed for disobedience. Moreover, the unscrupulous were using *sati* as a guise for murder when there was a prospect of dispute over inherited property. Crime encourages creativity. Variations had been introduced. They might burn a widow if the husband had died in a distant place by using 'his garments, his slippers, his walking staff' as a substitute for corpse.[22]

---

[19] Ibid., 99.
[20] Ibid., 92.
[21] Ibid., 93.
[22] Ibid., 240–41.

On 4 December 1829, the Bengal Sati Regulation banned this practice in all jurisdictions of British India. It was also the year in which the bishop's journal was published in London.

The young but wise bishop was careful about saving Indian souls in too much of a hurry, for any impression 'that we mean to impose Christianity on them by force' would retard the progress of conversion 'to an almost indefinite period'.[23] He was genuinely upset when he learnt that the principal mosque in Allahabad on the banks of the Jumna river had been turned into the residence of the general after the British took over. It then became an 'assembly-room' before it was restored as a mosque. 'Nevertheless', writes Heber, 'the original desecration was undoubtedly offensive and unjust; and the restitution a proper and popular measure.'[24]

Nothing in India was more labyrinthine than religion. Heber's 'Moonshee' introduced him to a book on *maya*, the 'Great Illusion', but the raw and physical aspects of religious practice were more prevalent than its philosophy. On 9 April 1825, Amelia and Reginald Heber went to the Calcutta maidan to witness the festival of 'Churruck Poojah' in honour of Goddess Kali. They saw devotees punish their bodies as 'miserable fanatics, torturing themselves in the most horrible manner, and each surround his own particular band of admirers, with music and torches'.[25]

The British could never comprehend the laissez-faire Indian attitude towards 'holy men', whether they took the form of impecunious beggars, fake madmen or genuine fakirs. Indians knew the difference, laughed away the dubious or the charlatan and revered the Hindu ascetic 'with a double quantity of dung and chalk on his face, who was singing in a plaintive monotonous tone to a little knot of peasants, who seemed to regard him with great veneration'.[26] In Benares, the bishop saw 'repeated instances of that penance of which I had heard much in Europe, of men with their legs or arms involuntarily distorted by keeping them in one position, and their hands clenched till the nails grew out at the backs'.[27] The ambivalence

---

[23] Ibid., 82.
[24] Ibid., 292.
[25] Ibid., 96.
[26] Ibid., 227.
[27] Ibid., 252.

never left British consciousness. In the 1930s, Winston Churchill underestimated a 'half-naked *fakir*' called Gandhi who could survive without food for three weeks.

The Indian mind worked on a very different trajectory from the British. One evening, Heber tried to push his oarsmen to row through the night because a sudden favourable breeze had arisen on the Ganges. He argued that one night's sail with such a tailwind was far better than a day's tracking. Mohammed, head of the oarsmen, answered: 'Yes, my lord, but toil is better than peril, and the eye of the day than the blindness of the night.'[28]

Indians were wary, for death lurked everywhere. In April 1824, cholera was ravaging the streets and shanties of Calcutta. Bishop Heber noted in his diaries: 'Few Europeans have yet died of it, but to all it is sufficiently near to remind us of our utter dependence on God's mercy, and how near we are in the midst of life to death!'[29] The bewildered bishop could never comprehend how scorpions, cockroaches, ants, spiders and snakes managed to enter his 16-oared pinnace: '...the idea of a snake in the boat seemed so improbable, that I attributed it to different causes, or to fancy.'[30]

Nothing, however, was improbable:

> I had heard at Patna of a lady who once lay a whole night with a *cobra di capello* under her pillow; she repeatedly thought during the night that something moved, and in the morning when she snatched her pillow away, she found the thick black throat, the square head, the green diamond-like eye, advanced within two inches of her neck. The snake was without malice, his hood was uninflated, and he was merely enjoying the warmth of his nest...[31]

The bishop always took leave of friends on his travels with a heavy heart, uncertain whether they would meet again. Amelia could not accompany her husband because of the potential risk to her infant. This was unfortunate for a loving couple but proved to be very

---

[28] Ibid., 179.
[29] Ibid., 99.
[30] Ibid., 280.
[31] Ibid., 280.

fortunate for posterity. Heber resolved to write detailed letters to her, which grew into the content of a book.

He reached Dhaka in 18 days, having tasted the local delicacy, *hilsa*, or sable fish, without being overly impressed. Nawab Shumsheddowlah (Shams ud-Daula), now living on a Company pension of Rs 10,000 a month, called on the bishop on the morning of 6 July, accompanied by his 30-year-old son. The 'good-looking elderly' nawab spoke fluent English and conversed about the Spanish war while smoking his hookah. They wore jewels on their turbans and 'splendid diamond rings'. At the end of their meeting, Bishop Heber offered the traditional *paan* and rosewater. The charmed nawab smiled and said: 'What, has your Lordship learned our customs?'[32]

The nawab of Dhaka had lost authority, but his entourage had not lost its chutzpah. His departure was accompanied with chants from the magical kingdom of nostalgia: 'Lion of war!', 'Prudent in Counsel!', 'High and Mighty Prince!' Every day the nawab sent baskets of fruit, pastry and 'dressed dishes' which did not quite suit the English palate: Heber could think of no better term for them than 'greasy dainties'.[33] On his farewell call, Bishop Heber gave the nawab his standard gift, a well-bound 'Hindoostanee' prayer-book. In return, he received 'trifles' like muslin and a walking stick made from a solid piece of beautifully carved ivory. There was no doubt about who was in power.[34]

We shall meet Bishop Heber intermittently through the book, as we examine the varied strands that, like a glistening cobweb, held the British Empire together but left wide gaps which might have been occupied by Indians but were left empty.

Had the bishop been a seer, he could have predicted how it would all end, for in Benaras he witnessed a traditional form of mass protest, whose logic he immediately recognized but whose impact he could not foretell. The government had just added to the economic burden with a heavy tax on houses, which was personal property. The Indian argument was unambiguous. If the British could tax a man's personal property today, they could well impose a tax on his children tomorrow.

---

[32] Ibid., 150–51.
[33] Ibid., 334.
[34] Ibid., 156.

'The whole population of Benares and its neighbourhood determined to sit *dhurna* till their grievances were redressed,' writes Bishop Heber. He was astonished by this unique demonstration of silence, self-denial and fasting by some 300,000 people. He continues:

To sit *dhurna* or mourning is to remain motionless in that posture, without food, and exposed to the weather, till the person against whom it is deployed consents to the request offered; and the Hindoos believe that whoever dies under such a process becomes a tormenting spirit to haunt and afflict his inflexible antagonist.[35]

It was a *bhook-hartal,* or hunger-strike.

The administration was perplexed. It could not send in police armed with batons or troops with guns because the protest was non-violent. On the other hand, any surrender would embolden Indians. There was relief when the *dhurna* began to dissipate due to inclement weather and prolonged hunger. Once the crisis abated, the Calcutta government turned sensible: 'The supreme Government followed up their success most wisely by a repeal of the obnoxious tax, and thus ended a disturbance which, if it had been harshly or improperly managed, might have put all India in a flame.'[36]

Bishop Heber realized what his 20th-century successors could not comprehend: that non-violent non-cooperation, led by a leader with steely resolve, could ignite India.

A French botanist, Victor Jacquemont, who came to India on an assignment from his government four years after Bishop Heber's sudden death in 1826, remarked perceptively in his letters to Paris that a Frenchman thought of himself first, while the Englishman regarded himself as alone. Bishop Heber asked himself a similar question when in Agra: whom did Indians prefer between the English and the French? The French, he concluded, might be 'often oppressive and avaricious' but were more popular than the English because many of them

had completely adopted the Indian dress and customs, and most of them were free from that exclusive and intolerant spirit, which the English, wherever they go, a caste by themselves,

[35] Ibid., 286–87.
[36] Ibid., 288.

disliking and disliked by their neighbours. Of this foolish, surly, national pride, I see but too many instances daily, and I am convinced it does us much harm in this country. We are not guilty of injustice or wilful oppression, but we shut out the natives from our society, and a bullying, insolent manner is continually assumed in speaking to them.[37]

Doolally Sahib was a caste by himself. Disliking and disliked. Foolish and surly with national pride. Bullying. Insolent. Insular. The Black Zemindar served, survived and lay in wait.

---

[37] Ibid., 491.

The Wise Fly

In life and its reflection, literature, music or poetry, the might of feudal India's rulers was traditionally tested by two voices raised on behalf of the people: the sage, empowered by a moral mystique, and the satirist, armed with pungent common sense. Whether sant, sufi or sadhu, the sage occupied a parallel realm, his authority derived from the divine right of mendicants. He identified with poverty and was rarely seen in court, although the court might send emissaries to him.

The wit sat in the company of kings, charged with the delicate and even dangerous responsibility of puncturing hubris without lese-majesty, while the redemptive twist in his tales entered the language and imagination of commoners. Humour was not rebellion—it was a bond of confidence which sought to prevent power from becoming pompous. Laughter was a reality check rather than doctrinaire disagreement or adversarial confrontation. Monarchs without tolerance for laughter lost their compact with the people. The wit was not a clown. The royal clown was tasked with making the king laugh; a satirist forced him to think. The greater a king, the more he needed a counterintuitive mind to preserve his benevolent rule. In the political lore of India, the iconic king was blessed with an iconic jester.

Such laughter spluttered during British rule, which grew from a revenue district of Bengal in 1757 to hegemony over the subcontinent within a hundred years. Master and subject still laughed, but generally at their own foibles or fate. Sometimes they laughed at each other, but rarely with each other. Nor did the British communicate with the ascetic, dismissing the Hindu 'holy man' as a regressive exhibit of heathen superstition playing 'magical' tricks upon the gullible and the Muslim pir as a relic who hid extremism in his beard.

The British were rarely in sync with Indian sensibility. Previous rulers, of whatever faith or community, had been lords with absolute rights. There was little distinction between the state treasury and their personal wealth. But even if they began as invaders, they learnt to adapt to the culture and kinship of their subjects, or *praja*, if they wanted to survive. The British ate differently, dressed differently, thought differently and indeed laughed for very different reasons from the Indian.

The most famous name in the hierarchy of Indian humour is Mahesh Das, better known as Birbal, one of the Navaratna, the nine brilliant jewels in the glittering court of Jalaluddin Akbar, the Mughal emperor from 1556 to 1605. Das, born in 1528, was a Bhatt-Brahmin (some accounts call him a Kayastha) from Kalpi who made his reputation as a poet at regional courts before coming to the attention of the monarch. Birbal rose quickly in royal affections, being appointed 'Kavi Raj' (Prince of Poets), and subsequently a commander of 2,000 horse with the title of 'Raja Birbal', or 'Birbar' (from *Vir Vara*, which means 'the best warrior').

Birbal's status can be gauged by the 25 honorifics before his name in a letter written by Abul Fazl on the emperor's behalf to another of the 'jewels', Mirza Abdur Rahim Khan-Khanan, praising Birbal for his poetry, wit and spiritual excellence. His influence can be equally measured by the vituperative jealousy of a foe, Abdul Qadir Badayuni, whose contrarian chronicle, *Muntakhabut Tawarikh,* is written from the perspective of those who opposed the inclusive policies central to Akbar's statecraft. Badayuni can barely conceal his bile against the Brahmin, Birbal, who rose inexorably till Akbar treated him as 'flesh of my flesh, and blood of my blood'.

Neither Abul Fazl nor Badayuni record any specific Birbal anecdote, although Abul Fazl notes that Birbal stories were popular and later commentators affirm their wide currency. Perhaps jokes were not considered worthy of inclusion in the rarefied literary environment of the royal narrative.

Birbal was both a real personality and a metaphor, whose repartee symbolized the right to tell the mightiest monarch that he was only human. It did not matter whether the stories were apocryphal; what is relevant is that they were believed. Whether literary, homely or political, they served as a synchronized engagement between absolute authority and cleverly crafted counterpoint. An emperor's trust offered space for careful indulgence. This delicate balance was woven into the tapestry of courteous language and exquisitely measured etiquette.

Once, during dinner, Akbar sniffed disparagingly at a dish of brinjals. Birbal obediently denounced the brinjal as a vegetable from hell, unworthy of a lord as magnificent as His Majesty. A few weeks later, at another meal, Akbar praised brinjals as delicious. Birbal went into raptures. Akbar reminded Birbal of his previous criticism. 'Sire,' replied Birbal, 'this brinjal is not my emperor. You are.'

Prof. C.M. Naim, professor emeritus at Chicago University, has cited some instances of ego-deflation in his essay, *Popular Jokes and Political History: The Case of Akbar, Birbal and Mulla Do-Piyaza.*[1]

Some stories pirouette around literary devices like subtle puns or riddles wrapped in phonetic gauze. Akbar once asked Birbal to answer two questions in one sentence: *Brahmin kyon pyaasa? Gadha kyon udasa?* (Why was the Brahmin thirsty? Why was the donkey sad?). Birbal replied: *Lota na tha* (He did not have a *lota*). *Lota* is the Hindi for metal pot from which the Brahmin could drink—he was thirsty as he did not have one. But *lota* is also a verb, meaning 'rolling in the dust'—the donkey was sad as he had not been able to roll in the dust. Birbal proved more than a match in a linguistic joust.

Akbar and Birbal were once enjoying a boat ride on the Jamuna river when a *mala* (garland) floated past. The emperor said, *Birbal, mala de* (Birbal, bring me a garland). If, however, you break up *mala*, into *ma* and *la*, it also means 'Birbal, bring your mother'. Birbal replied: *Jahan-numa, bahne do* (Lord of the World, let it float). *Bahne* is also a Hindi term for sisters and could thus imply, 'Bring your sisters'. No fingerprints on the stiletto.

Birbal's ripostes were comfort food for the people from the high table of an empire. His verbal victories were reassuring evidence of the limits of power, while the emperor rose in esteem because these encounters were proof of his innate humility.

Akbar and his son Saleem were out hunting. As the day became warm, they handed their coats to Birbal. Akbar told Birbal that the weight of the coats seemed as heavy as an ass-load. Birbal replied: 'No, Your Majesty, it was likely to be of two asses.'

When the emperor announced that he had merged two months into one in his new calendar, Birbal commented that this was extremely gracious of His Majesty: previously people enjoyed fifteen days of moonlight, now they could have thirty.

Such stories were buttressed by facts which reinforced the relationship in the public consciousness. Prof. Naim narrates an incident he has sourced to an 18th-century manuscript. It was once suggested to Birbal that he convert to Islam. Birbal replied, 'Your Majesty, I am already totally devoted to you, but I shall not recite the *kalima* that would ruin my religion.' Birbal wins plaudits for integrity, and Akbar for honouring that integrity.

Birbal received special privileges. In Fatehpur Sikri, the new capital, Birbal was favoured with a residence near the emperor's palace. Akbar was Birbal's guest on four occasions, an honour not bestowed on any other noble. Akbar once risked his life to save Birbal from being trampled by an elephant. When Birbal, commander of the campaign against rebellious Yusufzai tribes, was killed in 1586 near the Swat valley, the emperor was inconsolable—he did not eat for two days. A day of official mourning was ordered. Even Badayuni concedes: 'His Majesty cared for the death of no grandee more than that of Birbal.'

Raja Man Singh of Amber, Akbar's nephew by marriage and one of his great generals, also rejected a suggestion that he convert to Islam, with no deleterious consequences on his continuous rise in court. Man Singh was en route to Bengal to take over as governor. At Monghyr, he called on Qutub al-Aqtab Shah Daulat, who urged the Raja to become a Muslim. Man Singh quoted the Quran to say that until his heart had changed there could be no conversion. If Shah Daulat had access to Allah, could he persuade the Almighty to change the Raja's heart? Raja Man Singh's heart did not change, and nor did his religion.[2]

Raja Man Singh became the first *mansabdar* to be raised to the rank of 7,000 horse, and, according to Abul Fazl, was given the titles of 'Mirza Raja' and 'Farzand' (son). In 1581, he was commander of the army which subdued Akbar's rebellious brother Hakim in Kabul; there could be no greater proof of trust.

Akbar, the first Mughal ruler to be born on Indian soil, was a child of eclectic fortunes. His father Humayun was a Sunni Turk-Mongol who knew enough astrology to chart horoscopes; his mother Hamida Begum was an independent-minded princess from an Iranian family. Akbar was born in 1542, at the Umarkot fortress of Rana Prasad in the Sind desert, while his father was in flight, having lost his kingdom to Sher Shah Suri. In the winter of 1543, the infant was left in the care of loving aunts and a cynical uncle at Kandahar as his parents fled to Persia for sanctuary. Whimsical destiny had a better fate in store; in 1556, when he was a little more than 13, Akbar became ruler of an uncertain domain which he enhanced into a magnificent empire.

According to his authorized biographer Abul Fazl, Akbar asked his array of intellectuals to answer a central question of theology with implications for social harmony within a multi-faith empire: have the different religions no common ground? For the ruler, the answer was not complicated. Consideration for the beliefs of every subject's faith was necessary for the emotional integration of the people. According to Prof. Mohammad Mujeeb, the emperor knew that the Muslim practice of 'sacrificing cows created a gulf between the Muslims and the Hindus that could not be bridged, and he used both his personal influence and his political authority to reduce the eating of meat and to prohibit cow-sacrifice'. Further, 'he abolished the *jizyah* [a hated poll tax on Hindus] in 1564... Hindus who, in childhood or otherwise, had from pressure become Musalmans, were allowed to go back to the faith of their fathers'.[3] Conversion was permitted from Hinduism to Islam and Islam to Hinduism, but only if voluntary. The previous norm requiring Muslims to pray five times a day in court was abandoned, the decision being left to the individual. The eminent Shia, Mir Fathullah, could say his namaz in the manner of his sect, a deviation which angered the orthodox Sunni clergy.[4]

As he grew older, Akbar turned vegetarian on most days and famously wondered why men should turn their stomachs into a graveyard for animals. Sanskrit religious texts like the *Atharva Veda*, Mahabharata and Ramayana were rendered into Persian under the aegis of the translation bureau headed by Abul Fazl. Akbar's drinking water came from the Ganges, which he described as the water of immortality. When he was on the march, supplies were brought on camel-back. Akbar was the first Mughal to marry into Rajput royalty; his Hindu wives prayed in temples within the palace complex. His son and successor Jahangir was born of a Rajput Hindu mother, as was his grandson Shah Jahan.

Long before Akbar, saints and mystics had sought harmony through concepts like *wahdah al-wajud,* the unity of all existence. This philosophy of integration underlay the message of the great 13th-century sufi mystic, Shaikh Nizamuddin Auliya, who was considered the patron saint of the capital, and his disciple Nasiruddin Mahmud, who was given the title Roshan Chiragh Dehalvi (Light of Delhi) by Sultan Feroze Shah Tughlaq (1351–1388). As Shaikh Gesu Daraz, another influential sufi of the Chishti order, put it: the human seed is the same for everyone. The sufi argument was logical. The Quran called Allah *Rabb-ul aal-ameen,* or the Creator of all existence, not just of Muslims; hence, a ruler could not discriminate on the basis of sect or faith, for every human being was a creation of the same God.

The sage, whether Hindu or Muslim, was instrumental in fusing this philosophy of coexistence into the daily life of the people. Music was a potent vehicle of this message. Prof. Mujeeb explains:

> [by the end of the 14th century] the devotional character of Hindi songs and the appeal which the language made to the *sufis* brought Hindus and Muslims closer together than any other influence. Several instances are recorded in the *Siyar al-Awliya* and the *Jawami al-Kalim* in which Hindi songs and refrains brought a feeling of ecstasy. Shaikh Nizamuddin was very sensitive to the music of words and to the tender charm of the Hindi of those days. Sometimes Hindi songs moved him where Persian *ghazals* left him cold. In the *Jawami al-Kalim,* there is a discussion which indicates that by the time of Shaikh Gesu Daraz Indian music had been studied and Hindi devotional songs had come to occupy a very significant position in the *sama*.[5]

The most committed Mughal ideologue of confluence was the man who could have become the sixth Mughal emperor, Dara Shikoh, designated heir of Shah Jahan. Prof. Mujeeb writes:

> This prince had many faults, most of which arose out of his inability to face difficult situations. He was weak, incompetent

and irritable, unable to control others or himself. But we are not judging him here as a politician or an administrator. What he represents socially is the culmination of that understanding between Muslims and non-Muslims of which Akbar laid the foundation and which led to the creation of a mixed governing class with a common code of behaviour. This understanding reached its highest point symbolically in Dara Shikoh's translation of the Upanishads and in Sheikh Muhibullah Allahabadi's verdict that a ruler who believed in a Prophet called 'the Blessing for All Humanity' could not discriminate between his Muslim and non-Muslim subjects. The translation of the Upanishads was not due to literary curiosity… it was the result of a passionate search for truth, and Dara Shikoh must have felt that in the Upanishads the goal, 'the Confluence of the two Oceans', had been reached.[6]

Upa means near; *ni* is down; *shad* means to sit: the Upanishad is an indication to the pupil to sit near the teacher to learn the secrets of *sruti,* or revealed literature.

Francois Bernier, the French physician who visited India between 1656 to 1668, records an encounter between Shah Jahan and the widow of a well-known Hindu moneylender who refused to share a legacy of ₹200,000 with her son because of his profligate habits. The son took his case to the emperor. Shah Jahan ordered the lady to hand over ₹100,000 to the treasury, give ₹50,000 to the son and keep the rest.

As court attendants tried to push her out after the verdict, the courageous widow called out to the king. Shah Jahan responded: 'Let us hear what she has to say!' She replied: '*Hazrat Salamat*! It is not perhaps without some reason that my son claims the property of his father; he is our son, and consequently our heir. But I would humbly inquire what kinship there may have been between Your Majesty and my deceased husband to warrant the demand of ₹100,000?' Bernier comments:

Chah-Jehan [Shah Jahan] was so well pleased with this short and artless harangue, and so amused with the idea of a *banyane* [from the *bania* caste], or Gentile tradesman, having

been related to the Sovereign of the *Indies*, that he burst forth
into a fit of laughter, and commanded that the widow should
be left in the undisturbed enjoyment of the money of her
deceased husband.[7]

Niccolao Manucci, the Venetian doctor and traveller who joined the
retinue of Henry Bard, First Viscount Bellomont, the ambassador of
Charles II to Persia and India in 1653 and remained in India till his
death in 1717, has left a striking account of the people, polity and
power during the diametrically different reigns of Shah Jahan and
Aurangzeb. In 1701, Manucci sent his manuscript to Europe through
a Jesuit priest, Pere Catrou, which was published in 1705. Upset
at what he felt was Jesuit appropriation of his text, Manucci sent
a second version, *Storia do Magor,* to the Venetian Senate through
Father Eusebius, a Capuchin.

Manucci describes how once, while hunting between Agra and
Delhi, Shah Jahan got separated from his men and came upon a
Brahmin serving water to wayfarers. The thirsty emperor drank
eagerly but was disconcerted to find a little grass in the water vessel.
He wanted to know the reason. The Brahmin replied: 'It is what I
do for my asses when they are tired, so that they may not get colic
pains.' Shah Jahan said nothing and went to rest under the shade
of a tree. Eventually his fellow-hunters and soldiers found him. The
terrified Brahmin, prostrating himself, asked for pardon. Instead,
he got a reward, the grant of a village which became known as the
'Brahmin's village'. This was the kind of liberal gesture which lent
popular legitimacy to the throne.

The people's theory of power was sound. A ruler's authority does
not extend to injustice or tyranny. Kings require alter egos who can
keep them grounded. An alternative view burnishes the king, while
the king exalts the corrective nudge. There are many examples of a
legendary ruler paired with a legendary wit: Krishnadevaraya and
Tenali Rama in the Deccan, Krishnachandra and Gopal Bhar in
Bengal.

David Dean Shulman links the comic trinity:

What can be said with assurance is that Tenali Rama serves
with equal prominence in premodern Tamil and Telegu folk

literature as the major exemplar of the court jester; that as such he is immensely popular, a heroic figure in more ways than one; and that he is clearly related to Indian counterparts such as Birbal, the jester (sometimes said to be from Andhra) associated with the Mughal Emperor Akbar, and the beloved Gopal Bhar of Bengal. It is entirely possible that this symbolic type emerges in its full scope only with a more powerfully structured political system such as that of the Vijayanagar kings, and in particular in connection with some royal figure who comes to be perceived as prototypical or symbolically dominant... we could apply to the jester what has been said of human endeavour generally—that while laughter is in the realm of ends, the means, on the contrary, are always serious.[8]

There is no documented evidence that Tenali Ramakrishnudu, a Brahmin from Tenali in Guntur district, was a courtier of King Krishnadevaraya of Vijayanagara (1509–1529), but his reputation thrives in oral tradition. He is renowned as *Vikata Kavi*, or the laughing poet.

The gods have their own, if occasionally peculiar, ways of determining a man's destiny. Shulman narrates how Tenali Rama became the laughing poet. Searching for a vocation, Tenali went to the temple of the Goddess Kali and, on the instructions of a seer, recited a mantra 30 million times in a single night. The Goddess appeared in her most awesome aspect, with a thousand heads, carrying two pots, one filled with wisdom and the other with wealth. She asked Rama to choose—he drank both and began to laugh, explaining that he, with only one head, had so much trouble when he got a runny nose; how much worse must it be for a goddess with her thousand heads! The curse of an angry goddess made him a laughing poet.

Laughter is saddled with risk. Once when Tenali's tongue got him into trouble, Krishnadevaraya ordered that his head pay the price. Tenali pleaded with the two executioners to allow him a final purifying bath, emerged from the water tank and signalled that they could proceed. As they swung their swords he dipped back into the tank, and the executioners decapitated each other.

Those brains also rescued the king from wily priests. Krishnadevaraya's mother had a craving for a mango as she lay on her deathbed. But the season was over, and the king feared that his mother's ghost would haunt eternity in search of a mango. The hundred Brahmins in his court offered a solution: if each was given a golden mango, her soul would rest in peace. It was decided that the gift would be distributed at a special dinner. Tenali Rama stood at the entrance of the banquet hall, carrying an iron-hot rod. He told the priests that if any of them agreed to be hit by the rod twice or thrice, the golden gift would increase proportionately. Many agreed at once. However, there were no extra mangoes, and the priests complained to the king, who demanded an answer. Tenali Rama explained that his mother had died of rheumatism because he could not place hot irons on her joints, as advised by the doctor; his only desire was to ensure the peace of his mother's soul by placing burning rods on the priests' joints.

Sometimes, the king needed a reproach. Depressed by his astrologer's ominous prediction that he had only a month or two to live, a worried Tenali informed the king that he had made no provision for his family. Krishnadevaraya reassured him that the family would be cared for. A few weeks later Tenali climbed into the chest which contained all his gold and spread word that he had died. The king immediately ordered his soldiers to seize Tenali's treasure. When they lifted the lid, Tenali emerged. The embarrassed king cried, 'What! Aren't you dead?' Replied Tenali, 'With someone like you as my family guardian, how could I afford to die?'

Krishnadevaraya, who loved horses, was so pleased by the purchase of a superb Arabian steed that he gave the dealer 5,000 gold coins as an advance on two more. Some days later the king saw Tenali jotting down names: it was a list of the biggest fools in the kingdom, with the king's name at the top. Krishnadevaraya asked what Tenali would do if the dealer brought the promised horses. In that case, Tenali replied, the trader's name would replace that of the king at the top of the list.

One night the king dreamt of a palace in the air. When he awoke, Krishnadevaraya offered 100,000 gold coins to anyone who could construct such a palace. No one had the courage to tell him that a palace could not be built on air. Tenali Rama was asked to rid the king of such illusions. A few days later an old man came to court, complaining that he had been looted of everything he possessed.

Krishnadevaraya asked for the thief's name so that he could be hanged. The old man dithered, until assured that he would not suffer any ill consequences because of his candour. The culprit, said the old man, was the king himself; he had dreamt that he had been robbed by the king. Krishnadevaraya roared, 'You fool! How can you pretend that a dream is reality?' 'Precisely,' replied the old man. He whipped off his false beard. It was Tenali Rama.

'Tenali Rama is a folk creation cast into the world of the royal court. The link he suggests between comedy and royal symbolism is basic to the perception of kingship in the popular culture...' writes Shulman.[9] This culture was prevalent across India. From Bengal we have the stories of Gopal Bhar in the court of Raja Krishnachandra of Nadia.

Gopal Bhar, sated by a magnificent dinner given to celebrate the birth of the Raja's grandson, decided to sleep overnight at the palace guest house. The following morning while on his walk, Raja Krishnachandra saw Gopal Bhar, wished him a good day, returned to his palace and settled down for a shave. Unfortunately, he got a nick which drew blood. The fearful barber made Gopal Bhar the scapegoat. It had been an ill omen to see Bhar's face; the razor had never misbehaved before. Gopal Bhar was sentenced to death. A rueful Gopal Bhar told Krishnachandra, 'Your Highness, you saw my face the first thing in the morning and got a nick. I saw your face the first thing in the morning and am about to lose my head. Tell me, whose face is more unlucky?' A contrite king set aside the death sentence and plied Gopal Bhar with gifts.

The king might be above the law, but he is never above laughter. The jester's salutary wit is incisive rather than aggressive—as an idiom from Mughal times puts it, the best joke is one which peels off folly without inciting anger.

The shared laughter began to ebb from the Mughal court in Delhi after 1658, when 40-year-old Aurangzeb defeated his elder brother and heir apparent Dara Shikoh at the battle of Samugarh near Agra, imprisoned his ill father Shah Jahan and seized the throne. For half a century, till his death in 1707, Mughal rule became militant instead of being benign. Aurangzeb alienated the majority of his subjects by imposing a totalitarian legal code, reviving *jiziya* against Hindus, promoting Sunni Islam supremacy, and damaging the framework of a fraternal culture.

The British in Surat had got a foretaste of what was to come when Aurangzeb became governor of Gujarat in 1645. Jain temples were desecrated. In 1667, nine years after Aurangzeb seized the throne, Sir George Oxden, president of the East India Company in Bombay, reported to London that Aurangzeb's religious zeal had 'greatly disturbed' the kingdom and forced non-Muslims to seek sanctuary in European towns.[10] An eminent surgeon from London, Dr John Fryer, employed by the East India Company in 1673, noted the persecution of Hindus and Shias, members of the Muslim sect considered apostate by the militant Sunni clergy.

Dr Fryer accuses Aurangzeb of bigotry:

> This Religious Bigot of an Emperor, Auren Zeeb, seeks not to suppress it (the Shia procession during Mohurrum) utterly, but to reduce the Celebration (sic), to preserve their Memories by a pious Respect, suitable to the Gravity of the Moors: For, says he, hereby Opportunity is offered to the Cophers (Kafirs, or Unbelievers) to think Musselmen (Mussalmans, or Muslims) favor the Lewd Worship of the heathens.[11]

Fryer describes the severity and implications of *jiziya*:

> For even at this instant he is on a Project to bring them all over to his Faith, and has already begun by two several Taxes or Polls, very severe ones, especially upon the Brachmins (Brahmins), making them pay a Gold Rupee an Head, and the inferior Tribes proportionate; which has made some Rajahs revolt...[12]

The equilibrium of a century had been destabilized.

Aurangzeb began his campaign for Islamic orthodoxy predictably enough, with a ban on alcohol and *bhang,* a somersault from existing practice. His grandfather Jahangir was a sot, and although his father Shah Jahan did not drink, others had the liberty to imbibe as they pleased. In fact, writes Manucci, wine was consumed so liberally that 'when Aurangzeb ascended the throne... he said in a passion that in all Hindustan no more than two men could be found who did not drink, namely, himself and Abdul Wahab, the chief *qazi* appointed by him'.[13]

Ironically, Aurangzeb did not know how right he was. The women in his own household, not to mention the wife of the chief *qazi,* loved a drink or three. Many of the women in Aurangzeb's palace ignored the ban on alcohol, arguing ingeniously that the edict applied only to men. In 1666, Aurangzeb was forced by his more fanatic mullahs to clarify that the prohibition applied to women as well; in addition, he ordered women to wear only loose cotton trousers instead of the tight and fashionable fits that presumably were more alluring. Aurangzeb's wife, Begum Sahib, was not amused.

Manucci writes:

[When Begum Sahib] learnt of this new rule, she invited the wives of the *qazi* (Abdul Wahab) and the other learned men to her mansion, and gave them wine until they were drunk. Aurangzeb came to her palace and referred to the restrictions under which he had placed women. He made excuses, saying that he was under an obligation to make the laws obeyed. She had never heard, she said, that those things were entered in the book of the Law. But Aurangzeb told her that such was the opinion of the learned. Thereupon Padshah Begam invited the king within the *pardah,* where he saw the wives of the said learned men all lying drunk and in disorder, and also wearing tight trousers on their legs![14]

The empress pointed out that the so-called pious men should first regulate their own bibulous households before they tried to impose upon others. Aurangzeb kept quiet, or as Manucci puts it, 'Thus was appeased the storm that had been raised against women.'[15]

Begum Sahib had the last word.

Manucci writes about Aurangzeb's favourite, or 'much-loved', wife Udaypuri Begum:

[She was] in the habit of drinking spirits, and that more liberally than discretion allows; thus frequently she was intoxicated. The other wives and concubines were jealous that Aurangzeb was so fond of Udepuri [*sic*]. They waited until one day this queen was in liquor, then went all in a body to the presence of Aurangzeb. He was pleased at such a visit, chiefly because they came in great glee, and resorted on this occasion to those cajoling ways, which never fail women when they mean to conquer their husbands' heart. After a little talk, they prayed him to call for the attendance of Queen Udepuri, so that the conversation might take a more elevated tone. He sent a message to his beloved asking her to come and enjoy the cheerful hour. The maidservant replied that Udepuri was somewhat indisposed. This answer caused the other ladies to laugh loudly, hoping to arouse the king's suspicions of something wrong.[16]

A second message evoked the same response. Aurangzeb went in person to see his 'indisposed' wife.

She was all in disorder, her hair flying loose and her head full of drink. Aurangzeb seated himself by her, and touched her with his hand. Thinking it was her servant-girl she asked (drunk though she was) for more. Aurangzeb was upset by the odour of spirits and by such a request. He came downcast out of her apartments and, although she did not lose the love he had for her, he turned in a fury upon the doorkeepers, who were bastinadoed for want of vigilance over the gates.[17]

Aurangzeb ordered that anyone caught drinking would have one hand and one foot cut off, but clearly his favourites were exempt. The inevitable happened: 'The regulations were strict at first, but little by little they were relaxed; and during the period of strictness the nobles, who found it hard to live without spirits, distilled in their houses, there being few who did not drink secretly'.[18] The emperor appointed vigilantes, known as *muhtasib,* to enforce his orders. 'But, seeing that the ministers themselves also drank and loved to get drunk, the rigour of prohibition was lightened by degrees.'[19]

The hypocrisy was apparent to the highest in the land. Jafar Khan, the trusted, fastidious, soft-spoken, civilized, courteous and extremely effective vizier, had the most eloquent reasons for drinking, and he did not disguise them when confronted by the emperor.

Manucci writes:

> This man used to drink his drop of liquor, and on this account Aurangzeb, as a strict Mussulman, caused him to be spoken to several times, and in the end spoke to him himself, saying that it was not a fit thing for the first minister in a kingdom of the faithful to drink wine, he being under an obligation to set a good example. Jafar Khan replied that he was an old man, without strength in his hands or firmness in his feet, had little sight in his eyes, and was very poor. By drinking wine he got sight for seeing, power for wielding the pen in the service of His Majesty, felt strength in his feet to run to court when His Majesty called, and seemed in imagination to become rich. For these reasons he drank. Wine could make the poor rich, the blind to see, the fragile robust, and the cripple whole. Aurangzeb laughed at this speech, and Jafar Khan told him that, whenever His Majesty desired, he would produce demonstrations, in substance, of these assertions.[20]

Aurangzeb had the good sense to laugh, surely aware that his injunctions had become impotent. Jafar Khan maintained his friendly relations with wine until his death in 1669.

Two years earlier, in 1667, the highest-ranking Rajput in Aurangzeb's court Raja Jai Singh had passed away in Burhanpur. The death of two grandees seemed to lift the restraint from the emperor's decisions. There was a spate of temple destruction, including at Mathura. 'Not content with this,' writes Manucci, 'he expelled the *jogis* or *sanyasis,* who are the ascetics and saints of the Hindus. He directed that the higher officers at the court who were Hindus should no longer hold their charges, but into their places Mahomedans should be put. He hindered the Hindus from enjoying their merry-making or carnival (the festival of Holi), on which occasion Mahomedans also resort to pranks...'[21] As is evident, Holi had become a shared festival in the north of India.

Fanaticism is often an invitation to parody. Orders were passed that all beards could only be as long as four 'finger-breadths'. An official was appointed to measure beards in the middle of the street, a risky responsibility for if he dared to touch the beard of a noble, he was beaten up. He took his revenge on commoners:

> It was, however, amusing to see the official in charge of beards rushing hither and thither, laying hold of wretched men by the beard, in order to measure and cut off the excess, and clipping their moustaches to uncover their lips. This last was done so that, when pronouncing the name Ala [Allah], there might be no impediment to the sound ascending straight to heaven. It was equally quaint to see the soldiers and others covering their faces with their shawls when they beheld afar off the said official, for fear of some affront.[22]

Delhi's urbane gentry was appalled when Aurangzeb banned music, an ancient art which had risen to fresh heights of glory with the patronage of Emperor Akbar. Orders were issued to destroy musical instruments. Delhi organized creative forms of protest. During one Friday afternoon prayer, about a thousand musicians assembled at Delhi's Jama Masjid, lamenting loudly as they carried 'over twenty highly-ornamented biers'. Aurangzeb saw them from a distance, and enquired. Music, they said, had been killed and they were bearing the cortege to the graveyard. Aurangzeb calmly replied that they should ensure that music was thoroughly buried and pray for her soul. Music, defiantly immortal, merely went into hiding.[23]

Clerics tried to justify such joyless edicts by citing the Quranic verse 76 of Surah 28 to suggest that Allah did not love those who rejoiced. It was a deliberate misquotation. The correct translation of the verse is: 'Exult not, for Allah loveth not those who exult in riches.'[24] The holy book condemns those who boast about their wealth, not those who take pride in their culture.

Critics began to mock Aurangzeb's martinet militancy, and even accused him of appointing generals because of their religious views rather than ability. This was popularly called *taza-gui,* or 'fresh' speech: not quite free speech, but a long way from silence. One of the most pugnacious critics was a disgruntled noble, Mirza Muhammad Niamat Khan. Unusually, he could not be bought off. Aurangzeb refrained from punitive action only because he felt it might become counterproductive. He wrote on the margins of one petition against Niamat Khan: 'It is not possible to cut out his tongue and sever his neck. One must burn [inwardly] and accept it.'[25]

Aurangzeb's successor Bahadur Shah attempted to revive the old convivial spirit. He raised Niamat Khan's title to 'Danishmand' (the learned) and gave him the much-sought assignment of writing imperial history. But Bahadur Shah, who died in 1712, did not live long enough to repair a damaged polity. The consequences were profound.

P.J. Marshall, former Rhodes Professor of Imperial History at King's College, London, describes the ensuing century of dislocation:

> Resistance to Mughal authority was widespread well before Aurangzeb's death. By then Mughal attempts to absorb what the Marathas claimed as their homeland in the western Deccan, either by conquest or by incorporating individual Maratha leaders into the imperial system, had failed. Rajput chiefs had long been generally reliable allies of the empire, but attempts to bring their territory more closely under imperial authority provoked fierce resistance during Aurangzeb's reign. In the Punjab, the writ of the Mughal governor was being contested at the end of the seventeenth century by communities of Sikhs. South of Delhi imperial communications were blocked by Jat insurgency, which had not been brought under control by the end of Aurangzeb's reign. Afghan groups constantly challenged Mughal rule in the province of Kabul and they were migrating into India in increasing numbers as traders or soldiers, nominally in Mughal service but often with ambitions of their own.[26]

A succession of heirs watched helplessly as the Mughal Empire crumbled. After 1739, when the Persian invader Nadir Shah fell upon Delhi's citizens, the hapless capital was repeatedly looted and massacred by marauding armies, while in the by-lanes of a lost city, entertainers like the *naqqal* and the *bhand* consoled one another with irreverent stories.

Within a decade after Aurangzeb's death, the Rajput chiefs of Rajasthan began to reassert their independence. In 1724, Asaf Jah, the Nizam ul Mulk of eastern Deccan, proclaimed his own dominion; in 1739 Awadh became virtually independent under Safdar Jang; the following year, Murshid Kuli Khan disengaged Bengal. By the 1730s, Marathas had taken Khandesh, Malwa, Gujarat, Berar, Agra and large parts of Orissa under rising clans like the Scindias, Gaikwads, Holkars and Bhonsales. In Punjab, the Sikhs created autonomous principalities before Maharaja Ranjit Singh wrought the first united Sikh state in 1799.

Tasweer Sahib

In October 1876, an English artist, Val C. Prinsep, was commissioned by the Viceroy, Lord Lytton, to paint pictures which might be suitable as a gift for Queen Victoria on her assumption of the title of Empress of India. Prinsep, though a resident of London, was India-born and India-savvy. His grandfather had left Warwickshire for Calcutta when Warren Hastings was governor-general. His father joined the East India Company in 1809, became proficient in Hindustani, Persian and Arabic, and rose to become member of the governor-general's council and then director, eventually retiring in 1874. A *ghat,* or landing place, on the Hooghly river in Calcutta was named after Val's uncle James Prinsep. Val Prinsep started in the Indian Civil Service but left after two years of training for a career in art.

Quickly given the *nom de plume* 'Tasweer Sahib' (Picture Sahib), Prinsep wrote a travel diary that became a collection of picturesque descriptions of old and changing India. His book, published in 1878, contains an appendix in which Prinsep includes a letter which Rana Raj Singh of Mewar (1629–1680) purportedly wrote to Aurangzeb after the imposition of *jiziya*. The Rana recalled that Emperor Akbar was known as a 'Juggut Gooroo' (World Leader) because people of every faith lived in ease and happiness during his reign, whether 'followers of Jesus or of Moses, of David or Mohammed; were they Brahmins, were they of the sect of Dharians, which denies the eternity of matter...' Jahangir and Shah Jahan followed these principles so that

conquest and prosperity went before them... During Your Majesty's reign many have been alienated from the empire, and further loss of territory must necessarily follow, since devastation and rapine now universally prevail without restraint. Your subjects are trampled underfoot, and every province of your empire is impoverished; depopulation spreads, and difficulties accumulate... As to the soldiery, there are murmurs, the merchants complaining, the Mohammedans discontented, the Hindoos destitute, and multitudes of people, wretched even to the want of their nightly meal, are beating their heads throughout the day in rage and desperation.[27]

Prinsep had twin concerns. He narrated the lasting damage done by Aurangzeb's folly, but he was also worried by the absence of empathy between the British and Indians, despite the seeming stability of the British Raj. He suggested a rather modern solution: two-way tourism 'to create a kindly feeling between natives and their rulers'.

A contemporary south Indian aristocrat has analysed the reasons for this lack of 'kindly feeling'.

Sir Mir Turab Ali Khan, or Salar Jung I, Prime Minister of Hyderabad between 1853 till his death in 1883, served three Nizams, created a modern administration in the princely state and became, through the marriage of his daughter Amat-uz-Zehra to Asaf Jah IV, maternal grandfather of the last Nizam, Mir Osman Ali Khan. Salar Jung had been a steadfast ally of the British through their worst crisis. In 1857 he moved quickly to quell the spread of the 'sepoy uprising' to Hyderabad. In 1876, *Vanity Fair* published his portrait by Leslie Ward (who used the pseudonym Spy), with the legend 'An Indian Statesman'.

His friendship with the British did not blind him to their faults: principally, the distance between them and Indians. Salar Jung told Richard Temple, the British Resident, that while India might have had worse despots, like Aurangzeb, the Mughals survived because they had 'amalgamated themselves with the people'. The British, he said, were 'utterly foreign' to India.[28]

The apotheosis may have come during the three generations of Akbar, Jahangir and Shah Jahan, but this amalgamation was a slow process nurtured across a wide timespan.

In the 14th century, Abul Hasan Yamin al-Din Khusrau, or Amir Khusrau Dahlawi, invented the musical form known as 'qawwali', for devotional songs. Khusrau, variously a courtier, soldier, musician, astrologer, poet and inconsistent commentator, could be a man for all seasons, but ended his life as a devoted disciple of Hazrat Nizamuddin Auliya. He died, literally of grief, within six months of his master's death in 1325 and was buried near Hazrat Nizamuddin's grave. Khusrau wrote:

> *Woh zulf-e shab gun hai ahl-e-saamaan,*
> *Woh roo-e anwar hai ahl-e-imaan;*
> *Azeez donon hain dil ko merey*
> *Kabhi hoon kaafir, kabhi Musalmaan.*

Says the poet: *The face glows with the light of faith alongside flowing locks of dark hair. Every belief is candescent; I can be a Hindu one day, a Muslim the next.* This civilizational construct, inspired by a desire for integration, reinforced by common sense, flourished as the creed of the people.

Kabir Das, born in 1498 into a family of weavers, is arguably the most influential north Indian poet of the last six centuries. He challenged the superficial differences of the caste system, fashioned by the artifice of priests who had made religion into a paying profession. The only people who could be called 'lower', he said, were those who did not have the name of God, or Lord Ram, on their lips. His ideology transcended conventional boundaries. In a Brahmin's home, he wrote, he became a Brahmin, and in a Muslim's home he recited the *kalima* ('In the name of Allah the beneficent and the merciful'). There was no conflict between *nirgun* and *sagun,* the invisible God and the deity in the form of an idol; the essence was important, not the detail. He asked whether the pilgrim's destination was more relevant than the pilgrim and eviscerated those who had reduced worship from ecstasy to ritual.

> *Nangey phiren jog jau hoi,*
> *ban ka mrig mukti gaya koi.*
> *Mudh mudhaye jau siddhi hoi,*
> *sargahin bher na pahunchi koi.*
> *Bindu rakhi jau tariyye bhai,*
> *tau khusrey kyon na param gati paai.*

Kahey Kabir sunon re bhai,
    Ram naam bina kin siddhi paai.

(*If wandering naked could bring liberation, the forest deer would
be the first to be free; if a shaven pate was piety, the shorn sheep
would be holy; if holding your semen could take you to heaven, a
steer might lead the way. Says Kabir: Listen to me, brother, the only
liberation is in the name of Ram!*)

And again:

Jau paye karta baran bicharey,
    tau jantaye teeni daarhi kin saarai.
Je tu baman bamani jaaya,
    tau aan baat hoi kaahe se aaya.
Je tu Turk Turkini jaaya,
    tau bhetar khatna kyon na karaya?

(*If God had wanted caste, says Kabir, the child would be born with
a caste mark on the forehead; had the Brahmin infant left the womb
through some special canal? If circumcision was the mark of Islam,
why wasn't every Muslim male born circumcised?*)

Mirza Abdur Rahim Khan Khanam (1556–1626), son of Bairam
Khan, is remembered today not for his military campaigns on behalf
of Emperor Akbar, but for his famously memorable couplets. There
is no need for a sword, he says, where a needle can serve. Although a
Muslim, he evokes Hindu gods in his verse, a conscious affirmation
of shared cultural heritage:

Ab Rahim muskil parhi garhe do-u kaam
Saanche se to jag nahin, jhootey miley na Ram.

(*Rahim now faces a difficult dilemma, for the world has no use for
truth, but falsehood will not take him to Lord Ram.*)

The road to God, said Rahim, was not wide enough to accommodate
an ego. There were many paths to God; he could not forsake Ram
or Hari. God could be reached only through love; those who loved

God preferred death to separation. This was the poet's 'first-hand experience over second-hand knowledge', in the phrase of Arundhati Subramaniam.[29]

Prof. Mujeeb points out that while Aurangzeb might have been 'responsible for the disintegration of an empire and the collapse of a social and cultural system', the message of cultural synthesis survived him 'by over a century, and the concept of cultural unity remained till long after the possibility and the desire for political unity had vanished.'[30]

Ironically, radical verse touched an exhilarating peak in the phantom phase of Mughal rule in the first half of the 19th century, when power had shifted into the British grasp. A generation of poets, high priests of Delhi culture, lit the gloom with sparkling imagery: Mir Taqi Meer (1723–1810); Shaikh Muhammad Ibrahim Zauq (1790–1854; poet laureate from the age of 19 till his death); Momin Khan Momin (1800–1852); Nawab Mirza Khan Dagh Dehlavi (1831–1905; his father Nawab Shamshuddin Khan of Loharu was hanged by the British in Delhi for conspiracy to murder William Fraser in 1835); Nawab Mustafa Khan Shefta (1809–1869); the last Mughal king Bahadur Shah Zafar (1775–1862); Munshi Hargopal Tufta (1799–1879); and the greatest of them all, Mirza Muhammad Asadullah Beg Khan (1797–1899), who adopted the *takhallus* or pen name Ghalib, or conqueror, a brave claim in the age of defeat. They teased obscurantism and turned the fractious sermons of doctrinaire puritans upside down. Four couplets, the first two by Mir, the third by Zauq and the last by Ghalib, are powerful illustrations:

*Mir ke deen-o-mazhab ka poochtey kya ho, un-nay toh
Kashka khaincha, dair mein batha, kab ka tark Islam kiya.*

(*Why do you ask about Mir's faith? He has a tilak on his forehead and sits in a temple, having left Islam long ago.*)

*Us ke farogh-e-husn se jhamkey hai sab mein noor
Shaam-e-haram ho ya ho diya Somnath ka.*

(*From that divine beauty sparkles light for all, whether it is the evening of the Kaaba mosque or the lamp of the Somnath temple.*)

> *Zahid sharab peeney sey kaafir hua main kyon,*
> *Kya derh chullu paani mein imaan bah gaya?*

(*Priest, have I become an infidel by drinking wine? Has my faith drowned in a mere fistful-and-half of water?*)

> *Kahan maikhaane ka darwaza Ghalib aur kahan waaiz*
> *Par itna jantey hain kal woh jaata tha ki ham nikley.*

(*Where be the door of the tavern, Ghalib, and where the priest? But this I know, that last night the priest was entering when I left.*)

Ghalib's ancestors were freewheeling military men. The family was typical of the late Mughal period, at ease with all faiths and sects. His paternal grandfather Mirza Qoqan Beg, a Seljuk Turk from Samarkand, came to India in the 1750s and joined the army of the last Mughal minister with any authority, Najaf Khan, vizier of Shah Alam. His father Mirza Abdullah Beg fought variously for the Shia Nawab Asaf ud-Daula of Awadh, the Sunni Nizam Asaf Ali Jah II of Hyderabad and the Rajput Raja Bakhtawar Singh of Alwar, who conferred the revenue of two villages as reward. Abdullah Beg died fighting for Alwar in 1802, when Ghalib was only five years old. Ghalib's uncle Mirza Nasrullah Beg had served the Maratha prince Daulat Rao Scindia as a subedar of Agra; his brother-in-law Ahmed Baksh Khan was Alwar's ambassador to the court of Lord Lake, the British General who took Delhi from the Scindias in 1803.

The British were regarded as intruders with little understanding of what the academic P. Hardy has described as 'India's polite civilization' in his essay *Ghalib and the British*:

Indeed, in reading the travels of Bishop Heber, Victor Jacquemont and Colonel William Sleeman, as well as the writings of the Delhi *alim*, Shah Abd al-Aziz, one is impressed by how little in feeling and in style of life, the educated classes of upper India were touched by the British presence before 1857. Muslims might be forgiven for hoping that if they shifted their gaze to cultural horizons for a while, when they shifted it back to the immediate surroundings, the British might be found to have merged completely into a familiar Indian environment.[31]

If that hope ever did exist, it was in vain.

Ghalib, too confident of his genius to waste time on modesty, relied on wit to negotiate his way through authority. Like any poet before the era of publishing royalties, he needed patronage from the aristocracy to survive, but he was always a fierce guardian of self-respect. His cool relations with the last Mughal, Bahadur Shah Zafar, warmed a little in 1850, when he was commissioned to write a history of Mughal rule. Heavily in debt, he was much in need of the 'balm' of remuneration, but a wounded Ghalib was not a defeated Ghalib. Bahadur Shah Zafar had not done him any favours, he wrote; instead, it was Zafar's good fortune to have 'a slave' like Ghalib, 'whose song has all the power of fire'.

The scholar Ralph Russell writes:

> He (Ghalib) was always very free in his behaviour towards the king. Ghalib rarely allowed any serious discussion of (his religious obligations), and nearly always turned aside any serious criticism with a joke. When a man read him a lecture against wine-drinking and told him that the prayers of the wine-drinker are never granted, Ghalib replied: 'My friend, if a man has wine, what does he *need* to pray for?'[32]

Such spirited liberty was intrinsic to India's 'polite civilization'. A famous exchange between the poet and the king has been recorded, after Ghalib recited these famous lines:

Yeh masaail-e-tasawwuf, yeh tera bayan Ghalib,
Tujhe ham wali samajhtey jo nah badah-khwar hota.

(*Ghalib, you write so well upon these mystic themes of love divine;*
We would have counted you a saint, but that we knew your love
of wine.)

According to Ghalib's protégé and biographer Altaf Hussain Hali, Zafar replied that he would never have described Ghalib as a saint.

The poet answered: 'Your Majesty counts me one even now, and only speaks like this lest my sainthood should go to my head'.[33] Such a bridge of intelligent banter was never built between Indians and the British.

Ghalib recognized that the sun would now rise from the west, but he expected the new conquerors to respect Delhi's old etiquette. In 1842, Ghalib was offered the position of professor of Persian at Delhi College, for which he had to go through the formality of an interview with James Thomason, a government official. Ghalib walked away from Thomason's tent because the officer did not rise from his chair to greet him at the entrance. As Ghalib put it, his intention was to enhance family honour by becoming a professor, not to sacrifice it.

The last vestiges of Mughal Delhi, said Ghalib, were destroyed by the five invasions of 1857: the sepoys robbed Delhi of its good name, the British of its wealth and honour, famine of its existence, cholera of its life and a pandemic fever of its resistance. He remained in Delhi through 1857, when it became a city of corpses. Ghalib wrote that he was among the helpless, shut in his room with his family, as the cries of infantry and cavalry rose from all sides, food and water became scarce and an eclipse on 18 September 1857 frightened the 'misguided' rebels. The British recaptured the city three days after the eclipse. The earth was stained with blood and every corner of the garden had turned into a graveyard, he wrote in *Dastanubuy*, a memoir of the upheaval which appeared in 1858.

On 5 October, Ghalib was taken to Colonel Brown, now ensconced in a merchant's house in Chandni Chowk. The colonel asked, gently, if Ghalib was a Muslim. The poet replied that he was half a Muslim: he drank wine but did not eat pork. It was possibly the last instance of high wit in the discourse between different civilizations. The bemused colonel did not pursue his enquiry.

A joke upon a British officer was trivial compared to laughter at the divine. In 1862, Ghalib admonished a friend, Mirza Mihr, whose grief at the death of his courtesan-mistress, Chunna Jan, had become tendentious. Ghalib wrote:

In the days of my lusty youth a man of perfect wisdom counselled me, 'Abstinence I do not approve: dissoluteness I do not forbid. Eat, drink and be merry. But remember that the wise fly settles on the sugar, and not on the honey'... And if you love your chains so much, then a Munna Jan is as good as a Chunna Jan. When I think of Paradise and consider how if my sins are forgiven me and I am installed in a palace with a *houri*, to live for ever in the worthy woman's company, I am filled with dismay and fear brings my heart into my mouth. How wearisome to find her always there!—a greater burden than a man could bear. The same old palace, all of emerald made; the same fruit-laden tree to cast its shade. And—God preserve her from all harm—the same old *houri* on my arm! Come to your senses, brother, and get yourself another.[34]

Ghalib's scorn was directed not only at the prospect of a boring paradise, but also at the humbug of mullahs who touted the *houri* as the heavenly reward for earthly virtue. Ghalib ignored the fulminations of self-righteous clergy and cheerfully prepared his taste buds for the promised *tasneem* (wine) of heaven. He had the power, he said, of a poet whose rhymes were on the lips of both the singer in her *kotha* (house) and the beggar on the street.

His personal faith, said Ghalib, was derived from 'the essential truth of God's reality'. Ghalib was never an agnostic or an atheist. His God was the creator of all existence: 'Hell is for those who deny the oneness of God... My belief in God's oneness is untainted, and my faith perfect. My tongue repeats, "There is no God but God," and my heart believes, "Nothing exists but God, and God alone is manifest in all things".' He told Hargopal Tufta: 'I hold all mankind to be my kin and look upon all men—Muslim, Hindu, Christian—as my brothers, no matter what others may think.'[35]

Ghalib wrote to Queen Victoria, pointing out that her conquest brought obligations:

I indicated what my expectations were by saying that the emperors of Rum and of Persia, and other conquering kings, had been accustomed to bestow all manner of bounties on their poets and panegyrists. They would fill a poet's mouth with pearls, or weight him in gold, or grant him villages in fief or open the door of their treasuries to shower wealth upon him. 'And so your poet and panegyrist seeks a title bestowed by the imperial tongue, and a robe of honour conferred by the imperial command, and a crust of bread from the imperial table.'[36]

All he received was polite acknowledgement that the letter had been received. The thought of distributing pearls might have put the Sahib off. Or he might have missed the tacit message that he had to come to terms with Indians if Indians were to come to terms with him. Ghalib and his peers became no more than flotsam from the past floating upon the Jumna, the river flowing past Delhi.

Ghalib died in 1869, the year in which Mohandas Karamchand Gandhi was born.

Indians accepted, if a trifle ruefully, British rule after 1857 but they never quite surrendered one weapon—subaltern laughter. In 1880, the leading publishing house of Lucknow, Naval Kishore Press, published 100 copies of *Manohar Kahaniyan*, a collection of 100 Hindi stories in the style of *kataksh* (reflection), or the art of saying the opposite of what you mean, a useful precaution in an age when police could seize a printing press on a charge of sedition.

A guru, or *gosai,* and his disciple stop at a village called Haribhumipur (Land of Hari, or God) while on pilgrimage. To their surprise, they find that every item in the market is being sold at the same price. The sagacious guru, fearful that such inverted values can only lead to disaster, wants to resume his pilgrimage. But the disciple, tempted by rich butter at the price of straw, buys quantities of *ghee* (clarified butter), sugar and flour to indulge in his favourite savoury, *maleeda*. Within a year, the disciple has become so fat that he is unrecognizable.

There comes a day when a thief is due to be hanged. The *kotwal* (police chief) discovers that the noose is too big for the neck of the thief. The king orders that a fat man be hanged instead. It is a land where the price of everything is the same, so one man will do as well as another. The disciple is chosen because he has become fat enough for the noose. The guru intervenes and offers his own neck instead. The *kotwal* is puzzled. The guru replies that whoever is hanged that day will become the king of heaven, which is what he has always aspired to be. The governor demands, on hearing the news, that he be sent to the gallows. The *diwan,* or prime minister, pulls rank, and gets ready to become king of heaven. There is however one authority above them all: the king decides to hang himself.

In Andher Nagri, or the Dark Town, the price of camphor and cotton is the same because both are white.

A man, seeking retribution after his goat is killed by rubble from a falling wall, finds that the king and his ministers are drunk. He goes to court in search of justice. The judge gives instructions for the wall to be arrested; then, on better advice, puts the owner of the wall on trial. The owner blames the mason. The mason accuses the shopkeeper who sold the limestone. The shopkeeper points his finger at the worker who diluted the limestone with too much water. The worker claims that there was excessive water in the leather water bag. The bag maker is summoned. He accuses the shepherd of selling a sheep which was too big, so that its leather made the bag larger than it should have been. The shepherd turns to the *kotwal*, who was on an inspection tour of the market while the sheep was being sold. He got so unnerved, says the shepherd, by the presence of the police, that he sold the wrong sheep.

The *kotwal* is hanged.

The Punch and Vindaloo Show

The Mughal dynasty, which traced its maternal lineage to Genghis Khan and paternal ancestry to Amir Taimur, found a foothold in Delhi when Babur defeated Sultan Sikandar Lodi at Panipat in 1526. The victor, conscious that the route to Delhi's heart lay through the mystic, offered prayers of gratitude at the shrines of two Sufi saints, Shaikh Nizamuddin Auliya and Qutb al-Din Bakhtiyar Kaki Ushi upon reaching the capital. The process of gradual Mughal integration into the multi-ethnic framework of northern India began with his son Humayun, who became emperor in 1530.

Humayun's reign was disrupted by defeat; in 1540, he lost his kingdom to Sher Shah Suri, the ruler of Bengal and Bihar, and was driven into exile in Persia. His fortunes turned in 1544 when the Persian monarch Shah Tahmasp provided an army for what proved to be a long but successful campaign back to Delhi. Just prior to his departure from Persia, Humayun hosted a dinner in honour of the Shah. The highlight of the menu was the very Indian, vegetarian khichri, which the Persians had never tasted before. Humayun's grandson Jahangir would make the Gujarati khichri his main meal on those days of the week when he became vegetarian.

There was no 'home leave' for officials and soldiers of the Mughal Empire. India became their home.

The British established a presence in 1608 as traders, remained to rule from 1757, but never to stay. For them, home was always the island they had left behind.

Emperor Akbar, whose reign of nearly 50 years began in 1556, encouraged intellectual and commercial interaction with Europe, meeting travellers, traders and priests. He exempted Europeans from prohibition because, as he said, they were 'born in the element of wine, as fish are produced in that of water', according to the authorized history, *Ain-i-Akbari*. In 1562, he married the Armenian-Christian Mariam Zamani and permitted this vibrant community to build a church in Agra. He was keen to develop relations with the Portuguese entrenched in Goa. Since his realm did not extend to Bijapur, adjoining Goa, he gave instructions that any Portuguese merchant visiting Bengal should be sent to Fatehpur Sikri, his capital from 1569.

In 1578, Pedro Tavares, following the monsoon winds, sailed from Goa to the Hooghly river in Bengal. Like others before him, he constructed thatched huts as habitation, and a trading base, for the four months it took for the winds to change direction. When the imperial summons came, Tavares had no option. Taking three colleagues and a retinue of servants, he travelled upriver in a Mughal flotilla to Patna, and then took the road to Agra and thence to Fatehpur Sikri.

The prosperity of Agra amazed the Europeans. The way to Fatehpur Sikri was lined with shops and stalls selling silk, cloth and precious stones. The capital's Mughal standing royal army included 30,000 horses and 1,000 elephants. Such prosperity did not necessarily extend to villages, where the peasantry were forced to pay the cost of maintaining an elitist military-feudal polity driven by institutionalized wealth acquisition. But by the standards of the existing global feudal order, the average Indian was significantly better off, according to every European commentator of that age.

Tavares, although a bit deficient on Akbar's preferred subject, theology, was the emperor's guest for over a year. He departed with handsome gifts and permission to establish a trading post on the Hooghly. This town, named after the river, became the first European settlement in Bengal. 'Alongside the lay population, another significant constituency at Hooghly was the ecclesiastics. When Akbar granted Tavares permission to found the city he also permitted the construction of churches and monasteries and guaranteed the right to practice and propagate Christianity,' writes Robert Ivermee.[1]

One part of Hooghly was reserved for commerce and entertainment, the second, known as Bandel, for worship. A splendid Portuguese church stands there till today on the riverfront, with illustrations of the original experience on the walls. By 1580 Jesuit priests had reached Akbar's court and, overwhelmed by optimism, convinced themselves that they had managed to convert the 'Great Mogul' to Christianity.

Francois Bernier describes Bengal's trade in the 17th century: paddy went north up the river and south by sea to Ceylon and the Maldives; sugar was exported to Golconda in the Deccan, Mecca in Arabia, Basra in Iraq and Bandar Abbas in Persia. Its silk might not have been as fine as Persia's or Beirut's, but the price was extremely competitive; the Dutch had between 700 to 800 employees in their silk factory at Kassembazar in Murshidabad. Huge quantities of saltpetre reached Europe, along with lac, opium, wax and medicines.[2]

The East India Company was founded 5 years before Akbar's death, on the last day of 1600, with a capital of £72,000. Its initial exploratory initiative left in 1601 for Bantam in Indonesia and returned by 1603. William Hawkins was captain of the first Company ship to reach India, in 1608. The enterprising Hawkins travelled to Jahangir's court in Agra and negotiated successfully for trading rights.

On 3 February 1615, an official mission led by Sir Thomas Roe, James I's ambassador to Jahangir, set sail from Gravesend in England. But it was not till 9 March that a north-east wind enabled the fleet of 6—*Charles, Unicorn, James, Globe, Swan* and the *Rose*—to proceed towards 'East India'. The journey was smooth, taking only 6 months. Hazards were endemic to sea travel; more than a century later, in 1743, the 17-year-old Robert Clive took 15 months to reach Madras because his ship was blown off course towards Brazil.

Sir Thomas Roe's chaplain, Reverend Edward Terry, has left a picturesque memoir of the expedition. The title leaves little room for speculation: *A Voyage to East-India wherein some things are taken notice of in our passage thither, but many more in our abode there, within that rich and spacious empire of the Great Mogul, mixt with some Parallel Observations and Inferences upon the Story, to profit as well as delight the Reader.*[3]

Terry records the impressive geography and prosperity of the Mughal Empire which extended from Kandahar, Kabul, Balochistan, Sind and Punjab to Malwa, Deccan, Bihar and Bengal. After a brief soliloquy on a 'sad truth', that 'hunger is the most powerful commander, the most absolute conqueror in the world... A man may fly from the sword, the arrow of pestilence may miss him; but there is no defence nor resistance against hunger, against thirst'[4], and quotations from the Bible on how famine forced people to eat their own dung and women to eat their own children (2 Kings, Old Testament), Terry describes Gujarat as 'a very goodly, large, and exceedingly rich province'. He is impressed by reports of the treasury of Gwalior, the road between Agra and Lahore shaded by great trees, the beauty of Hardwar and the trade and topography of Bengal, a most 'fruitful province, but more properly called a kingdom, which hath two very large provinces within it... the one lying to the east, the other on the west side of the river Ganges'.[5]

Terry explains why Europeans were chasing one another to the shores of the Mughal Empire:

> The most spacious and fertile monarchy, called by the inhabitants Indostan, so much abounds in all necessaries for the use and service of man, to feed, and cloath (clothe), and enrich him, as that it is able to subsist and flourish of itself, without the least help from any neighbour-prince or nation. Here I shall speak first of that which nature requires most, food, which this empire brings forth in abundance; as, singular good wheat, rice barley, with divers other kinds of good grain to make bread, (the staff of life) and all these sorts of corn in their kinds, very good and exceeding cheap...[6]

The Reverend compares Indian bread to the food that the patriarch Abraham's wife, Sarah, made for the visiting angels who promised her a son—exalted praise from a chaplain. He lauds the butter and cheese, the plentiful deer, fowl and birds, the abundance of sugar and salt, the variety of exquisite fruit, including the luscious mango and the pleasing pineapple which he likes best of all. There is toddy to top it off.

He adds:

> And here I cannot chuse [choose] but take notice of a very pleasant and clear liquor, called Toddy, issuing from a spongy tree, that grows strait [straight] and tall without boughs to the top, and there spreads out its tender branches [where]

they make incisions which they open and stop again as they please, under which they hang pots made of large and light gourds... That which thus distils forth in the night, if it be taken very early in the morning, is as pleasing to the taste as any new white wine, and much clearer than it. It is very piercing, medicinable, and inoffensive drink...[7]

Sailors preferred to wait till the heat of the day, when the toddy became heady, and was able to 'turn their brains'.

Terry admired Indian agriculture—the tobacco reminded him of the leaf grown in the West Indies. He noted that Jahangir drank water only from the Ganges:

The Mogul, wheresoever he is, hath water brought him from that river, that he may drink thereof, by some appointed for that service... The water is brought to the King in fine copper jars, excellently well tinn'd on the inside, and seal'd up when they are delivered to the water-bearers for the King's use...[8]

Terry also finds scorpions of Biblical ferocity, snakes who would not let a man rest quietly in his grave, lions, tigers and other beasts of prey, and whining mosquitoes. He loves the majestic elephant.

The people are mainly Hindus, followed by Muslims and Armenian Christians who make wine from raisins, sugar and other ingredients. There are Jews in small pockets of India, although their main abode is Cairo in Egypt. Hindus and Muslims would rather die, he writes, like the Rachabites in the holy book (Jeremiah, Old Testament) than 'eat or drink anything their law forbids them'[9]. Terry reproaches the drunkards, pointing out archly that Noah, who got intoxicated on the wine of his own vineyard, 'had laid open his nakedness in his tent' and thereby exposed in one hour's excess what 600 years of sobriety had concealed (Genesis). Terry finds Muslims to be largely idle and Hindus industrious and diligent. The people who upset Terry most are the Christians, at that time mainly Portuguese Catholic; Terry, naturally, belonged to the Church of England.

The Reverend writes:

It is a most sad and horrible thing to consider what scandal there is brought upon the Christian religion, by the looseness and remissness, by the exorbitances of many, which come amongst them, who profess themselves Christians, of whom I have often heard the natives (who live near the port where our ships arrive) say thus, in broken English which they have gotten, 'Christian religion, Devil religion, Christian much drunk, Christian much do wrong, much beat, much abuse others'. The unmatcht [unmatched] extremities of tyranny and cruelty (to which nothing could be added to make it more cruel) practiced by the Spaniards upon the people of West India, is above all example, and almost belief, when their bloody outrages were such, as made those wretched natives to submit under any kind of death, which they would voluntarily impose upon themselves, rather than endure the Spaniards tyranny.[10]

Terry includes the Iberian Portuguese in his 'Spaniard' classification.

Sir Thomas travelled to the court of Jahangir in 1616, while the emperor was on a pilgrimage to Ajmer, to present the formal letter from King James I. The English ambassador was well received. A high noble, Asaf Khan, hosted a banquet of 50 dishes for Sir Thomas; Terry, as a lower ranking guest, was served only 40, but tried them all out of curiosity. He loved the *pilau*. The Company had received trading rights for Surat, then India's largest port, in 1612; Sir Thomas was allowed to open factories in other parts of the Mughal Empire. When he returned to England, Roe advised the East India Company to concentrate on business and avoid involvement in local wars. His advice held good for more than half a century.

There were handsome dividends from textiles, indigo, pepper, silk, medicines, perfume and precious stones. The Company did business through Indians like Virji Vora, a Jain who converted European bullion into local currency, bought coral, spices and textiles from local markets and financed the East India Company as well as its officials in their individual capacity from 1619 to 1675. (Vora, or Bohra, originally a caste name for moneylenders, is still a common surname among Hindus and Muslims. It derives from the Sanskrit *vyavahar*, through *beohar*, according to Sir Jadunath Sarkar's *A History of Jaipur*.[11])

Indian traders of the time like Abdul Gafur could send out 20 ships in a single year between the Red Sea and China. Their vessels were among the best in the world. Marco Polo records the size and sophistication of India's merchant ships in the 13th century:

> They have a single deck, and below this the space is divided into about sixty small cabins, fewer, or more, according to the size of the vessel, each of them affording accommodation for one merchant. They are provided with a good helm. They have four masts, with as many sails, and some of them have two masts, which can be set up or lowered again, as may be found necessary. Some ships of the larger class have as many as thirteen bulkheads or divisions in the hold, formed of thick planks mortised into each other... Ships of the largest size require a crew of three hundred men; others, two hundred; and some, one hundred and fifty only, according to their greater or less bulk. They carry from five to six thousand baskets, or mat bags, of pepper.[12]

In contrast, Indian rulers never invested seriously in a navy because there was no perception of a significant military threat from across the waters. Mughals called themselves masters of the seas, but that was hyperbole. Their strategic thinking was consumed by land armies. Heavily armed European merchantmen had a free ride. Both trade and pilgrimage became vulnerable to Portuguese marauders, the habitual offenders. As early as in 1502, the Portuguese looted 12,000 ducats and a near-equivalent value in goods, before setting the Haj pilgrim vessel *Miri* on fire, killing all 380 men and women aboard.

Aurangzeb asked his able vizier, Jafar Khan, to examine the possibility of creating a 'war navy'. The biggest problem was also the most apparent: they had money and timber, but not men with experience and skill in sea warfare. Aurangzeb thought that mercenaries could be hired, but Jafar Khan advised that it was dangerous to employ those who would inevitably be foreign fugitives from their own lands. Aurangzeb nevertheless ordered a warship to be constructed. The assignment was given to a Venetian, Ortencio Bronzoni.

Manucci writes that his countryman 'made a small ship with its sails and riggings, guns and flags'.[13] A demonstration was arranged in a 'great tank' before Aurangzeb and all his court:

> Here the European artillerymen, accustomed to navigation, went aboard the vessel, and caused it to move in all directions by adjusting the sails and working the helm with great dexterity and cleverness. Then, as if engaging some other man-of-war, they discharged the cannon, turning in all directions. On seeing all this, after reflecting on the construction of the boat and the dexterity required in handling it, Aurangzeb concluded that to sail over and fight on the ocean were not things for the people of Hindustan, but only suited to European alertness and boldness. Thus at last he abandoned the project entertained with such obstinacy.[14]

And that was that.

The Eternal Mosquito

English confidence in its sea power soared after the victory over the Spanish Armada in 1588; international trade was a supplementary benefit. The East India Company began operations from Surat, which teemed with hundreds of ships, from Arab dhows to Chinese junks. The Company's growing network of inland agents brought information that the best cotton and silk were to be found in Bengal, and Robert Hughes and John Parker were sent to investigate in 1618. They lived in Patna for three years and recommended relocation, but the directors were unwilling.[15]

The British, who had come in search of what was right with India, very quickly began to dwell on what was wrong with Indians. Dr John Fryer (circa 1650–1733) was hired by the Company on a salary of 50 shillings a month 'to commence on his arriveall'. He left England on 9 December 1672, reached Masulipatnam on the Coromandel coast on 26 June 1673, and travelled through Golconda and Goa up to Surat, which he reached in 1674. Fryer's account was published in the Historical Print Editions of the British Library in the collection titled *Travels in India in the Seventeenth Century: by*

Sir Thomas Roe and Dr John Fryer. Although tinted with prejudice, it describes a complex society absorbing, or rejecting, the influence of Europe.

Dr Fryer was quite certain that all Indians were inherently inferior; even Armenians, although Christian, got verbal stick because they dressed like 'natives'. The 'grave and haughty' Muslims were uneducated and jealous. 'The Moors, who are by Nature slothful, will not take pains; being proud, scorn to be taught; and jealous of the Baseness of Mankind, dare not trust their Children under tuition, whereby few of their Great Men or Merchants can read, but keep a Scrivan of the Gentues [the word merges Gentile and Hindu],' Fryer writes.[16] Hindus were intelligent, but timid and untrustworthy. He was vitriolic about the *banias*, who handled all financial transactions, calling them cheats and vermin, for they sucked out your money from the moment you set foot on land. They were 'worse Brokers than Jews'[17] which, for a European from an anti-Semitic culture, was serious condemnation. Dissembling was their 'Masterpiece: Their whole desire is to have Money pass through their Fingers, to which a great part is sure to stick'.[18]

'Brachmins', or Brahmins, the doctors of divinity, did not have much indigenous knowledge, but taught the Pythagorean theory of transmigration of souls, and if they saw a tree twined into another, they proclaimed that the soul of a debtor had entered the tree and was being held fast by the other. Dr Fryer was convinced that Hindus worshipped household gods and 'devils', and that Islam had emerged from an 'impostor'.

No Indian was safe from this harangue. The Parsis, he added, were 'entertained and allowed to live' in Gujarat, permitted to drink wine and continue with their traditional customs, including feeding their corpses to the vultures. His verdict on these refugees from Persia? 'These are somewhat Whiter, and, I think, Nastier than the Gentues.'[19]

Fryer acknowledged that there was freedom to practise one's faith in India: 'Religions of all Inventions are licens'd'[20], but did not dwell on the difference with Europe, then riven by schismatic conflict between Catholics and Protestants. The Portuguese priest, Fray Sebastien Maurique, who was in Bengal during the reign of Shah Jehan, made a similar observation. He noted that Christian priests would have been driven out of Bengal for encouraging people to eat pork and drink wine but the 'Nababo' of Dhaka rejected the demands of clergy to punish the Catholic priests for breaking the Islamic code.[21]

Despite Aurangzeb's restrictive policies, Dr Fryer wrote, Shias could take out Muharram processions mourning the martyrdom of 'Hossen Gosseen', a linguistic corruption of the brothers Hasan and Hussain, grandsons of the Prophet Muhammad. Fryer mistakenly believed that Imam Hussain 'perished by Thirst in the Deserts, fighting the Christians'[22]; Imam Hussain's foes in the battle of Karbala were Muslims.

In Gujarat, Hindus celebrated Holi with panache. Fryer wrote:

March begins with a Licentious Week of Sports and Rejoycing, wherein they are not wanting for Lascivious Discourse, nor are they to be offended at any Jest or Waggery. And to show their Beneficence at the beginning of the Rains, they Treat the Ants and Flies with Sweatmeats and Waters, studiously setting Hony [sic], Syrups, or any thing that may entice them to their own death, out of their way; allowing them Sugar, or any other dried Confects for their Repast...[23]

Dr Fryer's remonstrance against Indian weather was more rational from the perspective of a north European used to nine months of grey cold and three months of nippy sunshine. He found the wind in south India and Gujarat from November to May as hot as an oven, so that perspiration dried up in the pores. Rains brought relief, but also swarms of ants, 'muskeetoes', flies and blisters.[24] The blisters were what was known as 'prickly heat', an itching malady which could shred skin from scratching. Foreigners tried every cure, from cold baths to germicidal soap, but little worked. R.V. Vernede records a burning ode to prickly heat[25]:

In the symptomatic stage, savage warfare did I wage
'Gainst a trifling erubescence on the arm,
For I scratched it night and day till I heard some idiot say
That a little iodine would do no harm.
When it spread to hip and shoulder,
*   then I grew a little bolder*

And agreed with all the experts at the club
That germicidal soap was the only certain hope,
Used gently in the matutinal tub.
But each little feverish pore became a flaming sore
So I cursed and bathed three hours a day instead,
And I used up quite a crowd o' tins of
*   different coloured powder,*
And I oiled myself before I went to bed.
But each day I'm getting worse
*   (which explains the scratchy verse)*
So my own advice I'll sell you for a song—
Every nincompoop you meet, has a cure for prickly heat,
And every single one of them is wrong.

Fryer praised Surat's Hindu women, who enjoyed the open air, the rich among them wearing silver chains and golden earrings:

...their Noses stretched with weighty Jewels, on their Toes, Rings of Gold, about their Waste [waist] a painted Clout [cloth], over their Shoulders they cast a Mantle; their Hair tied behind their Head which both in Men and Women is naturally very long; a-top a Coronet of Gold beset with Stones.[26]

He witnessed female acrobats holding 'Nine Gilded Balls in play with their Hands and Feet, and the Muscles of their Arms and Legs, a long time together without letting them fall: They are clearer complexion'd than the men'.[27]

Jewellers and diamond-cutters flourished in Gujarat, but pharmacy and medicine were in his view woeful, for people 'will submit to Spells and Charms, and the Advice of Old Women'[28]. But he was also amazed by the Brahmin who came each day to the English factory, diagnosed any illness by just the feel of the pulse and cured ague and fever with a powder of 'Naturel Cinnaber'. Fryer, a doctor, treated a wife of the governor of Gujarat, 'Mahmud Emir Caun... Son of Emir Jemla (Mir Jumla), who established Aurenzeeb in his Throne'[29]. On another occasion, he solved the delicate problem of a Muslim host's alcohol-free dinner by filling his 'Metarrah with Beveridge which passed for Water, being drunk out of a Leather Bottle Tipped with Silver, for Travel'.[30]

Personal and corporate gain made the hardship worthwhile. The trade through Surat included sugar, tea, porcelain, lacquered ware, quicksilver and copper from China; cowrie seashells (also used as small-change currency) from Siam and the Philippines; gold and ivory from Sumatra; drugs and wool from Persia. Ahmedabad produced silk and 'atlases wrought in gold'; Agra sent indigo and many kinds of cloth; and from Calicut and the Carnatic coast arrived the 'weightiest' pepper, spice, amber, granite, opium and saltpetre, then much in demand for gunpowder.[31]

This success was reflected in the luxury at Company headquarters; the president began to live like an Emir. In Surat 'a noise of trumpets' preceded the president, carried 'in a Palenkeen, a horse of state led before him, a Mirchal [a fan of ostrich's feathers] to keep off the sun, as the Omrahs [Mughal nobles] or great men have, none but the Emperor have a Sumbrero among the Moguls'.[32]

The ostentation was also a conscious advertisement of rising status:

> However, for the English Honour be it spoke, none of them surpass the Grandeur of our East India Company, who not only command, but oblige their utmost Respect, none of their Servants shewing themselves in Publick without a Company answerable to theirs, and exceeding them in civility of Garb and Manners. When the Chief made his Entry at his Return from the Fort, it was very Pompous, all the Merchants of Esteem going to meet him with loud Indian Musick and Led-Horses: Before his *Palankeen* an Horse of State, and two St George's Banners, with *English* Trumpeters; and after him the Factors on Horseback, and lusty Fellows running by their sides with *Arundells* (which are broad Umbrelloes held over their heads), Soldiers and Spearmen, Two hundred at least, and after these a Row of Palankeens belonging to English and other Merchants. At Meals their Domesticks wait on them with Obeisance suitable to great Potentates, enclosing their Tables, which are strewed liberally with Dainties served up in Plate of *China*; *Nam mulla aconita bibuntur fictibus*, says Juvenal, which crack when poysoned; which whether true or false (since it is so much practised in this Country by

way of Revenge) is but a necessary Caution by all means to avoid. They fan the Air with Peacocks Tails set in huge Silver Handles, and chiefly now, because the busy Flies would cover the Table, were they not beaten off.[33]

Indians had more piquant concerns. They were perplexed by the weight of garments Europeans wore despite the heat. Sir Thomas Roe was dressed in a red taffeta cloak fringed with green, ruffs of silk set three or four times and heavy folds of lace during his audience with Jahangir. One Mughal politely asked Dr Fryer if he slept in his clothes. Maratha nobles at Chhatrapati Shivaji's court were astonished at the sight of the English delegation wearing huge wigs with prodigious ringlets in the sun. Self-inflicted discomfort was an English virtue beyond the comprehension of Indians.

When the men in coats stuck to trade, there were no problems. Indian customs officials could be finicky, in one instance demanding duty on metal buttons each time Europeans came ashore, but such issues could always be resolved in the usual manner: in Fryer's phrase, when the fist was mollified. For more serious offences, like evasion of tariff, a great whip called a *chawbuck* was kept hanging on the wall.

Europeans of the 17th century took a liking to the *pilaus* and *biriyanis* during a long and lingering meal with an Indian host, and even *paan,* or betel leaf, afterwards. Such meals were generally formal rather than friendly. When Europeans returned the hospitality, alcohol appeared. Fryer reports:

> They [Muslim officials] drink no Wine Publickly, but Privately will be good Fellows, not content with such little Glasses as we drink out of, nor Claret or Rhenish (which they call Vinegar) but Sack and Brandy out of the Bottle they will Tipple, till they are well warmed.[34]

Western science could always score a minor success; some guests considered the bubbles and froth in a bottle of beer something wondrous. The British, in turn, took to the local arrack, which was considerably cheaper, despite tasting like Polish brandy to Dr Fryer. Too much of it led to jitters, he said, and there was no cure for a hangover except sleep.

There was plenty of 'Cabob' and 'dumpoked fowl' on the Company table, but neither beef nor pork was available at Surat in deference to local religious sentiment. European and Persian wines were served. When impecunious young English 'factors' tried to supplement their fare by shooting birds, tearful Hindu Gujaratis would offer money to save the lives of birds. This became a surreptitious means of income for underpaid clerks.

In Madras, a garrison town with wide streets and houses modelled on British lines, the 'Honourable President' of Fort St George welcomed the charter for trade issued on 17 August 1717 with a public parade that had 'Dancing Girls with the Country Music' while the 'Sherrif' waved a 'White Wand' as they proceeded through the 'Middle gate street into the Black Town, and so out at the Armenian bridge gate, through the Pedda Naik pettah to the Company's Garden'.[35]

Pests were the great English bugbear. There was a strong view that Indian mosquitoes had colour prejudice, feasting on a white man's blood with gluttonous intensity. Fryer's only protection against mosquito bites was to wear breeches up to the toes and mufflers on hands and face. Rev. John Ovington, a chaplain who lived in India for two years a little after Fryer, lamented the prodigious growth of vermin and venomous creatures during the rains—snakes were rife, spiders bulked up to the size of a thumb and toads to the size of a small duck.[36] He was hugely impressed, however, by the vegetarianism of Hindus.

The problem was perennial. Indian mosquitoes were equally inconsiderate to the lawyer-raconteur-diarist William Hickey in 1777, during his first night in Bengal, which he spent at a tavern. Hickey found the place 'uncomfortable and beastly dirty' but got 'excellent fish, tolerable fowl, with plenty of eggs and bacon, and what was a prodigious luxury to me who had been so long without it, capitally good bread'.[37] They had enough claret and madeira from the ship.

Sleep was, however, entirely out of the question because of the 'myriads of mosquitoes that assailed us. At the end of three hours' misery I arose and walked about the room, surprised at the hideous yells of jackals innumerable. Towards daybreak the troublesome insects quitted the apartment for the open air. I then lay down upon three chairs, and, being exhausted from want of rest, fell into a sound sleep, which continued upwards of two hours and refreshed me wonderfully.'[38]

Hickey also found 'not less than a dozen' bandicoot rats performing antics in his comfortable house in Calcutta when he was suddenly awakened at night. He was told the following morning at breakfast that he was lucky not to have lost all his hair.

Another half century passed, and matters had not improved. Writing in her fascinating journal on 7 August 1830, Fanny Parkes thought that the 'plagues of Egypt were not worse than the plagues of India. Last night the dinner-table was covered with white ants, having wings; these ants, at a certain period after a shower, rise from the earth with four large wings'. The only answer to mosquitoes was the *pankha* swinging over the bed, pulled by a man who had to be relieved every two hours. There were odious winged bugs emitting sickening effluvia; rats as large as bandicoots, who bit fingers and feet when you were asleep; in Calcutta yellow fever and small pox raged all year round. The worst afflicted were men in the Company's army, whose only remedy was *arak* mixed with *datura*.[39] Mrs Parkes repeats a ditty: *These cursed fleas, they bite and skip so, / In this island of Calypso.*

In 1848, Lady Falkland reported that dinner was a torment, for insects, attracted by candles, flew into the room in countless numbers. She writes of 'a long, dark yellow horned shaped insect, with no end of joints, which makes you shudder as it flies, with either ruby or emerald-coloured bodies; large beetles "armed to the teeth" in black, strong, shining armour, and with horns like formidable spears'. She continues, 'These beetles are so strong that, when placed under a wine-glass, they move it before them as they advance along the table.'[40]

But profits continued to trump mosquitoes.

In the beginning, the East India Company thought that martinet regulations would keep the men out of trouble. Anyone out at night without permission was fined 10 rupees, which went to charity, or a day in stocks. The profane use of God's name was less expensive; it set you back only 12 pence, equivalent to the punishment for lying. Sacrilege was unacceptable. An intoxicated Thomas Burrett was expelled for drinking a toast to the health of the devil. The normal fine for getting drunk and disorderly was 5 shillings or 6 hours in stocks.

Bad behaviour was a punishable offence. On 20 March 1699, Mr James Eustace called Mr George Shaw 'son of a —'. Mr Shaw, in retaliation, struck Mr Eustace at the Sea Gate entrance while going for evening service despite the governor's promise to adjudicate. Both were fined half a year's salary, confined to the fort for one month and forbidden to wear a sword or a cane for a year.[41]

Such rules worked only up to a point in an environment where alcohol and gambling were the principal means of relaxation. Betting was so endemic, and lucrative, that the best birds in cockfighting were imported from Thailand. As the Rev. Patrick Warner, chaplain at Fort St George, wrote to the Court of Directors on 31 January 1676, the behaviour of some 'writers', as Company employees were called, was a scandal to the Christian religion, so sinful was their gambling and drinking. An evening often ended in men carrying an inebriated companion naked to his dwelling.

According to Rev. Edward Terry, Sir Thomas Roe's cook once got drunk on Armenian wine, a pleasant change from shipboard rum. He rushed out into the street and, waving his sword, challenged a passer-by, shouting, 'Now then Heathen Dog!' The affronted person turned out to be the Mughal governor's brother, who shrugged off the incident when Sir Thomas rushed to apologize. The governor was clearly broad-minded. One evening Sir Thomas, who had left a newly wedded wife back home in England, found a woman at his door, with the compliments of the governor. The English knight disapproved.[42]

By the final years of Aurangzeb's rule, however, very few Europeans were quivering before Mughal authority. Fryer records the collapse of governance in Gujarat: 'Mahmud Emir Caun' could not quell 'Coolies from pilfering', or raids from Rajputs states, or Maratha invasion and plunder, despite his huge army.[43]

Mughal nobles seemed blinded by complacency, but at least Muslim beggars were asking the right questions. Fryer recalled an interesting encounter:

Going out to see the City of Surat, I passed without any incivility, the better because I understood not what they said; for though we meet not with Boys so rude as in England, to run after Strangers, yet here are a sort of bold, lusty, and most on end, drunken Beggars, of the Musslemen Cast

[Mussalman, or Muslim], that if they see a Christian in good Clothes, Mounted on a stately Horse, with rich Trappings, are presently upon their Punctilio's with God Almighty, and interrogate him, Why he suffers him to go afoot, and in Rags, and this Coffery [from *kafir*, Unbeliever] to vaunt it thus?[44]

The faithful were in rags and the foreigner on a horse because another age of history was around the corner.

Chilli, Chai and Church: The Portuguese Menu

The mummy of Ramses II, who died in 1213 BC, had pepper sealed in each nostril. The ancient Greek doctor Hippocrates, born circa 460 BC, mixed pepper with vinegar and honey to cure infections. Rome had pepper warehouses in the age of Caesars; the first-century author and naturalist Gaius Secundus, or Pliny the Elder, mentions long pepper, known as *pippali* or *pippalimula* in Sanskrit. By the end of the 14th century, pepper accounted for over 90 per cent of the spices imported by Venice. The medicinal properties of pepper and other spices have been widely recognized; true believers once thought it could cure plague during contagion and impotence in dotage.

The great Tamil Chola Empire, whose dynasty ruled from circa 300 BC to 1279, traded with both China and Arabia. Romila Thapar writes:

> South India exported textiles, spices, medicinal plants, jewels, ivory, horn, ebony and camphor to China. The same commodities were also exported to the west, to ports such as Dhofar and Aden and, in addition, Siraf received cargoes of aloe wood, perfumes, sandalwood and condiments. Persia, Arabia and Egypt were the destinations of those trading with the west, with Siraf on the Persian Gulf as an entrepot...[45]

Pliny claims that Indian spice, silk and pearls were draining the gold of Rome, but it was not one-way traffic. India imported red coral, cosmetics and pigment from Italy. The trade surplus was, however, in India's favour. Rev. Edward Terry, seeing bejewelled Gujaratis in 1617, was reminded of Rome in its splendour:

Now the Mogul having such an abundance of Jewels, wears many of them daily, enough to exceed those women, which Rome was wont to shew in their starlike dresses, who in the height and prosperity of that empire *Were said to wear/ The spoils of nations in one ear.*[46]

The land route between Europe and India was known from antiquity, but there was no direct sea route. Cargo went from Indian ports to Aden or Jeddah, up the Red Sea in smaller vessels, by caravan to the Nile and by boat to Alexandria, where galleys from Venice, Genoa and Constantinople were waiting.

Marco Polo, who travelled from San Thome (now in Madras, where he visited the shrine of St Thomas the Apostle) to Cape Comorin and then north to Gujarat in the 13th century, saw peaceable Hindus, Muslims and Christian communities in 'Maabar', or Malabar, selling commodities to ships 'from Ormus, Chisti, Aden, and various ports of Arabia—laden with merchandise and horses'.[47] Arabian horses were prized, as India had a poor record in horse-breeding. Marco Polo mentions that Indian ginger, pepper and indigo were much in demand in Europe, while the fame of Golconda diamonds was widespread.

Indian kingdoms had diplomatic relations with west Asian countries. Persia exchanged ambassadors not only with Delhi but also with the Vijayanagara Empire in the south. According to Manucci, 'During Aurangzeb's journey from Kashmir, before he had reached Dihli [Delhi], there arrived ambassadors from Ethiopia, from Mecca, and from Basrah [Basra in Iraq], to congratulate him on his accession.' The diplomats from Ethiopia apparently short-changed Aurangzeb on the gifts, but there was no controversy about the other two.

The objective of European explorer-seafarers was not to discover India, but to reduce the cost of business. In 1488, Bartolomeo Dias sailed around, and named, the Cape of Good Hope. Four years later, Columbus headed in the wrong direction, but thought he had found pepper when he discovered Caribbean islanders eating *aji*, a chilli. In 1494, the Catholic powers Spain and Portugal signed the Treaty of Tordesillas, with the blessings of the papacy, drawing a line in the ocean by which Spain was allotted the right to territories 370 leagues west of Cape Verde; Portugal was awarded the east.

The first Portuguese explorer to reach Malabar, Pera de Covilha, came by the traditional land route in 1488, to verify the extent of the Indian Ocean trade. On 8 July 1497, Vasco da Gama left Portugal in command of 4 ships searching for a direct sea route to Calicut; we are often misled by the long grey beard in his portraits, but he was only about 37 years old then. Alvaro Velho, on board the *Sao Rafael*, has left an eyewitness account of this historic journey: the surviving manuscript is a copy of the original 16th-century document preserved in the Convent of the Holy Cross at Coimbra till 1834.[48]

Da Gama anchored at Malindi, a busy port on the east coast of Africa, on 14 April 1498, after ten months at sea, to find four merchant ships from India. According to Charles Allen, the switch of the Indian trade from Arabs to Europeans owes a debt to Shaykh Ahmad ibn Majid, who on 22 April 1498 'climbed aboard Vasco da Gama's San Gabriel flagship of the First India Armada, in the East African port of Malindi. This was an exceptional stroke of luck for da Gama because ibn Majid happened to be the greatest navigator of the age. He came from a long line of master mariners from eastern Oman who had made names for themselves as pilots "of the two coasts" (meaning the east coast of Africa and the west coast of India) and he was already famous as the author of two books on seamanship that were to remain in use for centuries...'[49] There are other versions of this story, but what is not disputed is that Vasco da Gama received help from a local navigator who knew the sea route. Vasco da Gama's fleet, led by the 84-foot *Sao Gabriel*, with 6 sails on 3 masts and a high forecastle and stern to give its 20 cannons greater range, sighted Calicut on 20 May, in a heavy thunderstorm.

Language did not prove to be a problem. The Portuguese, who had brought along an Arabic speaker, were surprised to find two Tunisian merchants in the port city who understood Castilian. Velho told the Tunisians that they had come in search of Christians and spices. The Portuguese believed in the legend of a 'Prete Jani' (Prester John), a Christian king who ruled the 'Indies', and expected him to become a natural ally against the *mouros*, or Muslims, the principal threat to Christian Europe after the fall of Constantinople to the Ottomans in 1453.

Alvaro Velho observed that Indian men covered only their 'lower extremities' with fine cotton cloth, while the women wore 'many jewels of gold round the neck, numerous bracelets on their arms, and rings set with precious stones on their toes' but were 'ugly and of small stature'. The people seemed mild, but 'covetous and ignorant'.[50]

The call on the Malabar ruler, known as the Zamorin, was scheduled for 28 May in the palace at Calicut. Vasco da Gama took 13 men, including Velho, in their best attire for what would in effect be the first direct bilateral trade negotiations between Europe and India. Discussions began on a cordial note but ended in the first exercise of Western gunboat diplomacy in Asia.

The delegation was served rice and 'excellent boiled fish' when it disembarked. Vasco da Gama was the only one who did not eat. On their way to the palace, they saw an idol of the infant Lord Krishna being nursed by his mother in a temple and assumed that this was a representation of a 'black Jesus' with Mary.

The Zamorin (a Portuguese misappropriation of Samoothri, or one whose domain is on the ocean) reclined on a green velvet couch under a golden canopy, with a very large golden cup in his left hand which he used as a spittoon; on his right was a gold basin 'so large that a man might just encircle it with his arms' which contained betel leaves. The scene might have been virtually unchanged from Marco Polo's time. The Venetian has thus described a ruler of 'Maabar' (or Malabar):

> The king is no more clothed that the rest, except that he has a piece of richer cloth, and is honourably distinguished by various kinds of ornaments, such as a collar set with jewels, sapphires, emeralds, and rubies, of immense value. He also wears, suspended from the neck and reaching to the breast, a fine silken string containing one hundred and four large handsome pearls and rubies... On each arm he wears three gold bracelets, adorned with pearls and jewels; on three different parts of the leg, golden bands ornamented in the same manner; and on the toes of his feet, as well as on his fingers, rings of great value.[51]

The royal treasure survived because each generation left it intact, for any diminution would be a reflection on an heir's ability to add to the inheritance.

In their first 24 hours, Vasco da Gama got a sense of the Zamorin's confidence and a taste of Kerala's weather; it rained so heavily that night that the streets ran with water. Negotiations went downhill when, the following morning, da Gama presented the gifts he had brought from his monarch, Dom Manuel: 'twelve pieces of *lambel* (striped cloth), four scarlet hoods, six hats, four strings of coral, a case containing six wash-hand basins, a case of sugar, two casks of oil, and two of honey'.[52] Courtiers began to laugh, adding that the poorest Indian or Arabian merchant brought gifts of more value.

The Zamorin was perfectly amenable to direct trade with Europe, but he wanted gold for his goods. The pathetic gifts raised suspicions about the Portuguese ability to pay for merchandise. At their next meeting, Vasco da Gama was made to wait four hours. Negotiations ended in acrimony. Vasco da Gama returned to his ships with difficulty, where his crew 'rendered thanks to God for having extricated us from the hands of people who had no more sense than beasts.'[53] When matters calmed down, the men were given time for shopping. They went ashore in twos and threes and bought shirts worth 300 *reis* in Portugal for only one tenth the price in the Kerala market. As he prepared to depart, Vasco da Gama loaded his ships with cloves, cinnamon and precious stones. More disputes arose when the port authorities ordered him to pay customs duty. Vasco da Gama slipped out of harbour under a barrage of cannon fire and the cover of a thunderstorm.[54]

For Portugal the expedition was a triumph. Vasco da Gama reached Lisbon's Targus river on 18 September 1499. The profits on spices alone covered the cost of the expedition, financed by King Manuel 1 (who ruled from 1495 to 1521), 60 times over. The king added these titles to his name: 'Lord of Guinea and the Conquest, Navigation and Commerce of Ethiopia, Arabia, Persia and India'. Vasco da Gama was knighted and, along with a lifelong pension, gifted the right to import duty-free 200 ducats worth of spices every year.

In 1500, a royal favourite, Pedro Alvares Cabral, commanded Portugal's second and much larger expedition to India. Vasco da Gama advised him to avoid the Gulf of Guinea, where he had been becalmed. In doing so, Cabral went west and became the first European to touch Brazil. He stopped in Latin America for only ten days but claimed a vaguely defined region for his king; Brazil thereby became the only exception to the rule set down in the Treaty of Tordesillas.

Spain and Portugal discovered both north and south America in their quest for India.

On 13 September 1500, Pedro Cabral's fleet received permission from an amenable Zamorin of Calicut to set up a fortified post. In December, local Muslim traders, resentful of competition, attacked this post; over 30 Portuguese died. Cabral's retaliation was a foretaste of European military capability. He bombarded Calicut for 2 days, seized 10 Muslim vessels, killed their crew and sailed south to Cochin, where the ruler of Travancore welcomed him. In 1502, Vasco da Gama returned with 20 ships; this time, his guns talked as often as he did. He made one more trip to India, in 1524, but died within a few months. His body was sent back to Portugal in 1539.

In 1506 Afonso de Albuquerque was appointed admiral of the 'fleet of the Arabian and Persian sea' and governor of Portuguese establishments in India. He identified Goa, then about 75 sq kms in area, as the potential safe harbour, administrative sanctuary and strategic headquarters of his country's rapidly expanding economic interests, surrounded as it was by the sea and protected by the Western Ghat mountains along the mainland.

Goa was then part of Bijapur, one of the five kingdoms to emerge from the collapse of the Bahmani Sultanate, ruled by Yusuf Adil Shah since 1490. Afonso de Albuquerque's first assault on Goa, between March and May 1510, failed. But Yusuf Shah died, and while the court's attention was concentrated on transition to a young heir, Ismail, Afonso de Albuquerque struck again. On 10 December 1510, Goa capitulated after a 2-day battle, in which an estimated 6,000 of the 8,000 defenders were killed.

Goa became first European colony in India. The Portuguese surrendered to the Indian Army in December 1961, four and a half centuries after they arrived and 14 years after the British went back home.

'The conquest of Goa advanced a Portuguese agenda that grew ever clearer in subsequent decades: armed supremacy over the Indian Ocean, commercial monopoly on targeted commodities, and a religious mission that carried the energy and anti-Muslim zeal of Europe's Counter-Reformation,' writes Richard Eaton.[55] This religious fervour was in sharp contrast to the prevailing culture of southern Indian rulers, whether the lords were Muslim Adil Shahis of Bijapur and Qutb Shahis of Golconda or Hindu maharajas of Vijayanagara. Eaton provides the example of Ibrahim Qutb Shah, who ruled for three decades from around 1550:

> [He was] steeped in the traditions of Andhra's regional culture. The sultan not only patronised Telegu literature, supported Brahmins and temples, and engaged in large-scale irrigation works in the style of a Kakatiya raja. He also assimilated into Qutb Shahi service many *nayaka* chieftains who proudly claimed descent from warrior-servants of the Kakatiya house, especially those serving its last dynast, Pratapa Rudra.[56]

Ibrahim Shah entrusted traditional Hindu 'warrior-servants' with command of the most important forts and used the idiom and style of a Kakatiya or Reddy king.

Portuguese rule in Goa had the flexibility and contradictions of a paradox. In some ways, the Portuguese assimilated far more easily than the British, but they also introduced the European maxim of *cujus regio, illius religio*: whoever's realm, his religion. Their priority was political consolidation and commercial expansion. In 1511, Afonso de Albuquerque conquered Malacca, famous for its straits and a key strategic base in the Indian Ocean. Now titled Duke of Goa, he was head of the Estado da India till his death in 1515, at the age of 52.

From Malacca, Portuguese ships were able to move into the Bay of Bengal towards India's wealthiest province. According to travellers, the average Bengali market was full of every variety of fish, meat and vegetable; butter, oils, pepper, salt, sweetmeats, silk and textiles, all at the lowest prices. The kingdom of Bengal, as Francois Bernier picturesquely put it, had a hundred gates to enter but not one through which to leave. The Portuguese opened an European door from the sea.

In 1517, Goa sent Joao Coelho on an exploratory trip to Chittagong, the eastern port of Bengal, later dubbed the 'Porto Grande'. He remained there till 1518, when the first official envoy, D. Joao de Silveira, came to seek trading rights from the provincial government based in Gaur. The reception was incendiary, for Portuguese pirates had seized two Bengali ships, but he succeeded in obtaining an agreement for *carreira de Bengala*. Along with traders, the Portuguese sent pirates, or *fidalgos*, operating on behalf of Portuguese nobles, who made a fortune out of brigandage, smuggling and mercenary services.

It was not long before local potentates, including the ruler of Arakan in Burma, began to enlist Portuguese buccaneers with superior military skills. In 1535–1536 the Portuguese governor in Bengal, Martim Afonso de Mello, helped Sultan Mahmud Shah stave off, albeit temporarily, the ruler of Bihar, Sher Shah Suri. In return, he received the right to collect customs duties at Chittagong and Satgaon in an individual capacity and permission to build factories. By the 1560s, most of the Portuguese trade with south-east Asia and China was in private hands. As demand grew, ships got bigger and began to offload their cargo onto smaller barks near the mouth of the Hooghly, the entrance of which was filled with treacherous sandbanks. These smaller vessels followed the tide upriver. Bengal was a centre of multinational trade: there was pepper from Malabar; cinnamon from Sri Lanka; cowrie shells from the Maldives; cloves, nutmeg and mace from Malacca; sandalwood from Timor; porcelain and pearls from China; camphor from Borneo and velvet, satin and muslin from Sumatra. The Bengal administration charged a duty of 2.5 per cent.

Fray (or Frey) Sebastian Manrique of Porto was among the Augustinian priests assigned to Hooghly. His account of life during the zenith of the Mughal Empire, *Travels of Fray Sebastien Manrique 1629–1643*, is a treasury of piquant detail. The Portuguese were far more comfortable in Indian dress than other Europeans, writes the priest, wearing silk or cotton robes, jewellery and Indian slippers. Homes in Hooghly ranged from splendid mansions to straw huts; superior rice was plentiful; the local sweets were delicious and mangoes unsurpassed.

Gambling and drinking were the preferred modes of entertainment. Gambling rooms were segregated according to social hierarchy. Trader-settlers were *casados*; soldier-traders were *soldados*; mercenaries were known as *chatins* and pirates were *arrenegados*. Those born in Portugal were *homo blanco* or *firangi*; children of white parents born in India were *casticos*; while those of mixed marriage were *mestizos*. Bengali introduced a word for pirates, *harmad*, a variation of armada; it is still in use. The rich drank wine from overseas, while others quaffed local rice liquor or thick arrack made with brown sugar. Local *bhang*, from cannabis, was either smoked or drunk in water flavoured with nutmeg, cloves or other spices. Opium and *bhang* were used as aphrodisiacs, and if that didn't work, they could at least guarantee sound sleep.

For those at the lower end of pay scales, there was no alternative to 'country liquor'. Robert Ivermee describes how some Englishmen experimented with *bhang*. The majority became merry, but one of them sat on the floor and wept all afternoon; another stuck his head into a large jar and kept it there for more than four hours; four or five began complimenting one another till they turned into emperors; one had a serious fight with a wooden pillar until the skin on his knuckles wore out and two sweated for three hours till they were nearly dehydrated.[57]

Manrique stayed in Hooghly till 1628, when he was sent to Arakan in Burma. He travelled across Bengal, making friends with Brahmins, Muslims and Mughal officials. He mentions that the law of every faith was respected in the Mughal Empire and narrates an incident where an official ordered that the hands of a Muslim be cut off because he had stolen a revered bird, the peacock, from a Hindu village. He was impressed by the beauty of mosques and splendour of temples and fascinated by the homage paid to the Hooghly river, an extension of the sacred Ganges. Indians working on Portuguese ships bottled the Hooghly river water and sold it as 'holy water' in other parts of the country (in 1585, the church forced Goa to make this illegal). Manrique described Bengali men as languorous and pusillanimous and the women as impetuous, assertive and fond of sex. Reflecting 16th-century Catholic doctrine, he called Hinduism 'pagan', 'stupid' and 'abominable', while Islam was dismissed as 'false' and 'wicked'.

Other European travellers, such as the French physician François Bernier, were sharply critical of Portuguese hypocrisy. In May 1666, Manucci called Goa a place 'where treachery is great and prevalent, where there is little fear of God and no concern for strangers'.[58] But he praised the fruit, particularly the Nicolao Afonso mango. Bernier accused the Portuguese of vanity and depravity, called their pirates the scourge of the seas and held them singularly responsible for a sharp escalation in 17th-century slave trade.[59] Hooghly's slave market was conducted in the heart of town.

Shah Jahan had reason to be unhappy with the Portuguese in Bengal. They had ignored his request for help when he rebelled against his father Jahangir, and he was wary of their amicable equation with Arakan, which continually challenged the eastern borders of his empire. But he made this flagrant slave trade the *casus belli*. In 1632, the commander of his forces, Nawab Qasim Khan Juvayni, sent an ultimatum: either the Portuguese give up slavery or there would be war.

The pragmatic merchants were ready to compromise, but priests, duty-bound to worry about the afterlife, were adamant. They argued that the slaves, converted to Christianity after purchase, would revert to their former faith if turned over to the Mughals. Their souls could not be abandoned. The priests prevailed. In a brief war, the Portuguese were outmanoeuvred and crushed.

Shah Jahan, unwilling to throw the baby out with the bathwater, restored commercial privileges in 1633 and granted 777 bighas of rent-free land to the Augustinian fathers at Bandel. But Portuguese domination was over. In 1635, a Dutch fleet holding a license sailed up to Hooghly town, now an imperial possession, to purchase cotton and silk for Japan. By 1636, the English had a factory in Hooghly. In 1653, the Dutch erected Fort Gustave in nearby Chinsurah; 20 years later, the French founded Chandernagore, about 5 miles downstream from Hooghly.

Portugal's memory has lasted in bits of Bengal's common parlance, like *chai* for tea and *biskut* for biscuit: the Porguguese brought tea to Bengal from their posts in Macau and South China. They also introduced potatoes, tomatoes, papaya and the ubiquitous chilli from Brazil, enabling Bengal to add a further creative dimension to its exceptional cooking.

In Goa, Indians embellished the chilli with mustard oil, salt and ginger, grinding the mix into a paste. The chilli became a staple for the poor, adding inexpensive bite to regular fare. The Portuguese also brought the custard apple, guava, cashew, groundnut, prickly pear, pineapple, marigold, maize and tobacco to India. In 1617, Jahangir became the only Indian ruler to ban tobacco, but the effort was futile. The hookah prevailed.

Roy Moxham writes:

The one great contribution the Portuguese made to India was to bring in the useful plants of the Americas. An extraordinary number of the fruits and vegetables that the Indians tend to regard as indigenous in fact came from South and Central America... The most commonly cultivated flower in today's India is the marigold. It adorns almost every deity and ancestral photograph in temple, shop, home or office. This plant was native to Mexico. The Portuguese probably introduced it to India for their own religious ceremonies.[60]

What astonished early European contemporaries was the Portuguese willingness to marry Indian women. The reasons were practical rather than altruistic. It was an attempt to create a new loyal population through integration. Goa could be defended with forts, walls, ditches and cannon, but a long-term strategy required numbers. Afonso de Albuquerque wrote to King Manuel that the Portuguese needed not only to build stone houses but to raise sons and daughters—with Indian wives—who would have a vested interest in Portuguese rule. This policy was approved but proved too radical for consensus and was discontinued after two years. Social legitimacy, however, could not be so easily withdrawn in practice.

Manuel's successor, Joao III 'the Pious', famously ruled between 1521 and 1557 with the sword in one hand and a crucifix in the other. In 1522, Bishop Duarte Nunes advised the new king that it was a grave error to tolerate Hindu festivals and temples in Goa. In 1533, Pope Clement VII authorized the diocese of Goa with jurisdiction from the Cape of Good Hope to China and Japan, while King Joao reinforced his piety by introducing the Inquisition to Portugal in 1536. The Society of Jesus arrived in 1540. The charismatic Jesuit icon, St Francis Xavier, reached Goa in May 1542, on board the same ship as the new viceroy, Martim Afonso de Souza. The two dined at the same table. Francis Xavier, bearing the title of Papal Nuncio, carried letters of introduction from the king to major rulers of the east. Goa's Vicar General Miguel Vaz had already done some vigorous proselytization with the support of the government, implementing the policy of *rigor de misericordia* (pressure of moral force, which had been successfully used to expel Jews and Muslims in Portugal).[61] Xavier's mission was to multiply the number of saved souls through conversion. He established institutions for religious administration and schools before he died on the Chinese island of Sancian in 1552. Miraculously, his corpse did not deteriorate and was sent back to Goa in 1554, where it is preserved in the Basilica of Bom Jesus. Dr Fryer, as both an Anglican visitor and a medical doctor, was awed by the 'Miraculous Relick'. Francis Xavier was canonized in 1622.

Portuguese policy served both God and Caesar. The church counted its blessings in numbers of new Catholics; the state needed loyalists in administration, military and trading. Privileges were granted to converts. By 1539, the five islands under Portuguese rule— Tiswadi, Divar, Chorao, Juv and Kumbarjuv—had an estimated 10,000 Catholics out of a population of about 40,000. Priests of other Catholic orders flooded Goa. Conversion became competitive, and a saying became popular: viceroys come and go, Jesuits stay on forever.

The converts were reluctant to abandon all aspects of their traditional or 'heathen' culture, a fact which grated on the priests. While drinking water, for instance, they held the vessel above the mouth in the Indian manner and poured, for touching the vessel might invite 'pollution'. There was relentless pressure to uproot tradition, inexorably linked as it was to the Hindu faith. King Joao III ordered all temples to be razed.

The Inquisition used torture in the service of religion. Dr Fryer describes a torture machine:

> Going the next Morning to the Palace-stairs, we saw their Sessions house, the bloody Prison of the Inquisition; and, in a principal Market-place, was raised an Engine a great height, at top like a Gibbet, with a Pulley, with steppings to go upon, as on a Flag staff, for the Strapado, which unhinges a man's joints; a cruel Torture. Over against these Stairs, is an Island, where they burn (after exposing them to the Multitude) all those condemned by the Inquisitor, which are brought from

the Sancto Officio dress'd up in the most horrid Shapes of Imps and Devils, and so delivered to the Executioner.[62]

Fryer was prudent enough to ask no questions.

The tribunal was particularly harsh on lower caste converts who, often attracted only by the worldly advantages of adopting Christianity, maintained convivial relations with 'Gentoo' relatives or went to local doctors when ill. They were consigned to the flames for apostasy or sorcery. There were instances of Hindus being smeared with beef. Soldiers were ordered to disperse any multitude at a Hindu festival; idol-worship was forbidden and many Brahmins decided to sell their property and leave. Official jobs were reserved for Catholics. During the century of intense oppression, between 1550 and 1650, the Christian population rose from one-fifth to two-thirds. High-caste converts managed to protect their privileged cocoons, retaining old surnames, marrying and socializing within their old kin, creating a Catholic Christianity with Hindu characteristics.

Edicts were often ignored rather than resisted—the church had to keep renewing its list of taboos. Try as they might, the authorities could not force people to end their reverence for the cow. When temples were destroyed, worshippers hid their deities or sent them to a sanctuary outside Goa, bringing them back to the village annually to display their true fealty. There were economic reasons as well for the survival of Hinduism—a mass departure of Hindus would have led to scarcity in farm labour, artisans and sailing crew, thereby undermining the colonial project. Business required existing expertise. Merchants, tax collectors and bankers were Hindus, while most contracts were handled by the elite Saraswat Brahmins.

The Goan Indian kitchen, allied with clothes and manners, won a splendid victory over any attempt at ostracization or European snobbery. In her fascinating study of food and colonial culture, Lizzie Collingham writes:

> When the Dutchman Jan Huyghen van Linschoten arrived in Goa in September 1583, almost a century after Vasco da Gama landed at Calicut, he was surprised to discover the wives of the Portuguese eating Indian food. A typical meal was boiled rice with a thin watery soup poured over it, salt fish, mango

pickle, and a fish or meat sauce. These were dishes strange to a 16th century European whose staple diet was wheat bread and roast meats. Not only did the Portuguese in India eat unfamiliar food, they ate it with their hands in the Indian manner. Indeed, the women laughed at anyone they observed using a spoon.[63]

The Portuguese were equally flexible in dress and personal habits. Adds Collingham:

> Many of the Portuguese settlers had adopted a variety of Indian habits. The men had discarded their tight knee-length hose for 'a sort of breeches, called Candales, the like whereof I never saw in any part of Europe; for when they are ty'd they leave something like the tops of Boots on the Leg. Others under a short Doublet, wear wide silk Breeches; and some have them hand down to their Ankles'. Even more peculiar, they regularly changed their underclothes. In Europe, it was customary to rub oneself down with one's old linen underclothes before putting on a fresh undershirt, and a bath was out of the question. In contrast, the Portuguese in India were scrupulously clean. Besides regularly changing their linen, they took a bath at least once, and sometimes twice, a day. Nor did the women ever fail to wash 'as often as they ease themselves or make water, or use the companie of their husbands'... The women observed purdah, and wore veils when they went outside. Although the wealthy hung themselves with 'jewels, and rosaries of Gold and Silver many times double', to indicate their Christian faith, they wore Indian clothes: thin, almost transparent, swathes of material above the waist and petticoats, bare legs and colourful slippers below... the wives were said to spend their days idly chewing betel nut, and washing and rubbing themselves with sweet-smelling perfumes and sandalwood. These were all practices, Linschoten observed, they had learned and 'received of the Indian Heathens, which have these customs of long time'.[64]

Despite the ruthless demands of the Inquisition, which began to peter out towards the second half of the 18th century, the Portuguese were more comfortable with eastern culture than the English who followed them, perhaps because they understood the east far better than north Europeans. Portugal was ruled by Arab-Moor Muslims for more than five centuries, between 712 and 1249.

Goan fishermen found an effective way to keep churchmen content: the best of the daily catch was reserved for priests. Food was a synthesizer, if not an equalizer. Portuguese-Goan cooks used toddy, in the absence of yeast, to ferment dough, adding to the repertoire of a staple like bread. The Bebinca cake was made from milk, eggs and jaggery, a local substitute for sugar. They introduced confections like the marzipan, tart and Florentine. The spicy vindaloo was a meat preparation, a chilli-soaked variation of *carne de vinho e alhos,* or pork cooked in wine vinegar and garlic. The fame of Goan cooks spread.

John Ovington records in 1689 that the East India Company kitchen in Surat had an Indian and a Portuguese cook in addition to an Englishman. This eclectic popularity became more mainstream when the British took along Goan cooks to their Raj in 1814 at the end of their friendly occupation of Goa during the Napoleonic wars. Lizzie Collingham writes that by the middle of the 19th century:

> Goan cooks were especially sought after... These cooks introduced *vindaloo* into the repertoire of Anglo-Indian curries... Goan cookery books referred to it as a 'Portuguese curry'. For the British, the Goans applied the techniques of *vindaloo* to all sorts of meats, with duck being the favourite. By the 1920s a Goan cook had become a marker of status... The Goans had preserved the Portuguese talent for magical desserts and the British enthused over their chocolate fondants and sugar-coated fruits. A classic Anglo-Indian dish known as beveca, made from sugar, rice flour, coconut cream and rose water, was a simplified version of the Goan layered coconut cake, *bebinca.*[65]

Cooking remains one of the great fine arts of Goa. During Mughal rule, Aurangzeb's sister Roshan Ara Begum put a Portuguese lady named Thomazia Martins in charge of her table. She had been among those captured and taken to Delhi after the fall of Hooghly in 1632. Roshan Ara Begum had an unusually independent life for a Mughal princess—she never married and was apparently happy with a succession of good-looking lovers.

The only Portuguese officials in Goa who insisted on maintaining an undiluted European profile were the small number of high officials who came on three-year tours of duty. They wore heavy and expensive European attire and walked at the unhurried pace of assured power, while Indian slaves protected their hatted heads with an umbrella and passing natives cringed in a low salute. It was acerbically said that a new viceroy spent his first year furnishing his palace—he had to, because it had been cleaned out by his predecessor. In the second year, he amassed a fortune. In the third, he prepared for departure.

The dazzling naval prowess of Portugal and Spain set the course for European commerce, colonization and slave trade in the 16th century. The contempt of the Iberian powers for contemporary England is summed up in John Hawkins' experience at Surat in 1608. The Portuguese based there tried to kill him and called James I a king of fishermen and England an island of no importance.[66] Such self-confidence was punctured 4 years later, when on 29 November 1612, Captain Thomas Best routed a Portuguese fleet of 4 galleons and 26 oared barks at Suvali, 19 km northwest of Surat, with 4 ships of the East India Company under his command. It marked the beginning of the end Portuguese ascendancy.

Portugal's Empire of the oceans effectively imploded between 1620 and 1665. Portugal lost Hormuz in 1622, Mombasa in 1631, Hooghly in 1632, Malacca in 1641, Muscat in 1650, Sao Tome in 1658, Sri Lanka in 1658, Kollam in 1661, Kochi and Kannur in 1663 and Bombay by 1665. Bombay disappeared in the dowry of the English king Charles II; the other strategic strongholds were lost in battle. The seas opened for a British advance.

But chilli, chai and *biskut* flourished, and they remain an intrinsic part of the daily cuisine of the Indian people.

English Intoxication, Indian Hallucination

The quest for wealth exacted a human cost. Dr John Fryer's diagnosis of the fate of the average European was bleak:

> What then is to be expected here, where sordid Thrift is the only Science? After which, notwithstanding there is so general an Inquest, few there be acquite [sic] it: For in Five hundred, One hundred survive not; of that One hundred, one quarter get not Estates; of those that do, it has not been recorded above One in Ten Years has seen his Country...[1]

Convolutions of 17th-century English grammar apart, the sense is obvious. He added that it was hardly worth a sober man's while to dream of wealth, which became as much of a mirage to the 'Vulgar' as the Greek deity Zeus was to Aesop's frogs.

Fryer had an instructive point. Aesop's frogs beseeched Zeus to send them a king. Zeus dropped a log into their pond, terrifying them. Eventually one of the frogs peeped above the water and realized that it was only a piece of wood. They hopped on to the log, began to make fun of their wooden god and prayed for another king. This time Zeus sent a water snake, which ate them all up.

Fryer mentions the salary structure: 'The Writers are obliged to serve Five Years for 10 *l*. [pounds] per Ann. [annum]' and rise to Senior Factors in three years and Merchants in another three. The President or Governor received £500 a year, but only half was paid in India, as indemnity against any misdemeanour. The accountant got £72, with 22 of them paid in London. The private income and high commissions were the 'Jacob's Ladder by which they ascend'.[2]

Salaries might seem comparatively parsimonious, but you were allowed compensation through private transactions and could even trade with the Company. Sir John Child, chief of Surat and Bombay, made a fortune of over £100,000 apart from his wages before his death in 1690, according to John Ovington.

Fryer did not wait for Jacob's ladder; he returned home. He found India and Indian food disagreeable. When he first saw the fabled Indian *pilau,* rice grains delicately hued by master-chefs in blue and green and yellow and red, his reaction was bemused: the 'Cooks are wittie', he wrote. His peers had a more attractive view of India's kitchens.

Johann Albrecht von Mandelslo, a page in the court of the German Duke of Holstein, came as part of a trade delegation to Persia in 1638. From there, he took an English boat in April to Surat, where he stayed as a guest of the Company. He came ashore near 'the Sulthan's Palace' on the Tapti river, found customs officials so exacting 'that they think it not enough to open chests and portmantles, but examine people's clothes and pockets' (spellings in quotations have been left as in the original). The sultan, or local governor, turned up at the customs house himself, determined to purchase both the diamond and the yellow amber bracelet in Mandelslo's possession. They were not for sale. The governor returned the diamond immediately and the bracelet later.

Mandelslo's journey of exploration was clear evidence of German interest in the profits and exotic treasure being reported by traders and travellers. The Frenchman Jean-Baptiste Tavernier made his first eastern journey in 1631 to Isfahan in Safawid Persia, at the age of 26. He was back in Persia in 1640 and this time took a ship to Surat, from where he travelled to Golconda, Goa, Dhaka, Patna and Agra. Even in the smallest village, he writes, he found plenty of rice, flour, butter, milk, vegetables, sugar and sweetmeats. He witnessed Shah Jahan going to Friday prayers in a procession of 80 elephants and being weighed on his birthday against jewels whose value would be distributed as alms. He was dazzled by Shah Jahan's famous peacock throne, which contained 108 rubies above 100 carats, 160 emeralds above 30 carats, along with innumerable diamonds and pearls, all surpassed in splendour by a great ruby and a pearl of 50 carats on the peacock's breast. Tavernier claims he saw an uncut stone of 500 carats in Golconda.

In 1666, Tavernier purchased a pristine blue-tinted diamond from the Kollur mines, weighing 112 carats, of perfect clarity. Louis XIV bought the Tavernier Blue and other diamonds for three million livres in 1668 and raised the jewel merchant to Baron of Aubonne. The gem was stolen during the French Revolution, reappeared in London in 1839 and has since 1958 found a home in the Natural History Museum in Washington DC.

The English traders at Surat, working for a company in the staid business of textiles and spice rather than fabulous stones, contented themselves with a comfortable rather than a glamorous life. As many as 15 or 16 meat dishes were served at dinner, since game was cheap as Gujaratis were largely vegetarian. The main drink was arrack (dubbed 'Fool's Rack'), except on Sundays, when better wine reached the table. They smoked the hubble-bubble and often watched dancing girls after dinner in 'native' style. They drank far too many toasts to the health of absent wives on a cocktail of arrack, rosewater, citric juice and sugar called 'palepuntz', or punch. Those who wanted an excuse for arrack praised its medicinal virtues as a morning laxative and an evening astringent. The daytime drink was either tea or *kawha*, favoured by Persian merchants and sailors.

Mandelslo got a heady taste of hospitality when he travelled across Gujarat. He was too puritan when in the company of Englishmen to take off his clothes before 'some local women', but he enjoyed the excellent *bhang* offered by the Mughal governor in Ahmedabad.[3] *Bhang*, generally taken with milk, was literally the opiate of the Indian masses. The entry on 'Indian Bhang' in the 1849 series of *Chambers's Edinburgh Journal* is sniffy about this 'Hindoo' indulgence and cautionary about addiction, but comprehensive in the report of its usage and variety:

> *Bhang* is the leaf of the male plant of the hemp, dried in the sun; when fresh, the leaf has a pleasing odour; but I am not certain whether it retains it when dried. *Ganja* is the same leaf; but being rubbed down in the hand to powder, and smoked in a *nariella* [a kind of *hookah*], retains the name of the plant;

the epithet of churres [*charas*] is given to the dried flower and
stamen, which must naturally be more delicate and scarce,
and on that account dearer. Churres is frequently made
into tablet and *laddoos,* or balls of sugar candy—a dainty
sweet-meat for the Hindoo, who gets bemused as he sucks or
nibbles the sweets; and I have heard the feeling they occasion
described by a friend as that of being plunged into a pleasing
reverie, which was, however, every now and then broken by a
sensation of being hoisted up into the air, and let down again
with a shock. The preparation of a *lotah,* or jug of *bhang,*
is accompanied by as much joviality and gossip among the
partakers as the mixture of a bowl of punch or negus [a mix
of wine, hot water, sugar, nutmeg and lemon] is with us, and
many a time have I noticed an old favourite servant as he sat
over the orgies of the *bhang.* Wherever Peerun travelled, his
bundle of *bhang* went with him...[4]

Indian *bhang* never became part of the sahib's relaxation—it remained
the preserve of Peerun, although the low-paid Company soldier could
not always be prevented from purchasing this gateway to a more
colourful world.

The English preferred intoxication to Indian hallucination.

The opulence of the dining table became an institutionalized
reward for the rigours of existence in India. Reverend John Ovington,
chaplain at Surat for two years from 1689, has left an account of a
Company dinner.[5] They sat at table according to seniority. Everyone
washed their hands when a servant brought a silver ewer and basin.
European wines and English beer were in much demand, and to
'please the curiosity of every Palate at the times of Eating, an *English,
Portuguese,* and an *Indian Cook,* are all entertain'd to dress the Meat
in different ways for the gratification of every Stomach'. He continues,
'Palau, that is Rice boil'd so artificially, that every grain lies singly
without being clodded together, with Spices intermixt, and a boil'd
Fowl in the middle, is the most common *Indian* Dish'.[6] On Sundays
and public holidays, deer, antelope, peacocks, hares, partridges and
Persian wines were served.

Food, drink and money were the priorities of a hard, short and
pestilential life. Numbers were small. Dr Fryer mentions that there

were only about 300 Englishmen in Madras in 1673, compared to some 3,000 Portuguese settlers and 40,000 Indians in the 'Heathen Town' just outside the walls. Rough statistics indicated that till the British victory in Bengal at Plassey in 1757, two-thirds of the 'writers' who came to India never saw England again.

Life was also lonely. Initially, the Company insisted that its employees lead a bachelor's existence, but this inevitably led to liaisons with Indian women. According to Roy Moxham, John Leachland, who had arrived as a purser's mate in 1615 and stayed on as a factor in Surat, married an Indian lady called Manya. The union became public when a daughter, whom he named Mary, was born in 1626. Leachland refused to abandon his wife and family despite threats from the president and left service. He was reemployed in 1632 during a staff shortage caused by disease. On his deathbed in 1634, Leachland requested that his dues be given to his wife and daughter. London did not approve, and the money was withheld. His colleagues had a larger heart than Company directors—they supported Manya and Mary financially. In 1643, Mary married the English tailor William Appleton in a ceremony conducted by the Company chaplain.

Not every priest was as virtuous as the rules. Moxham writes:

A chaplain, William Leske, had an affair with a sweeper woman in 1616. He also used a whip on some Indian brokers and was expelled. Later, however, it would become common for the Company's men, if not the clergy, to imitate their neighbours and maintain a *zenana*, a harem.[7]

It was not until 1670 that the East India Company tried to send English women to their Indian settlements, according to J. Talboys Wheeler, who retired as the assistant secretary for foreign affairs.[8] Three or four 'plain' and 'honest' women, tolerably educated, reached 'Madraspatanam', or Madras, but two of them remained unmarried and survived in the fort on a small allowance given by the Company. The experiment was a failure.

The Company's focus by this time had shifted east. Surat was closer to England, but Siam and China were easier to reach from the Coromandel coast while Bengal was better for the balance sheet. In 1681, Bengal became a separate agency, with inland posts at

Kasimbazar, Malda, Dhaka and Patna. Bengal's textiles had become high fashion in England, in dress and furnishing. Society women demanded Indian chintz for petticoats and outer garments. The Company paid for Indian goods in bullion: between 1681 and 1685, this amounted to nearly 7,000 kg of gold and 240,000 kg of silver.

The principal Company agent in Kasimbazar, Job Charnock, was in continual trouble both with his hosts and his mentors. The authorities forced him out of Hooghly in 1686 but let him purchase, two years later, three adjacent villages downriver—Gobindpur, Kalikata and Sutanuti—from a landlord named Sabarna Raychaudhuri. Calcutta was born. The present Fort William sits on what was once Gobindpur; Kalikata is the region from there to Burrabazar; and Sutanuti became the abode of the Bengali gentry and indigenous population, now Shyambazar in the north. Charnock died in 1693, but a fortified factory was in business by 1696.

Bengal was where the money was. 'The Indian subcontinent,' writes Nick Robbins, 'was then the workshop of the world, accounting for almost a quarter of global manufacturing output in 1750, compared with just 1.9 per cent for Britain. Within the Mughal Empire, Bengal was the richest province, described by Aurangzeb as "the Paradise of nations...".'[9] By 1690, over 40 per cent of the East India Company's imports were from Bengal; within another five decades this had grown to over 65 per cent.

Dhaka's exquisite, light, translucent, gossamer-thin muslin, described as 'woven air', became the high point of fashion in 18th-century London and Paris. The puritan Aurangzeb famously scolded his daughter for immodesty when she wore a dress made of seven layers of cotton muslin; for more liberal Europe, less was sufficient. Marie Antoinette wore muslin around her neck on her way to the guillotine. Napoleon banned its import to protect domestic textiles (despite Josephine's patronage) and Britain used taxes to curtail its import in the 19th century. (The art of spinning such labour-intensive muslin, with thread counts ranging from 350 to over 1,000, was lost; in the 2010s Bangladesh began to train weavers to revive that extraordinary skill, according to the *Times*, London, of 20 March 2021).

Indian weave was available at half the cost of English fabrics. Bengal added some 150 names for cloth to the English dictionary, including silk, calico, muslin, chintz, gingham, dungaree, taffeta, seersucker and bandana, the best of these made from *phuti* cotton grown beside the Meghna, a beautiful river in east Bengal. In the 1760s, the Company's declared profits rose by 75 per cent or higher, as supplies to China began to include opium.[10]

The British were only one amid the many *kulah poshan* (or hat-wearing) Europeans lined up on the western bank of the Hooghly. Their main rivals were the French, who had begun operations in 1674 from Pondicherry on the Coromandel coast, and established a second base in Chandernagore on the Hooghly, in 1676.

The British strengthened their position with the 1717 grant of a *firman* by the dilettante Mughal Emperor Farrukhsiyar, who had spent part of his childhood in Bengal playing with toys presented by Company officials. Those toys proved an excellent investment. All customs taxes for inland trade in commodities like salt, saltpetre, opium and tobacco were waived.[11]

The Company mission to Delhi included the Armenian Khwaja Sarhad, who was on a straight commission of ₹50,000 as a success fee, and the doctor William Hamilton, who cured His Imperial Highness of two large swellings in his groin. The groin possibly sealed the deal.

Hamilton received an elephant and solid gold medical instruments; the Company got commercial and territorial privileges (but not rights) greater than any granted to a European company. Private trade by officials was, however, not permitted. But as Delhi's authority weakened, such qualifications were ignored with impunity. The empire that had stretched from central Asia to Burma two decades before began to disintegrate rapidly and irretrievably. The psyche of the Mughal aristocracy split between self-entitlement and self-pity, without the confidence to ward off an enemy or the honesty to laugh at itself. Regional satraps became the de facto rulers of India.

In 1739, the Persian invader Nadir Shah smashed what little remained of Mughal credibility and massacred the citizens of Delhi while the 'emperor' Muhammad Shah (nicknamed 'Rangila' or 'colourful') sat silent on an impotent and tenuous throne, kept in Mughal possession till 1857 by the strange glue of everyone else's convenience. Regional powers, each individually stronger than the Mughal, never felt strong enough to replace the nominal ruler in Delhi.

Three years after Nadir Shah's invasion, the Marathas tested Bengal's defences when in 1742 Bhaskar Pant Kolhatkar led his armies deep into the province before wheeling back. In the north, the Marathas drove out the Afghans from Punjab between 1757 and 1758, taking Delhi, Lahore, Multan and Attock on the banks of the Indus near the Khyber Pass. They were checked by the Afghans under Ahmed Shah Abdali at the third battle of Panipat in 1761, but they resumed their grip on central and north India by the end of the decade. Their inability to seize the throne of Delhi created an opening for a trading company which had mastered the art of opportunism and backed its ambitions with brilliant victories on battlefields from Plassey to Buxar to Seringapatnam to Assaye, Agra and Delhi.

The British journey to Delhi began in 1757, from Bengal.

France lost momentum after a vigorous bid for influence led by Joseph Francois Dupleix, son of a director in La Compagnie Perpetuelle des Indes, who had been in Pondicherry since 1720. Dupleix strengthened the French in Bengal after his appointment as superintendent of Chandernagore in 1731; in 1742 he was promoted to governor-general of all French operations. In 1746, he captured Madras but had to return the city to the Company under the terms of the Treaty of Aix-la-Chapelle. In 1754, the charismatic Dupleix was suddenly recalled to France, a victim of petty vindictiveness, and died in poverty a decade later.

The young Siraj ud-Daula succeeded his grandfather Alivardi Khan as Nawab of Bengal in 1756, initiating a series of immature mistakes with fatal consequences. Spurred by ego rather than understanding, he captured poorly defended Calcutta on 20 June 1756. Fifty-five British prisoners, including the magistrate Josiah Holwell, were locked up that midsummer night in a cell meant for drunkards, commonly nicknamed the 'Black Hole'. According to Holwell, 43 died of suffocation. The British prepared for revenge. Their reputation and their fortunes were at stake.

Jesse Norman writes:

Trade with the Indian subcontinent accounted for roughly one-fifth of world trade in the early 18th century. The Indian trade had long been extremely profitable for the Company, but those profits were raised to almost unimaginable levels as a result of the exploits of Robert Clive. A natural troublemaker who had been expelled by a succession of English schools, Clive entered the Company on the bottom rung in the usual position of 'writer' or junior clerk.[12]

Clive became an unlikely star in Madras, when in 1751 he led Company forces to victory against Chanda Sahib, a claimant to the principality of Arcot with French support. Clive and Admiral Watson mobilized after the fall of Calcutta, sailed to Bengal and first neutralized the French. On 2 January 1757 they took Chandernagore with a riverside attack. Clive next split the strength of his principal adversary by bribing Mir Jafar, commander of the Nawab's forces, and defeated Siraj ud-Daula at Plassey on 23 June 1757. While he loaded the spoils of victory on to boats, the coup de grace was delivered by Jafar's son, Mir Miran, who pursued and killed Siraj ud-Daula. Jesse Norman writes:

> The effect of these actions was to unleash a bonanza of personal enrichment for the Company, its shareholders and above all its local agents. Bengal… was now effectively controlled by a few hundred Company men. Indian nobles had been quickly elbowed out of the markets after Plassey as the British took over the lucrative trade in betel nuts, salt and opium. But now the Company possessed something far greater; control of the tax revenue of Bengal, amounting to some £33 million a year.[13]

Clive immediately strengthened the Company's ability to protect its wealthy possessions by raising a standing army while he and his colleagues filled their pockets.

With typical insouciance, Clive had made the Bengal government's 'unfulfilled' pledges a reason for his war. Now, taking a long stride, he acquired the right from his puppet, Nawab Mir Jafar, to punish anyone who dared to ask the English for any tax or duty, however trifling. The East India Company became zamindars, or landlords, of 24-Parganas, Nadia, Hooghly, part of Dhaka and the Hijli island. Clive received a controversial *jagir* or personal fiefdom, whose value he took in a cash equivalent from the Company on his return to England in 1760. While retaining its monopoly over the lucrative sale of salt, the East India Company began production of opium in 1761.

Massacre by Famine

Ten Sufis can sleep under the same blanket, goes an Indian proverb, but two kings cannot live in the same kingdom. Tensions escalated between the Company, which wielded true authority, and the second puppet nawab of Bengal, Mir Kasim, a virtual pensioner with a title. War was inevitable. Three allies—the Mughal Emperor Shah Alam and the nawabs of Bengal and Awadh—made an effort to abort the East India Company's political ambitions. They were defeated decisively by the British at the battle of Buxar in 1764. The Company struck its own coins to confirm its sovereign status.

Company officials celebrated their good fortune with unbridled loot, to the point where Robert Clive was sent back to restore some sanity. On his return in May 1765, the first decision he made was to curb 'gifts', a euphemism for rampant corruption. All presents between ₹1,000 and ₹4,000 now required permission—anything above that went into Company coffers. This shocked and infuriated Company officials, who believed that they needed £3,000 a year to maintain their lifestyle, and thrice that amount to take back as retirement benefits, at a time when the salary of a member of the governor's council was £330.

The historian Percival Spear, using florid metaphors appropriate to colourful larceny, writes: 'The brotherhood of exploitation, the freemasonry of graft, had been violated. Clive had put himself outside the pale. They sharpened their mental knives of revenge on the grindstone of hate while dipping their quills of complaint in the ink of defamation.' The resurrected Clive compared Gomorrah favourably to Calcutta. He declared, in a letter to Sir Francis Sykes in July 1765:

> I will pronounce Calcutta to be one of the most wicked Places in the Universe. Corruption Licentiousness and a want of Principle seem to have possessed the Minds of all the Civil Servants, by frequent bad Examples they are grown callous, Rapacious and Luxurious beyond Conception...[14]

Clive secured the Company's finances through a covenant signed with Shah Alam on 12 August 1765, which assigned the *diwani,* or revenue rights, of Bengal to the East India Company. The price of East India Company stock shot up, and dividends rose from 6 per cent to 10 per cent even as it ensured the autonomy of India operations by giving the British government a subvention of £400,000 a year.

Clive, back in England by 1767, was confident when he rose to defend himself in Parliament against accusations of unbridled avarice. Nicholas Dirks writes: 'Clive used his most recent sojourn in Bengal as reformer to buttress his claim for approbation rather than condemnation, and he gave several speeches before Parliament that were judged brilliant, if sometimes excessive, rhetorical performances.'[15] He had made the East India Company 'Sovereign' over 15,000,000 people, he argued. As for the English 'Nabobs', their conduct was 'strictly honourable'. They were never 'authors of those acts of violence and oppression of which it is the fashion to accuse them. Such crimes are committed by the Natives of the Country, acting as their agents, and for the most part without their knowledge'.[16]

As for the famous gifts:

When presents are received as the price of services to the Nation, to the Company and to that Prince who bestowed those presents; when they are not exacted from him by compulsion; when he is in a state of independence and can do with his money what he pleases; and when they are not received to the disadvantage of the Company, he holds presents so received not dishonourable.[17]

If the narrative was limited to the denudation of a Mughal aristocracy that had passed its sell-by date by a new commercial-colonial class, it would have merited some attention but not excessive approbation. What makes the first five years of British rule in Bengal chilling is the death by starvation of uncounted millions because of barbaric exploitation by the East India Company. This fact has been carefully excised from common knowledge.

In 1769, the monsoon failed in Bengal; by 1770 drought had deteriorated into a catastrophic famine. According to confidential records of the Company, this apocalyptic tragedy killed an estimated number between a third and half of the population of lower Bengal. Instead of providing relief to parents selling their children and people resorting to cannibalism, Company officials, making full use of their monopoly on inland trade, gloated while they raised taxes and harvested money out of death: 'the revenue assessment was in fact increased by ten per cent during the height of the famine and there were several accusations of British collusion in the inevitable hoarding and profiteering'.[18]

John Keay quotes a report compiled by the eminent civil servant Sir William Hunter a century later from official records:

> All through the stifling summer of 1770 the people went on dying. The husbandmen sold their cattle; they sold their implements of agriculture; they devoured their seed-grain; they sold their sons and daughters till at length no buyer of children could be found; they ate the leaves of the trees and the grass of the field; and in June 1770 the [British] Resident at the Darbar [of Murshidabad] affirmed that the living were feeding on the dead. Day and night a torrent of famished and disease-ridden wretches poured into the great cities... The streets were blocked up with promiscuous heaps of the dying and the dead.[19]

Warren Hastings, the governor of Bengal, wrote to the Court of Directors on 3 November 1772 with a sense of achievement at having raised tax revenues during this horrific disaster:

> Notwithstanding the loss of at least one-third of the inhabitants of the province, and the consequent decrease of the cultivation, the net collections of the year 1771 exceeded even those of 1768... it was naturally to be expected that the diminution of the revenue should have kept an equal pace with the other consequences of so great a calamity. That it did not was owing to its being violently kept up to its former standard.[20]

Hastings mentions, without a tremor, that violence was used to extract money from the 'dying and the dead'.

One of the inexplicable—even bizarre—facts is that the Indian poor died of starvation in their millions in 1770 but did not rise against the British dispensation. It was easy for the British to take Indians for granted.

In London, the Company's inflated stock and overstretched borrowings led to a familiar bubble. No one had forgotten the investor panic after the collapse of the South Sea Company half a century earlier as a consequence of mass greed for profits from the slave trade. The 1715 Treaty of Utrecht, negotiated between the belligerents of the War of Spanish Succession, gave Britain, in addition to Gibraltar and Minorca, monopoly rights over the export of African slaves to the Spanish Empire in Latin America for thirty years. The South Sea Company was formed to supply slaves to the Atlantic shores of Spanish America. Among its shareholders were King George I, Sir Isaac Newton, the Bishop of Oxford, and a horde of celebrities, including the poet Alexander Pope and the writers Jonathan Swift and Daniel Defoe. Such was the craze for its stock, pushing its price into ether, that the bubble had to burst, which it did in 1720. Thousands were ruined. The British government could not afford another implosion of confidence in colonial profiteering.

The East India Company received a loan of £1,000,000 in 1772, with a few strings attached. The 1773 Regulating Act created a Governing Council of 5, with 3 members appointed by the government. A Supreme Court was established. The East India Company got a monopoly on the supply of tea to America, with permission to claim back customs duties. The Company immediately began to dump its tea on America. On 16 December 1773, Americans dumped this tea into the sea. A butterfly effect was in place.

Warren Hastings, son of a vicar at Balliol, Oxford, and ward of a Company director, had seen and suffered in both his professional and personal lives during his early days in India. He lost his first wife and two children to diphtheria. In 1756, he was imprisoned by Siraj ud-Daula until a Dutch friend bailed him out and helped him escape to the Dutch enclave at Chinsurah. When Hastings returned to Kasimbazar after 1757, he sold coffee and salt on the side for personal profit. In his first year as governor, he sent 50 chests of opium to China, where he also invested Spanish dollars.

Bribery was par for this acquisitive course. Hastings was 'caught accepting a suspicious £15,000 from one of Mir Jafar's wives, the Munny [or Munni] Begum, who was an ex-dancing girl from Agra sophisticated enough to smoke the hookah and to talk non-stop to visiting Englishmen from behind her scarlet purdah'[21]. In 1776, he sold diamonds worth £25,000 sent from India to London dealers. A different dimension to his personality enriched Bengal intellectually. He learnt Sanskrit, Arabic and Persian and founded the Asiatic Society of Bengal in 1784, which began the modern study of ancient Indian texts. As Sumanta Banerjee puts it: 'Hastings seemed to have smoothly moved in and out from his role as a connoisseur of oriental classics to that of a rapacious felon of the highest order.'[22]

Hastings did not drink, rarely dined out and went to bed by 10. His virtues paused at probity. Hastings had a simple theory of power: he would help friends but not his friends' friends.

He was hardly alone in his avarice. Sir Robert Baker, commander-in-chief of the Army, ran a lucrative business in saltpetre and opium. Richard Barwell, who sat on Hastings's council, became famous for winning a fortune in private business and losing it at cards, as well as flicking bread pellets at boisterous dinners with such accuracy that he could snuff out a candle at four yards. It was a jolly good time.

Hastings identified, in 1786, the 'sources of opulence' in Bengal: fertility of its soil, size of its population and the skilful industry of its people which yielded one crore of rupees annually, a sum, he boasted, greater than could be made in any other country in the world. By 1793, the East India Company was not only able to finance its wars of expansion, but increase its contribution to the British government to £500,000.

Success encourages pomp and circumstance. The fourth Governor-general Richard Wellesley (brother of the future Duke of Wellington, Arthur Wellesley) built a palace for his Calcutta residence, still in use, now known as the Raj Bhavan (Government House). By the 1830s, Governor-general Lord Auckland's travelling entourage consisted of 850 camels, 140 elephants, 250 horses and 12,000 men, including a French chef at the head of a battalion of cooks. This compares quite well with the Mughals at the apex of their power: in the 1610s, Jahangir marched, according to his memoirs, with a travelling town of tents. His kitchen was carried by 50 camels and 200 men with baskets on their heads at 10 pm the previous night to the next halt, so that breakfast might be ready for the emperor, his nobles and his forces when they followed the next morning.

By the first decade of the 19th century, Europeans and Indians had learned to work together in administration as they had earlier cooperated in commerce, but the social distance was always a gulf. In an interesting paradox, the more they learnt about each other's ways, the more aloof they became. As Colonel Thomas Broughton, a fine example of the straight-talking soldier, said in his letter to his brother written in 1809, Indians and the British did not mix.

Jadoo Ka Chukkur

When the young Napoleon Bonaparte was thinking about career options, he told his brother Lucien that the East India Company might be worth a thought.[23] Fortune took him elsewhere, but if he had come east, he could have well been fighting under the command of the man who would become his *bête noire*, Arthur Wellesley.

Alternatively, Napoleon could have served the Maratha ruler Mahadji Scindia, whose principal commander was the French officer Benoît de Boigne. De Boigne retired and left India when Mahadji Scindia passed away in 1794, after a reign of 33 years. The young Napoleon might have taken de Boigne's place and met Wellesley on the fields of India rather than Europe. The possibilities are intriguing. Given his military genius, Napoleon could have helped establish a Scindia Empire across India.

The principal Maratha clans—the Scindias of Gwalior, the Holkars from Indore, the Bhonsales of Nagpur, the Gaekwads in Baroda and the Peshwas of Pune—were the only Indian kingdoms capable of aborting British ascendancy. The Scindias owed their pre-eminence to Meherban Shrimant Sardar Bahadur Mahadji Scindia, Vakil-ul-Mutlaq (Regent of the Mughal Empire) and Amir-ul-Umra (Head of the Nobles), youngest son of the founder of the dynasty, Ranoji Rao. A Scindia held the key to Delhi's gates until it was wrested by the British.

Daulat Rao Scindia, who ruled between 1794 and 1827, came to terms with the Company in 1803 after losing four battles to General Gerald Lake. He was forced to cede Delhi but retained most of his other territories. In 1809, Colonel Thomas Broughton was posted to his court. Broughton, educated at Eton, began his career as a cadet in 1795, fought with the victorious army which defeated Tipu Sultan at Srirangapattna in 1799 and served as honorary secretary of the Royal Asiatic Society at the same time as the more famous Lieutenant-colonel James Tod, author of *Annals and Antiquities of Rajasthan*, who was the librarian. In a coincidence, both died within two days of each other in 1835.

Broughton has left a fascinating account of life, culture and politics in the Gwalior kingdom, in the form of letters to his brother in England, written during his march with the Scindia camp in 1809. They constitute a narrative portrait of the ruler, his bonhomie with the people, his respect for every faith, the multi-ethnic nature of his forces which included Hindu and Muslim contingents and the vibrant mix of religion and popular culture. This panoramic portrait is etched in acute observation.

Broughton's first letter, written from 'Kiruolee' on 26 December 1808, entered a caveat: he would describe events as they happened, but there would be no military secrets. He had no illusions about war, 'the offspring of systematic meanness, bad faith and constitutional cunning' on all sides. But as 'the intrigues and common politics of a Mahratta Durbar are, however, always matters of public notoriety and discussion, I shall be able to lay before you enough of each to convey a tolerably correct idea of that policy....'[24]

Broughton noted that the British and Indians lived in different worlds, their links limited to political discourse. There was not much chance of the gap narrowing. He accepted that British prejudice and Indian inhibitions were insurmountable obstacles:

> Secondly, I must beg you to bear in mind, that when an English gentleman undertakes to give an account of Indian manners and habits of private life, he labours under many disadvantages. The obstacles which prevent our ever viewing the natives of India in their domestic circles are great and insuperable; such as the restrictions of caste on their side, rank and situation on ours, &c. We do not intermarry with them, as the Portuguese did; nor do we ever mix with them, in the common duties of social life on terms of equality.

What knowledge we have of their domestic arrangements has been gained chiefly by inquiry; and hence we are often led to describe customs and institutions unfavourably, because our own prejudices render us incompetent to feel their propriety, or correctly to judge of their effects... As it is probable, therefore, that I may often view things in an imperfect light, or perhaps with a prejudiced eye, I shall confine myself as much as possible to plain matters of fact, and leave you to draw your own conclusions.[25]

The Marathas and the British kept a wary eye on the other. In his second letter, from Soopoor, written on 1 January 1809, Broughton mentions that Scindia had a spy in the English camp known as *khabardar*, or keeper of news, who reported directly to the maharaja; and 'we of course another in his'. The problem with the Indian spy in British pay for more than four decades was that he had 'picked up a collection of anecdotes of the most extraordinary nature: most of them are entertaining enough; but many not over delicate, and perhaps not always restrained within the strict line of truth'.

Broughton missed the blazing fire of an English hearth; the substitute was 'a large chafing dish of live coals; over which we enjoy a bottle of old port with as keen a relish as you can do in the more northern climate'.[26]

Indians needed warmth in the evenings as well, but they got it from 'Mouah' or *mahua,* distilled from the fruit of a tree, about as strong as cheap gin but with a smell sufficient to churn an English stomach. The march of British civilization had reached the vendors; some of the *mahua* was being sold in discarded English bottles.

Broughton notes the difference between an Indian camp and the British—the first sprawled into a bazaar, while the second was confined and disciplined. The most noted 'native' corps were the *Barah Bhaees,* or Twelve Brothers, entirely Mahratta. These were descendants of the original leaders of the community, whose power terrified the peasant. The maharaja's baggage was in charge of the *Shohdas,* a Muslim group with a fearsome reputation in battle and unflinching loyalty to their chief, Fazil Khan. As reward, Fazil Khan was given control of gambling houses.

Broughton saw Hindus and Muslims celebrating festivals amicably at Kota, in January: Muslims marked 'Bukree Eed' with meat-laden mass feasts, and Hindus 'Makar Sunkranti' by distributing packets of *til.* A shrewd moneylender gave a dinner for Brahmins, where each guest was gifted a new *dhoti,* blanket and linen jacket. But as soon as a Brahmin got the presents, he was locked up in a ruined fort so that he could not return to the queue. They were all seen the following morning in their new clothes.

The seventh letter, written on 26 February, detailed a call upon Scindia in the royal camp. 'It is usual on such visits of ceremony for the company to be entertained by a *Nach,* but on this occasion there was none, in consequence of its being the *Moohurrum,*' writes Broughton. Respect for other faiths was ingrained in the culture of Indian rulers. More than a hundred *taziyas* in the night time Muharram procession were carried to the maharaja's tent before being immersed in the river. Broughton describes the scene:

> The flaming of torches, firing of matchlocks, and the harsh and discordant sounds of Mahratta drums and trumpets, united with the strange but animated groups passing on all sides, to produce the most extraordinary scene I ever beheld. Such of the Mahratta Surdars as are not Brahmuns frequently construct *Taziyas* at their own tents, and expend large sums of money on them...[27]

The Scindias also continued the Persian tradition of searching for a prediction in a verse of the poet Hafiz, chosen by opening a collection of his poetry at random. When Jahangir was waiting for news from the Deccan where his son Khurram (later Shah Jahan) was waging war, he turned to the poet.

> Some days before the news of this victory reached me, I took one night an augury from the *diwan* of Khwaja Hafiz as to what would be the end of this affair, and this ode turned up— *The day of absence and night of parting from the friend are o'er.* I took this augury; the star passed and fulfilment came. When the secret tongue (*lisanu-l-ghaib*) of Hafiz showed such an ending it gave me a strong hope, and accordingly, after twenty-five days, the news of victory arrived. In many of my

desires I have resorted to the Khwaja's *diwan,* and (generally) the result has coincided with what I found there. It is seldom that the opposite happened.[28]

Broughton dismissed this as superstition, although he did mention that Virgil was similarly considered an omen in earlier times. The syncretic, multicultural spirit of Daulat Rao Scindia's reign is evident from this passage in the colonel's letter of 14 August 1809, written from Kuliawas:

Several *Kafilus* [Kafilas, or processions] of pilgrims, both Moosulmans and Hindoos, have lately gone from camp; the former to pay their vows at the tomb of Kwaja Moouen-oo-deen Chishtee [Khwaja Moinuddin Chishti], at Ajmeer; the latter to worship at and bathe in the sacred lakes of Pokur [Pushkar]—a town but a few miles distant from Ajmeer, and esteemed one of the holiest, as it is the most ancient, *teeruts,* or places of religious resort, in India.[29]

British policy towards religion was quite in contrast; it invested in conflict between Hindus and Muslims, not harmony.

In his ninth letter, written on 15 March from Doonee, Broughton describes the fun and frolic of the Holi carnival. His British colleagues were a trifle reluctant to see their white linen jackets and pantaloons get colourfully wet, but the colonel insisted he would honour tradition and greet the maharaja. Daulat Rao sat in a special tent, with his courtiers in rank and dancing girls assembled. Each guest was given a large silver squirter after being seated, along with a vase of coloured water. The maharaja began proceedings by sprinkling water from a *goolabdan,* or small perforated vessel used for rosewater. Court etiquette forbade anyone from throwing colour on the maharaja but Broughton made it clear that if anyone pelted him, he would pelt right back.

The maharaja was ready for all comers. Broughton reports:

We soon found, however, that we have not the slightest chance with him; for, besides a cloth which his attendants held before his face he had in a few minutes the pipe of a large fire-engine put into his hands, filled with yellow water, and worked by

half a dozen men: and with this he played about him with
such effect, that in a short time there was not a man in the
whole tent who had a dry suit upon his back.[30]

There had never been anything remotely akin to Holi in Broughton's
English life. His description was detailed, if self-righteous:

> Figure to yourself successive groups of dancing girls, bedecked
> with gold and silver lace; their tawdry trappings stained with
> patches of *abeer,* and dripping, like so many Naiads, with
> orange-coloured water; now chaunting the Hohlee songs with
> all the airs of practised libertinism, and now shrinking with
> affected screams beneath a fresh shower from the Muha Raj's
> engine: the discord of drums, trumpets, fiddles, and cymbals,
> sounding as if only to drown the other noises that arose
> around them; the triumph of those who successfully threw
> the *abeer,* and the clamours of others who suffered from their
> attacks; the loud shouts of laughter and applause which burst
> on all sides from the joyous crowd...[31]

Holi was a feast of merriment, when authority was dismantled by
gaiety and coarse humour.

> The utmost licence is permitted to all ranks; the men, old and
> young, parade about the streets, or the camp, in large groups,
> singing *Kuveers,* or extraordinary stanzas, full of the grossest
> indelicacy, into which they freely introduce the names of their
> superiors, coupled with the most abominable allusions; the
> whole party joining in the chorus, and expressing their delight
> by loud peals of laughter, hallooing, and almost frantic
> gestures.[32]

This was the India which the British could never fully understand.
Broughton repeats the one Holi song which passed his delicacy
test; he translated the lyrics himself:

> *While some his loosen'd turban seize,*
> *And ask for* Phag, *and laughing teaze;*
> *Others approach with roguish leer,*

And softly whisper in his ear.
With many a scoff, and many a taunt,
The Phagoon *some fair Gopees chaunt;*
While others, as he bends his way,
Sing at their doors Dhumaree *gay.*
One boldly strikes a loving slap;
One brings the powder in her lap;
And clouds of crimson dust arise
About the youth with lotus-eyes.
Then all the colour'd water pour,
And whelm him in a saffron shower;
And crowding round him bid him stand,
With wands of flowers in every hand.[33]

Having given the colonel a taste of Holi, the maharaja graciously exempted the British from the 'ordeal' thereafter.

The British never quite adapted to the physical proximity that came so naturally to Indians. Indians might be inured to the beggars who crowded around the court at Dussehra, but for Broughton they were an 'intolerable nuisance': 'The Moohumedans are the worst, many of them going about on horseback, and asking for rupees with as much assurance as others beg for *pice*; and the more impertinent they are, the greater is the idea entertained of their sanctity'. But he liked their singing.[34]

Broughton is dismissive about Indian faith in the malignancy of the 'evil eye'. Mahadji Scindia's loss of several infant sons was widely attributed to *Nuzur*, or this evil eye. Indeed, Daulat Rao, a nephew, was crowned successor because Madhoji had no male heirs. Broughton, as a champion of Western rationality, was contemptuous about Indians beating drums and blaring trumpets to drive away Rahu during an eclipse.

Indians, in turn, were awed by British science and technology—for them, inventions like the 'perambulator' which measured distances was magical. In his 17th letter, written on 30 June, Broughton says: 'They call it *Jadoo-ka-chukkur*, the magic wheel; and being, from the highest to the lowest, implicit believers in witchcraft, they find a satisfaction in attributing to its influence everything wherein they feel our superiority over themselves'.[35]

The British were not merely calculating distance; they were also constantly measuring Indian character: the chronic rivalry between rulers, the continuous shifts of influence within a durbar, and bitter jealousies that made the maharaja's spy, the *khabardar,* one of their most valued employees. Corruption was common. Even a maharaja's orders were not sacrosanct. When Daulat Rao settled a sum of ₹1,000 from the treasury for a relative, all the latter could realistically expect was ₹700, as the rest of the money would be taken by treasury officials. Broughton witnessed the quicksilver change in factional equations that could be wrought by a dancing girl and the rising venality within a structure that had begun to totter before it could reach its prime.

Broughton was a bit of a prig when it came to dancing girls. He thought the *Nach* to be the least joyous entertainment imaginable, although European men seemed fascinated by the roguish air of the woman. He was censorious about 'indecent' gestures used in the 'Kuharwa' dance, meant to arouse desire but serving only to excite his disgust. He was appalled when a powerful Mahratta noble became bewitched by a dancing girl.

The noble in question was 'Surjee Rao', the maharaja's influential father-in-law, then in charge of the campaign against the Rajput state of Jaipur. In his tenth letter, sent on 7 April, Broughton claims that Surjee Rao had acquired a nickname, 'Bapoo Sahib', because his whims included appearing at the head of his troops entirely in European dress, including a hat. But this was the least of Surjee Rao's problems.

Our British correspondent writes:

The minister is notoriously addicted to the bottle and is said to be frequently drunk: like most other great men, too, of Hindustan, he indulges freely with women; and has so much injured his constitution by excess, that he has constant recourse to provocatives to excite his appetite and stimulate his failing powers: dishes of young pigeons, and goat's flesh stewed down to rich jellies, are daily served up at his table; and the female, or, as she is generally termed, the queen, of the white ants, a sovereign remedy in cases of exhausted vigour, is carefully sought after and preserved for his use... This eccentric minister is at present under the all-powerful sway of a common Nach girl, named Juwahir; who has so completely captivated his affections, that he is miserable when separated from her, even for the shortest space of time: she lives at his tents; accompanies him in a palanquin whenever he goes abroad; and is herself attended by a far more numerous train than that of her venerable lover.[36]

Surjee Rao established an espionage network which, Broughton predicted, would in all probability lead to an explosion. Daulat Rao intervened, but at arm's length, after Rao apparently spent ₹40,000 meant for troops on his mistress. The state's principal banker, 'Gokul Paruk', sent an ultimatum: as long as Surjee Rao was in charge, the kingdom's affairs could never prosper. On 26 July, Surjee Rao was killed by nobles acting on Daulat Rao's behalf. Juwahir was imprisoned and her wealth seized. Surjee Rao had the last, if eerie, laugh—his ghost was reputed to haunt the camp.

What Broughton and his contemporaries carried away from such experience was a simple lesson. Half of India was in their hands; the rest was waiting to be conquered. Perhaps the people of Gwalior had a premonition. On 14 August, Broughton wrote about a superstition which seized the camp when the British detachment changed their flag because the old Union Jack was worn out; the new one was a white ensign with the 'union' limited to a corner. 'It was immediately asserted that the English were about to assume the general sovereignty of Hindoostan, of which the white flag was the emblem; while the coloured canton represented the contracted space which the Mahrattas were still permitted to occupy.'[37] As a premonition it was logical; as a prediction it was accurate. In another decade, the Marathas had been reduced to allies, in what has been called 'honourable subservience'. The fate of most other Indian princes was less honorable.

The English may have won the field, but they did not command affection. A dozen years after Broughton's letters, the Rev. Reginald Heber, the second bishop of Calcutta, heard on his travels that although French officers in the service of Scindia were oppressive and avaricious, they were more popular than English sahibs with their 'intolerant spirit' and 'foolish surly national pride'.

Broughton reiterates, in his penultimate letter of 31 December 1809, the point he made in his first. He hopes that his brother has understood how blessed it was to be born an Englishman after this 'perusal of my attempts to depict the manners and customs of a people as much separated from Englishmen by character as they are by actual distance upon the face of the globe'.[38] The most exotic difference was the place of magic in the Indian consciousness, and a rear-magical ability to deal with the incredible, an art that would become a trope in the British view of mysterious India.

In his letter of 16 June, Broughton is spellbound by the mastery of snake-charmers, but not by their claims of supernatural ability:

> We are not here quite so much troubled with thieves as at
> our last halting place; but instead of them we are pestered
> with snakes, scorpions, and a large species of yellow spider,
> whose body is nearly an inch in length, though the animal
> is quite innoxious. It is not uncommon to see men who will
> take up the most venomous snakes, and allow them to creep
> about their persons with impunity: they pretend to do this
> by a certain *muntur*, or charm; and if we refuse them their
> claim to supernatural powers, we must at least acknowledge
> some art by which they render so dangerous a creature quite
> harmless. I have known a Sipahee [sepoy] dig out one of these
> snakes, and keep him for several days in a cloth tied about his
> loins, feeding him daily with the utmost care and assiduity.
> Scorpions are easily rendered innocent by pinching their tails
> just below the sting; which deprives the animal of the power
> of darting forward.[39]

Through the 19th century the British were bewitched by Indian magic and *muntur*, which reason told them must be artifice against the evidence of their eyes. They were not the first to confuse yogic powers with sorcery. Long before Broughton, travellers had enchanted Europe with tales beyond the scope of Western imagination. Marco Polo spoke of Kashmiri magicians who could turn the sky dark and change the weather. The 14th-century Berber-Moroccan jurist and explorer Muhammad Ibn Battuta fainted when he saw a cubic figure and sandals floating in the air in the court of the Sultan in Delhi, Muhammad bin Tughlaq. Stories circulated about the Mughal Emperor Jahangir watching a dog, hog, panther, lion and tiger being sent up a chain to vanish into thin air and seeing magicians make a tree blossom, or indeed an egg hatch, in five minutes.

Such was the demand for the incredulous that:

> [Jahangir's] memoirs were translated into English in 1829, and extracts were printed in the popular *Illustrated London News,* though they did not mention the chain trick at all. Instead, their large readership was faced with the Emperor's account of how jugglers had 'produced a man whom they divided limb from limb, actually severing his head from his body. They scattered these mutilated members along the ground,' then covered him with a sheet. Moments later, the man was in 'perfect health and condition, and one might have safely sworn that he had never received wound or injury'... In 1832, stories began to appear in the British press of a 'man that sat in the air'. Readers of the *Saturday Magazine* must have been taken aback by the illustration of a *fakir* sitting cross-legged four feet from the ground. Turning to the story, they would have read of Sheshal, a Madras Brahmin who had floated in the air while engaged in prayer.[40]

For the British, India's abracadabra added an extra patina of exotica to a people whose secret life seemed incomprehensible.

By the early 19th century, Britain came under the influence of 'utilitarian' ethicists who saw colonialism as an opportunity for reform and wanted to do India a favour by getting rid of such superstitious 'barbarism'.

The Raj was still far from its apogee when James Mill began writing his six-volume *The History of British India* in 1806. Mill divided Indian history into Hindu, Muslim and British parts, a simplistic and inaccurate classification which became the staple of school texts and invigorated the process of dividing the principal communities of India, Hindus and Muslims, towards competitive politics. British rule had found the historian it required.

4

Beef, Beer, Ham and Baboo Hurry Mohan

Four years after Colonel Broughton's correspondence with his brother, the British government renewed the charter for governance of 'British territories in India' for twenty years through The East India Company Act. This significant turning point formalized the transformation of mercantile buccaneers into warrior-statesmen of an empire. The Company's trade was restricted to tea and opium, with long-term consequences that could hardly be foreseen in 1813. The Calcutta government was also charged with the responsibility of reviving Indian learning and promoting science, on an annual budget of ₹100,000. In practice, Indian learning disappeared into an academic cloister, and the 'new' education became an opportunity to seed the mind of Bengal's intelligentsia with a colonial interpretation of India's past and future.

A clause in the Charter Act permitted missionary activity in India. Old India hands like Sir Thomas Munro, the governor of Madras in the 1820s, were apprehensive. Sir Thomas believed that it was not the job of the East India Company to turn India into England or Scotland, but to enable Indians to create a modern administration for themselves in their own languages. As a gesture of respect, Munro instituted a daily offering to Sri Venkateswara at the Tirumala temple, which became known as the Munro Gangalam.

But colonial fervour had its own momentum, reinforced by popular support. As influential a liberal as William Wilberforce, 'the indefatigable opponent of slavery, believed that the conversion of India was still more important than the abolition of the slave trade' writes David Gilmour, and letting Indian subjects remain 'under the grossest, the darkest and most degrading system of idolatrous superstition that almost ever existed upon the earth' was the foulest blot on British moral character.[1] This vigorous advocate of social reform was also the voice of an evangelical ideology that equated civilization with white Christianity. The 'religious and moral improvement' of Indians became a policy imperative for a Company which had thus far exercised religious neutrality. One of Wilberforce's closest allies, Charles Grant, a former civil servant, was convinced that Hindus ware so mired in cruelty, superstition and vice that it was a moral duty to introduce them to Christianity and save widows from being burnt and the girl child from being killed.

The Church of England established the diocese of Calcutta in 1813, with jurisdiction up to Australia and parts of southern Africa. The first Bishop of Calcutta, Thomas Fanshaw Middleton, arrived in 1814 and died in 1822 at the age of 53. Life was as vulnerable for servants of the Lord as it was for servants of the Company. The second Bishop, Rev. Reginald Heber, reached Calcutta in October 1823 with his wife Amelia and daughter Emily. He has left a travelogue which ranks as an invaluable addition to the remarkable library bequeathed by British India.

On 15 June 1824, Bishop Heber set out to explore the subcontinent. His tour began in Dhaka and then moved west to Almora in the Kumaon Himalayas, Delhi, Bombay and Ceylon. He was back by ship to Calcutta by October 1825. Three months later, on 30 January 1826, he left again, this time for Madras and Travancore. He was in Tanjore on 26 March, Easter Day, and in Trichinopoly on 3 April. After an early morning service during which he gave a blessing in Tamil, he returned to his bungalow, took a cold bath and was found dead at the young age of 42.

The India which the reverend saw was beginning to absorb the multifaceted impact of an unfamiliar and ascendant foreign power. The temperamentally charitable reverend described Nawab Shams-ud-Daula of Dhaka as a 'poor humbled potentate', which was correct, but dismissed his food as too greasy and common, which may have been a reflection of his own palate rather than the nawab's kitchen. Hindus, Bishop Heber observed, were more socially reticent, as 'few of them' would 'eat with us'. The reverend dined mainly with fellow-Englishmen on his travels: Mr Warner in Dhaka, Sir Charles D'Oyly at Dinapore, Mr Brooke in Benaras, Mr Boulderson in Shahi, Colonel Robertson in Chunar, or Mr Traill in Kumaon.

A small but growing group of aspirational Indians tried to flatter the new rulers with imitation, to the pecuniary delight of tailors and the happy surprise of wine merchants. The Irish journalist James Augustus Hicky, who started India's first printed English newspaper, *Hicky's Bengal Gazette,* in January 1780, satirised the Bengali 'Banyans and Sarkers' who had made money as Company contractors by publishing a *faux* complaint from the 'Juty-wallah' (shoemakers) of Calcutta and Patna. These shoemakers wailed that they were facing a shortage of customers because the nouveau riche Indian was driving in a chariot or a phaeton, thus preserving footwear for months which had earlier worn out in mere days of trudging. Hicky displayed mock concern about a future when the Indian chariot might have the temerity to drive over a European in a road accident.

Hicky sniggered at a certain Raja Ramlochan:

The attachment of the natives of Bengal to the English laws begins now... Raja Ramlochan a very opulent Gentoo of high caste and family [who had] lately paid a visit to a very eminent attorney, equipped in Boots, Buckskin, Breeches, Hunting Frock and Jockey cap; the Lawyer... waked from his reverie in great astonishment at the lively transportation of his grave Gentoo client who it seems was dressed in the exact hunting character of Lord March and had borrowed the Fancy from one of Darley's Comic Prints.[2]

Behind such comic excess lay the hope of upward mobility.

There was much to laugh at. Saadat Ali Khan, who would rule as the sixth Nawab of Awadh between 1798 and 1814, spent some years in Calcutta. Hicky reported that he had employed a famous tailor to make '2 Suits of Regimentals, 2 Do of an English Admirals uniform and two suits of canonicals. At the same time he sent for an English peruke maker and gave him orders to make him two wigs, of every denomination according to English fashion'.[3] The family had form: Saadat Ali Khan's grandfather Asaf ud-Daula had requested Warren Hastings to send the best wines available in Calcutta. Saadat Ali Khan's weakness for alcohol proved to be more expensive—

he would hand out generous gifts when intoxicated and repent when sober.

The nawab was very much in his senses when he invited the British elite in Lucknow for breakfast to show off a set of Worcestershire china he had ordered from England. The table looked splendid, writes Lizzie Collingham, except for twenty chamber pots filled with milk. The servants had mistaken them for milk pots. When the guests, straining to keep a straight face, seemed reluctant to take milk, the host remarked that he thought the English liked milk.

Lizzie Collingham explains the dilemma:

> British attitudes to Indian attempts to assimilate European culture into their courts were often condescending. Central to the justification of British rule was the assertion that Indians were incapable of achieving civilization on their own. It therefore undermined British self-confidence to acknowledge that Indians did understand and suavely adopt their ways.[4]

The Mughal King Akbar Shah II's favourite son Mirza Jahangir comforted himself with Hoffman's cherry brandy, in his eminent view the only English liquor worth drinking. During bouts of restraint, he reduced his intake to one glass every hour, till he passed out. In 1814, the Anglo-Irish Earl of Moira Francis Edward Rawdon-Hastings, governor-general during the transitional decade between 1813 and 1823, granted an interview only after Mirza Jahangir promised to limit himself to one bottle of port a day. The Mirza died in 1821 at the age of 31. His brother Mirza Babur built a European-style house with Corinthian columns in the courtyard behind the Diwan-i-Aam at Red Fort. He wore boots and a coat with stars on the breast, carried a walking stick, and drove around in a coach with six horses.[5]

Bishop Heber wrote in his journal that wealthy Bengalis were starting to copy Western architecture, constructing Corinthian pillars in their homes and speaking 'tolerable English'. Many of their sons were in English schools.

Hindu (or Hindoo) College, the first Asian institution of higher learning with a Western curriculum, opened in Calcutta on 20 January 1817 with 20 male scholars. Among its founders was David Hare, a Scottish watchmaker who had turned so 'native' that the authorities did not permit a Christian burial when he died of cholera in 1842. The secondary school on the campus, begun in 1818, was named after Hare. Its motto was 'Illuminate the darkness'.

From its first decade, Hindu College acquired a reputation for radicalism. It appointed the brilliant 17-year-old avant-garde poet Henry Louis Vivian Derozio as a teacher of English literature. Derozio inspired what became known as the 'Young Bengal' or 'Young India' movement, which challenged Indian religious dogma, flaunted western notions of 'modernity' and 'masculinity', harnessed a rising intellectual ferment in the cause of reform and scandalized Hindu society by eating beef.

As Rosinka Chaudhuri puts it:

> Among Indians, however, the drive for reform, based on the redemptive idea of a mission to reform India, had become the domain of an entire class since at least 1826, when Derozio joined the Hindu College. This reform movement, downplayed in postcolonial perspectives, was constituted, paradoxically, of radical dimensions co-existing with forms of imitation and parody, cutting across assumptions about colonial societies.[6]

There was nothing 'Western' per se about beef—it had been part of Muslim food. But no section of Hindus had ever tried to ingratiate themselves with sultans and nawabs by eating beef. If anything, some Muslim rulers showed sensitivity towards Hindu sentiment by placing voluntary restrictions on the consumption of beef.

An insidious objective of colonial history was to reinvent the past as perpetual conflict between Muslim invaders and Hindu patriots. Central to this thesis was the proposition that British rule had rescued Hindus from Muslim fanaticism and initiated the enlightenment of Bengal. When facts interfered with theory, they were excised out of the story.

The history of Bengal's last nawabs began around 1660, when a Hindu boy from the Deccan named Surya Narayan Mishra was sold by his impoverished parents to a Muslim called Haji Shafi Ispahani. The child was converted to Islam and renamed Muhammad Hadi. Haji Ispahani took him to Persia, but Hadi returned to India after his foster-father's death, entered Mughal service in Berar and rose to become diwan of Golconda by 1687.

In 1700, he was transferred to Bengal with the title of Murshid Quli Khan to take over administrative control from Aurangzeb's grandson Muhammad Azim al-Din, who had stopped sending revenues to Delhi in order to finance an independent bid for power. The grandson was shifted to Bihar. He reasserted his rule over Bengal, India's richest province, after Aurangzeb's death in 1707, and Quli Khan was sent to the Deccan. Three years later, Quli Khan was back in Bengal, with greater authority to restore good governance. In 1717, he was recognized as Nawab Nazim, giving him virtual independence.

Robert Ivermee, historian at SOAS University of London and the Catholic University of Paris, categorically rejects the colonial projection of the nawabs as communal despots:

> Despite recent attempts to re-read Indian history as Hindu versus Muslim, the rule of nawabs was not the Muslim oppression of Bengal's predominantly Hindu population, nor was it the spread of Islam at the point of a sword. In spite of external threats faced, the kingdom of the nawabs of Bengal was consistently cosmopolitan and pluralist, witnessing encounters between heterogenous peoples and cultures through which striking new syntheses emerged.[7]

Disputes over revenue were cited by the British as evidence of Quli Khan's 'cruelty' against Hindus, as in the case of Sitaram, zamindar of Bhushna, or Udai Narayan of Rajshahi. The British view is stressed repeatedly without question, by empire authors like J. Talboys Wheeler, who insists that Quli Khan 'put into practice a system of the greatest oppression upon the Zemindars or Hindu landholders; which, although it much augmented the revenue of the state, rendered his name dreaded and detested throughout the province'.[8] Robert Ivermee explains:

> The circumstances of these depositions differ little from those of other defaulting or rebellious zamindars, whether Hindu or Muslim. Both Sitaram and Udai Narayan defied Quli Khan's authority, refusing to submit revenues, resorting

to armed opposition, and making incursions into other
zamindars' estates. Their suppression followed a very similar
course to that of the insurgent Afghan zamindars Shujat
and Najat Khan. Though Quli Khan's revenue settlement in
Bengal may have displaced members of a pre-Mughal Hindu
landowning elite whose position had been confirmed under
Akbar, the zamindars who stepped into their shoes were more
often Hindu than Muslim. The successors to Sitaram, Udai
Narayan, Shujat Khan and Najat Khan were all Hindu.[9]

Among Quli Khan's private secretaries was Kishen Ray; Maharaja
Nandakumar Ray was in charge of revenue collection with Lahori
Mull as a high official; Raghunandan was appointed head of the mint.

The best example of 'cosmopolitan pluralism' is Hiranand
Galera, a Rajput-Jain banker and saltpetre trader in Patna. His son
Manikchand persuaded Murshid Quli Khan to shift the capital in
1703 to the smaller town of Maksudabad, renamed Murshidabad.
Manikchand was appointed deputy diwan, with the additional
responsibility of managing the nawab's personal finances. During
the drought of 1715 this banking family helped save lives by
giving loans to distressed peasants and farmers. Manikchand's heir
Fatehchand controlled the minting of coins and thereby the price of
bullion, becoming the richest moneylender in Bengal, with a personal
protection force of 2,000 men. In addition to a palatial home,
Fatehchand built Jain temples in Murshidabad which remain open
for worship. In 1723, he was honoured with the title of Jagat Seth, or
'banker to the world'.

Quli Khan kept the East India Company in check. He did not
permit the Company to mint coin or expand its settlement with an
additional purchase of 38 villages. A successor, Alivardi Khan, who
became nawab in 1740, famously compared European businesses to
beehives: leave them alone, and they would provide honey; disturb
them, and the bees would sting you to death. His heir Siraj ud-Daula
shook the hive in 1756 and was fatally stung within less than a year.

The intellectual offensive against Muslim rulers was led by
historians like Robert Orme, author of *Fragments of the Mughal
Empire*, which castigated the Mughals as 'licentious', 'corrupt'
and 'cruel', and Alexander Dow who celebrated the 'freedom' and

'happiness' of Indians under British rule after Mughal 'despotism'. For Thomas Maurice, Muslim rule was a period of sustained spoilation and 'rooted depravity'.

James Mill's six-volume *The History of British India*, published in 1817, used fallacy and concoction to shape a patronizing justification for colonization. For him, Hindus were prone to 'deceit and perfidy' and, like the Chinese, both Hindus and Muslims displayed the 'same insincerity, mendacity, and perfidy, the same indifference to the feeling of others'. In addition, Muslims were cruel and devoted to pleasure and lust. India's history became a sequence of faults and perversities, and Indians a people in existential need of the west's civilizing touch. Mill's book was taught at Haileybury, the alma mater of the Company's senior bureaucracy. Thomas Macaulay praised the tome as the greatest intellectual achievement since Edward Gibbons's *Decline and Fall of the Roman Empire*, which had been published in 1776. In an essay in *Edinburgh Review*, Macaulay described Siraj ud-Daula as a drunken tyrant who terrorized Hindus, tortured birds and animals and had once tipped a boatload of people into the Hooghly because he enjoyed watching them drown.[10]

Rosinka Chaudhuri describes James Mill's work as 'the most influential single work on Indian history to appear in the 19th century, and published well before Derozio's death [which] would also have had a huge impact on Calcutta intellectuals of the time'.[11]

Derozio identified himself as an Indian rather than European, although his father Francis was Portuguese and his mother Sophia Johnson an Englishwoman from Hampshire. As a child, he went to the David Drummond Dharamtala Academy, started by a Scottish sceptic, philosopher and freethinker. Where the 'Muslim past' was concerned, Derozio endorsed colonial tropes, so starkly different from Bengal's experience, or indeed the bonhomie between Marathas and Muslims which Broughton had witnessed at the Scindia camp in 1809, the year Derozio was born. Derozio's poem, *The Enchantress of the Cave*, is a relevant example:

> *The Moslem brings his turban'd band,*
> *To win the peaceful, golden land,*
> *The crescent on his banner shines,*
> *The watchword's 'Alla' in his lines,*

And on his blade the Koran verse
Bespeaks for every foe a curse.
The Hindoo courts the bloody broil,
To fight or fall for his parent soil,
And he must go forth in the battle to bleed
For all that is dear—country, kindred, and creed;
But evil betide him and fair Hindoostan
If ever he yield to the proud Mussulman!

Derozio and his disciples were more concerned, however, with curing the superstition which had, in their view, turned Hindus into supine weaklings. They assaulted conventional tenets with heavy artillery. They denied the sanctity of the Ganges, rejected the sacred thread (*poitey*) worn by Brahmins, recited lines from Homer as prayer and declared that John Dryden and Alexander Pope deserved higher praise than the *shastras*. Beef became medicine for the backbone.

The prescription was too harsh for the Hindu College to swallow. In May 1831, Derozio was dismissed because:

> Native managers of the Hindu College were alarmed at the progress which some of the pupils were making under Derozio, by actually *cutting* their way through ham and beef, and wading to liberalism through tumblers of beer. From this new feature of Hindu education, the praise or blame of which must rest on the memory of Derozio, the managers dreaded the worst consequences.[12]

On the evening of 22 August 1831, a group of 'Derozions' met in the home of one of their group, Krishnamohan Bandopadhyay, a Kulin Brahmin teacher at Hare School. They ate bread and beef curry and threw the bones into a neighbour's house. This was high religious and cultural treason; they were chased away by outraged neighbours. Thrown out of home, Krishnamohan took refuge in Christianity and embarked upon a career as a prolific writer. His most famous work, *Vidyakalpadrum*, was an encyclopaedia aimed at cleansing Indian 'ignorance' and 'confusion' through the curative powers of European science and history.

Derozio died of cholera on 17 October 1931, at the age of just 22, but he had created a moment in social history. Beefsteak became an exotic icon for modernists who quoted Shakespeare, Johnson, Marlow, Webster and Ford, while Wordsworth, Shelley, Byron and Keats tripped off the tongue.

The subaltern attraction of sacrilege spread to Muslims. Many 'excellent Mussulmans', writes Percival Spear, 'on their part experimented with English food and drink', adding that they often ate ham if it was designated 'Belatty [Vilayati, or foreign] Heron or English venison'.[13] There was less public outrage because they sinned on the sly.

As British rule took root, stereotypes were injected into Indian consciousness. No influential Indian was immune from caustic exaggeration. Alongside the barbaric Muslim emerged the Hindu bania, or business caste, with crafty brains, sharp teeth and flexible bookkeeping. Educated Bengalis were lampooned as talkative and languorous, full of hot air and rice. The success of this propaganda was best confirmed by a paradox: Hindus and Muslims began to see each other through British eyes.

A mid-century Brahmo social reformer like Sibnath Sastri (1847–1919) attributed the 'decay' and 'corruption' in Hindu life to Muslim degradation. Rosinka Chaudhuri provides a sample of Sastri's eloquence:

It troubles me to say so, and my grief makes it difficult for me to restrain my tears when I think that in the years before Muslim domination, in the dawn and glory of Hindu rule, the ancient Greek and Chinese travellers had described the Hindu race (*jati*) as brave, honest, simple in character, hospitable, and generous, and now, after a few centuries of subjugation, that very race seems to have been deprived of all those good qualities. The Muslims set up their capitals in one place after the other, and proximity to their corrupt court culture destroyed first the wealthy Hindus, and subsequently, by following their example, the entire country's morals were tarnished.[14]

Many contemporaries protested against distortion. Bhudev
Mukhopadhyay, who studied in Hindu College in the 1840s, wrote
in *Samajik Prabhanda*:

> Many English historians suggest, explicitly at times, through
> hints at others, that the Muslims perpetrated unspeakable
> oppression on Hindus when they held political power. Thus
> English historians are sowing a seed of deep resentment
> against the Muslims in the minds of the Hindus. The kind of
> resentment against Muslims and the Islamic religion among
> modern English educated youth, one would not have found
> half of that in traditional cultivated Brahmins who were often
> educated in Persian.[15]

The inclusive view of Indian society was encapsulated in the dictum
of the sage Gadadhar Chattopadhyay, more famous as Ramakrishna
Paramahansa (1836–1886): *Jata mat, tato path* (There are as many
paths to God as there are views). But newly minted 'modern English
educated youth' were in no mood to listen to homilies about harmony.
Rosinka Chaudhuri quotes a satirical poem on the 'Young Bengal'
phenomenon written by the Anglo-Indian poet Henry Meredith
Parker (1796–1868) in which Hurry (an Anglicized rendering of
Hari) Mohun says:

> *Kings, Priests, and Laws, and Creeds, are but the tools*
> *Which cunning knaves employ to govern fools,*
> *Down with Kings, Laws and Creeds then, and in chief*
> *With any creed prohibiting roast beef.*

The Brown Sahib

In 1832, a select committee enquiring into the sales of British
goods discovered that Indians had developed a preference for wine,
brandy, beer and champagne. Europeans in India had always turned
to alcohol as a palliative for loneliness and hardship. In the 1690s,
John Ovington moaned that they courted death by 'carousing these
cheerful liquors', consuming 'immoderate draughts' in the Indian heat
and sleeping drunk in open fields. But Western liquor did not become

popular with the Indian elite until the British became politically powerful and intellectually fashionable. Tapan Raychaudhuri quotes Bhudev Mukhopadhyay as saying that open defiance by many students of Hindu customs in food and drink was almost *de rigeur* on the Hindu College campus—to be 'civilized', one had to eat beef and drink alcohol.[16]

The 'vigour' of meat, in contrast to the lethargy induced by Indian vegetables and rice, became a defining issue. Collingham writes:

> Meat-eating among educated Indians was a response to the British claim that vegetarianism was at the root of Indian weakness... British arrogance, the fact of their ability ruthlessly to subdue Indians and impose their rule over them, and the assertion that this overwhelming power was, at least in part, derived from their meat-based diet, all gnawed away at Indian self-confidence. Faced with the incontrovertible fact that they were a subject people, educated Indians worried that their diet had made them feeble.[17]

This seemed persuasive to Indians, who could not quite fully comprehend the reasons for British invincibility. Among the many who bought this brittle claim was a Gujarati schoolboy, Mohandas Karamchand Gandhi. It was not until Gandhi proved that you could take on South African racism and British imperialism on a diet of nuts, fruit and horrid-tasting vegetable paste—there were spells in his life when the Mahatma became a nutarian or a fruitarian—that such myths began to dissipate.

With so much churn in the Raj capital, the stage was set for Thomas Babington Macaulay, historian, Whig MP for Leeds and flag-waver of the Empire. Macaulay served as law member in the Council of Lord William Bentinck, governor-general from 1834 to 1838. Macaulay can justifiably be considered paterfamilias of 'Brown Sahibs', Indians who preened occidental feathers in the hope of graduating to a superior class. Macaulay's certainties were uncomplicated. Britain, at the pinnacle of civilization, could help India play slow catch-up by turning natives into miniature Englishmen. His central project was to shift education from an implicitly useless Sanskrit or Persian-based knowledge to 'useful learning'.

Macaulay asserted in his *Minute on Education*, presented on 2 February 1835, that he had not met any Oriental scholar 'who could deny that a single shelf of a good European library was worth the whole native literature of India and Arabia'[18] or venture to compare Sanskrit verse with any European poetry.

> It is, I believe, no exaggeration to say that all the historical information which has been collected from all the books written in the Sanskrit language is less valuable than what may be found in the most paltry abridgements used at preparatory schools in England. In every branch of physical or moral philosophy, the relative position of the two nations is nearly the same.[19]

The whole corpus of Sanskrit literature and philosophy, in other words, was worth less than the abridged books taught in English prep schools. Speaking in Parliament, Macaulay dismissed Indian culture as inferior and Indian rulers as tyrannical and debased. It was Britain's humane duty to rescue Indians from 'bloody and degrading superstitions'. His route map for Indian enlightenment was unambiguous. English must become the language of administration and the higher courts. A Western education would fashion 'a class of persons, Indian in blood and colour, but English in taste, in opinions, in morals and in intellect'.[20] The study of Sanskrit could be restricted to the Sanskrit College in Benaras and Persian to the 'Mohamaten College' in Delhi.

Lord Bentinck was pleased to pass the English Education Act 1835, just before the end of his term. Macaulay incorporated the dialectics of white supremacy into British Indian policy.

One cannot say how many scholars of Sanskrit Macaulay actually met before coming to his conclusions about Asia's contribution to the world library, but there was one way he could have evaluated the range and quality of Bengal's erudition: through a compendium of books printed during seven decades of Company rule from Calcutta.

While block printing was known in ancient India, the Portuguese were the pioneers of modern printing. The first press arrived in Goa from Portugal on 6 September 1556. A year later, St Francis Xavier's *Catecismo da Doutrina Christa* was published. Within a decade, there were books on medicine; by 1578, translations in Tamil had appeared. The Church was at the forefront of change. The first Tamil New Testament appeared in 1714, and by the end of the century, Sanskrit and Marathi texts were appearing in Tanjore under Maratha patronage, while the East India Company published Tamil-English dictionaries. A Gujarati press was founded in Bombay by the Parsi entrepreneur Fardunji Marzban in 1812. The British joined this enterprise only after Sir Eyre Coote captured Pondicherry from the French in 1761 and discovered a printing press in the governor's house.

For reasons which have never been fully studied, the Mughal Empire remained aloof, although there was nothing in either religious law or secular practice to prohibit printing. Printing was, however, opposed by court scribes, who were convinced that calligraphers in charge of records and archives would lose their jobs. It was a classic case of a Luddite mentality sabotaging progress. This single mistake held India back in innumerable ways.

Bengal's advance had to await the arrival of British rule. In 1778, a blacksmith, Panchanan Karmakar, produced a complete set of Bengali types for the East India Company. The first book in Bengali script, a grammar of the language by the civil servant Nathaniel Halhad, was printed at the St Andrews Press at Hooghly. The Company set up its own facilities under Sir Charles Wilkins, a Sanskrit scholar who translated a range of classics including the *Geeta, Hitopadesha* and *Sakuntala*. The 1790s saw Bengali translations of legal codes and regulations and bilingual educational texts like *The Tutor* by John Miller and *A Vocabulary in Two Parts* by H.P. Forster.

Macaulay might have done well to take a look at the work of his fellow Englishman, William Carey, the son of an indigent schoolteacher from Northamptonshire. Carey, a Baptist, had left for India on a Danish ship in 1792 along with his wife and sister, to bring the light of the Gospel to the 'poor dark idolatrous heathen'. Since missionary activity was not yet permitted by the Company, he took a job as manager of an indigo plantation in Malda for five years and learnt Bengali and Sanskrit. In 1800, his mission bought a house with a garden in the Danish settlement of Serampore, or Srirampur, with help from Governor Ole Bie and donations from England. Carey hired Panchanan Karmakar. The Baptist Mission Press produced the first Bengali Bible, the *Dharma Pustaka* (Book of Religion), in 1800.

Between 1800 and 1815, Carey published evangelical texts like *Mangal Samachar Matiur Rakhita* (Good News from the Gospel of St Matthew) and the Pentateuch, as well as authentic Indian writing which would have helped expand Macaulay's knowledge: *Raja Protapaditya Charita* (A History of King Protapaditya of Jessore) by Ram Ram Basu; a Bengali version of the *Mahabharata* by Kashee Ram Das; *Ramayan* by Kirtee Dash; *Batrish Simhasan* by Mrityunjay Sharma; *Lipimala* by Ram Ram Basu; *Hitopadesha* by Golaknath Sharma; a translation of the *Oriental Fabulist* by H.P. Forster; *Maharaja Krishna Chandra Royasha Charitram* by Rajiblochana Mukherjee; *Tota Itihasa*, translated from Hindi into Bengali by Chandi Charan Munshi; grammars of Marathi and Sanskrit by Carey himself; *Itihasamala*, a collection of stories in Bengali; *Simhasana Battisi* by Vaijnath Sarma; and *Purusha Pariksha* by Hara Prasad Roy. Other companies had also become active, printing books like *Prem Sagar* (translated from Brajbhasha into Hindi by Lallolal Kavi, the language *munshee* at Fort William; Sanskrit Press); *Kulliyat-i-Mir*, a collection of the Urdu poet Mir's verse and *Meghaduta*, which were published by Hindoostani Press, founded by John Gilchrist in 1802.

If Macaulay wanted thought-provoking debate, he could have turned to Raja Rammohun Roy. Born in 1772 into a wealthy zamindar Kulin Brahmin family of Burdwan, Roy studied Persian, Sufi philosophy, Arabic science and the Quran at Patna; then Sanskrit and the Vedas in Benaras and Buddhism in Tibet. He settled down in Calcutta in the 1790s.

Roy did not question British rule; no one yet did. But he did question British behaviour, which few had the courage to do. He demanded legal reform, a free press and the restoration of Indians in government service. He was equally trenchant with his fellow Indians. He campaigned against polygamy, noting that as a Kulin Brahmin he had been married thrice before he was nine. He condemned *sati* and sought inheritance rights for widows at a time when a wife was, in British law, her husband's property.

His Persian treatise, *Tuhfat-ul-Muwahhdin*, was published in 1804. It argued that polytheism constituted an erroneous reading of Hinduism. He translated the Vedanta and Upanishads into Bengali and English to stress an underlying monotheism and believed that the way towards a transcendent Divine lay through individual meditation rather than the shackles of organized religion. The publication of *Vedanta Grantha* and *Vedantasar* in 1815 was followed by English versions in 1816, published in Calcutta and London, titled *Translation of an Abridgement of the Vedanta*.

Roy's public advocacy of wide-ranging reform ruffled conventional feathers. A traditionalist like Sankara Sastri of Madras responded, in 1817, with *A Defence of Hindu Idolatry*. In Calcutta, Mrityunjoy Vidyalankar was critical of Roy in *Vedanta Chandrika* (which appeared in English as *An Apology of the Present System of Hindu Worship*), but conceded that a life of piety for widows was better than death on a funeral pyre. Rammohun Roy replied with *A Defence of Hindu Theism, A Second Defence of the Monotheistical System* and *Bhattacharjer Sahit Bichar*.

Roy met Carey at Serampore in 1816. He praised Christian morality but argued that the concept of Trinity was polytheism and hence a deviation from the Abrahamic indivisible God. Roy ventured to suggest that Jesus's miracles were irrational implants which could be excised from the New Testament without loss to Christianity, which distressed the Baptist mission's English newspaper, *Friend of India*.

On 20 August 1828, Raja Rammohun Roy established Brahmo Samaj, the Society of Brahma. Its monotheist congregation included some of the best and brightest of Bengal. One prominent founding-member was the landowner aristocrat Debendranath Tagore, father of Rabindranath, the iconic philosopher-poet of Bengal, author of India's and Bangladesh's national anthems and the first Indian to win the Nobel Prize. Rabindranath Tagore became head of the Brahmo Samaj in 1911.

Macaulay could have joined the nuanced debate and accessed this Indian bookshelf had he the broad mind of a William Carey.

Babu Moshai and the Ingabanga

The British response to a Bengali identity with foreign characteristics was ambiguous. The Raj wanted British Indians in its edifice without granting them British rights. Lodged in the limbo between white rule and brown subjugation, the Bengali babu found a niche in either the upper tier of inherited riches or across the high and middling professions: lawyers, doctors, magistrates, teachers, clerks. The prototype of the government employee was soon recognizable. Sedentary by inclination, garrulous by preference, supremely self-assured about his skewered grammar and hybrid diction, the babu confidently fished for favour through his skill at *shaheb-dhara*, or netting the sahib.

The sahib maintained a polite distance from his creation, his derision quite vehement in private. David Gilmour writes:

> The type managed to stir every prejudice and preconception in the minds of the [British] arrivals, who were soon writing home to describe babus as 'soapy', 'fat', 'oily', 'smooth-talking', 'devious', 'dishonest', 'servile', 'cowardly' and 'cringing villains'; if they were also Bengali, that only made things worse. It is not easy to understand how young British men reacted so strongly to these perceived defects of character when they would surely have been aware of worse failings among their often drunken, violent and foul-mouthed fellow countrymen.[21]

Gilmour tries to explain this thesaurus of negative epithets as the subconscious contempt felt by the victor for a race which had repeatedly succumbed to small armies under British officers despite possessing a phenomenal advantage in battlefield numbers.

Even an ICS officer sympathetic to India like Henry Beveridge would write that the 'besetting sin of Bengalees' was that they would 'think and talk and talk and think for ever but... will not act'. Beveridge's ICS colleague Sir A.C. Lyall was less polite in *The Old Pindaree*, quoted by *Hobson-Jobson* in the entry for 'babu': 'But I'd sooner be robbed by a tall man who showed me a yard of steel/ Than be fleeced by a sneaking Baboo, with a peon and badge at his heel'. The dictionary adds:

> In Bengal and elsewhere, among Anglo-Indians, it is often used with a slight savour of disparagement, as characterizing a superficially cultivated, but too often effeminate, Bengali. And from the extensive employment of the class, to which

the term was employed as a title, in the capacity of clerks in English offices, the word has come to signify 'a native clerk who writes English'.[22]

It did not seem to occur to the imperial mind that the Bengali babu's attitude might also lie in an awkward combination of ambition, dipping self-esteem and frustration. *Hobson-Jobson* quotes Sir H.M. Elliot as writing, in 1850, that the babus would 'rave about patriotism, and the degradation of their present position'.[23] In any case, the babu would not have survived if he had been inept. Rudyard Kipling saw virtue in the clerk, or *kerani*, of Calcutta, the 'City of Dreadful Night':

> The Babus make beautiful accountants, and if we could only see it, a merciful Providence has made the Babu for figures and detail. Without him on the Bengal side, the dividends of any company would be eaten up by the expenses of English or country-bred clerks. The Babu is a great man, and, to respect him, you must see five score or so of him in a room of hundred yards long bending over ledgers, ledgers, and yet more ledgers—silent as the Sphinx and busy as a bee.[24]

These mechanics of the government's financial mill took pride in being part of a social elite known as the *bhadralok*, with the suffix *Moshay* (a variation of *Mahashoy*, or respected), attached as an accolade.

Such babus had status but were forced to subsist on the salary of a clerk, which led to the saying '*moner babu, taka-ey kabu*', or 'Babu in his mind, but short of cash'. It was the babu, however, who displayed the sharpest instincts in the fluid game of upward mobility, sending daughters to the Calcutta Female School, founded in 1849 by John Elliot Drinkwater Bethune, with financial assistance from Raja Dakshinaranjan Mukherjee, an alumnus of Hare School and activist of the Young Bengal movement.

The first premises of the school, with 21 girls, were in Mukherjee's home, before moving to the west of Cornwallis Square. The government took it over in 1856 and renamed it Bethune. Two students, Kadambini Ganguly and Chandramukhi Basu, became the first female graduates in the British Empire. The other haven of the babu, Hindu College, was renamed Presidency College in 1855. Presidency became co-educational only in 1944, although Calcutta University had started graduate courses for women in 1878.

The wealthy babu, or the *dhanilok*, enriched through trade, banking and brokerage, prospered under British patronage but lost his way in the maze of self-indulgence. Narasingha Sil quotes a description of dissipation:

> They could be identified by deep crow's feet under the eyes, a sign of their nocturnal orgies, shoulder long haircut [*babri*], black powder [*misi*] on their teeth, diaphanous *dhoti*... with black borders, chemise or shirt... made of cambric or the finest muslin, delicately creased... scarf around the neck [*udani*] and buckled Chinese leather shoes. These characters sleep by day, enjoy kite flying [in the afternoon] and songbird [*bulbul*] fights.[25]

By the second half of the 19th century, the hybrid babu was disdained by the British for finding a voice and ridiculed by nationalists for finding a dubious one. Pearychand Mittra lambasted the dandy babu in his novel *Alaler Gharey Dulal* (The Rich Man's Spoilt Child), which appeared in 1858. An advertisement for Lipton tea, reproduced in *Freedom and Beefsteaks,* shows three men in the babu's drawing room seated at a table, wearing English coats over the Bengali *dhoti*, while a bearer in turban and native attire stands in the corner with a large teapot. The wallpaper and furniture are Western. Rosinka Chaudhuri quotes the Bengali journalist Girishchandra Ghosh, who lamented in 1862 that previous British generations had looked on Indians as heirs of a ruined noble, but Indians had now become slaves, with a bleak past and a blinkered future.

Bankim Chandra Chatterjee's scathing depiction of an Anglophile babu, written in 1874, is memorable. I paraphrase: *One word in the mind of the Babu becomes ten when he speaks, a hundred when he writes and thousands when he quarrels. He has the strength of one in his hands, ten in his mouth, a hundred behind your back and of none when the time comes for action. His deity is the Englishman, his preceptor the Brahmo preacher, his scripture the newspaper and his pilgrimage the National Theatre. He becomes a Christian before missionaries, a Brahmo before their leader, a Hindu in front of his father and an atheist before the doleful Brahmin. He drinks water at home and alcohol at his friend's…*

The high-end product of this confluence was a class that came to be known as the 'Ingabanga', or English-Bengali. By the last quarter of the 19th century, the 'Ingabanga' constituted the Indian cream of Calcutta society. Their diction was Victorian (*thet* instead of *that*), their table manners irreproachable in the allocation of duties to knives and forks, their literature Tennyson and Shakespeare, their dream a job in the ICS with a place on the honours list. This made them useful, but not equal to the British. If they sat at the same table, conversation was strictly functional.

Well-meaning doyens of the Raj tried to camouflage the superiority complex; the ill-intentioned wallowed in it. Lord Lytton, who proclaimed Queen Victoria as Empress of India during his tenure as viceroy, gave censure a new dimension when he described British officials in the 1880s who had started to express public sympathy for Indian aspirations as 'White Babus'. Lytton checked the career of the brilliant but fractious Allan Octavian Hume, who had reached the rank of secretary, for crossing an invisible line. In 1885, Hume became a founder-president of the Indian National Congress, along with William Wedderburn, W.C. Bonnerjee, Surendranath Banerjee, Monomohun Ghose, Lalmohan Ghosh, Badruddin Tyabji, M.G. Ranade, Dadabhai Naoroji, Dinshaw Wacha and Pherozeshah Mehta. Wedderburn, a Scot, was superseded by the Bombay government for helping debt-laden tenant farmers in the Deccan. He retired early and served as president of Congress in 1889 and 1910.

Some grandees like Evelyn Baring, finance member in Lord Ripon's Council, argued that the British Empire could hardly be subverted 'by allowing the Bengali Baboo to discuss his own schools and drains'.[26] Sir Henry Cotton, a third-generation officer who was born in Kumbakonam and served as chief commissioner of Assam and chief secretary of Bengal, condemned the violence of European planters and reached out to Indians. He maintained publicly that British prejudice had become a barrier to legitimate Indian aspirations, which were becoming 'more reasonable and more irresistible'. Sir Henry attended a session of the Indian National Congress in 1886 and was elected Congress President in 1904.

These liberals wanted a more inclusive dispensation, not the end of British rule. No one believed that the independence of India was a realistic prospect.

The War of the Palate

There was one art in which India never lost its independence: cuisine. In the war of the palate, it was the British who ceded ground. A new spirit of laissez-faire entered the English kitchen.

Victorian memsahibs might have found Indian food too 'acid' when they arrived but returned home with altered tastebuds. Recipe books in English on 'Indian cookery' became bestsellers, and explanatory notes found avid readers. The *shaami kebab*, said one, may have originated in central Asia, but Lucknow's chefs had refined it to a velvety softness when Nawab Asaf ud-Daula, who had lost his teeth, expressed a desire for this delicacy.

Vendors for Edmunds' Empress Currie Powder, sold in bottles, reminded customers that it was not necessary to live in a hot climate to enjoy spicy food. Edmunds had serious competition from the likes of Manoekjee Poojajee's curry powders and pickles exported from Bombay or the array of flavours from Belatee Bungalow in Calcutta.

British chefs introduced appetising variations. As Lizzie Collingham puts it:

> [Once curries became] firmly established in Victorian food culture, distinctively European herbs such as thyme and marjoram began to find their way into Indian recipes. Anglo-Indian dishes such as mulligatawny soup and kedgeree underwent further Anglicisation in the hands of British cooks. Richard Terry of the Oriental Club not only added the by now standard apples to his mulligatawny but also bay leaves, ham and turnips. Mrs Beeton included bacon in hers, while Eliza Acton strove for authenticity with 'part of a pickled mango' and grated coconut, but gave herself away by also suggesting the addition of the 'pre-cooked flesh of part of a calf's head' and offal, as well as 'a large cupful of thick cream'. Meanwhile, the transformation of the ever-versatile *khichari* continued. The Anglo-Indians had already added

fried onions, fish and hard-boiled eggs to the rice and lentil dish. Now the aristocracy, who served kedgeree for breakfast during their country-house weekends, settled on smoked haddock as the definitive fish to add to the rice, and almost invariably abandoned the lentils.[27]

A recipe for 'Bengal chicken curry' from Richard Terry's *Indian Cookery* bears repetition:

> Cut into small dice 2 onions, and fry with 2 pats of butter: add your chicken cut into small joints, with one tablespoonfull [sic] of curry paste, ½ of powder, ½ of Bengal chutnee, ½ pickled lime, and ½ pickled mango; stir the whole over a slow fire 10 minutes, cover the chicken with broth or water, and let simmer 1½ hours—by this time the curry will be almost dry—add 1 teaspoonful of cream, and serve with rice, separate.[28]

'Curry' was first used by the Portuguese as 'caril' or 'caree', adapted from the Malayalam and Kannada *karil* and Tamil *kari*. Soon a great variety of food was being curried in England, including lobster and oyster, till the English version became unrecognizable to an Indian like Rakhal Haldar, a professor of Sanskrit at University College London in the 1840s. Curry spread to other colonies; Australians made curry out of wattlebird and kangaroo tail.

A Western meal is linear. Europeans eat in sequence, one dish at a time. Indians prefer a sort of circular harmony, choosing at will from different items arrayed on the rim of a large dish called the *thali*. There is no set starting course, although there is, alas, an end. The creative cooks of Madras turned out a unique soup as a starter for Anglo-India.

They took a local staple, *rasam*, made from black pepper, tamarind and water, added some rice and vegetables and named it *milagu tanni*. They were doing their masters a favour, for pepper water, or *molo tanni*, was a traditional recipe for fever, dyspepsia, cholera and even haemorrhoids. The 'mull', short for mulligatawny, became hugely popular across British India, with discretionary variations. The pretentious promoted it to *potage de Madras*. Richard Terry's recipe for an 'Anglicised Mulligatawny Soup' took over four hours to cook and included lean ham, chicken, carrots, turnips, cloves, mace, mixed herbs, onions, sliced apples, butter, curry powder, potato flour, garlic, salt, sugar and rice.[29]

In Bombay, the British took a fancy to the Parsi *dhansak*, a collation of brown rice, four pulses, vegetables, fried onions and either chicken or mutton. The small fish known as Bombay Duck, so called because it swam so close to the surface, was another favourite.

From their earliest presence, the British found a hint of adventure—and perhaps a whiff of danger—in Indian food. Survival was perilous for a dozen other reasons, mainly disease; in 1690, Reverend Ovington was startled to discover that 20 of the 24 Europeans who had been on board his ship to India two years before had died by the time he left from Bombay. But even savoury food and much-needed drink could become a hazard in the dramatically different Indian climate and conditions.

Percival Spear quotes C. Niebuhr's *Journal of Travels to Arabia and the East*:

> It is true that many Englishmen die here very suddenly, but in my opinion the fault is chiefly their own; they eat much succulent food, particularly beef and pork, which the ancient legislators have forbidden for good reason, to the Indians; they drink very strong Portugal wines, at the hottest time of day: in addition they wear as in Europe tight-fitting clothes, which are useless in these countries, since they are much more sensitive to the heat than the Indians with their long and flowing garments.[30]

'Much succulent food' was if anything an understatement. Ovington mentions that the Company kitchen catered to the 'gratification of every stomach', with pilau and *cabob* as the most commonly cooked meal. On Sundays, there was peacock and antelope. Beer and European wine were served regularly and Persian wines on special occasions.

Eliza Fay was told, before she left for India in 1779, that Bengal's heat destroyed the appetite, only to find on arrival that she had never consumed so much at dinner, which was at two in the afternoon. The table was laden with fish, fowl, turkey and half a sheep at dinner parties; four times as much food was generally served as in England. Every lady, noted Mrs Fay, 'even your humble servant', drank at least a bottle at dinner. She was, moreover, quite certain that she was living cheap. One presumes that leftover fish, fowl and flesh were thrown into the Burdwan stew.

Dinner time varied. Lord Cornwallis changed it to three in winter and four in summer, before it advanced in stages to eight in the evening, creating time for a 'tiffin' around mid-day. Newcomers were forgiven if they thought the banana was a kind of sausage. The mango became immensely popular.

An illustration of 'The Sahib at Table' in Hilton Brown's collection shows a dinner table in post-prandial uproar, the fun watched beadily by amused Hindu and sardonic Muslim waiters. There are three memsahibs and eight men, all high and happy. A servant examines an empty bottle of wine, a slight smile on his face, in the background. Even the hookah is tipsy.

Calcutta's Mayor, Alexander Mackrabie, recorded in his journal of 3 November 1775 that there were great joints of roasted goat and endless cold dishes at a party given by the Claverings, but the cooking was detestable and the conversation stupid. The ladies pelted one another with bread pills and got drunk on cherry brandy.[31]

The Frenchman Count de Warren, who came to India around 1800, was 'thunderstruck at the enormous quantity of beer and wine absorbed by these English ladies, in appearance so pale and delicate', according to Major Henry Hobbs. De Warren says he could 'scarcely recover from my astonishment at seeing my fair neighbour quickly dispose of a bottle and a half of very strong beer, eked out with a fair allowance of claret, and wind up with five or six glasses of light but spirited champagne, taken with her dessert'.[32] In 1830, George Johnson heard about four 'Burra Bebbees' (Senior Memsahibs) who drank a dozen bottles of Hodgson's pale ale before they retired from the table and witnessed a lady put away six quarts of Allsops beer, an imitation of India Pale Ale, without moving from her chair.

The Company merchants and administrators took full advantage of low prices and high availability. Lizzie Collingham writes:

[They] gained a reputation for consuming immense amounts of meat, in contrast to the vegetarian Indians, and even the meat-eating Mughal nobility. Once the British were established in India, they continued to replicate the consumption patterns of the wealthy at home and loaded their tables with 'Turkies that you could not see over—round of Beef, boiled roast Beef, stewed Beef, loin of Veal for a side dish and roast big capons as large as Hen Turkies'. Large bowls of curry and rice were placed along the table, in between the turkeys and beef. This was just the first course.[33]

Lifestyles began to reflect Calcutta's emergence as the best-fed capital of the 18th century. An everyday meal might consist of soup, roast fowl, curry, rice, mutton pie, rice pudding, tarts and cheese, washed down with wine.

One commentator, writes Kincaid, was 'disgusted' by the sight of 'one of the *prettiest girls* in Calcutta eat about two pounds of mutton-chops at one sitting!' There were, as a rule, two glasses by every plate, one for 'loll shrub' (*laal sharab*, or red wine), and the other for any other kind of alcohol; and after dinner the men sat down for the really serious part of the repast, which was drinking three bottles of claret each. A siesta was necessary, for most Europeans got drunk and developed expertise at silly games like snuffing out a candle at a distance of four yards with a bread-pellet—the champion could do that at a length of four yards. The fun paused when a certain Captain Morrison lost his temper after being hit by a pellet, threw a leg of mutton at the 'assailant' and incited a duel in which the pellet-assailant nearly died. Those who wanted to flaunt their wealth entertained on a river barge (an equivalent to the modern yacht in social-mobility rankings) with the highest bragging rights going to those who could afford slaves from Mauritius to row their boats.[34]

There was the famous case of the newly arrived, beautiful 20-year-old Miss Rose Aylmer, niece of Justice Russel, her memory now restricted to a grave in the Calcutta cemetery. She contracted severe constipation by over-indulging in pineapples and within a few days died a martyr to excess. Colonel Arthur Wellesley was stationed in Calcutta when a young army chaplain called Mr Blunt got so inebriated that he ran amok, stark naked, amidst soldiers and sailors, singing ribald songs. Wellesley was generous—even the most cautious men, he said, were liable to be led astray by convivial society, and such 'cursory debauch' should not be taken too seriously. But the man of God died within ten days of depression.

The future victor of Waterloo was a guest of the lawyer William Hickey on 4 June 1797, to celebrate the king's birthday. An eminent French cook prepared a 'tolerably fat deer' and 'a very fine turtle', while the host took 'especial care to lay in a *quantum sufficit* of the best champagne that was procurable' in addition to claret, hock and madeira. There was great hilarity and much singing. The party went on till three in the morning, and everyone woke up with a dreadful hangover.

Such consumption was moderate 'when compared with that in the officers' mess of the 33rd Foot, over which Colonel Wellesley presided, and in the house of Wesley's second-in-command, Lieutenant Colonel John Sherbrooke, at Alypore, three miles from Calcutta. Here the drinking was astonishing,' writes Christopher Hibbert.[35]

If there were complaints, they were minor. An anonymous mid-19th-century housewife found Indian meat inferior to that found in England, the eggs smaller and English bacon extremely expensive. Her recipes included 21 Western soups, including Palestine Soup (3 lbs of artichokes. 3 pints of clear mutton broth, ½ pint of milk, little cayenne and salt) and a distinctly multicultural mulligatawny (1 fowl sliced, 4 onions sliced, 6 cloves, 2 tablespoons batter), with variations that had antelope venison.[36]

The Colonial Menu had Scotch mutton broth, pot-au-feu, beef à la mode, mould of beef, *polpetti*, Saunders, Breslau of beef, *beef en Persillade*, German tongues, spiced beef, salt beef, beef-steak pie, four kinds of veal, three kinds of pork, Oxford sauce, ten forms of mutton including the delightfully named Chaddy Maddy, seven kinds of poultry, five kinds of game, oyster patties, buttered crab, Bengal stew, sheep's head, sheep's tongue, debris pudding, kidney toast, anchovy toast, macaroni pie and scrambled eggs.

'In India there are only a few good sorts of fish; the *seir*, which, though white, somewhat resembles salmon, the pomfret or turbot, and the murrell. English salmon and herrings are sold in tins, and sardines are very commonly used for all sorts of cutlets, omelettes, &c,' she says. Kedgeree was made with 'One tea-cup of rice boiled as for curry; mix this with any cold fish, a little butter, pepper, and three beaten eggs; stir over the fire till very hot, and serve'.

There was also oyster pilau. India came into its own with the curries, which 'every native' knew how to make: Madras curry paste, curry powder, mint chutney, hot chutney and Tapp sauce, Delhi chutney, Bengal chutney and Bolarum chutney (3 lbs each of *kismis*, tamarinds, green ginger and brown sugar; 1 lb of onions; 15 ounces of green chillies; 4 or 5 mangoes and 3 dessertspoons of salt) which are straight out of the Indian palate. The sauces and sweets were Western.

Fact wandered into fiction. William Makepeace Thackeray's Jos Sedley, who had made his money as Collector of Boggley Wollah, was a typical overfed 'English Nabob' in *Vanity Fair*, published in 1848: fat to the point of bursting, smug to the verge of idiocy. Thackeray's grandfather, also William Makepeace, got a salary of £62 a year as the collector in Sylhet, Bengal, but amassed a minor fortune by selling captured elephants to the East India Company. He retired at the happy age of 27.

An intrepid Calcutta businessman promoted soda water as a cure for such a gourmand culture. An advertisement appeared in the *Calcutta Gazette* selling 'Soda Water, for the Hot Weather', advocating its 'medicinal qualities' as 'so numerous, and of such importance, that the most eminent Physicians recommend it, on account of the very great number of cases in which it has been highly beneficial, particularly in calculous complaints and in habitual stranguarie [sic]'. It added, 'and it is besides a cool and grateful beverage, particularly adapted for this climate...'[37] *Plus ça change.* Coca Cola, the world champion sugar-soaked teeth-rattler, also began life in an American pharmacy as a 'medicine' at five cents a glass.

If anyone was fooled by the advertising in 1816, it was not for long. *Hobson-Jobson* says that soda water was called *Bilayuti pawnee*, or English water; foreign scents were known as *Khushboo pawnee*, or perfumed water. A sprightly ode in Hindi underscores the vital importance of potable water at a time when the well was its principal source: *Pani kua, pani tal; Pani ata, pani dal; Pani bagh, pani ramna; Pani Ganga, pani Jamuna; Pani hansta, pani rota; Pani jagta, pani sota; Pani bap, pani ma; Bara nam pani ka.* A simple translation would be: *Water is wells, water is tanks; Water is flour, water is cereal; Water is fruit, water is flower; Water is Ganga, water is Jamuna; Water is laughter, water is tears; Water wakes, water sleeps; Water is father, water is mother. Glorious is the name of water!*

Ingenuity being the mother of protocol, the British devised innovative ways to ensure Western etiquette within the framework of Indian logistics. Lizzie Collingham, referring to Thomas Williamson's *Guide to Gentlemen Intended for the Civil, Military or Naval Service of the Honourable East India Company* of 1810, notes that an *aub-dar* (*aabdar*, or the Indian servant in charge of drinks) ensured that the water, champagne, Madeira, claret or pale ale were chilled. A guest's *hookkahburdar* went ahead, carrying his master's hubble-bubble to the host's residence; the hookah was smoked with aplomb before it became too oriental for the master race of Victorians. A second servant might accompany the guest, charged with the onerous duty of keeping flies away with a *chowrie* (fan made of peacock feathers) or discreetly chuck out an advancing cockroach. The British were not squeamish, although eyes would be politely averted when minute insects were calmly picked out from the food. In a sparse military outpost, where a host might be short of tableware, thoughtful guests would send a servant ahead with cutlery and napkins.

There was not much need to worry about any embarrassment before Indian guests, for 'natives' were rarely invited to dinners at home. Nor were most Indians eager to be invited. The sepoys fought for the East India Company, and gave their lives in battle, but were not quite eager to eat with the foreigner, as John Nicholson, posted with the 27th regiment of the Bengal Army discovered. 'Like other infantry regiments of the Bengal Army, the 27th was composed to high-caste Hindus—Brahmins and Rajputs recruited from Oude and Bihar. Caste obligations dominated their thinking and affected their military performance in ways that Nicholson must have found incomprehensible at first. Before taking meals, they had to purify themselves by bathing, changing their clothes and performing prayers. The meal itself had to be fresh, cooked by persons of the same caste as themselves, and eaten in ritually pure circumstances without risk of pollution. All this could take hours, so that no fast marches were possible,' writes Charles Allen.[38]

In 1824, the brilliant diarist Fanny Parkes had 22 servants in attendance at a dinner for eight despite her husband's comparatively modest salary. A rich sahib's budget could rise to as much as

£10,000 for annual household expenses, but the average household spending on hospitality was around £700. Being stingy was a social contretemps. Since no caste Hindu, however poor, would touch food from an English kitchen, leftovers from a *burra khana* (the big dinner) were sent to the Christian poor. The cooks were mainly Muslim, having slowly gravitated from the diminished Mughal aristocracy which had lost its old income and was incapable of finding a new one. Without much fuss, they began to shift foreign tastebuds to accommodate chilli-hot chutney and choreographed the triumphant march of mulligatawny soup through the heart and soul of British India. By the 1830s, the British staple for breakfast, lunch and dinner included curry to spice up the bland boiled or roasted meats.[39]

W.H. Dawe's *The Wife's Help to Indian Cookery* (1888) pays tribute to the 'Madras Karhi', while Edward Palmer's *Indian Cookery* (1936) tells you how to make kedgeree with green or red chillies, enhanced by fish (preferably caught early that morning), hard-boiled eggs and onions. There were happy experiments. Mango was added to Bengal's famous prawn curry, and poppadom appeared beside crispy bacon. But the signature dish of Anglo-India remained mulligatawny soup, served at every formal event, even when it caused discomfort instead of settling any dyspepsia. *The Police-Wallah's Little Dinner* by 'Aliph Cheem', a pseudonym of the British officer Major Walter Yeldham, published in 1888, tells a tale of a district meal with the collector, his conceited 'sub', the pompous judge, the thirsty surgeon and the priest:

> *There's the Padre, the Reverend Michael Whine,*
> *The sorrowfullest of men,*
> *Who tells you he's crushed with his children nine,*
> *And what'll he do with ten?*
> ...
> *First we had Mulligatawny soup,*
> *Which made us all perspire,*
> *For the cook, that obstinate nincompoop,*
> *Had flavoured it hot as fire.*
> *Next a tremendous fragmentary dish*
> *Of salmon was carried in,—*

The taste was rather of oil than fish,
With a palpable touch of tin.
Then, when the salmon was swept away,
We'd a duckey shtew, with peas,
And the principal feature of that entrée
Was its circumambient grease.[40]

Hot, oily *shtew* and grease: the British certainly got closer to Indian food than they did to any Indian. Salmon and duck gained prominence as the late Victorians started course correction, to use a mild pun. But the European fare still had to transit the greasy rigours of an Indian cook, even after travelling thousands of unnecessary miles imprisoned in a tin.

Margaret MacMillan writes:

By the second half of the nineteenth century, the British were trying to distance themselves from India even in their food. When tinned food came in, it was considered a compliment to guests to give them Home-grown delicacies out of the tins; one naïve lady, who had never been out of India, was overheard to say, 'doubtless nothing else was ever used at Her Majesty's table'. Generations of Indian cooks learnt to make the right sort of dishes: the soups, the puddings, the savouries on toast, the cakes for tea... Taking its cue from upper-class behaviour at Home, etiquette in India forbade the discussion of food. It was impolite to compliment the hostess on the cooking; it suggested that she had actually done the work herself. Perhaps it was just as well, for often there was not much to praise.[41]

Mediocre cooking in the memsahib's home was often disguised in the French language: the potage would be followed by *poissons* (tinned salmon), *quenelles* of partridge, *releves* (boiled turkey, to be plain), *rots* (quails), *entremets* (meringues), cheese, ices and dessert.

One visiting Victorian was in no mood to compromise. Edward Lear, who spent 14 months in India as a guest of his friend Lord Northbrook, loved India although he dismissed British Calcutta as nothing but a Hustlefussabad. His meals were totally British: 'divine' boiled mutton, stewed rabbit, cutlets, beefsteak and eggs, with beer.

British assertion found expression in other aspects of lifestyle, most impressively in architecture. Massive structures were created on a European model unfit for India's inexorable heat. Percival Spear notes:

> The settlers were beginning to adopt English rather than Indian standards of living and amusement; the ideal of making every English settlement an exact replica, as far as possible, of an English town was just coming into fashion. Nowhere is this seen more clearly than in the architecture of the time. There was never any attempt to adopt the Indian style of a house opening inwards on a courtyard, which with the resources possessed by the Europeans of the time, could have been made cool and luxurious enough with verandahs, fountains and formal gardens. Instead the classical style was imported bodily, and the verandahs were not even lowered sufficiently by means of arches to keep out the sun.[42]

The luxury of fine dining and handsome bungalows was a privilege of upper-crust Raj society. Those at the nether end of the class structure, like the trooper and the plebeian, leavened their harsh discomforts with inexpensive local spirits like *bhang* and *arrack* and searched for hope in false optimism. But they helped navigate the Empire through the numerous bends and whirlpools of a stressful journey.

5

Love, Doolaly and the Coloured Races

The French botanist and traveller Victor Jacquemont, who was in India from 1828 till his sudden death in December 1832, praised the English for their success, strength, wealth and moral fibre but was critical of their arrogance and racism: they esteemed themselves too highly, and despised the 'coloured races' too much. In a letter to Porphyre Jacquemont, written on 5 December 1831, he teased English presumptions:

> I am an English gentleman: that is to say, one of the most brilliant animals in the creation. I have forsaken the joys of Europe, and the charms of the domestic circle: I have bid farewell to my friends, in order to come and live in this beast of a country. Ergo, in compensation for this, I have a right to eat, drink, dress, live, and ride, &c. &c. in the most magnificent style. And if my income is not sufficient, I will run in debt to meet this necessity.[1]

Every Englishman, he wrote, lived beyond his means; a captain earning ₹600 a month, or a surgeon ₹1,200, was quite content to owe ₹50,000 or ₹100,000: 'debts truly shameful, and for which there can be no excuse, except in the insanity of the debtors'.[2]

This 'despise' of the 'coloured races' did not translate into sexual abstinence. The day had its rules; the night was another story. Even priests were not immune to the charms of Indian women, although they presumably limited their admiration to prose. Edward Terry, Sir Thomas Roe's chaplain, called India a 'Paradise'. Always conscious of his role as minister of the Gospel, the censorious Terry frequently alludes to the Bible to make his point. David, Bathsheba and

Solomon with his famous 1,000 concubines are much on his mind, as are Samson and Delilah. Terry calls 17th-century India a 'most spacious and fertile monarchy (with) all necessaries for the use and service of man' but even the 'garden of Eden had a serpent in it'. In India, they are scorpions, snakes and mosquitoes. And vanity: Indian women 'varnish' themselves with make-up. There are women akin to a merchant's ship: 'always ready for trade, and therefore, sets herself as possibly she can with all variety of rigging'. This is liberty land: 'Here is a free toleration for harlots, who are enlisted and enrolled (as they say) before they can have liberty to keep such an open house... those base prostitutes are as little ashamed to entertain, as others are openly to frequent their houses.'[3]

In 18th-century Calcutta, the sahib could find a concubine for anything between three to five rupees a month. The sinuous and seductive nautch was a regular attraction at social get-togethers. The Portuguese called a nautch girl *bailadere* or *bayadere*; in Calcutta they were known as *baijis*; south India was familiar with the *bhogamdasi*; the north had various appellations like *kanchani, chunchuni* or *ramjani* (transliterated to Rum-Johnny), according to one of the great philological compilations of the world, *Hobson-Johnson: A Glossary of Colloquial Anglo-Indian Words and Phrases, and of Kindred Terms, Etymological, Historical, Geographical and Discursive,* by the British civil servants Henry Yule and Arthur Burnell, completed by 1882.

Abdul Halim Sharar (1860–1926), author of the exquisite *Guzishta Lucknow*, a virtuoso anecdotal study of Awadhi culture and lifestyle, writes that Lucknow's courtesans could be divided into five categories: *kanchanis*, who came from Punjab; *chunnawalis*, or lime-sellers who had graduated into song and dance; the *nagrant*, of Gujarati origin; the *takiyas*, who served the poor; and the sophisticated *randis*, who had formal training in music and dance.

Nautch cut across class and region. Francois Bernier reports that the Mughal Emperor Shah Jahan admitted dancing girls into the seraglio. He added:

They were not indeed the prostitutes seen in bazaars, but those of a more private and respectable class, who attend the grand weddings of *Omrahs* [aristocrats] and *Mansebdars* for the purpose of singing and dancing. Most of these *Kenchens* are handsome and well dressed, and sing to perfection; and their limbs being extremely supple, they dance with wonderful agility, and are always correct in regard to time.[4]

Unsurprisingly, Shah Jahan's puritan son Aurangzeb restricted their entry into the palace. They could make their salutations at the Diwan-i-Aam (public audience) from afar and go away.

In 1673, Fryer wrote about a nautch at a Company event at Surat: 'After supper they treated us with the Dancing Wenches, and good soops [sic] of Brandy and Delf Beer, till it was late enough.'[5] In 1701, Talboys Wheeler recorded that 'the Governor (of Madras) conducted the Nabob into the Consultation Room... after dinner they were diverted with the Dancing Wenches'.[6] Robert Orme, Clive's friend and publicist-historian, who lived in India between 1743 and 1758, claimed that a Gujarat nawab had beheaded dancing girls because they did not answer his summons immediately. Orme was among those historians determined to prove that the British had rescued India from Mughal 'savagery'. However, he did concede that nature had showered Indian women with extraordinary beauty.

European men were obviously attracted to nautch; women were, understandably, more objective. Jemima Kindersley, whose letters were published in 1777, overcame her initial diffidence:

It is difficult to give you any proper idea of this entertainment; which is so very delightful, not only to black men, but to many Europeans. A large room is lighted up; at one end sit the great people who are to be entertained, at the other are the dancers and their attendants; one of the girls who are to dance comes forward, for there is seldom more than one of them dance at a time; the performance consists chiefly in a continual removing the shawl, first over the head, then off again; extending first one hand, then the other; the feet are likewise moved, though a yard of ground would be sufficient for the whole performance. But it is their languishing glances, wanton smiles, and attitudes not quite consistent with decency, which are so admired; and whoever excels most in these is the finest dancer.[7]

Rev. Heber's wife Amelia was less generous to 'the Nach, or dancing girls, if dancing that could be called, which consisted in strained movements of the arms, head, and body, the feet, though in perpetual slow motion, Seldom moving from the same spot'. However, she praised the singing of 'Viiki, the Catalami of the east', who had a 'low but sweet voice'. But the 'unmelodious nature music' was nearly as tiring as the 'swarms of moschetoes' [mosquitoes].[8] Amelia Heber did not understand why men made such a deal about nautch, but nobody had told her that the dancing girls were told to tone down their come-hither glances when ladies were present.

The *Annual Register* sniffed in 1782 that dancing girls were nothing but a form of prostitution; Charles Dowley was impressed in 1800 with their grace, having seen a performance at the home of a 'rich Native of Calcutta, named Sookma Roy, a person remarkable for many excellent qualities, especially for his attachment and hospitality towards Europeans'.[9] Talking of Lucknow, Percival Spear notes that on 'both sides there was much give-and-take; the English had long acquired a taste for nautches, and developed new ones for elephant fights and hookah smoking; the nawabs on their part experimented with English food and drink'.[10]

The taste was widespread. Nautch girls did brisk business at camps when the Company Army was on the move, and many of them settled in cantonments. Generals would be entertained with a troupe of up to a hundred dancers. Sir David Octherlony, the first resident of Delhi, entertained his colleagues, the military and civilian administrators who came to the Mughal capital after the British victory in 1803, to nautch parties in a city with the finest talent. It was not about the sexual innuendo alone, for sex was available with much less fuss down the road. Europeans had never seen the interplay of subtle grace, acting, lissom agility, insouciance and poetry put to music. The 'snake dance', in which the nautch girl would mimic the cobra's sway to the charmer's music was much in demand.

Jacquemont describes Maharaja Ranjit Singh's hospitality in a letter to his father despatched from Delhi on 10 January 1832. On his return from the court in Lahore, he found the dining table at the residence laid out 'luxuriously and tastefully, after the French fashion' and then some local entertainment:

The concert was execrable, Oriental music being one of the most disagreeable noises I know; but the slow-cadenced and voluptuous dance of Delhi and Cashmere is one of the most agreeable that can be executed. I will also admit that my Cashmerian *danseuses* had an inch of colour on their faces, vermillion on their lips, red and white on their cheeks, and black around their eyes. But this daubery was very pretty: it gives an extraordinary lustre to the already beautiful and extraordinary large eyes of the Eastern women. And as the *danseuses* of Lahore are quite as virtuous as those of Paris, it is useless to tell you more...[11]

As James Forbes pointed out, nautch girls did not need English to convey their meaning:

Two girls usually perform at the same time; their steps are not so many or active as ours, but much more interesting; as the song, the music and the motions of the dance combine to express love, hope, jealousy, despair, and the passions so well known to lovers, and very easily to be understood by those who are ignorant of other languages.[12]

Satirists were less subtle. A poem in *Adventures of Qui Hi*, published in 1815, describes husbands in a brothel: 'Here serious characters resort / And quit domestic broils for sport, / And in some sooty fair one's arms / Forget sweet matrimony's charms' (*Qui Hi* is a variation of *Koi hai?*, the standard call of a sahib in need of a servant).[13]

Not all English views were ecstatic. *Hobson-Jobson* records in its entry for 'Nautch' that the staid Colonel Broughton chastised Europeans for becoming victims of an illusion. The good Bishop Heber was even less impressed: 'The Nach women were, as usual, ugly, huddled up in huge bundles of red petticoats; and their exhibition as dull and insipid to an European taste, as could well be conceived.'[14] The champion of Western civilisation, Macaulay, lashed out at his fellow Christians in 1843 for decorating the temples of false gods, permitting dancing girls and gilding the images before which ignorant heathen Indians bowed.

Starch started to stick to the Victorian collar. The songs of 'Rum-Johnny', once a welcome diversion in a fleeting life, were now derided as 'barbarous' and 'horrid screeching', while Indian dance became no more than disgusting caterwauling of the Orient. How could nautch possibly compare with the cotillion? The dancing girls took their feeble revenge once the white clients had left, mimicking English expressions and their dance steps amidst peals of laughter.

British moralists, led by the powerful missionary lobby, were less successful in their counter-revolution than they expected. 'Purity Association' sprang up to urge a boycott of such moral degradation, aided by Indian reformers like Keshub Chandra Sen who saw the furies of hell in the eyes and comely waist of the nautch girl, a vast ocean of poison in her breasts and India's death in her smile. Hyper exaggeration was not very persuasive. Major Walter Yeldham's marvellously incisive verse-portraits in *Lays of Ind* includes *The Naughty Nautch*:

> *The Reverend McPherson believed that a nautch*
> *Was a most diabolical sort of debauch;*
> *He thought that the dance's voluptuous mazes*
> *Would turn a man's brain, and allure him to blazes!*
> *That almond-eyed girls,*
> *Dressed in bangles and pearls,*
> *And other scant jims*
> *Disclosing their limbs,*
> *With movement suggestive*
> *And harmony festive,*
> *With fire in their eyes, and love on their lips,*
> *And passion in each of their elegant skips,*
> *As beauteous as angels, as wicked as devils,*
> *Performed at these highly indelicate revels.*[15]

When Rev. McPherson actually saw a nautch at a dinner hosted by the raja, in the company of the cantonment's officers—General Smart, Major Spruce, Colonel Byles, Captain Quill and Major Stock, along with the commissioner and his wife—all he could conclude was that the devil did not have good taste:

The Rajah he bowed and he bowed and he bowed,
Shaking hands as they came with the whole of the crowd;
And he led to a couch the Commissioner's wife,
And said 'twas the happiest hour of his life.
Then suddenly sounded a loud-clanging gong,
And there burst on the eyes of the wondering throng
A bevy of girls
Dressed in bangles and pearls
And other rich gems.
With fat podgy limbs...
And sang a wild air
Which affected your hair
While behind them a circle of men and of boys,
With tomtoms and pipes, made a terrible noise.[16]

Missionaries on a warpath cited, among the 'ill-effects' of nautch, physical weakness and disease. The Madras Christian Literature Society was livid in 1892 after Indian gentry entertained British dignitaries with a nautch. The government, sensibly, dismissed the protests as intolerant, but chose discretion over valour at the reception for the future King George V when he visited Madras in 1905. The proposed nautch was dropped.

Indians were more concerned about hospitality than morality. The British rarely felt the need to return their munificent generosity. Percival Spear makes the pertinent point that even during the rule of Warren Hastings there was never any resistance to a free meal despite the talk of Indian perfidy in 1756: 'Significantly enough no memories of the Black Hole prevented European intercourse with the Muslim princes; wherever they were assured of a luxurious and hospitable welcome they gathered like flies to the honey-pot.' The same rule applied to the 'East Indians', at that time segregated from English society; 'anyone of this class', says F.J. Shore, 'whose circumstances will allow him to give good entertainments, will not find the English (in Bengal at least) at all backward in partaking of them.'[17]

To add insult to injury, the flies sneered at the honeypot after getting sated. Dennis Kincaid comments:

It occurred to very few of the Calcutta gentry, who patronised a local prince by accepting his invitations, what hours of anxiety preceded the despatch of an invitation, what alternating moods of gratitude and panic succeeded its acceptance; what expense to procure the materials of European food from Calcutta, to engage cooks skilled in the mysteries of the European kitchen; what shedding of religious prejudices to provide the guests with beef and wine. Dancing-girls ordered from Lucknow and Delhi—surely Rahema Bibi with her incredibly graceful gestures, surely Zebunissa with her delightful wit and the wonderful memory that enabled her to cap appropriately any Persian quotation—surely these would be to the taste of the scornful strangers, so that they would give a good account of the host to authorities in Calcutta?[18]

Kincaid adds, perceptively, that the nautch party worked because it was the one social occasion at which the British and Indians could gloss over their mutual dislike. By the 19th century, he writes:

[The two] neither understood nor liked each other as a general rule; but the Indian nobles had learnt their manners in the Mogul court and the English residents or soldiers were men of the world with something of the cynical tolerance and outward polish of that century. Some of the famous breakfasts given by the Nawab of Lucknow, that charming and futile prince, were evidently enjoyed by everyone: and between the almost endless courses there would be animal-fights or processions of rare beasts such as a 'greyish elephant'. But that strange society of Lucknow, with its Europeanised Musulmans and Indianised Europeans was not typical of India. The younger factors met few of the Indian gentry; their contacts were chiefly with the moneylenders and traders of the capital, whom they would only meet in business hours or at an occasional, inevitable nautch.[19]

Sahibs were loath to admit that Indian hospitality was usually less boring than their parties, where conversation would circle around the idiosyncrasies of colleagues or gentle queries about how on earth

'Tubby' had got a CSI in the birthday honours. There was music after the meal, when a memsahib would inflict her repertoire upon a caged audience or a sahib attempt a comic song. If all else failed, there were parlour games. When the butler arrived bearing whisky an hour after dinner, it signalled departure, to general relief.

The Doolaly Syndrome

A report in the Bengali paper *Samachar Darpan* on 3 November 1827 described the behaviour of a fresh batch of British troops lodged at Fort William. They took leave, wandered in the sun, drank and whored so much that many of them 'kicked the bucket' even before they could join their regiments.[20] Their officers in class-riven Britain shrugged; you could hardly expect better behaviour from working-class 'Tommies'. Their drunken brawls were the price for keeping order in perilous circumstances.

An assessment made in 1834 indicated that a corps of 1,000 men would, within ten years in India, either be dead from war or disease or physically wrecked. Officers were given six months' leave every two years, enough for a four-month visit to England after the Suez Canal opened. The 'British Other Ranks', or non-commissioned officers, were forced to do five years or more of continuous duty. Tommies had to wait even longer for a break. The departure parade for soldiers returning home, predictably, was a loud and drunken affair. The regiment turned out to say goodbye, with beer and whisky and music. The band played *Rolling home to dear old Blighty* as soldiers marched to the railway station.

From the Indian side of the pageantry, a wail would be heard, the cry of abandoned girlfriends and their parents. A father's lament captures the pathos:

> *Oh doolally sahib, fifteen years you've had my daughter,*
> *and now you go to Blighty, sahib;*
> *May the boat that takes you over sink to the bottom of*
> *the pani, sahib!*[21]

'Doolally' derives from Deolali, a transit camp situated in Nashik about a 100 miles from Bombay and referred to the feverish eccentricity of the English soldier waiting to go home; *pani* meant water, or the seas. Few, if any, British civilians or soldiers married an Indian paramour. As the saying went, they wanted the comforts of betrothal without the 'plague' of marriage.

Wedding rings were reserved for home. The *British Magazine and Review* published, in September 1782, 'A Love Elegy' by a certain 'JW':

Ye, nymphs of India! Flushed with charms sublime
Which your own Phoebus guards, and still inspires;
Who boast the native ardour of your clime,
That favours love, and nurses warm desires.
Still may you captivate Indostan's swains
And purchase love by ev'ry winning art
But simple is the conquest Laura gains
For me in vain would Indus pour her store...[22]

The practical answer was brothels. Some over-optimistic Victorian army commanders thought that they could 'sweat the sex out' of the soldier with rigorous drill and endless football games. Neither the football nor the morals improved. It was a no-contest between reality and virtue. Brothels came up within reach of the cantonment. In Calcutta, the troops frequented Coolootola, Taltala, Bowbazar, Fenwick Bazar, Watgunge, Bhowanipore or Sona-gaji, an area named after a Muslim divine whose grave is in its by-lanes. This red light area is better known as 'Sona-gachi', which translates to 'golden tree'. Delhi's major haunt was G.B. Road; Agra had the 'Rag' and Bombay its Grant Road. Women on Grant Road stood behind bars for their protection from violence. The upper echelons went to Karaya Road in Calcutta or the Turkish Baths in Delhi.

The Raj was prudent. Gilmour writes:

Sexual scandal seldom damaged careers in Victorian India. Most Civilians [ICS officers] did not lead lives about which scandals could be spread; those who did usually got away with them. In the view of Sir Denzil Ibbetson, a Member of Curzon's Council, the Government should not be 'ordinarily concerned with the private morals of its officers, unless they constitute a scandal which is calculated to bring discredit upon Govt or the Service, or impair the efficiency of the officer as a public servant'. As a result, blind eyes were generally turned to men who discreetly kept Burmese mistresses or pursued love affairs with Anglo-Indian widows or even had adulterous liaisons in hill stations. Homosexuals, however, would not have been viewed with such tolerance. Sodomy, opined Ibbetson, 'put a man altogether outside the pale' and would have justified his dismissal, 'scandal or no scandal'. Yet homosexual civilians either sublimated their desires or else qualified them undetected. Sublimation was rarer in the Army, and scandal was more common. On learning of the sexual activities of Sir Hector MacDonald, who had risen from the ranks to command British forces in Ceylon, his fellow general, Lord Kitchener, wanted him court-martialled and shot. MacDonald decided it was preferable to shoot himself.[23]

The administration tried, periodically, to ring-fence prostitution. 'Obscene acts and songs' became punishable in the Indian Penal Code of 1860. This was followed by the Cantonment Act of 1864 and the Contagious Diseases Act of 1868, dubbed the 'Chouddo Ain', or 'Fourteen Law', which sought to control ever-rising venereal disease in the barracks through registration and medical treatment of prostitutes. There was obvious fear among them about any administrative interest in a clearly illegitimate business. Bengal's Lieutenant-governor Sir William Grey estimated that there were 30,000 courtesans in Calcutta in the 1870s, whereas the number registered was between 6,000 and 7,000, according to Sumanta Banerjee. A survey of Berhampore in January 1870 showed only 8 registered 'public women', but syphilis and gonorrhoea were rampant in the small town.

Many Calcutta courtesans resettled in the French colony, Chandernagore, where there were no such regulations. For bent policemen, a zone like Sona-gaji, with a brisk nocturnal business in food, flowers and alcohol, meant gratification in cash and kind. The constable had functional power—he could be protector or persecutor. There was a saying among prostitutes: *Mach khabi to ilish, nang dhorbi to pulish* (If you want fish, eat *ilish;* if you want a lover, keep a policeman).

Sumanta Banerjee identifies policy-driven poverty as a significant, although not the sole, reason for the mushroom growth in Bengal's red light areas:

> The close association of prostitution with the new dens of crime in an urban metropolis like Calcutta reflected the economic changes that were altering land relations in the countryside, driving thousands of unemployed villagers to the metropolis and other towns, many among whom found means of survival through new, non-traditional channels like running distilleries or gambling dens—institutions that emerged in 18th century Calcutta, initially to cater to the needs of the British soldiers and civilians, and extended later to embrace the Bengali parvenu.[24]

The nouveau riche brought their own variations to the fluid Calcutta culture. A common practice among the newly affluent 'babu' was keeping a mistress in a separate residence, who might even be a destitute widow of the high-caste Kulin Brahmin.

The origins of limitless polygamy among this select community of Kulin Brahmins is believed to lie in a decision made by the 12th-century king of Bengal, Ballal Sen, who wanted a network of powerful caste-and-class alliances. In practice this led to the neglect of wives and, as wealth depleted with generations, financial despair. If the husband died in middle age as frequently happened, wives— many of whom were barely children—were abandoned or subjected to cruel isolation and denial of anything that might 'excite' them, including spice or a preferred dish. The retrograde practice of child marriage was compounded by the Hindu ban on remarriage. By the 19th century, such victims of despair and destitution constituted a significant community of 'kept' women, technically different from those who would sell their wares to any *khodder* or customer.

Some of them found a more glamorous vocation as actresses when Bengali theatre became dominant from the 1870s. This had the side effect of providing a vicarious literary education, since the plays were as likely to be adaptations of Bengali fiction as of Shakespeare.

The most famous of such actresses, Binodini Dasi (1863–1941), narrates a story in her autobiography which is not too far from stage drama. She was 20 and a billboard name for Star Theatre when she changed her lover for someone with more means. The jilted and jealous reject stormed into her residence early one morning, threw ₹20,000 at her feet and asked her to give up acting. Binodini's answer was out of a script: 'I have made money, but money cannot make me.' The lover struck her with a sword but missed. She caught his hand and reminded him of the disgrace to his family if he was hanged for the murder of a prostitute. He threw away the sword and held his face in his hands in remorse. A babu was saved. The curtain came down.

Writers like Bhavanicharan Bandopadhyay caricatured this kind of babu for sacrificing his roots at the altar of Kamala, the goddess of material comforts. In his novel *Naba Babu Bilas*, a toady tells his master that it would require success in four p's and four kh's to make him an accomplished babu: *pasha* (dice), *paira* (pigeon-fights), *paradar* (adultery), *poshak* (dress), *khushi* (pleasure), *khanki* (prostitute), *khana* (feasts) and *khairat* (charity).

> The word Babu, popular in 19th century Bengali discourse, was a catch-all term that embraced respectable dignitaries... from one end of the contemporary Bengali social hierarchy to the members of that society's parvenu and their spoilt sons who occupied the other end, dissipating their wealth on drinking, whoring and other amusements. It was this latter section of the babus (from the 19th century) in Calcutta on whose patronage prostitution began to thrive in the city. This class of Bengali parvenu made money through the diverse transactions with the British traders and administrators in a hierarchically defined system—ranging from operations of the banians and dewans (who acted as direct agents of the colonial commercial and administrative systems respectively) at the top, to those of their subordinates, hangers-on, flunkeys and parasites (known as *mosahebs*) at the bottom. These upstart fortune-seekers, along with the 'absentee zemindars' (the new rentiers created by the Permanent Settlement) formed a distinct urban group of pleasure-hunters with new social habits, who were in search of entertainment to fill up their leisure time.[25]

The persistent reach of racism had to touch this world at some point. The second half of the 19th century witnessed a rising demand by white clients for women of their own colour. Some came from impoverished local communities, often derided as 'low-caste Christians'. This was supplemented by a larger foreign influx.

Their enclaves in Calcutta were Kalinga Bazar and Karaya Lane. Flaunting their skin, they protested against being mixed with darker professionals during medical examinations. The Calcutta authorities were sympathetic. White prostitutes were allotted facilities at Sealdah, while 'natives' were sent to a hospital in Alipore.[26] According to Banerjee, the records show that in 1872 there were 437 Europeans in a list of 6,871 prostitutes. Their countries of origin are remarkably diverse: England, Ireland, Russia, Austria, Poland, Hungary, Italy, France and Spain.[27] The Suez Canal, by cutting travel time from Europe, was working in mysterious ways its wonders to perform.

By the last quarter of the 19th century, even paid inter-racial sex had become taboo. David Gilmour records the horror of the Bombay establishment in 1891 when 20-year-old Fanny Epstein from Manchester opened a brothel. The police commissioner spoke to her personally; the Methodist Mission, the Church Missionary Society and a 'Home for Women' sent emissaries, only to learn that she was perfectly content managing her business. The controversy ended when she sold her establishment and took a ship to Marseille where she reinvented herself as 'Mademoiselle Kahn'.[28]

The stiff-necked Lord Curzon, viceroy between January 1899 and November 1905, wanted to ban British barmaids in Calcutta's hotels, not because he disapproved of Indians drinking whisky, but because he worried about any spillover into an inter-racial sexual liaison. With the Suez Canal opening for large passenger ships in November 1869, Calcutta's restaurants began to hire English barmaids on short-term contracts. These barmaids were, however, mainly employed in dock area taverns which catered to sailors and soldiers. Many of them had come in search of husbands, paying for their dreams with salaries from hiring companies like Spiers and Pond. When prospects of marriage receded, they drifted into extracurricular activity, taking lodgings in Kerr's Lane and Dacres Lane.

Curzon was a martinet with a strange angst. When King Edward VII asked for a contingent of Indian soldiers at his coronation parade,

Curzon frowned. Writing to London on 11 November 1901, Curzon felt that 'English women of the housemaid class and even higher' might offer themselves to these handsome Indian soldiers in London because of their powerful physiques and colourful uniforms.

The Enchanted Circle

Those Europeans who fell genuinely in love with India and its ways constitute an enchanting minority. They were not any less loyal to the Empire, but they certainly proved that it was possible to serve Britain without becoming hostile to Indians.

Job Charnock, founder of Calcutta, rescued a beautiful widow about to commit sati on her husband's pyre and took her home, shocking colleagues. According to William Hedges, then the Company governor of Bengal, the two 'lived lovingly for many years, and had several children'. Hedges was censorious: 'Mr Charnock did shamefully, to ye great scandall of our Nation, keep a Gentoo woman of his kindred, which he has had these 19 years'.[29] The 'Gentoo woman' refused to convert to Christianity, although Charnock had their three daughters baptized at St Mary's Church in Madras as Mary, Elizabeth and Katherine. The mother's name was not recorded.

Victor Jacquemont stayed in Delhi with William Fraser, a Scottish adventurer-administrator with the Company who died in India in 1835 at the age of 49:

I am alone in Mr Fraser's immense house, which is a kind of Gothic fortress, built by himself, at immense expense, upon the very place where Timour Lenggue [Emir Taimur] pitched his tent when he laid siege to Delhi. My host is at the camp with the Governor-General, whom he accompanies to the limits of his jurisdiction... The resident [representative of the Calcutta government] at Delhi received five thousand rupees per month (or 13,000 francs), for table money. As he seldom has more than five or six persons at dinner, and feels himself conscientiously bound to expend this extra allowance in the object for which it is given, you may easily imagine that the dinners I have at his house do not much resemble my ambulatory meals... I light an excellent Havannah cigar, and

folding my Cashmere morning gown round my limbs, mount
my horse, and, preceded by two men, who run before me
with torches in their hands, a short gallop soon brings me to
Fraser's fortress.[30]

A plentiful household lived in Fraser's fortress. He had Hindu and
Muslim wives whose children practised their mother's faith. Fraser
admired the poetry of Ghalib and commissioned Mughal miniature
paintings which were collected in what is known as the Fraser Album,
now in the British Library. His closest friend was the famous military
commander, Colonel James Skinner, whose father was Scottish and
mother a Rajput. They fought together in the First Regiment of
Irregular Horse, more famous as Skinner's Horse.

When Fraser was in charge of revenue, he used a system akin
to Indian panchayats to resolve disputes quickly and rapidly settled
over 300. He promised higher revenue and delivered. The resident,
Sir Charles Metcalfe, felt that Fraser could have risen higher in the
civil service were he free from some faults. Those 'faults', however,
made Fraser a hero to Indian villagers. Writes Percival Spear:

> The waywardness which barred the path to high office created
> his legend in the countryside. He roved the Territory in
> intimate touch with the people and was said to know more of
> land tenures than any living Englishman... He consorted with
> the grey-beards of Delhi, and so earned the disapproval of his
> fellow-officials. He lived as a solitary among his colleagues
> saying that they had no rational conversation... He won the
> Indian gentry by his insight into their ways, and exasperated
> them by his arbitrary temper.[31]

Jacquemont calls Fraser 'half-Asiatic in his habits' and notes that he
was a celebrity for 'a hundred leagues around', in his letter of 11
January to Victor de Tracy:

> He is a man who, delighting in the emotions of danger, goes
> to war as an amateur, whenever there is fighting going on, and
> never returns without a few gun-shot wounds; but his humanity
> is such, that in the midst of the many scenes of carnage to

which his monomania has hurried him, he has never struck a blow with his sword; his heart fails when his arm has been raised to cut his enemy down. He is half-Asiatic in his habits, but in other respects a Scotch highlander, and an excellent man, with great originality of thought, a metaphysician to boot, and enjoying the best possible reputation of being a country bear.[32]

Jacquemont commends Fraser for being the 'only officer of government' who, to his knowledge, kept up social relations with Indians, the infamous wrecks of Mughal nobility who had become psychologically unnerved. Jacquemont contrasts their behaviour with that of Bengalis: 'At Calcutta, where there are so many Europeans of every class, the lowest Bengalee burgher keeps his shoes on at the Governor-general's!! At Delhi, the greatest Mogul lord takes off his in the presence of a British ensign'.[33]

It is an irony that Fraser was killed by an assassin in the pay of the nawab of Firozpur, father of the poet Daagh Dehlavi, Shamshuddin Khan, who felt he had been denied his inheritance rights in the state of Loharu by the British.

Fraser's contemporary Major General Sir David Ochterlony, first baronet of Pitforthy GCB, first resident at the Mughal court after the capture of Delhi in 1803, embraced an Indian lifestyle, wore Indian dress and was accompanied by all of his wives when he went to 'take the air' in the evening, each wife seated on a separate elephant. The Mughal king Shah Alam gave him the title Nasir-ud-Daula, and the British named a cantonment in Rajputana, Nasirabad, after him. Ochterlony earned a place in military history in 1816, leading his forces to victory in the Anglo-Gurkha war when all seemed lost. Calcutta honoured this authentic war hero by erecting the Ochterlony Monument on the maidan in 1828, paid for by public subscription. In 1969, a coalition government in Bengal changed the name of the memorial.

Bishop Heber describes Ochterlony, whom he met in Rajputana, as a tall and pleasing-looking man, so wrapped up in shawls and a Mughal furred cap that he looked like a travelling Eastern prince. At other times, he wore the British uniform of collar, coat and trousers. Portraits show him completely at ease at home in Indian attire, presiding over a polygamous family, smoking a heavily coiled hookah. Europeans, either bemused or snide, called him 'Akhtar-loony'. His favourite wife was a former dancing girl, Bibi Mehrattan Mubarak ul Nissa Begum, a devout Muslim and mother of his youngest children. Europeans addressed her as Lady Ochterlony, while Indian visitors called her Qudsia Begum, a title reserved for the most powerful woman in the Mughal court. The people knew her as 'General Begum'. She received gifts and dresses of honour from visitors and ambassadors in the Mughal style. When Ochterlony died in 1825, she inherited what became known as Mubarak Bagh, her husband's country house to the north of the city.

The 'bridge culture' of Ochterlony, Skinner or Fraser was common till the 1820s. William Hickey, who lived in Calcutta between 1777 and 1808, has left a candid and colourful account in his memoirs, completed by 1810, of life in London, Calcutta, Madras, Jamaica and the many ports he visited.[34] Hickey was a rakish Irish-English lawyer whose father despaired of his prospects, with good reason. In December 1763, at the age of 14, William was expelled from his school, Westminster, for neglect of studies *and* dissipation in public houses. Three years later he joined his father's offices but was caught embezzling £500. In January 1769, he was packed off to the colonies. A recommendation from Edmund Burke enabled him to practice in the newly upgraded Calcutta Supreme Court.

In 1783, Hickey's English mistress Charlotte Barry died. A short spell of chastity later, impelled by his 'amorous disposition', he sent one night for a 'native woman' but became impotent with 'horror' at the thought of a 'connection' with dark skin. The amorous disposition won the short battle. Hickey decided that many Indian women were not black at all, and many could even be considered 'very fair'.

Robert Pott, a British friend posted at Murshidabad, sent a good-looking woman called 'Kiraum' (or Kironbala) for his 'private use'. Within a year a 'suspiciously dark' son was born. The puzzle was solved when, returning early one day from work, he discovered Kiraum in bed with his *khidmatgar,* or attendant. The two were thrown out, but when Hickey discovered that mother and son were in difficulty, he provided her with a monthly allowance.

A beautiful, lively and clever 'Hindostanee' girl called Jemdanee used to come over to meet Hickey's housemate, Carter. When Carter left Bengal, Hickey invited Jemdanee to become 'intimate' with him. From that day to her death, they lived together. She was immensely popular with Hickey's friends because of her sprightly good humour and was a perfect hostess at dinner parties, although she never touched a drop of alcohol. They set up a country house in Chinsurah. She became pregnant and dreamt of a 'Chuta William Sahib' (Small William Sahib). Jemdanee lost her life during childbirth in 1796; a year later, the boy died of fever at the age of one.[35] An oil done in 1787, titled 'An Indian Lady', hangs in the National Gallery of Ireland in Dublin, is said to be a portrait of Jemdanee.

William Hickey records instances of interracial love that he witnessed in Calcutta: Dr Wilson was so miserable at the thought of returning to England for health reasons, and thereby leaving his *bibi* who had borne several children, that he chose to die in India; or a 'beautiful Hindostanee woman' who tried her best to stop her lover, Colonel Cooper, from turning into a sot. Many Europeans honoured such relationships in their wills. In 1817, Major Charles Hay Elliot left money to three illegitimate daughters, and ₹35,000 to the unborn child of his pregnant *bibi*. Captain James Nicholson wanted his estate to be divided equally between ten children, two from his British wife and eight from other women.

The third Governor-general, Sir John Shore, a deeply religious man, came to Bengal in 1769 at the age of 19 and had 2 children with a *bibi* before he returned home in 1785. In England, he married Charlotte in 1786, with whom he had 9 children. Shore was appointed president of the British and Foreign Bible Society after retirement in 1798.

His successor, the flamboyant Richard Wellesley, ruled in the style of kings. The bill for illuminations at one of his public receptions came to a staggering £3,248.[36] He was however a lonely monarch—his wife Hyacinthe had refused to join him. Wellesley was disarmingly honest in a letter to Hyacinthe: 'This climate excites one sexually most terribly... As for sex, one must have it in this climate.' Hyacinthe was cool. Both of them must live without sex, she replied. Wellesley was not so calm. He found an Indian mistress.[37]

It has been estimated that around three-fourths of British bachelors had concubines. Indian women, both Hindus and Muslims, were exalted as true models of symmetry and beauty, with large black eyes glowing with soft fire and so expressive as to make speech unnecessary, according to one anonymous admirer quoted by P. Thankappan Nair in *Calcutta in the 17th Century*, published by Firma KLM.

Sir Charles Metcalfe, who had come to India at the age of 19 in 1774 and had a faultless career culminating in the position of acting governor-general in 1835 for a year, had 3 sons from an Indian wife. His brother Thomas Theophilus Metcalfe who reached India in 1813 and spent 4 decades in Delhi, including 18 years as commissioner, was the ultimate *Pukka Sahib*. According to his daughter Emily, his clothes were made by a first-class tailor, Pulford in St James Street, and sent from London each year along with shoes and gloves. He smoked the hookah for half an hour every morning, the gurgle making an almost musical sound. He left for work at 10, returned at 2.30, dined at 3, read, played billiards, took a walk, had a light meal by 8 and went to bed immediately after. He built a dream house near the Qutub Minar in 1844, which he called *Dilkhoosha*, or delight of the heart, and never returned to England. India was his home.

He died, alas, an Indian death, victim of that terrible curse called Mughal succession politics. Percival Spear describes the circumstances:

> Sir Thomas died in 1853 at the age of fifty-eight. It was believed by his family that he was poisoned by Zinat Mahal [wife of the last Mughal king Bahadur Shah Zafar] in revenge for the part he played in excluding her son Jivan Bakht from the succession to the imperial title. The means were said to be either 'vegetable poisons prepared in such a way as to leave *no* trace behind them—a secret well known to the famous *Hakeems* or native doctors'; or alternatively ground diamonds.[38]

By the 1830s, inter-racial romance had turned into a stigma. David Gilmour explains:

> The disappearance of the *bibi* from British lives was followed by an attempt to efface her from British history. When Captain Williamson wrote *The East India Vade Mecum* in 1810, his book contained interesting information about *bibis*; when the second edition appeared in 1825, this had all been

removed. When in 1854 John Kaye published his life of Sir Charles Metcalfe, he suppressed the fact that his subject had had an Indian wife and three half-Indian sons, one of them a distinguished soldier who was awarded the Order of the Bath and an entry in the *Oxford Dictionary of National Biography*. It seemed that the whole idea of interracial physical relationships was so appalling that people had to pretend not just that they had stopped but that they had not even happened.[39]

Those few Englishman who persisted in the old ways were at best tolerated as eccentric. Emily Eden, Governor-general Lord Auckland's sister, wrote on 12 January 1840 from Gwalior:

We dined with Colonel J. yesterday. He lives, I believe, quite in the native style, with a few black Mrs J.'s gracing his domestic circle when we are not here, but he borrowed St Cloup and our cooks to dress the dinner, and it went off very well.[40]

As the 19th century broke into new directions, it left tantalizing evidence, in the lives of some extraordinary men and women, of what might have been.

Love in the Time of Distress

Delhi's citizens described the social and political devastation in the wake of Nadir Shah's conquest and devastation in 1739 *gardi ka waqt,* or a time of distress. Central authority, already wobbly, collapsed. Regional powers competed to fill the vacuum. They soon learnt from British victories that they needed to modernize their armies if they wanted to survive, and this could only be done by Europeans.

Once the French effectively abandoned their pursuit of power in India after their defeat at Wandiwash in 1740, their adventurer-mercenary officers sought, and got, employment with Indian princes.

Benoit de Boigne, born in 1751 in Savoy, became a conscript in the Russian army at the age of 20, was captured by the Turks and then found his way to India. He rose to eminence in the employ of the Scindias, eventually commanding a standing army of 20,000, with

2,000 cavalry and 200 cannon, consisting of Marathas, Rajputs, Mughals, Afghans, Persians and Sikhs. Mahadji Scindia granted him a *jaidad* (estate) near Aligarh with a revenue estimated at ₹300,000 a year. De Boigne made a separate fortune from selling indigo to France. He married a Muslim lady from Lucknow and had two children, a daughter Banu and a son Ali Baksh. They went to Europe with him when, with a fortune of £250,000, De Boigne sailed for England in 1797. He settled them in an English village and left for Savoy, where he made a second reputation as a philanthropist before he died in 1830.

Walter Joseph Reinhardt, born in 1725 at Strasbourg, is now remembered chiefly because of his adventurous marriage. Nicknamed 'Sombre' because of his comparatively dark complexion, he reached India on a French ship in 1750, enlisted in the East India Company Army under the name of Sommers, shifted allegiance to the French and then to the Bengal army of Siraj ud-Daula. He became a general in the service of Raja Jawahar Singh, the Jat ruler of Deeg. Indians called him Samru Sahib.

At the age of 40, he married a 14-year-old dancing girl from Delhi called Farzana, who became known as 'Samru ki Begum'. In 1774, he was given Sardhana as a *jagir*. Walter Samru wore Mughal dress, adopted their manners and spoke fluent Persian and Urdu. Begum Samru took over as ruler of Sardhana after his death in 1778 and raised a force of 5 battalions, led by European officers. In May 1781, she became a Catholic, took the name Joanna and built a magnificent church, strewn with marble statuary. She proved her political acumen when she rejected a proposed alliance with the ruthless Rohilla chief Ghulam Qadir against the Mughal ruler Shah Alam. Instead, she joined Mahadji Scindia, fielding an army of 4 battalions and 85 guns, to rescue Shah Alam from Ghulam Qadir, and was given the title of Zebun Nissa. Mahadji Scindia was named deputy regent of the Mughal Empire in 1784, although Shah Alam was in fact his vassal. Scindia was only one step away from the throne of Delhi, but it proved a step too far.

Stories about her reached every ear in her lifetime. Bishop Heber heard in Meerut, in December 1824, that she was 'a very little, queer-looking old woman, with brilliant, but wicked eyes, and the remains of beauty in her features.' She had 'considerable talent' and had earned the respect of her soldiers 'on account of both her supposed wisdom and her courage... riding at their head, into a heavy fire of the enemy'. However, she was also 'a sad tyranness, and, having the power of life and death within her own little territory, several stories are told of her cruelty, and the noses and ears which she orders to be cut off'.[41] Jacquemont met the Begum at Sardhana in 1830 and dismissed her as an 'old witch', although he was 'gallant' enough to kiss her hand and happy enough to drink wine at her table on Christmas day. He wrote:

> She must be a hundred years old, she is bent in two, and her face is shrivelled like dried raisins; she is, in fine, a sort of walking mummy, who still looks after all her affairs herself, listens to two or three secretaries at once, and at the same time dictates to as many others. Only four years ago, she caused some of her ministers and disgraced courtiers to be tied to the cannon's mouth, and fired off like shot. It is related of her, and the story is true, that about sixty or eighty years ago, she had a young female slave of whom she was jealous, buried alive, and that she gave her husband a nautch (a ball) upon this horrible tomb. Her two European husbands met with violent deaths. She was, however, as courageous as she was cruel.[42]

The Frenchman ruefully noted that she buried ₹400,000 from her annual income of ₹1,600,000 lakhs in her garden, and predicted that the money would all be taken by the British after she died.

The marble statue in her church shows Begum Samru clutching the royal *sanad* which confirmed her *jagir*. A European and an Indian stand to the right and left of her feet. The frieze at the base of the pedestal depicts her conversion. Begum Samru died in 1836 at the age of 86. Farzana, the dancing girl of Chawri Bazar, became the only Christian princess to rule an Indian state.

Fanny Parkes describes a fascinating love story in her diary, written at the zenith of British confidence. The date is February 1835. Fanny Parkes is in Agra and has just received an invitation from Colonel Gardner, once doyen of Lucknow, now over 70 and living in Khasganj, 60 miles from Agra. The colonel's granddaughter Susan will wed a Mughal prince. Susan also has a Muslim name, Shubbeah Begum, given by her mother, and has gone into purdah from the day of her engagement. She is married in the traditional Indian style. The glittering *baraat* (the groom's procession) is welcomed with playful theatre by the bride's family, and nuptials conducted in a *nikah* ceremony.

The colonel's son, James Gardner, wears 'handsome native attire'. His mother, Nawab Malmunzilool Nissa Begum, is a niece of Nawab Fakhrul Dowla of Cambay (or Khambat in Gujarat; the title of 'nawab' was used by both genders). James had gone to school in Calcutta; the rest of his education was at home. He speaks and writes Persian fluently. Unaffected by the sun, he rides through his villages and estates all day, farming indigo for substantial profit.

Colonel Gardner is at the court in Lucknow when he witnesses the nawab's roving eye fall on Mulka Begum, the daughter of Mirza Suliman Shekho and niece of the Mughal king Akbar Shah II. Mirza Suliman lives in Agra on a Company pension with 'some forty children', 'proud and poor'. The colonel rescues Mulka and brings her home. His son James sees Mulka and falls instantly in love. The father refuses to give his assent for marriage, and the couple flee to a jungle hideout. The indignant colonel will not relent. After two years in exile, James writes to his father, expressing his passion in verse:

> *Durd ishk-e kushidu'um ki m'purs*
> *Zahir hijree chush'du'um ki m'purs.*
> *Hum ne dil sanam ko diya*
> *Phir kissiko kya?*
> [*I have felt the pain of love, ask not of whom*
> *I have felt the pangs of absence, ask not of whom.*
> *I have given my heart to my beloved*
> *What is that to another?*]

Paternal love soothes anger. James and Mulka return home, marry and live happily at least till the time Fanny Parkes comes calling. Nawab Mulka Humanee Begum is a power in the family, and her word is accepted as law by the villagers. She and James have two sons and a daughter, who wear 'native dresses of silk and satin embroidered in gold and silver'. Their names echo a shared inheritance: the elder boy is Suliman, the second William Linnaeus, and their sister is called Noshaba.

The nawab of Cambay is a wedding guest—he drinks sherry in the presence of European women and brandy or a local white spirit with the men. Indian begums do not dine with their husbands, but they might send a favourite dish or two from their personal kitchen for a special guest. Fanny Parkes enjoys the local cuisine so much that she stops eating European meals as long as she is in this English-Mughal household.

She is welcomed by Mulka Begum on the morning of her arrival. The begum is sitting on a *charpai*, a bedcot, and delivers herself of all the English she knows: 'How do you do?' Her language is Urdu. Attendants fan her, driving away the omnipotent bane of India, mosquitoes. Some opium is brought. She takes a bite and then gives a tinge to each of the children—it will prevent them from catching a cold, she explains.

Mulka Begum comes into her own that evening. Her large apartment in the zenana is supported by eight double pillars and lit by brass lamps (*chiraghdans*) placed upon the floor. A carpet is spread at the centre, with pillows fringed with gold for the lady of the house, and more modest versions for visitors.

Fanny Parkes has left a vivid account of that evening:

A short time after our arrival, Mulka Begum entered the room, looking a dazzling apparition; you could not see her face, she having drawn her *dupatta* over it; her movements were graceful, and the magnificence and elegance of her drapery were surprising to the eye of the European. She seated herself on the *gaddi* and throwing her *dupatta* partly off her face, conversed with us. How beautiful she looked! How very beautiful! Her animated countenance was constantly varying, and her eyes struck fire when a joyous thought crossed her mind. The languor of the morning had disappeared; by lamplight she was a different creature; and I felt no surprise when I remembered the wondrous tales told by the men of the beauty of Eastern women. Mulka walks very gracefully, and is as straight as an arrow. In Europe, how rarely—how very rarely does a woman walk gracefully! Bound up in stays, the body stiff as a lobster in its shell; that snake-like, undulating movement—the poetry of motion—is lost, destroyed by the stiffness of the waist and hip, which impedes the free movement of the limbs. A lady in European attire gives me the idea of a German manikin; an Asiatic, in her flowing drapery, recalls the statues of antiquity. I had heard of Mulka's beauty long ere I beheld her, and she was described to me as the loveliest creature in existence.[43]

The Begum offers her guests sweetmeats on glass dishes, tea, coffee and the hookah. Dancing, writes Parkes, is considered disgraceful to a woman of rank. Muslim women live in purdah; never ride on horseback or swim, love their *atr* (rose-petal perfume) and hate foreign eau de cologne, which they consider as unwholesome as gin. 'Natives, especially native women, are curious beings; the whole pride of their lives consists in having had a grand wedding: they talk of it, and boast of it to the hour of their death,' says Fanny Parkes. Mulka Begum expresses one regret: 'Ah, you English ladies with your white faces, you run about where you will, like dolls, and are so happy.' It is a deep sigh over a lifetime of confinement behind a veil.[44]

The Begum and Rev. Tally-ho

There was one formidable English lady in the annals of Anglo-India who decided that her real home was Calcutta despite being part of a privileged and powerful English family, her grandson would become a prime minister of Britain. She was known as Begum Johnson.

Frances Croke was born on 10 April 1728 at Fort St David in Madras, the daughter of a Governor, Edward Croke. Her mother, Isabella Bezoir, was Portuguese. She was barely in her teens when she married Perry Templar in Calcutta; her husband and two infant children were dead within five years. Her second husband, the merchant James Altman, died of small pox within 12 days of the wedding in 1748. The third marriage to William Watts, an East India Company agent at Kassembazar, was long and happy. They had four children, among them a daughter, Amelia.

Frances and William Watts returned to England in 1759, where William passed away five years later. Frances returned to Calcutta to make her home at 12 Clive Street.

Her daughter Amelia's husband Charles Jenkinson, a close adviser to King George III, was raised into the peerage, becoming the first earl of Liverpool. Amelia died at the young age of 19 due to complications after the birth of her son Robert Banks Jenkinson.

Robert Jenkinson, second earl of Liverpool, had a remarkable career: secretary of state for foreign affairs at the age of 31; home secretary at 37; secretary for war and the colonies at 39; and finally prime minister on 8 June 1812, a post he held till 1827. He led his nation through the Peninsular wars and the epic victory over Napoleon at Waterloo.[45]

The serene Frances preferred to reign over Calcutta, where she became known as 'Begum', as a matriarch of the city, and Johnson, because of marital overreach.

William Johnson, an Oxford graduate, reached Calcutta in 1772 as assistant chaplain of Calcutta's Fort William. Within two years, he became her fourth husband, despite being 16 years younger. His great professional achievement was the 1787 consecration of St John's Church, the first Anglican cathedral. But his temperament proved to be too smug for both his wife and the congregation. Calcutta nicknamed him 'Reverend Tally-ho'. Begum Johnson got her marriage annulled and packed William off to London with an annuity. The husband got the alimony. She kept the surname.

The highest in the British hierarchy were Begum Johnson's guests at dinner in Calcutta. Dressed in lace, truffles, buttons in bows, she entertained from 4 in the afternoon till late at night. She died on 3 February 1812, a few weeks before her grandson became prime minister. Governor-general Gilbert Elliot-Murray-Kynynmound, First Earl of Minto, led her funeral procession, followed by members of his council and judges in their coaches, to the St John's churchyard. The redoubtable begum did not leave a single rupee to her surviving husband, although she did mention his name in her will. Her portrait hangs in the India Office Library. Begum Johnson's epitaph does not exaggerate: 'The oldest British resident in Bengal, universally beloved, respected and revered.'

On a less exalted level, the case of Colonel Fugleman is a charming colonial version of a morganatic marriage. The colonel became bound to India by a lifetime's service, debt and 'the rosy fetters of Cupid (or rather the coffee-coloured bands of Hymen)' when he met and wed coffee-coloured Miss Madeline Tommkyns, the very pretty daughter of a planter. Madeline had found a devoted English husband but discovered that this did not mean automatic access to her dream city, London, according to the ICS officer H.G. Keene.[46]

The dark and comely Madeline had been educated in Calcutta, but her diction was submerged in artless accents and her verbs were fractured from her nouns. Keene quotes Madeline's description, with some relish, of her first encounter with the colonel:

> In thee morning, ass sun as it was light, there we saw the Kunnal and, oh my! didn't he look splendeed? Of course, you know, we were riding in the Buggee, and he was on hees horse, in the centre of the rod and when we came by, of course, you know, hees horse commenced to hit a keek, and, oh my! wee got so frightened.[47]

They nursed and comforted the colonel, and love blossomed.

As a hostess, Madeline cooked a splendid *saddle-peroo khana* (saddle of mutton with roast peafowl) but was hopeless on wine. Their marriage was fruitful—an illustration shows eight 'tawny' children playing in the verandah or being nursed by an ayah in the family bungalow, while the colonel smokes a cheroot, a gin and water in his right hand, and his wife enjoys a hookah and chews paan. Madeline called England 'home', when, as her catty companions said behind her back, she could go home in 24 hours if she wanted to. How would she enter London society, someone asked. 'Oh! It will be very easee; we will give a dinner, don't you know, to the whole station,' she chirped.

Madeline never got the chance to feed the whole of London station. What began in India, ended in India.[48]

Such relationships were not one-dimensional. Vera Ogilvie told Charles Allen about her spirited grandmother 'who went out as a young bride of Ogilvie *Dandi-mar* or "Ogilvie Beat-with-a-stick".' Ogilvie continues:

> [The] first thing that confronted her in this very lonely station in the Punjab was a compound full of native women with whom he had solaced his solitude, and several suspiciously

pale-faced children running about. In keeping with the mores of the period, once my grandmother had arrived the native women were put aside. Nevertheless, it was not exactly a happy beginning for the bride and the story goes that my grandmother found a little comfort in the friendship of a very good-looking Pathan orderly who appears in many family photographs and is reputed to be the father of my eldest aunt, long since dead.[49]

In 2013, the American politician Joseph Robinette Biden mentioned that his great-great-great-great grandfather, George Biden, was a ship captain in the 'East India Trading Company'. Joe Biden meant the East India Company. There is no record of any George Biden. However, the author Ben Macintyre, basing his information on research by Tim Willasey-Wilsey, a visiting professor of war studies at King's College London, wrote in the London *Times*[50] that there were two Biden brothers from Derbyshire, William and Christopher, who joined the Company as teenagers.

Christopher was a fourth mate in 1807 on an Indiaman, the 1,333-ton *Royal George*. Macintyre continues:

[He] rose through the company ranks, steadily amassing a fortune. He discovered and named Nelson Island in Chagos Archipelago, and made a close study of life at sea, which he wrote up in a book entitled *Naval Discipline: Subordination Contrasted with Insubordination*. The book is packed with tales of drunkenness, mutiny, shipwrecks, theft and mayhem. But Captain Biden was fairly enlightened for the time. 'Flogging should only be resorted to when all other modes of punishment fail,' he wrote. By 1839, Christopher Biden and his English wife Harriott... settled in Madras, where he was appointed master attendant and marine storekeeper. The Bidens had a son and two daughters, one of whom died during the crossing from Britain and was buried at sea.[51]

Christopher set up a home for destitute seamen and campaigned actively against slavery. In his role as beach magistrate, he prosecuted captains of slave ships and helped pass a law commanding that all ships be inspected for kidnapped children. After his death in February 1858, a plaque was placed in the cathedral at Madras praising the 'universal respect his guileless and kindly heart won from every class of the community'. Christopher Biden lived and died in India.

Christopher Biden's great-great-great-great grandson was elected 46th president of the United States of America.

David Gilmour writes:

> At a personal level, they [British and Indians] were generally at their best towards the end of the eighteenth century, when men of the Enlightenment ruled and studied in Calcutta, when upper-class Indians and Europeans entertained each other at nautches and dinners, when British men married Indian wives, learned their languages and respected their religions. Not in great numbers of course, but enough to create a sense for cultural exchange even at a time when Indians were being defeated on the battlefield and excluded from political power. Parsi gentlemen would feast with the British in Bombay; nawabs and other Muslim noblemen would try European drink and food, even ham if it was labelled 'heron' or 'English venison'. The idea of cultural exchange went into decline, especially on the British side, as the nineteenth century got into its stride. Racial relations reached their lowest point, for understandable reasons, in the decade after the Rebellion [the war of 1857], but cultural separateness, promoted by Evangelical intolerance and Victorian rectitude, was well advanced by 1857.[52]

This cultural separation led inevitably to conflict.

Gifts of Fortune in a Land of Regrets

The Venetian traveller Niccolao Manucci reached India in 1656, joined the camp of Dara Shikoh, fought for him in the war against Aurangzeb, met Shivaji in 1665, shifted south and died in the British city of Madras in 1717 at the age of 78. He possessed many talents, but none more felicitous than a keen eye and a persuasive tongue. They kept him alive through the turbulent decades of gradual Mughal disintegration and growing British assertion. Two diplomatic encounters, 40 years apart, that he witnessed constitute a picturesque metaphor for decline.

In April 1661, Budaq Beg, the Persian envoy of Shah Abbas II was given precise instructions in Multan, en route to Delhi, on how to behave when he was received at Aurangzeb's court. He must bow before the emperor, who would not receive the Persian monarch's letter personally. This, by protocol, was the responsibility of the vizier. As a special gesture, however, Aurangzeb's son Shah Alam would accept the letter.

The date of the audience was set for 2 June.

Aurangzeb, seated on the peacock throne, kept his eyes deliberately averted as Budaq Beg approached. Instead of bowing before Aurangzeb, the ambassador placed both his hands on his breast in a Persian salutation. Manucci describes what followed:

> ...four strong men told off for this purpose came up; two took him by the hands, and two by the neck, and without force or violence, as if they were teaching him, they lowered his hands and bent his head. They told him that thus it was the fashion to make obeisance in the Mogul country. Upon

this the ambassador acted prudently, and allowed his whole body to bend without resisting, and performed his bow in the Indian manner.[1]

The message was decorous but firm. Mughal protocol was a display of its proclaimed power.

The Persian shah was irritated by the implied overlordship in Aurangzeb's title of Alamgir, or 'ruler of the world', but his ambassador Budaq Beg offered the letter to the Mughal prince with a smile. Shah Alam took it to his father, who passed it on to Danish, the eunuch in charge of his household. The gifts from Persia were then displayed. Gifts were an estimate of esteem, and therefore carefully scrutinized. If a host felt he had been devalued, there could be consequences.

Beg had brought:

Twenty-seven handsome, large, and powerful horses, each horse having two men to lead it by the reins. Nine of these horses were decked out with precious stones, and saddles decorated with pearls. The others had costly housing of brocade reaching to their feet. There were 18 large shaggy camels, taller than any in India or in the Balkh, clothed in lovely coverings; 60 cases of perfect rose-water, and 20 cases of another water, distilled from a flower which is only found in Persia and is called *bedemus (bed-i-mushk)*: it is a very comforting water against all fevers caused by heat; twelve carpets, fifteen cubits in length and five in breadth, very handsome and finely worked; four cases filled with brocade lengths, very rich, figures with pleasing flowers, and very costly; also four damascened short-swords, four poignards covered with precious stones; also a sealed box of gold, full of manna from the mountains of Shiraz.[2]

Manucci was not alone in recording such exaltation. His European fellow-traveller—to use the term in its literal sense—Francois Bernier arrived during the reign of Shah Jahan, the king who had commissioned the peacock throne but never sat on it because it was delivered after he had been dethroned. Bernier describes the environment in Shah Jahan's court:

Whenever a word escapes the lips of the King, if at all to the purpose, how trifling soever may be its import, it is immediately caught by the surrounding throng; and the chief *Omrahs*, extending their arms towards heaven, as it to receive some benediction, exclaim *Karamat! Karamat!* wonderful! wonderful! he has spoken wonders![3]

Bernier adds a piquant proverb in Persian verse:

Agner chah ronzra goyed cheb est in
Bubayed gouft inck mah ou peruin.

(*Should the king say that it is night at noon,*
Be sure to cry, Behold, I see the moon!)

With great power came great flattery. Noon became night because India was one of the two superpowers of the 17th century, the other being China. By 1701, the scales had tilted so sharply that an English merchant in Madras could afford to laugh at Aurangzeb's military governor of Carnatic as the latter got drunk on European wine and brandy.

The logistics of business persuaded the East India Company to shift its operational headquarters from Surat to the eastern coast of India. The best cotton and silk came from Bengal. In 1634, Shah Jahan permitted the East India Company to establish trading posts in Balasore and Hariharpur, but, ever wary of European ambitions, stopped them from taking larger ships up the Hooghly river.

The Company began to search for a secure base on the Coromandel coast. In August 1639, regional satrap Damarla Venkatadri Nayaka gave permission to Company agents Francis Day and Andrew Cogan to buy a seaside village called Madraspatnam. As a port, its merits were dubious. A reef of sand parallel to the beach thwarted anchorage of ships; people and goods had to be transported in catamarans across surf. Local gossip suggested that Francis Day, who enjoyed drinking with 'Moors and Persians', chose the spot for easier access to his mistress, who lived in the nearby Portuguese settlement of San Thome.

The English completed construction of their Madras fort on 23 April 1644, St George's Day, and named it after England's patron saint. By the 1670s Madras had an estimated population of 300 Englishmen, 3,000 Portuguese and 40,000 Indians in the 'Black [or Heathen] Town' beyond the walls. Their principal worries were death from disease and infirmity from alcohol. The authorities tried to check intemperance by imposing a limit of a pint of arrack or brandy and a quart of wine, although alcohol is rarely obedient to orders.

The Company, still loyal to the advice of Sir Thomas Roe, focused on profits and kept out of politics. This changed dramatically in 1686 when King James II issued a fresh charter that confirmed previous privileges and granted a new one: the right to raise troops. The Company decided that it had become a 'sovereign state in India' and went to war. It sent a fleet under the command of William Heath to Bengal, only to be badly bruised. The ships retreated to Madras. Possessions in Surat and Bombay were seized. A Company delegation hastily begged Aurangzeb's pardon, which was granted upon payment of a fine of ₹150,000.[4] This substantial sum was but a small price compared to the size of revenue and the extraordinary wealth being accumulated by the Company and its officials.

Madras became part of the Mughal realm with the conquest of Bijapur and Golconda in 1687. The Company reinforced its defences in 1690 with a second sanctuary at Cuddalore, about 100 miles south of Madras. This was named Fort St David after the patron saint of Wales since the incumbent Governor, Elihu Yale, was of Welsh ancestry.

The first Mughal mission to Madras in 1692 presented Elihu Yale with a horse covered in velvet, its saddle plated in gold, and flattered him with phrases like 'Excellent in Countenance and Elected to Great Favour'. Aurangzeb's delegation wanted an alliance against the Marathas in return for the licence to trade. Elihu Yale promised nothing. He had not become wealthy by making concessions under duress.

Yale lost his job as governor that year because he put his private interests above corporate profits. He and his brother Thomas were accused of 'mishandling' a trade expedition to Canton. Among Yale's more creative japes was buying tracts of land and collecting 'taxes' that went into his personal coffers. He returned to England in 1697 an extremely wealthy man and tried to improve his reputation with educational philanthropy. He made a significant donation to the

Collegiate School in Connecticut, America, where he had lived till the age of three. The grateful institution renamed itself Yale in 1718. They still like the name.

Elihu Yale died in 1721. His epitaph in Wrexham is a light-fingered compliment:

Born in America, in Europe bred.
In Africa travelled, in Asia wed;
Where long he lived and thrived, in London dead,
Much good, some ill he did, so hope all's even
And that his soul thro' mercy's gone to heaven.

Yale's old foe Thomas Pitt was appointed the governor of Madras in 1698, a post he held till 1709. Pitt was an old India hand, an interloper who made his first fortune as a private trader in Bengal. In 1683, at the age of 30, he came to terms with the law by paying a modest fine of £1,000, settled in England, bought the 'rotten borough' of Old Sarum and entered Parliament.

During his second stint in India, he earned the nickname 'Diamond Pitt' after buying a fabulous 410-carat diamond, discovered in the Kollur mines, from a merchant called 'Jamchaund' for 48,000 *pagodas*. He sent the invaluable jewel to London in 1701, hidden in the heel of his son Robert's shoe, on the East Indiaman *Loyal Cooke*. The stone was cut to 141 carats and sold in 1717 to Philippe II, Duke of Orleans, Regent of France, to embellish the crown. Napoleon transferred it to the pommel of his sword. It has been in the Louvre since 1877.

By the 1690s, it had become obvious that the edifice of the empire was under severe strain. Aurangzeb, generally in robust health, tried to calm apprehensions after he fell and dislocated his right knee while returning from the toilet by saying that a king needed only sight and speech to rule, but God had granted him 'the thirty sound teeth that I still possess' to bite with. The growing frailty was not lost on Europeans. As Manucci wrote: 'It looks as if everything in India were being made ready for some remarkable revolution.' As ever, the only people who could not see this were the commanders and bureaucrats of the empire.

In January 1701, the Mughal governor of the Carnatic Nawab Daud Khan camped at Arcot some 'sixty six miles west' of Madras. Pitt sent placatory gifts through Manucci:

> ...two cannon, several lengths of broadcloth in scarlet and other colours, other pieces of gold cloth of Europe and China, and several rareties such as mirrors of all sizes, different kinds of crystal vases, and some weapons such as fusils [sic], pistols, and sabres; also different kinds of wine; added to all of which was a sum of five thousand rupees.[5]

The wine was handed over publicly, but Manucci decided to pass on the money only when the two were alone. As he noted tartly, 'with the Mahomedans no present was better or more esteemed than money'.

Daud Khan thought that the quality of gifts was below his dignity; the Company had been 'cavalier... and gave him next to nothing'. The British, he told Manucci, had been left undisturbed while they 'enriched themselves in his country to a most extraordinary degree... they had rendered no account of their administration, good or bad, commencing with 1686. Nor had they accounted for the revenue from tobacco, *betel*, wine, *et cetera*, which reached a considerable sum every year'. If they thought they could fob off the government with 'four hundred *patacas*' (equivalent to ₹4,800) they were very much mistaken.[6]

Manucci was a persuasive intermediary, and his advocacy became easier after supper, when Daud Khan was in high spirits 'having drunk copiously of the European wines that I had brought for him'.[7] Manucci argued that the Mughals should do nothing that would force the Europeans to abandon India. The administration had earned revenues of more than 500,000 *patacas* from Madras alone, and the trade provided a livelihood to Indian weavers, printers and agents. The British picked up a separate signal from Daud Khan's behaviour. The ultra-pious Aurangzeb's generals could be plied with liquor and purchased with cash. Thomas Pitt made all the right gestures when Daud Khan visited him in July. He came out of the fort to welcome his guest while Company troops put on a display of drill which amazed Daud Khan. Pitt gave an expensive present which the nawab could keep for himself: a ball of ambergris mounted in gold, with a heavy gold chain. Then it was time for discussion over a wine-soaked meal.

The ever-present Manucci reports: 'When the talk was finished, the governor [Pitt] sent for wine, and drank to the health of King Aurangzeb to a salute of thirty one guns.'[8] As irony, this was in the supreme category. They were drinking alcohol in the name of Aurangzeb, a self-professed fundamentalist who had imposed prohibition in the name of faith.

The toast to Aurangzeb was the first of many.

> Daud Khan responded to this politeness by drinking the health of the King of England, to the sound of as many cannon as before. Then they drank the health of the chief minister (*wazir*), Asad Khan, who is nowadays Mirolo Morao [*Amir-ul-Umra*]—that is, 'Noble of Nobles'... A salute of 21 guns was fired. This was followed by a toast to Zulfiqar Khan, and one to Daud Khan himself, each with the same number of cannon. To end with, they drank to the *Diwan*, the chief minister of this general, and to his *bakshi*, each time to the sound of fifteen cannon... While these ceremonies were taking place, they made him a present of several cases of liqueurs, spirits, and wines of Europe of different sorts. All these he greatly prized.[9]

An inebriated Daud Khan slept for an hour before sitting down to 'a magnificent dinner'.

J. Talboys Wheeler records that on 'Tuesday 15th July 1701' the 'Nawab' was found in 'a Portuguese Chapel very drunk'. He had fallen asleep and upon waking up at 4, left. He did send word for the English to supply 'a dozen bottles of cordial waters'.[10]

The British had the measure of the Mughal. All talk of Islamic piety was hypocrisy; Aurangzeb's Empire was fading into the twilight of overreach and over-indulgence. Cases of wine and coin were sufficient to elide over disputes. More to the point, Daud Khan did not dare attack the English garrison of 800 well-trained soldiers backed by artillery. Aurangzeb might still have 30 teeth, but the jaws had lost their grip, and dimming eyes were shadowed by blinkers. A new aristocracy, entrenched along coastal India, had begun to take the wealth of India to Europe.

Familiarity about British loot from Bengal in the second half of the 18th century has tended to obscure just how much was being creamed away in Madras at the same time. George Pigot, governor of Madras between 1755 and 1763, collected over £1,000,000 from the pre-eminent local milch cow, the Nawab of Arcot Mohammad Ali. Like his peers and predecessors, Pigot converted the bribes he took into jewels for easier transport to England.

In 1762, Colonel Rennell

> ...wrote from Madras that the chairman was going home worth £300,000, adding, 'This is certainly a fine country for a young gentleman to improve a small fortune in. The inhabitants affect a deal of ostentation in their manner of living. Few private gentlemen live at less expence [sic] than £5-6,000 a year and those married about £8,000–£10,000. The Governor lives at the rate of £20,000 per annum'. In 1764, on his appointment as Surveyor-General in Bengal he hoped to return in a few years with £5,000 or £6,000 and wrote optimistically that, while he had an allowance of £900 and perquisites of £1,000, 'I can enjoy my Friends, my Bottle and all the Necessaries of Life for £400—Besides when I get acquainted with the Trade of this part of India I shall make much greater advantages as I shall always be able to command a Capital.'[11]

London's corrective endeavours wrought less change than the directors expected. Too many were complicit. In 1769, the directors decided to take action against the Madras Governor Charles Bouchier but were thwarted by divine intervention. The ship carrying the three-man committee to investigate a debt-scandal sank in 1770 off the Cape of Good Hope. Bouchier's successor Joshua Dupre made a fortune of some £300,000 by 'bribery, rapine, extortion and every species of corruption', according to George Paterson, the chief assistant to Sir John Lindsay. Paterson and Lindsay were members of yet another barren investigation committee. On reaching Madras, they found Arcot grease irresistible. Paterson made off with at least £40,000, but this did not stop him from pontificating in his diaries.

The Nawab of Arcot borrowed, entertained and made charming excuses to creditors. He kept several British MPs happy through an agent in London. There were 26 'nabob' MPs in the House of Commons after the 1774 general elections; the number rose to 45 after the 1784 polls. Arcot's investment paid off when he was 'asserted to have a large share in the arrest and imprisonment of Lord Pigot in 1776', according to Percival Spear. Spear quotes 'Asiaticus':

A dissatisfied group of creditors daily meet at the Nabob's. No sooner has the sun risen than every avenue to the palace is filled with palanquins and carriages and in the evening the same faces, the same surly looks are to be seen again. The Nabob receives everybody with politeness, apologizes for his want of punctuality (in paying), which he attributes to the loss of Tanjore, and repeats the hackneyed tale of the cruel treatment which he has received at the hands of Lord Pigot.[12]

The nawab looked upon every European with such majestic countenance and pleasing good nature that he aroused sympathy rather than ire. He blamed the British for the debts he owed to the British. They had denied him Tanjore's revenues, so how could he repay them? It was a delicate form of revenge.

Nicholas Dirks writes:

The failure to reform the corruption in Madras was made especially conspicuous when [Thomas] Rumbold returned to London in 1780, after a mere two years as governor, with a fortune of about £750,000, of which at least £180,000 had been procured as bribes from the nawab [of Carnatic]. Like other governors before him, he returned with a commission to act as the nawab's agent. He was soon elected to Parliament and apparently received a polite reception from Lord North [Prime Minister of Britain from 1770 to 1782]. The growing weakness of Lord North, and the news that no sooner had Rumbold left Madras than Haidar Ali asserted de facto control over the Carnatic hinterland, however, gave room to the [opposing] faction to agitate for inquiries into Rumbold's affairs. Edmund Burke, whose cousin William had been an agent for the raja of Tanjore, took up the charge.[13]

Edmund Burke, scourge of the 'nabobs', had a formidable finger in the Indian pie through his cousin William, who went to Madras in 1777. When Prime Minister William Pitt, or Pitt the Elder (later Lord Chatham), lashed out in 1770 against the new 'nabobs', he conveniently forgot to mention how his grandfather Thomas had enriched the family.

The arm of corruption was longer than the arm of the law. As for the nawab of Arcot, it was said that by the end of his days he owed everybody and therefore paid nobody.

Cash and Carry

The conflicts of Arcot produced one authentic British hero. After a dreary start to his career, during which he nearly committed suicide, 26-year-old Robert Clive led a force of 200 Europeans and 300 Indians to victory over Chanda Sahab, a claimant to Arcot supported by the French. Clive acquired a reputation but not a fortune from this achievement. Clive's great theatre would be Bengal.

No one strives to conquer a poor country; rewards must be commensurate with the investment. Bengal was the wealthiest part of the country when, according to statistics for 1750, India produced 24 per cent of the world's manufacturing output. Britain accounted for less than 2 per cent.

Maya Jasanoff writes:

From their capital at Murshidabad, the nawabs of Bengal presided over the richest province of the Mughal Empire. Cotton cloth, raw silk, saltpeter, sugar, indigo, and opium— the products of the region seemed inexhaustible, and all the European merchant companies set up factories to trade in them. Travelling downriver from Murshidabad was like travelling across a mixed-up map of Europe: there were the Portuguese at Hughli, the Dutch at Chinsura, the Danes at Serampore, the French at Chandernagore, and, of course, the British at Calcutta.[14]

In April 1756, an impetuous and partly delusional young man, Siraj ud-Daula, succeeded his grandfather Alivardi Khan as nawab of Bengal. Disputes with the East India Company had become chronic. Siraj ud-Daula's government accused the Company of replacing existing contractors with its own agents, or *gumastas*, to enhance incomes. It was assumed that negotiations would crease over disputes, as they had always done.

Siraj ud-Daula raised the ante; on 13 June his forces reached the outskirts of Calcutta. The disbelieving British were taken unawares. On the morning of 20 June, the president of the council Roger Drake fled by boat, along with most of the military command and women and children, to the Dutch station Fulta, leaving John Zephaniah Holwell in charge. By evening the fort was captured. According to Holwell, 146 British prisoners were packed into an 18-square-foot cell, and all but 23 died of suffocation overnight.

Many prisoners did die; what is not certain is the number, and whether this incident was inadvertent or deliberate. Holwell certainly understood the value of a scissored story. His *A Genuine Narrative of the Deplorable Deaths of the English Gentlemen, and Others, who were Suffocated in the Black-Hole, Fort William, at Calcutta* led to immediate outrage with its excruciating detail. Holwell became hero of his own tale:

> Death, attended with the most cruel train of circumstances, I plainly perceived must prove our inevitable destiny. I had seen this migration in too many shapes, and accustomed myself to think on the subject with much propriety to be alarmed at the prospect, and indeed felt much more for my wretched companions than myself... We had been but for a few minutes confined, before everyone fell into a perspiration so profuse, you can form no idea of it. This consequently brought on a raging thirst, which still increased in proportion as the body was drained of its moisture... Before nine o'clock every man's thirst grew intolerable, and respiration difficult.[15]

There were delirious cries for water, he says. He continues: 'The water appeared. Words cannot paint to you the universal agitation and raving the sight of it threw us into...' In a curious reflex, Holwell claims that the Indian guards 'took care to keep us supplied with water, that they might have the satisfaction of seeing us fight for it...'.[16] John Keay, who has written a definitive account of the East India Company, concludes that Holwell's 'figures are not reliable...'. He continues:

> How many [died] can never be known and scarcely matters. What does matter is that John Zephaniah Holwell was one of the twenty three survivors and that, for all his faults, was a brilliant publicist. If the sword failed him, the pen would not. He too sensed history in the making that 'must be published', and in the highly emotive language he crafted an account of it [so that] the mention of the Black Hole would yet conjure up a vivid hell. How the prisoners stripped off their clothes, fought for the window space, retched over 'the ruinous, volatile effluvia' and finally fell beneath the weight of their comrades became common knowledge. Schoolboys could recite the details—the precious water being passed around in hats, the gaolers leering through the bars, the prisoners sucking the perspiration from their underwear and, it was whispered, even drinking their own urine.[17]

Remarkably, neither the Company nor London's newspapers gave the event, dubbed the 'Black Hole of Calcutta', as much prominence as it got in retrospect. Henry Elmsley Busteed points out that Alexander Mackrabie, sheriff of Calcutta when he died in 1776, does not mention the 'Black Hole' incident:

> [A] consideration which often occurred to me, viz., that in any of the gossipy letters and accounts from and of Calcutta, written, say, twenty to twenty-five years after the recovery, there is little or nothing about the tragedy of 1756. Mackrabie, for instance, never recalls it, though he writes of the old Fort chapel and the Custom House there.[18]

Within another three decades, the site was demolished. 'Asiaticus' writes in the *Asiatic Journal of Bengal*:

> The formidable Black Hole is now no more. Early in the year 1812 I visited it. It was situated in the old fort of Calcutta,

and was then on the eve of demolition. Since that time the fort has come down, and on its site have been erected some extensive warehouses for the Company.[19]

Clive was ordered to mobilize in rapid response to the loss of Calcutta. His campaign was swift and comprehensive. He first neutralized the French by capturing Chandernagore. On 23 June 1757, despite being heavily outnumbered, he destroyed Siraj ud-Daula's army at the battle of Palashi, a village which took its name from *palash*, a tree with bright orange flowers. Palashi is more generally known as Plassey. The triumph changed Clive's, and India's, fortunes.

Prize money was standard reward for successful commanders, but Clive was not interested in an official dole. Gilmour writes:

> Princely gifts were for military officers, as well as for civil servants, the quickest way of making a large sum of money. Soldiers were rewarded for victories and other services by those nawabs of Bengal supported by the Company. They also had the chance of prize money when the wealth of a defeated foe was seized and distributed after a battle. Arthur Wellesley received £4000 for his capture of Seringapatnam in 1799, enough to make him a more acceptable son-in-law for the Pakenhams in Ireland, who had earlier scorned the penniless officer as a suitor for their daughter Kitty.[20]

Clive's sights were set on a different level.

The House of Commons select committee of 1772–73 calculated that Clive and his colleagues had extracted over £2,000,000 from the puppet nawabs of Bengal between 1757 and 1765. Clive left India with £180,000 (equivalent to £24,000,000 in 2020) plus a *jagir* with an annual income of £27,000 as a lifelong entitlement. As Clive reminded Parliament, he had turned the East India Company into a sovereign power, ruling over 20,000,000 people (more than the population of France and Spain combined) with an army of 50,000 men and officers, and revenues of £5,000,000–6,000,000 a year.

Endemic sleaze worried the Company. There was only one man, in its view, who could control extortion masquerading as gifts: Clive himself. In 1765, Clive was again in Calcutta, trying to curb what he had unleased. He merely increased resentment without reducing mendacity, and returned home after two years to fight other battles. A depressed Clive was widely believed to have committed suicide on 22 November 1774, although there was no suicide note. Samuel Johnson was certain that Clive had 'cut his own throat' because of a guilty 'consciousness'.

For an establishment in search of an alibi, the easy answer was to blame unscrupulous 'Asiatics' for infecting lily-white Englishmen with their corrupt ways. Large presents were the norm in India; what could the British do except politely accept such customary oblations? Lord Chatham tried to save the British baby in the Indian bathwater:

> The riches of Asia have been poured in upon us, and have brought with them not only Asiatic Luxury, but, I fear, Asiatic principles of government. Without connections, without any natural interest in the soil, the importers of foreign gold have forced their way into Parliament by such a torrent of private corruption as no hereditary fortune could resist.[21]

Lord Chatham was right in one respect: British 'nabobs' had no natural interest in India's soil. British fascination for the successful fortune-hunters, the 'white nabobs', was such that tickets for public seats at the impeachment trial of Warren Hastings sold for as much as 50 guineas apiece. Plays like *The Nabob*, produced in 1768, became hits. Popular tracts and pamphlets caricatured the white nabob as a wealthy rogue with a bad liver and worse heart.

The Regulating Act of 1773 raised Indian salaries (the governor-general's pay rose to a formidable £25,000 per annum) and further tightened rules, but London was too distant and a fortune was too close.

Edmund Burke's oratory has gained a grand posthumous reputation which ignores awkward facts like his nickname in Parliament: the 'Dinner Bell', for he could clear the House of Commons when he stood up for yet another long speech. But he had impact. He warned his countrymen that if the venality of 'white nabobs' was not checked, England might suffer its own version of the French Revolution. In 1783, speaking during the India Bill debate, he told fellow MPs that they had married into elite families, bought estates and made a mockery of Indian reform. Burke turned Warren Hastings, who was back in England by 1785, into the 'captain-general' of iniquity and embodiment of fraud, violence and tranny in his speech to the House of Lords in February 1788.[22]

Hastings's defence can be summarized in two sentences: in India, sovereignty was synonymous with despotism; there was no other way to govern. In any case, British rule was a substantial improvement on the desultory ruin which Indian potentates had wrought upon their own people.

Once again, it was all the fault of Indians.

Burke reserved his moral eloquence for opponents, not relatives like William or supporters like Philip Francis, who became a member of Hastings's council. Francis did little to hide his incessant itch for money, whether from graft or gambling. Busteed writes in his narrative of the Hastings era: 'Rumour credited Francis with having won thirty lakhs at whist, and lost ten thousand pounds at backgammon.' He quotes Francis's letters as evidence.

In March 1776, Francis wrote: 'An extraordinary stroke of fortune has made me independent. Two years will probably raise me to affluent circumstances.' In another letter he requested a friend in Benares to buy diamonds, which could be ferreted out much more easily than money, adding, 'I have actually won a fortune and must think of some means of realising it in England. Keep this stuff to yourself.' A third letter was to a friend in England: 'You must know, my friend, that on one blessed day of the present year of our Lord, I had won about twenty thousand pounds at whist. It is reduced to about twelve…'[23]

Francis insisted on feeling sorry for himself: the waste of spirits in accursed India was an unconquerable disease and unutterable misery, he moaned. If he could save £25,000, he might put this misery behind him. Sometimes he felt a little less would be adequate; at others, nothing short of £40,000 was enough.

Gambling was an expensive passion of the Company elite. The stakes were maniacal because the money was ill-gotten. Francis inevitably lost more than he won and was reduced to playing once a week, for trifles. Busteed claims that an ally of Francis, 'Mr Farrer', the first advocate admitted by the Supreme Court, earned a legitimate

£60,000 in less than four years but could have retired with more if he had not been such a sucker at the card table.

The most unscrupulous scoundrel on Hastings's council, Richard Barwell, could drop as much as £40,000 in a night. A marine officer named Henry Thompson published a 'scandalous' pamphlet about Barwell titled 'The Intrigues of a Nabob'. Francis wrote in his diary of September 1777 that Barwell, born in India, possessed 'all the bad qualities common to this climate and country'. This was kind compared to what followed:

> He is rapacious without industry, and ambitious without exertion of his faculties or steady application to affairs. He would be Governor-General if money could make him so, and in that station he would soon engross the wealth of the country. He will do whatever can be done by bribery and intrigue. He has no other resource. His mind is strictly effeminate and unequal to any serious constant occupation except gaming in which alone he is indefatigable.[24]

For good measure, Francis called him 'cunning, cruel, rapacious, tyrannical, and profligate beyond all European ideas of those qualities'.[25]

Burke summoned a reluctant and dilatory Barwell before the House of Commons committee investigating the 'nabobs'. The famed orator was in good form as he thundered:

> What your object is in such conduct, Mr Barwell, I acknowledge myself quite at a loss to say. Probably you scarcely know it yourself. I, however, take the liberty of assuring you it will not answer your purpose whatever that may be. If you expect to weary me or exhaust my patience or that of the honourable members constituting this committee, I can with confidence assert you will fail and have egregiously mistaken the characters of those you are now before, and likewise *that you know me not*! Answers! Intelligible and direct answers to such questions as I deem necessary and proper to put, I must and will have ere I have done with you. I therefore conceive it will tend to your own ease, and that it will be prudent in

you to drop the puerile and silly behaviour (to use no harsher epithets) you have hitherto adopted.[26]

Barwell's mentor Hastings was corrupt but not puerile. In India he dressed plainly in a green coat but understood the symbolic significance of a state occasion and could move swiftly to quell impending trouble, as he did with the raja of Benaras, from whom he also extracted £500,000. Hastings's supporters advertised his qualities in doggerel: *Hathi par howdah, ghore par zin, Jaldi bahar jaata hai Sahib Warren Hastin* (Howdah on an elephant, saddle on a horse, Very quickly moves Sahib Warren Hastings). The local wits of Benaras deftly altered this to *Hathi par howdah, ghore par zin, Jaldi bhaag jaata hai Sahib Warren Hastin* (Howdah on elephant, saddle on horse, Very quickly flees Sahib Warren Hastings).

Hastings's successor Lord Cornwallis ended cosy recommendations for jobs and changed the closed-door system of granting contracts over breakfast to a more transparent process. But his social zeal could be excessive. He so disapproved of public dancing that in 1786 he stopped the customary Christmas dinner, ball and supper. Guests at the few obligatory functions also found that the claret often ran out. Cornwallis would not have won an election in British Calcutta.

Lord Wellesley, governor-general between 1798 and 1805, restored the high-spending grandeur of dazzling receptions although he could not bide the 'ill-bred' familiarity of Calcutta society. 'The century which had come in with the sometimes riotous dining of obscure factors at a common table closed with an oriental adaptation of Vauxhall and the Brighton pavilion,' writes Percival Spear.[27] As Wellesley, an aggressive imperialist, pursued war financed by debt, the defeated Indian nobility ruefully recognized that an *inquilab* had taken place. The world had turned upside down.

'Druid's Head on a Welsh Halfpenny'

The economic exploitation of India intensified. *Hobson-Jobson* explains how British protectionist policies reversed India's initial advantage in its definition of 'piece-goods':

This, which is now the technical term for Manchester cottons imported into India, was originally applied in trade to the

Indian cottons exported to England, a trade which appears to have been deliberately killed by the heavy duties which Lancashire procured to be imposed in its own interest, as in its own interest it has recently procured the abolition of the small import duty on English piece-goods in India.[28]

It debunks the theory that Indian manufacture became a natural victim of technological advance in England:

But it is certain that this Indian trade was not killed by natural causes: *it was killed by prohibitory duties* [italics in original text]. These duties were so high in 1783 that they were declared to operate as a premium on smuggling, and they were *reduced* to 18 per cent. *ad valorem*. In the year 1796-97 the value of piece goods from India imported into England was £2,776,682, or one-third of the whole value of the imports from India, which was £8,252,309.[29]

The duties were raised again in 1799 and then in 1814. India was conquered by the British with Indian money. Apart from financing its wars from Indian revenues, the East India Company was earning £30,000,000 and remitting nearly 12 per cent back to London by the 1850s, its last decade of operations.

British expansion in India followed a very specific economic logic. Frank Perlin writes:

It was especially marked by piecemeal intrusion into the subcontinent by the East India Companies, which penetrated along many different regional 'fronts', took over rights, interfered in governments, and conquered one piece of territory after another: thus, the textile manufacturing and cotton-growing regions of Bihar and Bengal by 1765; much of what is now eastern Uttar Pradesh by 1775 (its important market entrepots); most of southern India south of the Kistna river between 1792 and 1801 (including the textile districts of Coromandel, Malabar and Mysore—marketing and textile towns, ports, cash-cropping districts); important cotton-growing districts and commercial towns in south

Gujarat between 1800 and 1805; large areas of Andhra and Orissa, also important for their export-oriented textile production, between 1753 and 1803; then in 1818–1819 most of Maharashtra among other territories. The latter were last because, commercially speaking, they were the least interesting for the Company, while the rest had obvious industrial and commercial functions.[30]

The three principal war aims were: control over natural resources and manufacturing centres; elimination of existing or potential threats; and eclipse of all vestiges of the ancien régime, the better to prevent any resurrection.

Tipu Sultan was defeated at Seringapatnam in 1799. In another five years, thanks to brilliant officers like Arthur Wellesley, who later became Duke of Wellington, the British had neutralized the formidable Marathas in central and north India. Wellington would describe his victory over Daulat Rao Scindia's army at Assaye on 23 September 1803 as closer than Waterloo. On 29 November of the same year, he defeated a second Maratha force, led by Scindia and Raghoji II Bhonsle, at Argaon in Akola district. On the second day of battle, three of Wellesley's battalions fled under fire, but Wellington rallied his troops, eventually taking all Maratha guns and baggage.

Agra fell in 1802. On 11 September 1803, General Gerard Lake defeated Scindia and his French general Louis Bourquin at Patparganj, across the Jamuna river from Humayun's tomb, and entered Delhi three days later. But the war was not over. Scindia and Bhonsle regrouped, and gave battle at Laswari, near Alwar on 1 November. Lake won but lost his son on the field and wrote that he had never been in 'so severe a business in my life'. The Mughal 'ruler' in Delhi, subservient to Scindia since 1770, became a British pawn.

The Marathas prevailed in the next military engagement at Bharatpur, leading to the treaty signed on 24 December 1805 that bought a decade's peace. The long conflict ended in 1818, with a British victory over the alliance of Peshwa Baji Rao II, Mudhoji Bhonsle of Nagpur and Malharrao Holkar III of Indore. Scindia remained on the sidelines, as he had made a separate peace in 1817. The British were masters of India east of Maharaja Ranjit Singh's Sikh kingdom in Punjab.

In Delhi, the Mughal court had been reduced to a pathetic farce. At 8.30 in the morning of 31 January 1823, Bishop Heber, riding an elephant and accompanied by Sir H.M. Elliot, entered the *Qila-i-Mualla*, or Red Fort, through the splendid arch of the gate tower into an exceedingly dirty stable-yard swarming with 'miserable beggars' and families of stable servants. They passed another richly carved but filthy gateway. A canvas which screened the hapless Mughal was drawn as attendants chanted, 'Lo, the ornament of the world! Lo, the asylum of nations! King of Kings! The Emperor Ackbar [sic] Shah! Just, fortunate, victorious!'[31]

Abu Nasir Muin-ud-din Muhammad Akbar Shah II, 'king' between 1806 and 1837, was seated on an open pavilion of white marble, 'richly carved, flanked by rose bushes and fountains, and some tapestry and striped curtains hanging in festoons about it...'. Elliot and Heber twice bowed three times. The king was pale, thin but handsome, with an aquiline nose, long white beard and a complexion almost as fair as any European. Wrapped up in shawls against the cold, he looked like a 'Druid's head on a Welsh halfpenny', records Heber. He made a ritual presentation of 51 gold mohurs in an embroidered purse and was given the traditional *khilat*, a kaftan. In a display of English power, Heber did not take off his hat, except when the 'poor old descendant of Tamerlane' tied a flimsy brocade turban around his head. Heber added four gold coins, an Arabic Bible and a Hindustani prayer book, bound in blue velvet laced in gold to his gifts. Akbar Shah II responded with a string of pearls and two worthless but glittering ornaments for the Bishop's turban, after which the prelate gave five more gold mohurs to his indigent majesty. Five gold coins were sent to the queen in her apartments before the British visitors took leave of this charade.[32]

At that moment, the Bishop recalled the famous Persian line: 'The spider hangs her tapestry in the palace of the Caesars'. He was clearly reminded of verse from the Persian poet Saadi which he had copied into his jornal on the sea voyage to India:

Brother! Know the world deceiveth!
Trust on Him who safety giveth!
Fix not on the world they trust,
She deeds us – but she turns to dust,

And the bare earth or kingly throne
Alike may serve to die upon.[33]

By 1831, all pretence was gone. The new resident Francis Hawkins 'was filled with the new ideas of superiority and stoutly believed that an Englishman should show deference to no man in India'. Percival Spear continues:

His first duty was to present a *nazr* to the king. This he regarded as humiliating and compromised with his conscience by presenting it with one hand only. Even standing before royalty irked him, so that on reaching the Queen's apartments he insisted on a chair to support his dignity. From such a start there soon developed open warfare. He refused to receive dishes of sweetmeats from the heir apparent, drove away in wrath gardeners who brought nosegays from the palace, and sent back royal *shuqas* on the ground of disrespectful wording.[34]

On a more prosaic note, when the Company's accountants did their sums later this was the balance sheet: '...the ornaments and shawls which I received from the Emperor were valued to me at two hundred and eighty-four sicca rupees. The horse was reported to be barely worth thirty rupees...'[35]

The British were more careful with allies like the ruler of Gwalior. In October 1837, Governor-general Lord Auckland set off on a 30-month-long grand tour accompanied by his sister, the author Emily Eden. Her letters are a brilliant portrait of personal and political relations between India's past and present.

They reached Dholepure and Gwalior in January 1840. The raja of Dholepure, said Emily Eden, seemed 'to run to size, in everything; wears eight of the largest pearls ever seen; rides the tallest elephant; his carriage has two stories and is drawn by six elephants, and he lives in a two-storied tent—rickety, but still nobody else has one so large'. If Dholepure had the tallest, Gwalior had the 'largest elephant in India; it is nearly twelve feet high, and G.'s [Governor-general Auckland's], which is generally thought a large one, looked like a little pony'. Visitors were obliged to take off their shoes before entering the 'native' durbars, but the English wore stockings over their shoes and kept their hats on.[36]

On 12 January 1840, Emily Eden called on Scindia's young queen:

> ...at the door of her own room was the little *ranee*, something like a little transformed cat in a fairy tale, covered with gold tissue, and clanking with diamonds. Her feet and hands were covered with rings fastened with diamond chains to her wrists and ankles. She laid hold of our hands and led us to her throne, which was like the rajah's, without a canopy, and her women lifted her up, and we sat on each side of her.[37]

Emily Eden saw some nautch; then it was time for presents.

The maharaja had 'ordered that she should put all the jewellery with her own little hands'. The jewels were spectacular.

> I had a diamond necklace and a collar, some native pearl earrings that hung nearly down to the waist, and a beautiful pair of diamond bracelets, and the great article of all was an immense diamond tiara. I luckily could not keep this on with a bonnet. They were valued altogether at 2,400*l.*, the mere stones.[38]

Lord Auckland was a 'pattern of patience' as he was garlanded with a string of pearls as big as peas. A diamond ring with a large sapphire was placed on his finger and a cocked hat embroidered with pearls on his head. The governor-general gave the maharaja a gold bed inlaid with rubies and a tent made of shawls with silver poles. Scindia had opened his vault to find suitable offerings for the lord; the British had merely done a bit of recycling. The bed and tent had been given by Maharaja Ranjit Singh of Punjab earlier on the tour.

Emily Eden called the fabulous Scindia jewellery 'an immense prize for the Company'.

Indian nobles who wanted to buy peace with the victorious British after 1857 turned up bearing gifts. Sir William Howard Russell, the eminent war correspondent of the *Times*, London, saw, on 19 February 1859, an anxious 'Rajah Hurdeo Bux' before the British chief commissioner of Lucknow. The raja had come with 'a magnificent horse, covered with splendid trappings, and trays of jewels—bracelets of emerald and diamond of considerable value, after which, a few civil speeches, on both sides, and he took his leave'.[39] One presumes that this array also went to the treasury.

The *Phal-Phool* Rule

The British Crown ruled India through a covenanted service, whose members had to pass a rigorous examination. The days of grace-and-favour appointments ended after 1857. Old-timers called this new breed the 'Competitionwallahs'. You could get away with a good deal as members of the Indian Civil Service, also known as the 'Heaven-born' Brahmins of the Raj. The one unpardonable sin was graft.

The ICS had its share of characters. The first modern market in Bombay, which opened in 1871, was named after the municipal commissioner Arthur Travers Crawford. Crawford had separated from his wife, and lived with two American actresses during one season in Pune. None of this harmed his career. But he was placed under house arrest when found accepting bribes. He escaped from Pune, was caught in Bombay wearing a false beard and dismissed without a pension.[40]

In 1888, the political agent in the princely state of Bhavnagar, Colonel Watson, was accused by an Indian journalist of receiving gifts, including horses, from the maharaja through his mistress, a Mrs Mills, then staying as a guest of the prince. The colonel responded with some hauteur, saying that his superiors had no business prying into his bedroom. It did not work. The Bombay government ordered him to return the horses and 'get rid' of Mrs Mills.[41]

The ICS took pride in its reputation for correct behaviour. Any officer who hit an Indian faced a severe reprimand or even dismissal, and momentary loss of temper could become a blot on the record. Sobriety was encouraged. William Gladstone, prime minister four times between 1868 and 1894, believed that one whisky and soda a day was enough for a bureaucrat in India, although he served his own guests claret for breakfast. The officer was generally abstemious, even in the solitude and insomnia of a distant posting. The intemperate paid a price. Thomas Fry, a sessions judge of Pune who was often drunk in court was demoted and shifted to Satara.[42]

A *phal-phool* (fruit-flower) rule became the new norm; officials could accept gifts of only fruit or flowers placed on trays known as dollies, which came around at Christmas. One army officer, John Morris (a member of two Everest expeditions, in 1922 and 1936) got a cauliflower on Christmas day from the contractor who supplied food to the troops. It was a very special cauliflower, since a gold sovereign popped out of it. Morris did the honourable thing: he kept the vegetable and returned the gold. According to Charles Allen, one resident in a princely state discovered 101 gold *mohurs* at the bottom of a huge dolly. The unnamed civil servant wrote an angry letter to the unnamed prince, only to receive a reply saying: 'I'm dreadfully sorry, but one hundred and one gold *mohurs* is what has been presented to the residency every year at Christmas and if the amount is not enough will you tell me what it is?' Five of the 101 coins were meant for the servants; the rest were for staff. The brown Christmas envelope was part of normal life in departments like the railways.[43]

The most straitlaced of the lords, George Nathaniel Curzon, First Marquess Curzon of Kedleston, viceroy of India from 1899 to 1905, was accused in 1903 of receiving expensive furniture from the maharaja of Benaras. The charge was made by the wife of an official who felt her husband had been denied the governorship of Burma, so one could discount the aspersion to that extent. What is indisputable is that Lord Wavell, the second last viceroy, was permitted to prolong his term in 1947 till the date of his daughter's wedding in February so that Indian grandees might come to the morning reception with gifts suitable for a viceroy's daughter. Wavell resigned the exact minute the reception was over.

The preferred extracurricular activity among Victorian bureaucrats tended to be writing: memoirs of course, but also satirical verse, fiction and quiet or anonymous forays into journalism. Some of it was a visceral outpouring of frustration, as for instance Alec McMillan's contribution to the *Pioneer*, reproduced in *Divers Ditties: Chiefly Written in India*:

> *My ruddy cheeks have long grown pale*
> *Beneath the sun's relentless fire,*
> *I dare not drink a glass of ale,*
> *And those damned seniors won't retire.*

Gifts of Fortune in a Land of Regrets

Black scorpions infest my shoes,
Ants batten on my best-loved books,
And last home mail brought out the news
My Maud had wed that blockhead Snooks.[44]

There was a hidden author in many a high-ranking soul. Alfred Lyall wanted to be the Trollope of his generation but went no further than becoming a mini-Matthew Arnold in poems like *The Land of Regrets*, the land being India and the regret British. Lyall was a sceptic: he expressed doubts about God in *Theology in Extremis*. Sir Henry Cotton, a well-wisher of Indians, wrote for the *Indian Observer*, a satirical weekly founded in 1870 which had the temerity to publish an attack on the Lieutenant-governor of Bengal, Sir George Campbell.

The most impressive ICS scholar was the Scottish bureaucrat Sir William Wilson Hunter, a graduate of Glasgow University who took a degree in Sanskrit before joining the service in 1862. His maxim became official doctrine: 'Nothing is more costly than ignorance.' He believed that knowledge was the crux of good governance. His recommendation led to the superb gazettes in which civil servants recorded an anthropological study of their districts. Hunter modelled his own work on *Ain-i-Akbari*. His nine-volume *Imperial Gazetteer of India* is a classic of the genre.

The Irish peer Richard Bourke, Lord Mayo, viceroy from 1869 till he was assassinated in Port Blair on 8 February 1872, gave Hunter two memorable assignments. He commissioned a statistical survey of India, which evolved into the first census of British India. In 1871, Lord Mayo asked Hunter to investigate a crucial question: were Indian Muslims 'bound by their religion to rebel against the Queen'[45]? The enquiry was made against the background of the long jihad waged by radical clerics against British rule from around 1830 to the 1870s. *The Indian Musulmans* was a serious attempt to examine the role of a holy war in Quranic doctrine. Hunter's conclusion, that Islam did not permit jihad if there was no interference in the practice of faith, served both a theological and political purpose, for it helped dilute controversies about the attitude of Indian Muslims towards the Raj. In 1882, Hunter presided over a Commission on Indian Education, and during the last year of service was elected vice chancellor of Calcutta University. He died at the comparatively young age of 60 in England, just three years after retirement.

ICS officers poured their intellectual genius into history, anthropology, philology and literature. William Muir published books on Islam in 1858 and 1883; his elder brother John worked on Hinduism. Bill Archer, a Cambridge graduate, studied the music and songs of the Uraons, a tribe in central India; his wife Mildred, from Oxford, wrote on traditional Indian painting. John Hutton, who served mainly in the Naga hills, recorded tribal dialects, and after retirement taught at Cambridge as professor of social anthropology.

George Grierson became famous for *Seven Grammars of the Dialects and Subdialects of the Bihari Language*, published between 1883 and 1887, and John Beames for *Comparative Grammar of the Modern Aryan Languages of India*. Foster Fitzgerald Arbuthnot translated the erotic Sanskrit text *Ananga Ranga* and collaborated with his friend Richard Burton on an English version of *Kama Sutra*. The book was printed only after Arbuthnot had retired as collector of Bombay. Herbert Risley considered his *Tribes and Castes of Bengal* an administrative necessity. Annette and Henry Beveridge did remarkable translations of Mughal texts like Abul Fazl's *Akbarnama* and Jahangir's *Tuzuk-i-Jahangiri*, published by the Royal Asiatic Society. Beveridge's *The Trial of Maharaja Nanda Kumar: A Narrative of a Judicial Murder* was the first history to expose a scandal which had long lingered in Bengal's memory.

The pay was good, the job secure and pension more than adequate. The young Hunter could write to his fiancée that they would be 'rich' when he retired, but he was referring to no more than the comfort of an assured income. Such rectitude was not necessarily true of those lower in the pecking order. Sir Penderel Moon, whose maternal ancestors had served in India from 1814 and who joined the ICS in 1929, found bribery amidst the 'subordinate' levels of administration appalling by his high standards. He told the BBC:

> I was perhaps much too hot in trying to check it. I ran in a large number of people of almost every rank for corruption, from the highest to the lowest. Tips I didn't object to. It was harassment, refusing to do a thing unless the palm was greased.[46]

Sir Penderel's intellectual contribution includes an epic history, *The British Conquest and Dominion of India.*

Good intentions did not melt race barriers. Although Lord Northbrook assured Queen Victoria in 1872 that the 'most enlightened' Hindus and Muslims were no longer reluctant to dine with him at Government House, the very fact that a viceroy had sent such a note indicates how distant the two races remained. The experience of James Sifton, an assistant magistrate in Bengal, was more representative of district-level truth. He said that 'he would shake hands with his host on arrival and departure but would not otherwise see him for the rest of the evening. Nor was he able to talk to many other Indians present' at a social event like a fireworks display by a wealthy local babu, 'because the seats for the Europeans were put in an area separate from all the others'.[47]

Lord Mayo echoed the establishment view when he told administrators: 'Teach your subordinates that we are all British gentlemen engaged in the magnificent work of governing an inferior race.'[48] He founded the Mayo College in Ajmer as part of his efforts to improve the scholastics of inferior princes. Several British voices worried that fair competition would induct a flood of intelligent Bengalis into the ICS, with unpredictable and perhaps dangerous implications.

A hesitant nostalgia for the 'good old days' when few questions were asked also began to creep in. There was a wistful air about T.F. Bignold's lament when, in 1871, this ICS officer wrote:

> *Oh! for the palmy days, the days of old!*
> *When writers revelled in barbaric gold;*
> *When each auspicious smile secured a gem*
> *From Merchant's store or Raja's diadem;*
> *When 'neath the* pankha *frill the Court reclined,*
> *When 'Almah wrote and Judges only signed;*
> *Or, lordlier still, beneath a virgin space*
> *Inscribed their names and hied them to the chase!*
> *Chained to the desk, the worn Civilian now*
> *Clears his parched throat and wipes his weary bow.*[49]

Sir Alfred Lyall cannot hide an autobiographical bitterness in *The Land of Regrets:*

He did list to the voice of the Siren,
He was caught by the clinking of gold,
And the slow toil of Europe seemed tiring
And the grey of his fatherland cold;
He must haste to the gardens of Circe;
What ails him, the slave, that he frets
In thy service? O Lady sans merci!
O Land of Regrets.
…

'Mid the crumbling of royalties rotting,
Each cursed by a knave or a fool,
Where Kings and fanatics are plotting,
He dreamt of a power and a rule;
Hath he come now, in season, to know thee;
Hath he seen what a stranger forgets,
All the graveyards of exiles below thee,
O Land of Regrets?[50]

*Abdul Wahab, Aurangzeb's Chief Qazi and enforcer of the
morality code. This miniature painting was published in
Niccolao Manucci's* Storia Do Mogor.

Rev. Reginald Heber, the second Bishop of Calcutta, reached the capital of British India in October 1823 with his wife Amelia and daughter Emily. He left a travel diary which ranks as an invaluable addition to the remarkable library bequeathed by the British.

Calcutta, from the Plassey Gate of Fort William, depicted in the Illustrated London News, 1870.

Robert Clive, his head held high, meeting Mir Jafar, who betrayed Nawab Siraj ud-Daulah at the Battle of Plassey in order to become the first British puppet Nawab of Bengal. Clive's victory established the East India Company as a military as well as a commercial power.

George Clive, a British civil servant, and his family with an Indian maid, or ayah. The ayah became the one Indian to get close to a British family. Painting by Joshua Reynolds.

*Portrait of Colonel James Skinner in uniform. Skinner's father Hercules
was Scottish and mother Jeany a Rajput. James Skinner raised the First
Regiment of Irregular Horse, known more famously as Skinner's Horse,
after he was denied a commission in the Company army
because he had an Indian mother.*

Job Charnock received the zemindari of three villages for an annual rent of Rs 1,195 from Azim-us-Shan, the Mughal governor of Bengal, according to J. Talboys Wheeler's Early Records of British India.

The front page of Hicky's Bengal Gazette, March 10, 1781; the Gazette was the first English newspaper in India. It positioned itself well: 'A weekly political and commercial paper open to all parties but influenced by none'. However, Hicky's readership was British and he had no particular desire to inform or influence Indians.

Indians did not laugh about British revelry in public, but privately disparaged British rule as an incomprehensible plague sent by malign destiny.

An illustration of 'The Sahib at Table' from Hilton Brown's anthology shows a dinner table in post-prandial uproar, the fun watched beadily by amused Hindu and sardonic Muslim waiters. There are three memsahibs and eight men, all high and happy. A servant examines an empty bottle of wine, a slight smile on his face, in the background. Even the hookah looks tipsy.

Famine in its most horrific dimensions was synonymous with British rule. The first 'Company famine' occurred in Bengal in 1770, and killed an astonishing one-third of the province's population through starvation, estimated at 10 million dead, as Warren Hastings informed London. In the same note, Hastings told the Directors that he had raised Company revenues during famine by using violent methods.

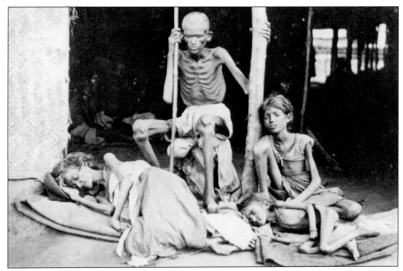

In British Raj continued its policy of 'forced export' of food from India in 1876–1879, while the famine swept through a region. Poverty, misery and disease wiped out millions periodically.

The site of the ever-controversial 'Black Hole of Calcutta' in Fort William. With conscious insensitivity, Curzon restored the memorial to the 'Black Hole' which had been demolished more than eight decades earlier by the British themselves.

An Indian Lady, most likely the beautiful 'Jemdanee', Bibi of the lawyer William Hickey. She was immensely popular with Hickey's friends because of her sprightly good humour and was a perfect hostess at bibulous dinner parties, although she never touched a drop of alcohol.

Frances Croke, better known as Begum Johnson, was a legendary name in Calcutta during the onset of British rule over the subcontinent. Her grandson, Robert Jenkinson, 2nd Earl of Liverpool, became Prime Minister of Britain. Her epitaph does not exaggerate: 'The oldest British resident in Bengal, universally beloved, respected and revered.'

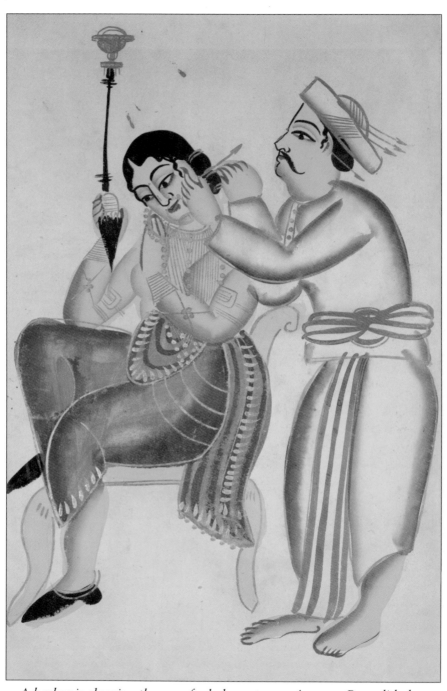

A barber is cleaning the ear of a lady customer. As some Bengali babus whiled away the hours with their mistresses and courtesans, neglected wives found creative ways of spending their time at home.

Newly rich Bengali babus acquired a hybrid culture in their search for upward unability in the British Raj. This classic Kalighat painting shows the babu and his wife dancing to a British tune. At another level, Rudyard Kipling saw virtue in the babu-clerk who worked in administration: 'The Babu is a great man, and, to respect him, you must see five score or so of him in a room of hundred yards long bending over ledgers, ledgers, and yet more ledgers—silent as the Sphinx and busy as a bee.'

Binodini Das, a billboard name for Calcutta's Star Theatre, when confronted by her jilted and jealous lover famously answered, 'I have made money, but money cannot make me.'

Nautch cut across class and region. The Burra Sahib went to a zemindar's parties to witness the finest dancing girls, while more modest soldiers invited less expensive dancers to the cantonment.

'Attack of the Mutineers on the Redan Battery at Lucknow, July 30, 1857.' Colonel A.R.D. Mackenzie, who witnessed the outbreak of the sepoy uprising at Meerut, wrote: 'Everyone remembers the mysterious chupattis or flat wheaten cakes which, shortly before the mutiny, were circulated from regiment to regiment. The messages conveyed by them have never been fathomed by Englishmen; but there can be no doubt that they were in some way a signal, understood by the sepoys, of warning to be in readiness for coming events.'

In September 1899, Maratha Punch dutifully depicted Curzon as Lord Krishna intent upon destroying the serpent Kalia; while Hindi Punch showed two Brahmins propitiating Lord Ganesh. The elephant god had the face of Curzon, while the mouse at his feet was captioned 'Loyalty'. This was excessive loyalty rather than sacrilege.

I Don't Care a *Damree*!

The most memorable contribution of service-scholars was surely the great dictionary of the Raj, *Hobson-Jobson: A Glossary of Colloquial Anglo-Indian Words and Phrases, and of Kindred Terms, Etymological, Historical, Geographical and Discursive*, a classic that has never gone out of print since it first appeared in 1886. It was compiled by Arthur Burnell of the Madras Civil Service, and an Army officer, Colonel Sir Henry Yule of the Bengal Engineers. Burnell won an honorary doctorate from Strasbourg University for his catalogue of Sanskrit manuscripts collected by the Tanjore royal family.

The dictionary defines its own title:

> A native festal excitement; a *tamasha*; but especially the Moharram ceremonies... It is in fact an Anglo-Saxon version of the wailings of the Mahommedans as they beat their breasts in the procession of the *Moharram*—'Ya Hasan! Ya Hosain!' It is to be remembered that these observances are *in India* by no means confined to Shi'as...[1]

By 1673, it says, the phrase had transmuted into 'Hossen Gosseen', and then 'Hossy-Gossy' before European bystanders decided that they were shouting 'Hobson Jobson' as mourners beat their bare breasts in penitential memory of the martyrdom of the Prophet's grandson Imam Hussain at the battle of Karbala in 680 AD.

It requires a monumental tin ear to go from *Ya Hasan! Ya Hosain* to 'Hobson-Jobson', but there we are. The British ear, not the Indian voice, was judge and jury.

There is much to delight the connoisseur in the vocabulary of shared experience. The origins of 'damn' lie in India. A *dam* was a copper coin, a fortieth part of a rupee; an *adhela* was half a *dam*, and the lowly *damree* one third of a *dam*. From this grew the expression: 'No, I won't give a *damree*!' This caught on in colloquial English as 'I don't care a *dam*!' *Hobson-Jobson* quotes Sir G. Trevelyan as saying: 'It was the Duke of Wellington who invented this oath, so disproportioned to the greatness of its author.'[2]

Uniquely, the patois diverged into two streams. The British created an English with Indian characteristics, while Indians translated their own language and diction into a continuous string of English words merged into Indian syntax and even grammar. Both have found a niche in 20th-century literature.

Hobson-Jobson gets a bit part in the conversation between protagonist Flora Crewe and the artist Anish Das in Tom Stoppard's *Indian Ink*, which opened at the Aldwych in London on 27 February 1995:

FLORA: While having tiffin on the verandah of my bungalow I spilled kedgeree on my dungarees and had to go to the gymkhana in my pyjamas looking like a coolie.

DAS: I was buying chutney in the bazaar when a thug escaped from the choky and killed a box-wallah for his loot, creating a hullabaloo and landing himself in the mulligatawny.

FLORA: I went doolally at the durbar and was sent back to Blighty in a dooley feeling rather dikki with a cup of char and a chit for a chotapeg.

DAS: Yes, and the burra sahib who looked so pukka in his topee sent a coolie to the memsahib—

FLORA: No, no. You can't have memsahib and sahib, that's cheating—and anyway I've already said coolie.

DAS: I concede, Miss Crewe. You are the Hobson-Jobson champion![3]

Anish Das's favourite author was Agatha Christie, but he wanted to write like Macaulay.

A hybrid tongue encourages wit, and G.V. Desani, who died in 2000 at the age of 91, was a master of self-caricature. *All About H. Hatterr*, his best and best-selling book, is set in 1939 and was published in 1952. It was written in incipient Indian English, dressed in credible exaggeration and delivered with raw humour. Banerjji discusses the merits of 'cock-sacrifice':

> Please let me go on, Mr H. Hatterr. We accept that man's nature is immoral to his sub-conscious foundations. We also accept that it must rise up and sublimate itself to the divine. Here the spiritual element comes in. Certain *yogis* have seen fit to overcome and conquer their procreation instinct. They hold it obligatory to be celibate and curb their sex-dynamo. If a man has controlled his erotic nature, he is qualified to serve others by all means at his command, and himself not at all. His *id* and libido are null and void. He is no longer a so and so, and a son of so and so, but rather, he is more like a mere x. I do not mean x the kiss symbol but, as we allude in algebra terminology, to denote an unknown quantity.
>
> What the hell this algebra's got to do with me, old feller?
>
> Your modesty amazes me! You have vanquished Kama, the Indian god of love, as well as the Persian goddess of Immorality, and you are so calm! This is true saintliness. I see, spiritually, you are ready for your mission! A thousand thanks! Thank you very much. In the words of the French Emperor Bonaparty, spoken for the bard Goethe, Voila un homme! You are both *universal* men, amen![4]

Both strands of language found their element in the more interactive mofussil rather than the insular compartments of Calcutta. *Hobson-Jobson* describes the mofussil as the second-tier

> country stations and districts, as contra-distinguished from 'the Presidency' [Calcutta, Bombay and Madras]; or, relatively, the rural localities of a district as contra-distinguished from the *sudder* or chief station, which is the residence of the district authorities. Thus if, in Calcutta, one talks of the Mofussil, he means anywhere in Bengal out of Calcutta; if one at Benares talks of going into the *Mofussil*, he means going anywhere in the Benares division or district (as the case might be) out of the city and station of Benares. And so over India.[5]

John Beames, who won the gold medal for Persian at Haileybury and served in Punjab, Ambala, Purnea, Champaran, Balasore and Chittagong for most of his career between 1858 and 1893, notes that '*Mofussil*, properly "mufassal", is an Arabic word meaning "scattered", "separated" and in Anglo-Indian slang is used to denote the rural parts of India'.[6]

A city like Lucknow, the capital of independent Awadh until 1856, was infused with mofussil culture. The nawab and the British Resident were the twin social luminaries, generating interaction between parallel cultures. The Anglophile Nawab Asaf ud-Daula displayed his love for things European in an exhibition room full of guns, pistols, watches, glassware and furniture. British civilians posted in places like Patna, Dhaka, Kasimbazar, Balasore, Masulipatnam, Cuddalore and Calicut boasted, legitimately, that their peers in Calcutta and Madras were ignorant of real India.

The sahibs of 'unreal India' added hues of class snobbery to intrinsic colour prejudice.

> Instead of the commercialism of the merchant balancing the jingoism of the gentleman, to produce a policy practical as well as spirited, fruitful of wealth as well as of glory, the opposite process… took place; the gentry were not exiled to their estates by the merchants, but the merchants were confined to their shops by the officials. The strength of a middle class is the union of commercial with professional interests but in India they were kept rigidly apart. The process was not complete till the turn of the century, but from the time of Wellesley, with his contempt for the 'cheesemongers of Leadenhall Street', it continued without a check.[7]

Bureaucrats, the elite snobs of British India, remained socially aloof from businessmen. Planters from upper Bengal, Bihar and Assam were expected to stay in the Spenser hotel when in Calcutta. Spenser had fine Victorian upholstery, good food and an excellent billiard room, but it was not D. Wilson's Hotel (later, the Great Eastern Hotel). The underclass in the Raj caste system, the 'Low Europeans' or the 'European Vagabonds', was kept at a distinct distance. These might be the retired soldier or sailor or NCO who had little money and no prospects in Britain, now working in a Presidency or mofussil tavern, a potential public nuisance as they preened about, uninhibitedly racist towards Indians and violent with everyone.

An honour system within the upper crust of the Raj cocoon reflected its 'Brahmin' culture. When you ordered whisky at Firpo's, the sniffy restaurant on Park Street, it came off the bar shelf rather than in a peg: the waiter checked consumption by the rule of the thumb, measuring levels in the bottle on the table 'before' and 'after' the meal. No one questioned the bill. In a more commercial environment, whisky arrived by the peg at Peliti's in Calcutta's Old Court Street, where you could get plastered for a rupee or two—during lunch.

Agra and Meerut were the premier mofussil towns in the Upper Provinces when John Lang, an Australian by birth and anti-establishment by preference, visited the region. Born in Sydney, Lang had studied law at Cambridge but enjoyed a parallel career as an editor and writer. He left Australia after a run-in with the authorities and headed, unusually, for Calcutta. He practised both journalism and law in India.

Lang was in Agra in 1854 when he received a letter written in Persian upon gold paper requesting him to call upon the Rani of Jhansi. Her state had been annexed by the British, and she wanted legal advice. Lang received a royal welcome. He entered the Jhansi palace on a white elephant, seated in a silver howdah trimmed with red velvet. He then ascended a steep staircase, took off his shoes and walked into a large room. Astrologers had determined the time of the meeting, between the setting of the sun and the rising of the moon. Lang waited in an armchair. The rani of Jhansi, then about 26 or 27 years old, sat behind a curtain which served as a purdah. Their conversation would continue till two in the morning.

Lang got a glimpse of the rani when the curtain was briefly, and inadvertently, lifted. He writes:

Her face must have been very handsome when she was younger, and even now it had many charms—though, according to my idea of beauty, it was too round. The expression also was very good, and very intelligent. The eyes were particularly fine, and the nose very delicately shaped. She was not very fair, though she was far from black. She had no ornaments, strange to say, upon her person, except a pair of gold ear-rings. Her dress was a plain white muslin, so fine in texture, and drawn about her in such a way, and so tightly, that the outline of her figure was plainly discernible—and a remarkably fine figure she had. What spoilt her was her voice, which was something between a whine and a croak. When the *purdah* was drawn aside, she was, or affected to be, very much annoyed; but presently she laughed, and good-humouredly expressed a hope that a sight of her head had not lessened my sympathy with her sufferings nor prejudiced her cause.[8]

Lang replied gallantly that if the governor-general could be so fortunate as to see such a beautiful queen, he would restore Jhansi at once. Although he was convinced that she had been wronged, Lang advised patience—to accept the annexation under protest and appeal to the Crown for redressal. The rani's reply was unequivocal: '*Main Jhansi kabhi naheen doongi!* (I will never cede Jhansi!)'. Lang left the following morning with splendid gifts: an elephant, a camel, an Arab horse, a pair of swift greyhounds, two Indian shawls, silks and a portrait of the rani.[9]

From Agra, Lang went to Delhi and then Meerut, a garrison town with around 10,000 British troops who could be rushed to Delhi in a crisis. He worked for six weeks in a British-owned newspaper called *The Mofussulite*. What impressed him was not the predictable mindset of British editors, but the simmering subaltern anger of Indians expressed through the insurrectionist journalism of an 'Oordoo', or Urdu, 'native print', *Jam-i-Jumsheed*.

Its owner-editor, who remains unnamed in the memoir, was a Brahmin who had a regular job as head pressman-cum-translator of the *Mofussulite*. *Jam-i-Jumsheed*

was founded without the knowledge, privity, or consent of the conductor of the European journal, by the head pressman, of his establishment, who was a Brahmin. The editor of this native print, which was lithographed in the Oordoo language, was the *moonshee* of the English press at Meerut. He was well skilled in English, and his chief employment was translating the native correspondence. Having constant access to the desks of the compositors, this press *moonshee* acquired a knowledge of every item of news furnished by European as well as native correspondents, and of this knowledge he failed not to avail himself.[10]

The intrepid Brahmin published in *Jam-i-Jumsheed* all the news suppressed or censored by the English paper. The most telling example was the way in which he broke the story of a Meerut magistrate's 'act of retributive justice' which was 'kept out of the columns of the Meerut paper [*Mofussulite*], at the instance of the friends of the gentleman who was guilty of the indiscretion'.

This magistrate, convinced that an escaped convict had taken shelter in a particular village, went there late at night, gave its residents half an hour to produce the culprit, and when they denied any knowledge of the convict's whereabouts, set fire to the entire village. Three men, four women (one in labour) and six children lost their lives, while 600 became homeless. The magistrate's protectors claimed his only fault was a touch of madness.

Jam-i-Jumsheed commented, sarcastically: 'Let us hope, however, that the Lieutenant-Governor [of the North West Provinces] will not heed such insinuations, but after complimenting the magistrate on his vigour and his zeal, appoint him to the first judgeship that may become vacant.' The report ended on a bitter note:

It remains for us to add that the escaped convict of whom the magistrate was in search, has been in Oude [Awadh] for the past month, and that no notice of this affair will appear in any of the papers printed in English and edited by the Sahib Logue.[11]

Lang praises the sophistication of Indian editors who 'used to wrap up the most bitter irony in the most complimentary phrases, and frequently their allusions, if viewed abstractedly, were both humorous and witty'. He cites a news report in which an intelligent schoolboy gave the correct answer to the visiting lieutenant-governor when asked about the earth's rotation. The editor of a 'native paper' predicted that this boy would come to a bad end for he should have flung science into the gutter before so potent a ruler, and replied, 'By your honour's grace, favour, and kindness, does this planet revolve upon its axis.'[12]

Satire could run close to the edge—the gullible provincial administration was convinced that one editor was being laudatory when extolling Lord Dalhousie for the way in which he rode an elephant to his meeting with Kashmir's Maharaja Gulab Singh. Lang realized what the editor was up to:

> This was the man who never lost an opportunity of bringing British rule in India into disgrace, ridicule, and contempt amongst his countrymen, and who, eventually, by producing his writings, and having them translated literally, succeeded in obtaining an appointment under the Government worth one hundred and fifty rupees per mensem![13]

John Lang eventually retired to Mussoorie, where he died in 1864. His book *The Weatherbys* was among the first works of English fiction to be set in India.

English journalism in British India began with the elan of rebellion but was quickly neutered into obedience.

James Augustus Hicky, the son of a weaver, was 32 when he reached Calcutta in 1772, paying for his passage by working as a surgeon's mate. Like so many others, he came in search of the metaphorical 'pagoda tree', driven by the illusion that all one had to do was shake it and fruit would plop into your lap. Till 1818, accounts at Madras were kept in *pagodas*, *fanams*, and *kas*. Eight *kas* made one *fanam*, and 42 *fanams* equalled one *pagoda*. The rupee became the standard currency in 1818, with the *pagoda* being equivalent to three and a half rupees.

Hicky prospered in business running cargo ships, but in October 1776 was jailed for failing to honour a bond of ₹ 4,000, in a suit brought by a 'few malignant Bengalis'. His lawyer William Hickey (near-namesake but no relation) describes how the jailbird was reborn as a media entrepreneur:

> At the time I first saw Hicky he had been about seven years in India. During his confinement [a prison sentence for debt] he met with a treatise upon printing, from which he collected

sufficient information to commence printer, there never having been a press in Calcutta. By indefatigable attention and unremitting labour he succeeded in cutting a rough set of types which answered very well for handbills and common advertisements, and as he could afford to work cheap he met with considerable encouragement. Having scraped together by this means a few hundred rupees he sent to England for a regular and proper set of materials for printing.[14]

While waiting for the press to arrive, Hicky realized that it might serve a better need, that of a weekly newspaper.

Hicky's Bengal Gazette; or The Original Calcutta General Advertiser appeared on 29 January 1780, the year in which the Company's administrative headquarters Writer's Building was completed and Warren Hastings fought a duel with his political rival Philip Francis (neither died, though Hastings had the better of the encounter). The *Gazette* positioned itself well: 'A weekly political and commercial paper open to all parties but influenced by none'. This was not strictly true: it was not very open to Indian readers and was certainly not influenced by them. The *Gazette* was an English paper for the English.

It was quickly full of advertisements for private sales and auctions of expensive silk from China and ham, sauce, salad oil, whisky, hats, swords, saddles, pianos and guitars from England sold by auctioneers like Joseph Baretto. Mrs Hodges announced a boarding school for young ladies and children near the Armenian church, where they could learn reading, writing, arithmetic and needlework. Another advertisement was plaintive:

> Mr Belvere, the Dancing Master, begs leave to acquaint the Ladies and Gentlemen of this settlement and the public in general that he proposes opening a dancing school for instructing the Ladies and Gentlemen the whole day till ten in the evening, two nights in the week except, viz., Wednesday and Saturday, and on those two nights he will give any lesson privately to his students as he proposes having two public Balls with music and illumination, agreeable to the Regulations of Europe.[15]

The *Gazette*'s columns were spiced by novelty, wit, salacious anecdotes and pseudonyms as a shield against libel. A certain 'Counsellor Feeble', who had lost his senses to a Miss Wringham, was reported as drinking 'W-g-h' eye-water till he retired tipsy. Another item reported: '*March 1781—Lost on the Course*, last Monday evening, Buxey Clumsey's heart whilst he stood simpering at the footstep of Hooka Turban's carriage'. This lady of variable virtue was also nicknamed 'Hooka Turban', 'Turban Conquest' and 'The St Helena Filly'.[16]

From the first issue, Hicky opened a section for local poetic aspirations called the 'Poet's Corner'. A husband, secure in the anonymity of a pen-name, could write an 'epigram on a scolding wife': *Mills, Wheels and Hammers lay aside your noise,/ For ye are whispers to my spouse's voice:/ She downs the noise of Mills, of Wheels, of hammers/ I wish that she would drown herself G-d D-m her*. Some of the verse was patriotic. When news of the treaty between France and America signed on 6 February 1778 reached Calcutta, Hicky taunted Britain's foes: *The treaty's sign'd with faithful France,/ And now like Frenchmen, sing and dance!/ Say, Yankies don't you feel compunction,/ At your unnatural, rash conjunction?*.[17]

Indians did not escape the paper's ribaldry. Two stanzas from Hicky's *A Description of India* leave little to the imagination:

> *Where insects settle on your meat*
> *Where scorpions crawl beneath your feet*
> *And deadly snakes infest;*
> *Mosquitoes ceaseless teasing sound*
> *And Jackalls direful howls confound*
> *Destroy your balmy rest.*
> *Where naked savages in Rows*
> *Present their offering to your nose.*
> *Wherever you chance to pass*
> *For here the privileges they claim*
> *Freely to squat devoid of shame*
> *And boldly sport an A____.*

Those deadly malarial mosquitoes never went away through the length and breadth of British rule. Lord Elgin, the viceroy between 1894 and 1899, had a favourite joke to fill up conversation gaps at stilted receptions: if they were not careful, mosquitoes would come through the windows and eat up the ladies for their supper. You had to be a viceroy to get away with such insipid humour.

Hicky's problems began when his acid nib began to expose corruption at the top. Commerce and gossip had found a voice. But, to the government's consternation, politics too had found a vehicle. The paper took up issues like atrocious sanitation, pathetic drinking water and corpses left lying on the road. Encouraged by readers and bolstered by notions of an Englishman's liberty, Hicky turned his caustic attention on Warren Hastings.

Hicky placed an 'Editor's Box' on the gate of his home for readers' letters, and many of the stories came from apparently anonymous correspondents. The first allegations against Hastings' conduct in the Rohilla war, which Edmund Burke would make famous through his oratory in Parliament, appeared as a letter to the editor in *Bengal Gazette*. Hicky made effective use of allusion when he could not print an accusation directly. All Calcutta gossiped about Marian Hastings's influence over her husband, and so Hicky published an anecdote about a lady who was so persuasive that she managed to take away the purse from a snatcher and returned home remarkably rich. *Poet's Corner* published a seven-stanza poem which appealed to Marian to correct her husband, in the true spirit of British wives.

Hicky began to call Hastings 'Great Mughal' and 'Grand Turk', epithets for tyrants, reported dissent in the army and extended his salvo towards Sir Elijah Impey, chief justice of the Supreme Court. A letter from a reader alleged that Impey had turned his home into a gaming house, where clients bribed the chief justice by losing money at the table.

Hastings helped competitors to set up a second newspaper, *India Gazette*, in 1780, and then manoeuvred to destroy Hicky by using the instruments of state, including renewal of the annual licence to print and the power of the courts. Hastings and Impey acted in collusion. Hicky reported his own misfortunes:

In January, 1782, was tried before Sir E. Impey an action brought by Warren Hastings, Esq., against J.A. Hicky on the same indictment on which the said Warren Hastings had the said J.A. Hicky tried and found guilty at the Assizes last June, and for which the said J.A. Hicky was sentenced to remain one year in prison and pay a fine of 2,000 rupees to the said Warren Hastings, who has on Wednesday last had damages given him by Sir E. Impey to the very heavy sum of 5,000 sicca rupees, which with the fine of June amount to 7,000 rupees, with a long confinement of one year in jail in this dangerous and scorching climate.[18]

Despite a court order that his machines should be left alone, Hicky's type and printing press were seized on 30 March 1782. Warren Hastings squashed this libertarian fly with a hammer.

The *Bengal Gazette* was too good to last, but it was good enough to be remembered. Hastings's successors kept their grip on the bludgeon although they applied it with a lighter touch. In 1831, the French visitor Victor Jacquemont mentioned in his letter of 26 December that there was 'the greatest sensation' in Calcutta when 'Mr Buckingham, the editor of a Calcutta paper, who was politely requested by an *acting* functionary at Calcutta, to leave the country, the tranquillity of which he endangered by his violent incendiary declarations'.[19] The troublesome editor was expelled to London. Jacquemont made the interesting observation that while the governor-general had the power to arrest even the governor of Madras or Bombay, in practice Europeans were rarely punished—only two or three had been arrested in 30 years. He adds that 6,000 European civilian and military officers and 20,000 troops were virtually above the law, and their behaviour was damaging the mystique of British rule.

Indians watched with careful eyes and spread stories about what they witnessed within the magic circle of bibulous rulers. A high point on the official social calendar each year was the king's birthday on 4 June, which the governor-general celebrated with suitable pomp, hosting a dinner and supper with dancing, at which everyone appeared in full dress despite the extreme heat. The first toast was to the king, the second to the queen and the royal family, the third to the East India Company, the fourth to the Army and Navy, the fifth to the commander-in-chief and the sixth to the success of British arms in India. Each toast was accompanied by a 21-gun salute, from cannon lined up in front of the Court House. The innumerable toasts were bibulous patriotism.

Private parties were more of an uproarious merry-go-round. The *Calcutta Gazette* recorded the proceedings of St Andrew's day on 30 November 1812 at Moore's Rooms, which started at 7 in the evening. The paper writes:

> After dinner a number of toasts suited to the day, succeeded in the following order: The Kirk of Scotland; The Pious Memory of St Andrew; The King, and God bless him; The Prince Regent; The Queen and Royal Family; The Land of Cakes—with three times three; The Land of Beef—with three times three; The Land of Potatoes—with three times three; The Immortal Memory of Wallace—followed by profound silence; The Duke of Clarence, and the Navy—with three times three; The Duke of York, and the Army—with three times three; Lord Minto—with three times three; Sir Samuel Hood, and the Squadron in India—with three times three; Sir George Nugent, and the Army in India, with three times three; Lord Wellington, and the Army of the Peninsula—with three times three, and accompanied with thunders of applause; Our Friends from the Thames and the Shannon, who now honour us with their presence—with three times three, and repeated bursts of applause from the Sons of Tweed—This compliment to the Guests was handsomely acknowledged in a suitable address to the President by a son of Shannon, in the name of all the visitors, which was received with loud applause; May the Rose, the Shamrock, and the Thistle, long flourish and twine in cordial Unison—with three times three, and the loudest applause; Honest and Bonny Lasses; Lady Nugent, and the Ladies of the Settlement, with three times three, and the loudest applauses; All absent Friends; The Beggar's Bennison.[20]

Any Indian reader would find this incomprehensible.

In 1777, William Hickey nearly died during his very first month in Calcutta because of excessive socializing,

> it being the custom in those days to drink freely. Having landed in Bengal with my blood in a ferment from the intemperance

committed on board ship, the evil was not lessened by daily superabundant notations of champagne and claret, the serious effects of which I began to experience by severe headaches and other feverish symptoms.[21]

On 13 November, a day after he had been sworn in as solicitor, attorney and proctor of the Supreme Court, Hickey was rebuked by Justice Hyde for excessive partying. But he could not resist going to Captain William Palmer's 'famous tavern dinner' on 14 November at the Harmonic and collapsed midway through the festivities.

All night he vomited in a delirium. There was a huge blister on his breast the following morning. Doctors gave up hope and generously felt the best form of farewell might be to let the patient drink away his final hours. Hickey writes:

I continued in this hopeless state ten days, the doctors in the morning thinking it impossible for me to survive until night, and the same from night to morning. In this forlorn condition I was allowed to drink as much claret as I pleased, and delicious it was to my palate. Equally grateful and refreshing were oranges which were given me several times a day. In the height of the fever I had frequently been lifted out of bed and put into the warm bath, though without deriving any benefit until the 30th [November] about noon, when just as they were taking me out of the bath a rash suddenly appeared all over my whole body, attended with a profuse perspiration. Dr Campbell, who happened to be present, ordered the attendants instantly to cover me with shawls, observing the crisis was arrived, and an hour would decide the business.[22]

At this last minute he gave Hickey a new medicine, and the lawyer gradually began to recover. It was not until the new year that Hickey was normal again. Everyone put his recovery in the category of a minor miracle.

With a hint of contrition, Hickey offers some useful advice on how to get through a long evening without getting drunk: eat sparingly when plain dishes come around, avoid malt liquor, instruct servants to take away the glass the moment it was put down and if the wine did 'revolt', chew two or three olives without swallowing the pulp. That would get you through half a dozen more glasses by the time the carousel ceased. Anglo-Indian nights did not end early.

Company doctors introduced a placebo as a prescription: they decided that wine was an antidote to fever in the heat of India if taken in moderate proportions, apart from being a substitute for bad drinking water—an elastic caveat which was interpreted variously. India's climate was certainly not conducive to wine production, so Shiraz was imported from Persia. After the 1770s, European madeira, claret and beer became available.

One aggressive importer in 1790 tried to win customers with a belligerent advertisement that was cheekily representative of its time: *Now drink Madeira and in scorn of knaves/ Leave continental wines to conquered slaves*[23]. Sixteen-year-old madeira was priced at about three rupees per bottle; the seven-year version at a bit over two rupees, which was also the cost of port. Gin was deliciously cheap, at one rupee and four annas a bottle. Madeira was drunk before dinner, claret with the meal and both afterwards. Many ladies were as spirited as the gentlemen. The first Indian breweries were set up to meet rising demand.

As to what and how Indians ate, the difference is best reflected in how high caste sepoys of the 27th regiment of the Bengal Army ate: 'Before taking meals they had to purity themselves by bathing, changing their clothes and performing prayers. The meal itself had to be fresh, cooked by persons of the same caste as themselves, and eaten in ritually pure circumstances without risk of pollution. All this could take hours, so that no fast marches were possible for all the martial qualities of the men themselves and their smartness of parade, their potential for effectiveness as a modern fighting force was bound to be a matter of concern...'[24]

Allen, misses the more important point. The sepoys were ready to die for the British that was professional. But they were not ready to eat with the British. This was personal.

The Medicine Men

In 1690, Rev. Thomas Ovington wrote in his journal that the biggest killer was fever, augmented by excessive eating and drinking. He

added, famously, that in Bombay two monsoons were the age of man.
A century later the number of monsoons were still being counted
on the fingers of one hand. According to Pramod Nayar, between
1707 and 1775, 57 per cent of Company employees died of illness in
Bengal, with a peak of 74 per cent between 1747 and 1756.[25] Between
1796 and 1820, the quarter century of regular warfare, only 203, or
one-seventh of the officers of the Bengal Army, retired on a pension.
During an epidemic, life vanished in hours.[26]

Hickey took his first holiday in 1779. Stuck in Madras for four
months on his way back to England, Hickey heard about six old
London acquaintances who had joined the East India Company,
'then the last resource of ruined profligates'. Of them, O'Hara, a
schoolfellow at Westminster and the son of an admiral, had died
young in Madras. Tompkins and Lee, who were in the Guards, fell
to the Indian weather. Williams, a captain of the Light Dragoons,
was killed in action. A sixth, called Bye but known as 'Bouquet Bye'
because of the nosegay he flaunted, disappeared.[27]

The most vulnerable, the men in the military, were perhaps
understandably the most conspicuous consumers. Hickey describes
one riotous dinner at the residence of Colonel Sherbrooke in 1797.
Arthur Wellesley, then in command of the 33rd Regiment, was among
the eight guests. Wellesley's schedule was normally disciplined: as he
wrote in 1798, he rose early and rode before breakfast between 8 and
9, worked till 4 in the hot weather, had dinner at 5 or 6 in the early
evening and then relaxed. At parties, the relaxation was pronounced.
Everyone toasted each other twice at Sherbrooke's home. Hickey had
another half a dozen drinks without hesitation after dinner, but began
to flag on the seventh round, for which he was chided by the host.
It was only after 22 'bumpers in glasses of considerable magnitude'
that they were allowed to refill at their own discretion. The guests
staggered home at 2 in the morning. The hangover headache lasted
48 hours.

At least a third of a junior Army officer's salary went to the mess.
Till the 1850s, each mess kept wheelbarrows to carry away drunken
officers. Winston Churchill, who came to India in 1896 as a lieutenant,
turned to moneylenders to finance his lifestyle and found them fat,
disagreeable and rapacious. The abstemious Bernard Montgomery,
the future hero of the Second World War, was appalled to discover

that non-alcoholic beverages were strictly prohibited in the mess at Peshawar before the First World War. Discussion of politics, religion and profession was taboo at the table, and anyone who made the mistake of mentioning a lady's name paid a fine: he had to buy a round of drinks.

The original name of Calcutta's Park Street was the self-evident Burial Ground Road. Maya Jasanoff writes:

> The vast majority of the 40,000 or so Europeans in India by 1800 were enlisted soldiers with limited chances of returning to Europe: one in four would die in India. A walk among the moss-caked obelisks and mausolea of Calcutta's Park Street Cemetery impresses one with the scale of civilian loss. These monuments are *huge*, as if sheer mass of bricks and mortar could stand in for lives ended too young, 'on distant shores from Kindred dust removed'. They are also insistent. THIS IS LAWRENCE GALL'S TOMB, pronounces one: IT WAS THY FATE, O GALL, TO LIVE LONG ENOUGH TO SEE THYSELF NEGLECTED BY THOSE FRIENDS WHO OUGHT TO HAVE SERVED THEE. TO THEE AND THINE FORTUNE HAS BEEN UNKIND. Another epitaph summarizes the life of Richard Becher, who had actually made it out of Bengal once alive, in 1771, returning to Britain a successful nabob; but he met ruin in London and travelled once more to Calcutta, where UNDER THE PANG OF DISAPPOINTMENT AND THE PRESSURE OF THE CLIMATE, A WORN MIND AND DEBILITATED BODY SUNK TO REST. He died in 1782. What also comes through so poignantly is how many of those who returned to Britain were emotional survivors, too, leaving loved ones beneath Indian soil. Becher had already buried his wife, Charlotte, in the graveyard of St John's Church, who died AFTER SUFFERING WITH PATIENCE A LONG ILLNESS OCCASIONED BY GRIEF FOR THE DEATH OF AN ONLY DAUGHTER.[28]

Disease was lethal. Cholera, typhoid, smallpox, enteric fever, dysentery, tetanus: death swooped relentlessly. There were no old

Anglo-Indians in India. They were either dead or had left for Britain after retirement. Disease did not respect high office. Two members of Hastings's Council, who reached Calcutta in 1774, died within three years: Col. George Monson by September 1776, nine months after his wife Anne, and General Sir John Clavering of boils and dysentery on 30 August 1777, just eight weeks after receiving the Order of the Bath. Philip Francis rages at the shadow of death which hung over the city: 'I hate the thought for my own part, of dying of the spleen, like a rat in a hole.'[29]

David Gilmour tells the story of George Yule, the resident at Hyderabad, who visited the grave of his child every morning, but never returned after his transfer to Simla. The only relic of such grief might be a strand of hair from the infant's corpse.

> Babies often died of typhoid or cholera or other diseases that might have killed them (though less frequently) in Britain. Sometimes they died with their mothers in childbirth. Sometimes their mothers died alone, leaving their fathers with an agonizing decision... Death could happen so abruptly in the Subcontinent that people who woke up with a headache often wondered whether it presaged a fatal illness. 'Everything is sudden in India,' observed one Anglo-Indian, 'the sudden twilights, the sudden death. A man can be talking to you at breakfast and be dead in the afternoon.' Cholera claimed its victims in such a way: when it hit a station, the inhabitants began measuring their lives in hours... The mortality rate in the eighteenth century had been enormous, partly because Anglo-Indians had been so careless of their health: they ate too much and drank too much and went out in the sun without a hat...[30]

Civic hygiene was unknown during the first century and more of Calcutta's existence, but public protests only began with the emergence of the media. Busteed writes:

> From 1780 and onwards correspondents in the newspapers make frequent complaints about the indescribably filthy condition of the streets and roads, which is fully confirmed by

the account of Grandpre in 1790, who tells of the canals and cesspools reeking with putrefying animal matter—the awful stench—the myriads of flies, and the crowds and flocks of animals and birds acting as scavengers.[31]

Mangy dogs played in the tank that provided the city's drinking water. In April 1780, a correspondent saw 'a string of parria [sic] dogs, without an ounce of hair on some of them, and in the last stage of the mange, plunge in and refresh themselves very comfortably in the great Tank'.[32] Tumours carried off people without warning. Chief Justice Impey had 'Cholera Morbus' once or twice a year.

Doctors were a subject of dark humour rather than a source of comfort. Those who commanded high fees, like Bartholomew Hartley, invited scorn for they could 'ruin your fortune to preserve your life':

What are Hartley and Hare to grim Dr Death
Who moves slowly, but perfects the cure?
Their prescriptions may rob me too soon of my breath,
And heighten the pains I endure.[33]

Busteed quotes satirical verse printed in a Calcutta newspaper of 1781:

Some doctors in India would make Plato smile;
If you fracture your skull they pronounce it the bile,
And with terrific phiz and a stare most sagacious,
Give a horse-ball of jalap and pills saponaceous.
A sprain in your toe or an aguish shiver,
The faculty here call a touch of the liver,
And with ointment mercurii and pills calomelli,
They reduce all the bones in your skin to a jelly.
...
If your wife has a headache, let Sangrado but touch her,
And he'll jab in his lancet like any hog butcher;
Tho' in putrid complaints dissolution is rapid,
He'll bleed you to render the serum more vapid.[34]

On 4 May 1786, the *Calcutta Gazette* reported a successful instance of inoculation in the Orphanage Society, as science took another cautious step forward, but there was little effective protection. As was said, people died one day, were buried the next; their furniture was sold on the third day and they were forgotten by the fourth. Mrs Christiana Berg was a singular exception: she died in June 1806 at Samulcottah at the age of 101 years, 5 months and 16 days.[35]

The collective dread was well described by Emily Eden in 1837:

> You cannot imagine in India how the *ranks close in* the very day after death. The most intimate friends never stay at home above two days, and they see everybody again directly... I should have thought grief might have taken just the other line, but I suppose they really could not bear it *alone* here... Dr _____ had more warm friends than anybody, but there was not one who stayed away from the races after his death.[36]

Vessels were washed in watered potassium. As late as in 1882, Annette Beveridge wrote about the danger from wild pigs, wild cats, mad jackals and a cobra nestling in the thatch, apart from 'a plague of pariah dogs going mad in the hot weather' in her letters from Faridpur and Rangpur in eastern Bengal. Annette Beveridge found the tombs of children at the Christian cemetery in Mussoorie heart-rending.[37] There was little time to waste on sentiment in the management of Empire. The Raj moved on. Rudyard Kipling, the laureate of imperial mores, is cool but not callous in *Possibilities*:

> *Ay, lay him 'neath the Simla pine—*
> *A fortnight fully to be missed,*
> *Behold, we lose our fourth at whist,*
> *A chair is vacant where we dine.*
> *His place forgets him; other men*
> *Have bought his ponies, guns, and traps.*
> *His fortune is the Great Perhaps*
> *And that cool rest-house down the glen.*
> *...*
>
> *And, when we leave the heated room,*
> *And when at four the lights expire,*
> *The crew shall gather round the fire*
> *And mock our laughter in the gloom.*

Talk as we talked, and they ere death—
First wanly, dance in ghostly-wise,
With ghosts of tunes for melodies,
And vanish at the morning's breath.[38]

By the high noon of Victorian Raj, the food had improved and appetites had calmed. The midday drink disappeared. The Army became more careful: only madeira before dinner and claret with the standard turkey, ham and curry, a collective noun for a variety of Indian dishes that crept into the vocabulary. On celebratory occasions, the band played songs like 'Kiss my lady', a favourite of women, and 'Money in both pockets', which the men preferred. The priorities were clear. When the colonel departed, drinking gathered momentum. If any officer left early, it was to boos of 'Shabby Fellow' or 'Milk Sop' or 'Cock Tail', but the abandon of bumper-magnitude consumption had waned.

One great leap forward for mankind was the availability of American ice from the 1830s, imported in enormous blocks and priced at two pence a pound, to cool the 'brandy-*pawnee*', or brandy-and-water, which was a favoured colonial drink till it was replaced by whisky in the 1870s. Other creature comforts turned up as well. A 'thermantidote', seven feet high and between four and five feet broad and ten to twelve feet long, blew cool air into a house, worked by two men standing outside. Labour was cheap.

These were partial remedies for India's long and fire-hot summers, which inflicted awkward forms of collateral damage. Eczema was common in the stifling weather and prickly heat inevitable. Rudyard Kipling was in such pain from fever and stomach cramps in the Lahore summer that he began to frequent opium dens, where he made friends with the Pathans who introduced the author to their code of honour, loyalty and revenge.

The only sensible option lay in the mountains, where the British could find relief from the India they had to rule. The climate was perfect, the landscape glorious, but what made the hill station a haven was that it was exclusive. The Indian presence was limited to the usual parade of servants and the occasional glimpse of native royalty.

White Simla

The epitome of the English Indian city was perched at a height of 7,467 feet in the Himalayas, on a ridge called Simla.

Simla came to the attention of Empire-builders in 1817, when two Scottish surveyors mapped the hill states conquered in the Anglo-Nepalese war that ended in 1816. In 1822, Commanding Officer and Political Agent Captain Charles Kennedy, a bachelor, built the first European residence. Five years later, Governor-general Lord Amherst spent two summer months at Kennedy House. Six more homes were constructed for his entourage. The East India Company acquired the territory in 1830, adding villages purchased on barter from the princely states of Patiala and Keonthal. By the time Kennedy retired in 1835, Simla had acquired some fame as a holiday spot and convalescence resort. Kennedy knew the recipe of retirement: he did an hour's work each day after breakfast and then settled down to a bottle of hock and another of champagne.

Governor-general Lord Dalhousie spent the summers between 1849 and 1851 in this Himalayan retreat. Its importance as a sanctuary was recognized in the war of 1857 when the hill chiefs supported the British. Sir John Lawrence described Simla as the strategic centre of British India, an eyrie from which the British could watch both ends of the sweeping arc from the Indus in the west to the Ganges in the east. Lawrence made Simla the summer capital when he became viceroy in 1864. Every year, hundreds of officials and thousands of files migrated 1,200 miles from Calcutta, by train, bullock cart and tonga for the long summer between April and October. Residences were built for the viceroy and the commander-in-chief of the Army. The government ignored the grumbles of those who were not invited, like editors. The only serious peril in Simla was riding off the precipice as you raced along the tracks.

Provinces developed their separate resorts: Madras society went to Ootacamund, Bombay to Mahabaleshwar, Rajasthan to Mount Abu, the Central Provinces to Panchmari, United Provinces to Nainital, Punjab to Muree and Bengal to Darjeeling after a train service started in 1880. Assam's permanent capital was a hill station, Shillong. The Burma administration went up to Maymyo in the Shaan hills. Every Englishman saw some part of this foreign field as forever England.

The houses were English, the weather was English, the evening fires were English and the morals were fluid. Conventions too needed a holiday. Most memsahibs took a long sojourn, while their husbands joined them for a shorter break. 'Grass-widows', wives temporarily separated from husbands working in remote outstations, and divorcees far preferred the mountains to hidebound plains. Most were on the 'sunny side of forty' and more fetching with maturity. Young men who came up were welcome guests at lawn tennis or dinner. The prolific Maud Diver, whose *The Englishwoman in India* was a stentorian effort to protect the reputation of her countrywomen, claimed that the real culprit at Simla was the Army officer on leave. Terms like 'poodle faker' for an officer wooing a married lady entered slang.

Edward Robert Lytton Bulwer-Lytton, first earl of Lytton, who was in India from 1876 to 1880, was the only viceroy suspected of breaking the seventh commandment—he was accused of having affairs with the wives of two ICS subordinates, George Batten and Trevor Plowden, in Simla. Nothing was ever proved, for the hills obeyed an eleventh commandment: discretion.

The viceroy's ball was the high point of the season. One story captures the ambience perfectly. Conrad Corfield, a former assistant private secretary to the viceroy, told Charles Allen:

The Viceroy had his own orchestra which used to play most evenings during dinner, and on one occasion Her Excellency enquired the title of the tune that was being played. No one could remember so an ADC was sent to enquire from the bandmaster. The conversation at the table changed to another subject during his absence. He slipped into his seat on return and waited for an opportunity to impart his information. At the next silence he leapt forward and in a penetrating voice said, 'I Will Remember Your Kisses, Your Excellency, When You Have Forgotten My Name'.[39]

Flirtation was complemented by gossip. *A letter from a lady in Calcutta to her Friend in England*, published in the 12 August 1784 issue of *Calcutta Gazette*, speaks of Simla's compensations once you had dealt with 'pois'nous insects out of number':

And yet, dear Girl! This place has charms
Such as my sprightly bosom warms!
No place, where at a bolder rate,
We females bear our sovereign state.
Beauty ne'er points its arms in vain,
Each glance subdues some melting swain.[40]

The beauty with a sprightly bosom never lost sight of practical requirements. While the swain's age, looks and intelligence mattered, she also wanted to know if in 'some strange place that ends with *pore*' he was making his lakhs and adding more'.[41] Everyone enjoyed a little scandal with their tea; while charming women recounted how, in turn, they had lost their complexions, manners and morals.

Iris Portal, a Simla enthusiast, thought that flirtation was inevitable when wives were bored, and husbands were

> fairly broad-minded and wouldn't really expect their wives to go up and live in monastic seclusion... It's difficult to convey how enormously romantic the atmosphere was in Simla, the warm starlit nights and bright, huge moon, those towering hills and mountains stretching away, silence and strange exotic smells...[42]

The 'Black Hearts', a group of bachelors who could afford to order expensive trinkets from Paris as prizes for party games, lit up the tennis court of Simla's United Services Club with coloured lights and special decorations for their gala dinner. The lights were discreet. In the shadows were spots called *kala jugga* (dark place), set aside for couples who wanted privacy.

The 'Gloom Club' held a 'wake'. A chief mourner sent invitations lined in black, and the dance card was shaped like a coffin decorated with skull and crossbones—every guest had to wear a costume suggested by the host. This last was not as innocent as it might seem. There was nothing mournful about The Gloom Club Dance Party of 1933, judging by the illustration in Vernede's *British Life in India*. Five of the young ladies in the picture have bare bosoms; two have stripped down to panties; one of them, with a martini in hand, is talking to an elderly man in a chair with nothing on but his shoes.

Others are in elegant evening dress; a few are masked. The only Indian present is a prince with a maharaja moustache and coat. He holds a brandy goblet and stares beadily at the company.

Excerpts from the poem accompanying the illustration, composed by the modest Mr Anonymous, tell a winsome story:

When Britons first took to the hills,
Preferring to the heat the chills
Of Nainital or Simla's thrills,
(Despite the cost of double bills)
Some genius, by design or chance,
Imported from the land of France
A very gay extravagance—
To wit—the famous Gloom Club Dance,
A very Fancy Dress affair,
Demanding nerve and also flair
For just how far 'twas safe to dare
In what the dancers chose to wear.
...
For every age there is a dress,
From Boadicea to Good Queen Bess,
From burka to a bead or less—
For men—well you would have to guess.
Two Adams and as many Eves
Dance to a lullaby of the leaves,
While here and there a dusky Jeeves
Ignores impassively what he perceives.
While svelte Sumerian ladies stare
With envy at Godiva's hair,
Their seniors' indignant glare,
For back and sides go bare, go bare.
...
Young Joan of Arc (that's her disguise)
Lisps sweetly and divinely sighs;
She may not win, but, if you're wise,
Be careful of those bedroom eyes.
And when the seniors have gone,
The fun goes on until the dawn,

With half the fancy dresses torn,
And some are drunk, while one forlorn
Seeks hopefully a kala jagah
And some young subaltern to hug her...[43]

Sir J.A. Thorne of the ICS remembered Simla with mock-regret:

It turned to a kill, I intended a quarrel.
Flirtatious young miss! (Yet it turned to a kiss.)
She pouted—and this robs my verse of a moral.
It turned to a kiss; I intended a quarrel!

Gossip was gospel; but to permit ordinary Indians into such banter
was an invitation to ruin. As George Orwell, who served in Burma,
has remarked, 'You cannot be memorably funny without at some
point raising topics which the rich, the powerful and the complacent
would prefer to see left alone.' The Raj, which had successfully defied
Indian rage, knew that it was unlikely to survive Indian ridicule.

The humourless imperialist Lord Curzon was the only viceroy
who abhorred Simla. That is to Simla's credit.

Simla's reputation was etched into public consciousness by
Rudyard Kipling's characters like Mrs Hauksbee. *Lessons for Mrs
Hauksbee: Tales of Passion, Intrigue and Scandal* comprises stories of
love, thwarted, sidestepped or fulfilled. Romance is filtered through a
beady eye: 'Then said Mrs Hauksbee to me—she looked a trifle faded
and jaded in the lamplight—"take my word for it, the silliest woman
can manage a clever man; but it needs a very clever woman to manage
a fool."'[44]

Kipling's fiction is the collective autobiography of the British Raj
at the apex of its self-confidence. A passage such as this from *Thrown
Away* captures the essence of two centuries:

Now India is a place beyond all others where one must not take
things too seriously—the mid-day sun always excepted. Too
much work and too much energy kill a man just as effectively
as too much assorted vice or too much drink. Flirtation does
not matter, because everyone is being transferred, and either
you or she leave the station and never return. Good work

does not matter, because a man is judged by his worst output, and another man takes all the credit of his best as a rule. Bad work does not matter, because other men do worse, and incompetents hang on longer in India than anywhere else. Amusements do not matter, because you must repeat them as soon as you have accomplished them once, and most amusements only mean trying to win another person's money. Sickness does not matter, because it's all in the day's work, and if you die, another man takes over your place and your office in the eight hours between your death and burial. Nothing matters except Home-furlough and acting allowances, and these only because they are scarce. It is a slack country, where all men work with imperfect instruments; and the wisest thing is to escape as soon as ever you can to some place where amusement is amusement and a reputation worth having.[45]

There was far more to Kipling than the single dimension of imperialism. He was never as racist as most of his contemporary civil or military officers or the upgraded 'Boxwallahs' who haunted the clubs. He saw more than one side of a story and wrote in marvellously evocative language. The human heart and foible were more resilient in his tales than prejudice and the gentle humour more poignant than anything painted with the stilted brush of arrogance. When Kipling meets India, we hear the enchanting echoes of two worlds speaking to each other from a distance, often across a vale of confusion and bias and sometimes with recognition and emotion, but always in touch.

Georgie Porgie is a bitter depiction of British betrayal. The nursery-rhyme title is awkward—Georgie kissed a Burmese girl and made her cry—but that should not undermine its genuine pathos.

Georgie Porgie buys the pretty daughter of a headman in Burma for ₹ 500, renames her Georgina, lives with her and then abandons her before he disappears to London on leave. Georgie marries an English girl and returns to the subcontinent; he is posted to a remote place called Sutrain. Burma is out of sight, out of mind and out of his life. But Georgina has not abandoned Georgie. She takes a steamer to India and painstakingly tracks Georgie along the colonial grapevine to a lonely hillside. As she nears his home, she sees him on the veranda with his new bride. Georgine stops, turns back and runs away.

'What is the noise down there?' asks Georgie's bride.

'Oh,' says Georgie Porgie, 'I suppose some brute of a hillman has been beating his wife.'

'But,' ends the story, 'it was Georgina crying, all by herself, down the hillside, among the stones of the water-course where the washermen wash the clothes.'[46]

A second short story is about Ameera and her 'king', the Englishman John Holden. They marry by Muslim rites in which John has given the ritual dower to his mother-in-law. Ameera and John love their first child even more than they love each other. Then the tragedies of India—famine, fever, cholera—intervene. The baby dies of fever. The rains fail. Famine drives families away, but John must remain at his post. Ameera refuses to leave the pestilent land when her mother decides to shift to some safer place. 'My lord and my love,' says Ameera, 'let there be no more foolish talk of going away. Where thou art, I am. It is enough.' Holden is suddenly despatched on an emergency mission. While he is away, cholera strikes. Holden gallops back on hearing the news. Ameera 'made no sign when Holden entered, because the human soul is a very lonely thing and, when it is getting ready to go away, hides itself in a misty borderland where the living may not follow. The black cholera does its work quietly and without explanation.' Ameera makes John promise, before she dies, that he will preserve nothing of hers, not even a strand of hair, for the Englishwoman he marries next will make him burn that strand. A bereaved Holden gives all their possessions away. The one thing he keeps is their bed.[47]

Two famous lines from Kipling's *The Ballad of East and West*, published in 1889, are quoted too often as the obituary of incompatible civilizations:

> *Oh, East is East, and West is West,*
>   *and never the twain shall meet,*
> *Till Earth and Sky stand presently at*
>   *God's great Judgement Seat.*

But Kipling is describing the brotherhood between the son of Kamal, a tribal chief of the Frontier, and the son of a British colonel who commands a troop of the Guides Cavalry. Kamal steals the colonel's prize mare. The colonel's son sets off in pursuit, despite being warned of the dangers. He finds Kamal, fires his pistol and misses. He then challenges Kamal's son to a riding contest, and the two ride till dawn, when the Britisher's horse stumbles while crossing a river. He is saved from the current by Kamal.

The Pathan chief claims that the young Englishman is alive only at his mercy. The colonel's son responds that Kamal is afraid of British reprisals. As a compromise, he offers to gift the disputed mare to Kamal, but the mare trots towards the colonel's son and nuzzles him. Kamal returns the horse. The British youth gives his pistol to Kamal, saying that he had lost his first pistol to a foe, but he is giving his second pistol to a friend. Kamal, moved, asks his son to accompany the colonel's son to the British fort. They go as blood brothers.

> *They have looked each other between the eyes,*
>   *and there they found no fault,*
> *They have taken the Oath of the Brother-in-Blood*
>   *on leavened bread and salt;*
> *They have taken the Oath of the Brother-in-Blood*
>   *on fire and fresh-cut sod,*
> *On the hilt and the haft of the Khyber knife,*
>   *and the Wondrous Names of God.*
> *…*
>
> *But there is neither East nor West,*
>   *Border, not Breed, nor Birth,*
> *When two strong men stand face to face,*
>   *tho' they come from the ends of the earth!*

But they never stood face to face in Simla.

8

Service with a Wile

The most unusual demand for an Indian slave was made by the profligate British monarch Charles II; he asked the East India Company to send him dwarves, both men and women, for his mistress the Duchess of Portsmouth. In 1683, the directors wrote to their governors in Surat and Madras:

> His Majesty hath required of us to send to India to provide him one male and two female blacks, but they must be dwarfs, and of the least size you can procure; the male to be about 17 years of age and the female about 14. We would have you, next to their littleness, to choose as may have the best features, and to send them home upon any of our ships, giving the commander great charge to take care of their accommodation, and in particular of the female, that she be in no way abused in the voyage by any of the seamen.[1]

Fortunately for the dwarves, Charles II died in 1685. The Company withdrew the order.

According to Roy Moxham:

> Slaves were commonplace in Madras. Not only were they kept by Company employees, but the Company itself purchased them for its own use. There was also a thriving export business. The accounts show that in the month of September 1687 no fewer than 665 slaves were exported.[2]

The East India Company, like others of its ilk, conducted a side-line in slavery while it was legal. The scale of slavery was lower than in

Africa because India had strong governments all through the 17th century who ensured, through diplomacy and war, that Europeans knew their place as traders on the fringe of Empire.

When the Mughal was overlord, an English guest deferred to local dress and etiquette. Edward Terry, the chaplain of the first English mission to a Mughal court in 1616, recalls the discomfort he felt sitting cross-legged on the floor during a sumptuous dinner, but sit with crossed legs he did. Spear writes:

> The early settlers wore 'banyan coats' and 'Moorsmen's trousers' as a matter of course in their houses, and some occasionally wore them in public. In 1686 the writers of Masulipatam were expressly forbidden to lounge on parade on Sundays in loose coats, but as late as 1738 a Council meeting was held in Calcutta in loose coats with hookahs and drinks in attendance.[3]

Indian dress made obvious sense in Indian weather.

If some English visitors felt superior, as Dr Fryer did, they kept their views confined to books meant for British readers. Fryer was forthright in London: 'The Moguls Feed high, Entertain much, and Whore not a little.'[4] As they gained confidence with time, Company merchants in Surat were not above a little mischief when it was their turn to entertain. Percival Spear, quoting the chaplain Rev. Ovington, writes:

> The Moghul magnates were the most welcome guests with their common hunting and drinking tastes; one [Mughal] Governor after his first visit particularly asked to be given some of the excellent roast kid then provided, upon which the English President sent out for the fattest pigs which could be found, to the great satisfaction of the Governor on his next visit.[5]

Spear notes how behaviour altered as the balance tilted:

> When the position of the East India Company changed towards the middle of the century, the character of racial

relations changed also. On the one hand the old merchants occupied new positions, and on the other the supply of Englishmen greatly increased, first as soldiers and then as administrators and traders. The result was to set in motion a double current, of increasing contact and knowledge of Indian life, and of increasing contempt for everything Indian as irrational, superstitious, barbaric and typical of an inferior civilization.[6]

At least some Englishmen thought a transition to a Western dress code ridiculous. Hugh Boyd wrote in *The Indian Observer* of 10 December 1793 that when he came to India in 1771, 'the young Writer and old senior merchant agreed in allowing themselves every decent chance of coolness and refreshment'. Two decades later he found that

> fashion in everything bears sovereign sway, and cloth coats, with hair dressed *a la mode d'Europe,* are now in vogue, the long buckskin meets the short boot, whilst the strings of the one and the straps of the other add not less weight than ornaments to the knees and ankles. Even the gingham waistcoats, which, stripped or plain, have so long stood their ground must, I hear, ultimately give way to the stronger Kerseymere, of which I have seen complete suits worn in the hottest weather. No longer a stock or anything like a cravat, but a monstrous roll of stuffed muslin surrounds the neck...[7]

The Mughal knee-length kurta and pyjama became the uniform of servants: *khansama, bawarchi, khidmatgar, chaprasi, chowkidar* and peon. Those further down the hierarchy, like the syce, *masalchi, mehtar, bheeshti, dhobi, darzi* and *malee* were left to their own devices, while the English masters flaunted tailored trousers and wigs during the day and reserved pyjamas for the night. *Hobson-Jobson* notes that when the pyjama found its way to the order books of tailors on Jermyn Street in 19th-century London, a few had feet sewn on to them. One tailor, asked why, replied: 'I believe, Sir, it is because of the White Ants!'[8]

Before there were servants, there were slaves. Even clergymen, most of whom were genteel parsons sent to cure the Indian soul of heathen ailments, were not immune to behaving like slave-lords. In Madras, a certain Rev. St J. Browne, who hit and kicked his servant till he fell 20 feet from a terrace, prevented others from saving the victim with a terse 'Let him go to hell'. The servant died. The priest was later removed from the parish.[9]

Calcutta newspapers published frequent advertisements such as this one in 1781:

To be Sold by Private Sale

Two Coffree boys, who play remarkably well on the French horn, about eighteen years of age: belonging to a Portuguese Paddrie lately deceased. For particulars, enquire of the Vicar of the Portuguese Church.[10]

'Coffree' meant black Africans; while 'Paddrie' was a variation of 'padre'.

Calcutta's Superintendent of Police C.S. Playdell has an entry in the charge sheet for 1778: 'A slave girl of Mr Anderson, Piggy, having run away from her master—*Order,* five strokes with a rattan and she be sent to her master.' The rattan cane, fashioned from the stem of a palm, bit sharply into the flesh. Any attempt by a slave to escape was a cognizable offence. A second girl, Peketase, owned by Birnarold Pinto, was caned five times. A third, Sarah, got 15 'rattans' for running away more than once.

Sumanta Banerjee writes:

[Playdell's chargesheet] is an important historical document which goes beyond the issue of slavery in 18th century Calcutta. The list of victims that he drew up illustrates how minor offences and innocuous acts of disobedience by Indian servants were often elevated to the status of serious crime by the Company's officials. Most of the accused in the twenty-odd cases listed in the chargesheet were Indian servants charged with non-compliance with orders, or escaping from their employers, or petty thefts. Thus we hear of one Captain Scott complaining against Banybub for not repairing his carriage, as a result of which the offender was punished by being thrashed ten times with slippers. Beating someone with shoes or slippers—termed in Bengali, respectively, as *jutomaro* and *chotimara*—had been traditionally regarded as the worst form of humiliation inflicted on anyone in Bengali society.[11]

Judges were more complicit than the police. Banerjee quotes a letter from Miller, Calcutta's police superintendent in 1793, saying that the government wanted to free slaves who had become self-sufficient but judges 'seldom declare a slave free, unless there be proofs of very severe ill-treatment; and I learn that a slave who was sometime ago declared free in the Cutcherry of Police was restored to her mistress by Order of the sitting judge'.[12]

Indian gangs collaborated in the slave trade, preying upon the weakest, particularly women from impoverished tribes. Col Broughton was genuinely distressed, as he wrote in his letter of 13 May 1809, when he learnt that girls were being auctioned in the bazaar while he was travelling with a Maratha camp:

> I mentioned to you in my last letter that the Meenas were in the habit of carrying off children and selling the girls... The poor creatures are from eight to ten years of age, and appear to feel keenly the indignities to which they are exposed. One of my own servants, whom curiosity led to see them, told me that their eyes were swollen with weeping, and that they presented altogether a most distressing spectacle.[13]

Broughton's servants wanted to buy four girls but thought that the asking price of ₹ 300 was too high, after which the girls were taken to the bazaar to be sold.

Portuguese traffickers plundered in the name of God. They converted their victims to Christianity and gave the men a black hat, trousers and stockings before selling them to affluent Europeans. The East India Company charged a duty of four annas on each transaction at registered depots in Baghbazar, Nimtala and Chitpur. Newspapers made money from advertisements: in 1781, the *Calcutta Gazette* offered a slave with the skills of a butler for 400 *sicca* rupees (Company currency, as distinct from the Mughal coin).

J.H. Valentin Dubois published a notice in the same paper on 2 December 1784 promising a reward of 100 'Sicca Rupees' to 'any black man' who could apprehend and deliver

Two slave boys (with the letters V.D. marked on each of their right arms, above the elbow, named Sam and Tom, about eleven years of age, and exactly of a size) run away, with a great quantity of plate, etc. This is to request, if they offer their service to any Gentlemen, they will be so kind as to examine their arms, keep them confined, and inform the owner.[14]

Between a permissive law, a biased judiciary and helpless victims, the grey difference between slave and servant was fudged in favour of the owner-employer even after slavery became socially reprehensible and then legally difficult. The British *nouveau riche,* imitating the old Indian gentry, maintained a large retinue of servants as evidence of their new status. The ruling dictum of India's ebbing aristocracy was summed up in a Hindi saying: *Thoda khana, par Banaras mein rahna* (Eat less, but live in Benares; or, live well).

It cost the British less to live in luxury. The Company kept servants' wages artificially depressed for more than a century. In 1759, two years after Clive's victory at Plassey, the Court of Zamindary decreed that anyone who paid more than the fixed rate would lose official protection, and servants who left without stipulated notice would be punished severely. The salary of a *khansama,* equivalent to a butler, was fixed at five rupees a month; a sweeper got three and a maidservant two. The *ayah,* whose childcare was invaluable, was among the better paid.

Indians were service-providers for a surging imperial temperament. William Mackintosh describes a day in the life of the sahib in the 1770s:

About the hour of seven in the morning, his *durvan* [doorkeeper] opens the gate, and the *viranda* [veranda] is free to his *circars, peons, harcarras* [messengers], *chubdars* [constables], *huccabardars* [those who prepare the hubble-bubble] and *consumas* [*khansamas,* or stewards], writers and solicitors [in the sense of those who come with requests]. The head-bearer and *jemmadar* enter the hall, and his bedroom at eight o'clock. A lady quits his side, and is conducted by a private staircase either to her own apartment, or out of the yard. The moment the master throws his legs out of bed, the whole posse in waiting rush into his room, each making three *salaams* [salutations; thrice indicates regal pomp], by bending the body and head very low, and touching the forehead with the inside of the fingers, and the floor with solicitors of his favour and protection. He condescends, perhaps, to nod or cast an eye towards the solicitors of his favour and protection. In about half an hour after undoing and taking off his long drawers, a clean shirt, breeches, stockings, and slippers are put upon his body, thighs, legs and feet, without any great exertion on his own part that if he were a statue. The barber enters, shaves him, cuts his nails, and cleans his ears. The *chillumjee* [for the *hookah*] and ewer are brought by a servant whose duty it is, who pours water upon his hands and face, and presents a towel. The superior then walks in state to his breakfast parlour in his waistcoat; is seated; the *consumah* makes and pours out his tea, and presents him with a plate of bread or toast. The hair-dresser comes behind, and begins his operation, while the *houccabardar* softly slips the upper end of the snake or tube of the *hucca* into his hand; while the hair-dresser is doing his duty, the gentleman is eating, sipping and smoking by turns...[15]

As the sahib retired to his bedroom at night, a woman was sent to 'amuse' him till she 'quit his side' in the morning.

When he left for England after a quarter century, Hickey settled accounts with 63 servants: nine valets, eight *chobdars* or guards, eight waiters, eight grooms for horses, two cooks, two bakers, one hairdresser, a wig-barber, a hookah-bearer, three grasscutters, a coachman et al. His favourite employee was 'Chaund', who once took along three ladies of leisure, one for the captain and two for himself, on a river trip along the Hooghly to Fulta. That, at least, is Hickey's sanitised version. It was common for bachelors to keep a trusted 'boy' who acted as procurer.

An intrepid bachelor, Thomas Twining, kept a staff of 44, including 20 boatmen, although he was quite convinced that the bullock cart was the best mode of transport. Most found the palanquin convenient, although newcomers could get distressed at the moans of carriers during the journey. Hickey explains that their moans 'did not indicate fatigue, and that the front bearer always noticed the sort of road they were passing over, pointing out any impediments, as "Here's a hole", "Here's a puddle of water", "Here's long grass", "Here's a parcel of bricks", &c'. The moans were a form of communication.[16]

Since the sahib insisted on his ablutions indoors, the bathroom required attendants. There was a zinc or galvanized iron bathtub, a large enamel or tin mug and an earthenware jar of cold water. The commode was wooden. The sweeper, who did the eventual cleaning, took care to announce his presence outside the bathroom with a light cough. Water was brought by the *bhishti* from the nearest well and boiled before drinking.

According to Lord Beveridge's letters and journals, in 1774 Sir Philip Francis and his brother-in-law Alexander Mackrabie 'had 110 servants to wait on a family of four people. Macrobie [sic] found both their number and their behaviour monstrous; he attributed to the servants every bad quality except drunkenness and insolence'. Mackrabie summed up his woes: 'To superintend this tribe of devils and their separate departments we have a monstrous collection of banyans chief and subordinate with their trains of clerks, who fill a large room and are constantly employed in controlling or rather conniving at one another's accounts.'[17] To place these numbers in perspective, a contemporary British officer in the Malay territories made do with three or four servants, including a Chinese cook and a Tamil butler.

If the servants made 'money besides wages', as Mackrabie alleged, they had ample justification. H.E. Busteed acknowledges in *Echoes from Old Calcutta* that average wages between 1760 and 1860 were 'pretty much the same'. He then accuses servants of filching, ignoring the reasons why they indulged in petty theft. Having lost the war of political power, Indians seemed to seek satisfaction in the skirmishes of household expenses. Gilmour writes:

When Georgina McRobert discovered that the sweeper was stealing her hens' eggs and then selling them to the cook, who afterwards sold them to his mistress as eggs from the bazaar, she decided to 'grin and bear it' because the servants 'have some good qualities after all'.[18]

Servants had no trade union to fight for their rights and so found surreptitious ways of supplementing their income. Mrs Eliza Fay wrote in her letters to England in 1780 that she was

> surrounded by a set of thieves. In England if servants are dishonest we punish them, or turn them away in disgrace... but these wretches have no sense of shame. My Khansama brought in a charge of a gallon of milk and thirteen eggs for making scarcely a pint and half of custard; this was so barefaced a cheat...[19]

Mrs Fay did not mention that servants' salaries in Calcutta were far lower than in London.

Such rights to comfort became part of Army life as well. A British captain on the Mysore campaign in the 1790s was accompanied by a steward, cook, valet, groom, assistant groom, barber, washerman and around 15 'coolies' to carry wine, brandy, tea, goats, poultry and other pleasantries required on a long march. The higher you rose, the grander it got. Sir Harry Fane, the commander-in-chief of the Army in the 1830s, had six waiters behind his chair at dinner while his daughter had three.[20]

An illustration done by William Taylor around 1840 shows a young British civilian at his morning toilette. A middle-aged barber is brushing his hair from behind the chair; a heavily bearded *khansama* holds a cup of tea; a pigtailed servant shows a mirror; a squatting menial presses the master's left leg; a glum boy fans the lord with a *punkah*.[21]

The wig-barber was not to be confused with the hairdresser, while the *hookaburdar* had to keep the silver of the hubble-bubble polished. For some now-unknown reason, it was considered an insult to step over another person's hookah tube at a dinner party. The choicest tobacco was sought, particularly the sweet-scented Persian laced with herbs, sugar and spice. Ladies began to smoke the hubble-bubble, the coils snaking across their waists, and it signalled intention if a lady offered a gentleman a puff of her hookah. It was only after the 1850s that the hookah gave way to the cheroot or the 'seegar'.

Emily Eden was astonished to discover in her brother Lord Auckland's Calcutta palace that five servants would 'glide' behind her when she moved from one room to another, and a sentry presented arms whenever she went to her bedroom to fetch a handkerchief. Four decades later, the Viceroy Lord Lytton had some 300 servants, including 100 cooks, many so magnificently attired that they could be, and were, mistaken for visiting Indian royalty.

Life was good for the fortunate, and glory awaited those who offered a splendid aperitif before dinner. John Collins (gin and lemon squash) and Billy Williams (ginger wine and lemon squash) are believed to have originated in British India. R.G. Gordon, of the ICS, became poetic about the gentle lady who offered her heart to anyone who could mix a great new cocktail:

> *I see a maid with flashing eyes*
> *Who, to a crowd of swains demented,*
> *Proclaimed her heart and hand the prize*
> *Of him who some new drink invented.*
> *Art in simplicity we find,*
> *And so the gentle maid bestowed her*
> *Sweet self on him whose taste combined*
> *Bitters, a lime and whisky soda.*[22]

The Indian *abdar* (server of drinks), dressed in a turban, long cotton coat and pyjamas, a red slanted slash from shoulder to waist, served these cocktails without the chance or even the wish to taste them.

Raw Power

The 19th century was one of political and social turbulence in Europe, but reform lost its pace on its way to its colonies. The ban on slavery ended one unmitigated evil, but mutations like 'indentured labour' were invented to fill the demand for a cheap workforce in far-flung plantation economies, with famine-refugees from India providing the bulk of the supply. There was much 'solemn discussion' in the drawing rooms of Calcutta and Madras on how far it was permissible, or indeed advisable, to flog one's domestic staff. Racism added its own degree of virulence. Since the perpetrators were confident that the law was on their side, brutality continued.

The famous war correspondent Sir William Russell recorded what he witnessed in 'Cawnpore' (Kanpur) on 26 February 1859:

As I was returning to the [Cawnpore] Hotel, I saw another exemplification of the mischiefs which are to be dreaded from a large infusion of Europeans into India… If Europeans are not restrained by education and humanity from giving vent to their angry passions, there is little chance of their being punished for anything short of murder—and of murder it has been oftentimes difficult to procure the conviction of Europeans at the hands of their countrymen. This is what happened. There were a number of coolies sitting idly under the shadow of a wall: suddenly there came upon them, with a bound and a roar, a great British lion—his eyes flashing fire, a tawny mane of long locks floating from under his pith helmet, and a huge stick in his fist—a veritable Thor in his anger. He rushed among the coolies, and they went down like grass, maimed and bleeding. I shouted out of the *gharry*, 'Good Heavens, stop! Why, you'll kill those men!' (One of them was holding up his arm, as if it were broken.) A furious growl, 'What the _____ business have you to interfere? It's no affair of yours.' 'Oh yes, sir, but it is. I am not going to be accessory to murder. See how you have maimed that man! You know they dared not raise a finger against you.' 'Well; but these lazy scoundrels are engaged to do our work, and they sneak off whenever they can, and how can I look after them!' Now I believe, from what I heard, these cases occur up-country frequently; and in one place there has been a sort of mutiny and murder among railway labourers; and in fact, the authorities have issued injunctions to the railway subordinates to be cautious how they commit excesses and violence among their labourers, and warn them they will be punished.[23]

Russell's conscience was repeatedly troubled, as when he saw two 'native servants, covered with plaisters [sic] and bandages, and bloody, who were lying on their *charpoys,* moaning'. They had been 'licked' by their master—'licking' was the colloquial term for a harsh beating. Russell described this as 'a savage, beastly, and degrading custom'. He had heard this practice being defended, and remarked that 'no man of feeling, education or goodness of heart can vindicate or practise it'. The master who had thus punished 'his delinquent domestics, sat sulky and sullen, and, I hope, ashamed of his violence, at the table; but he had no fears of any pains or penalties of the law'. British law protected British crimes.[24]

In Agra, Russell was overawed by the Taj Mahal, like any other visitor: 'It is wrong to call it a dream in marble; it is a thought—an idea—a conception of tenderness—a sigh, as it were, of eternal devotion and heroic love, caught and imbued with such immortality as the earth can give.' His companion, 'who loves not India or her races' but who possessed the necessary objectivity, made a startling point: 'If the people of this land really built the Taj, the sooner we English leave the country the better. We have no business to live here and be their masters'.[25]

Russell once asked an English officer what Indians thought of their English rulers. '*They?*' replied the officer, 'Why, they don't think anything about us at all. They look upon us as out-of-the-way inscrutable beings, whom it would be quite useless to perplex their heads about, and they're too well accustomed to this sort of thing to wonder at it.' The indifference was largely reciprocated. Hilton Brown quotes an English lady from Madras who was asked what she had seen of the country and the 'natives' since her arrival in India. 'Oh, nothing!' she said. 'Thank goodness, I know nothing at all about them, nor I don't wish to: really I think the less one sees and knows of them the better!' Brown wonders how much this type of 'English lady' cost the Raj and mentions that she was still there in force till 1947.[26]

Russell was distressed by the 'deep dislike' which the British felt for India 'and its inhabitants, which is evinced by a constant cry for "Home!"'.[27] Few sahibs disliked India more than Sir John Lawrence, the architect of the British victory in 1857. To be fair, he was not popular with anyone. The civil servant John Beames, who came to India in 1858, writes:

The signal services rendered by this great man have caused him to be regarded as a sort of popular hero, and it will

seem almost blasphemy to say a word against him. But it is
undeniably true that by those who served under him, he was
intensely disliked. He was a rough, coarse man; in appearance
more like a 'navvy' than a gentleman.[28]

Indians had good reason to despise him. Dennis Kincaid describes
how he regularly thrashed Indian servants for no apparent reason
outside a Lahore church, as if inspired by the sermon to be cruel:

> A number of servants gathered round the porch to watch
> him mount his pony. He swore at them in duty bound – for
> did not every Anglo-Indian do so? Was it not a pleasure in
> Lahore to watch John Lawrence emerge from morning prayer
> at the new church and, refreshed by his devotions, fall with
> furious blows upon the servants awaiting him at the church
> door? And then he trotted down the straight wide roads of
> the station, the grey dust rising under the horse's roofs, past
> dozens of whitewashed bungalows, looking sadly alike...[29]

The church priest was unperturbed. Kincaid mentions that this padre
kept the service short for he had a servant waiting in the vestry with
a cigar and a glass of beer.

Being beaten with 'furious blows' was the predestined fate of the
'blackey', as even brown or pale-skin Indians were called. Attitudes
began to improve only after liberals like Henry Beveridge entered the
civil service in 1857 at the age of 21; he would retire after 35 years.
He and his second wife, Annette, would become well-known for
their translation of Persian texts into English. They were benevolent
towards their domestic staff of 39, but salaries were still low. The
domestic payroll was an easily affordable ₹ 250 a month since Henry's
salary was ₹ 1,800. Ali Jan the *khansamah* earned ₹ 12; 'Hurree',
or Bisheswar, the major domo, Ramyad the bearer and Bogmonia
the *ayah* got ₹ 10 each. The Beveridges treated them like family.
Annette could become motherly, scolding them for eating opium and
threatening to cut their pay if they persisted.

Beveridge (later, Lord) writes that Hurree would eat only if
Annette Beveridge brought him food when he fell ill because he
trusted her:

You know that Hindus do not eat beef nor drink wine but when poor Hurree seemed likely to die we said he must take beef soup and drink and that we would give his brahmin priest money to forgive him. He does not know what he is getting but of course the other servants know and by-and-by when he is better, they will not eat with him, because he will have lost caste by eating our English food. It is better for him to eat it and die, is it not? I think he is ready to take anything I will give him. Poor fellow! He looks at me with such pitiful eyes when I go to see him.[30]

Food was, literally, a touchy issue. Boatmen on the river route from Calcutta to Benares preferred to throw away their food and break their pots if by any chance an English passenger stepped into their midst as they cooked their meals on the bank.

Edward Aitken, a founding member of the Bombay Natural History Society who served in the same years as Beveridge, hated his servants with a visceral passion. He described the lamp-handler as a greedy dogsbody in his autobiography *Behind the Bungalow*, which appeared in 1889:

The Mussaul's name is Mukkun, which means butter, and of this commodity I believe he absorbs as much as he can honestly or dishonestly come by. How else does the surface of him acquire that glossy oleaginous appearance, as if he would take fire easily and burn well?[31]

Mukkun was infuriating even when drying dishes (with the damask table napkin!) or sharpening knives: 'Hour after hour the squeaky, squeaky, squeaky sound of the board plays upon your nerves, not the nerves of the ear, but the nerves of the mind, for there is more in it than the ear can convey.'[32]

The *dhobie* (washerman) was a 'jubilant' butcher of clothes:

Destruction is so much easier than construction and so much more rapid and abundant in its physical results that the devastator feels a jubilant joy in his work. The *dhobie*, dashing your cambric and fine linen against the stones,

shattering a button, fraying a hem or rending a seam at every
stroke, feels a triumphant contempt for the miserable creature
whose plodding needle and thread put the garment together.
This feeling is the germ from which the *dhobie* has grown.
Day after day he has stood before that great black stone and
wreaked his rage upon shirt and trouser and coat and trouser
and shirt. Then he has wrung them as if he were wringing the
necks of poultry, and fixed them on his drying line with thorns
and spikes, and finally he has taken the battered garments
to his torture chamber and ploughed them with his iron,
longwise and crosswise and slantwise, and dropped glowing
cinders on their tenderest places. Son has followed father
through countless generations in cultivating this passion for
destruction, until it has become a monstrous growth which we
see and shudder at in the *dhobie*. He is not tolerable. Submit
to him we must, since resistance is futile; but his craven spirit
makes submission difficult and resignation impossible. If he
had the soul of the conqueror, if he wasted you like Attila, if
he flung his iron into the clothes-basket, and cried *Voe victis,*
then a feeling of respect would soften the bitterness of the
conquered; but he conceals his ravages like the white ant, and
you are betrayed in your hour of need.[33]

Aitken's fury extended to the *dirzee*, or tailor, and his language, while
thinly varnished with humour, dipped effortlessly into rank racism.
Hurree (Hari) was a 'little human animal', with *pan supare* (betel
leaf and nut) 'temporarily stowed away under that swelling in the left
cheek, where the fierce black patch of whisker grows. The survival of
a partial cheek pouch in some branches of the human race is a point
that escaped Darwin'.[34] Some militant victims of the *dhobi* advocated
aggression, suggesting that the only way to get even was to raid the
dhobi's hut and 'ruthlessly confiscate any clothes in process of being
washed or ironed, which do not belong to you'.[35]

Since the *dhobi* or the *dirzee* never published a memoir, we do
not know their version. But consider a telling fact: Indians who got
their refined cotton washed and ironed by the same *dhobi* rarely
had complaints. The *dhobi* turned into Attila the Hun only with his
Western clients.

By the time the long twilight of the Raj set in, the *khansama* had learnt to write accounts on paper. The artistry lay in the smaller sums, which seemed too trivial to dispute. Hence: 'Butons for master's trousers, 9 pies'; 'Tramwei for going to market, 1 anna 6 pies'; 'Making white of master's hat, 5 pies'. If you challenged any marked cost, you got a very patient explanation of how he had bargained to cut the price. Sometimes he took upon himself the duties of a conscience. One sahib, shopping while his wife was away, was on the point of buying a luxury when he heard a gentle murmur from his guardian servant: 'Missis never allowing, sir.'[36]

Sahibs might rail at the peon, the 'mother-in-law of liars', or the watchman who took a 'gift' to open the gate to an outsider, but as Aitken said about Mukkun Lal, 'submit to him we must'. Who else but the cook who made a bit on hens' eggs had the expertise to select the right fish from the *monjee, rowe, cutlah, quoye, sowle, mhagoor, tangra, chunah* and *hilsa* displayed on the wet stalls of a Calcutta market?

Indians had unusual ways of expressing their fluctuating feelings. One memsahib discovered that her cook had, despite strict instructions, brought his young son to the kitchen, dressed in a new pink shirt, his hands tinkling with silver bangles. The boy was sitting on the slab of beef purchased for dinner. She would have upbraided the cook, but the child looked so cherubic that she said nothing. The happy cook surpassed himself that evening. However, no beef was served.[37]

When one English hostess in the south found that the clear soup was rather muddy, she decided to rise from the table and investigate. The cook had used his *mundu*, or thin linen wrap-around, as a strainer. He was dismissed the next morning. It was slightly better, perhaps, than straining coffee through the master's socks, as reported by the anonymous author of a superb mid-19th-century guidebook for women on their way to India.

The author employed a modest 17 servants, at a total salary of ₹105 a month. The cook was her favourite—he had the skills to 'put to shame the performances of an English one' in soups, cutlets, jellies, and confectionaries. He was rewarded with a handsome ₹15 per month. She found the 'butler' the most expensive and most useless. The *chokera* was either the master's 'dressing boy' earning between six to nine rupees, or an unpaid intern who broke 'sufficient glass and china' to make his learning process an expensive one. The common view was that a 'native never speaks the truth except by accident' but the Lady Resident believed this to be an exaggeration.[38]

The following anecdote, from Chapter 6, was apparently not an exaggeration:

> 'Boy, how are master's socks so dirty?'
> 'I take, make e'strain coffee.'
> 'What, you dirty wretch, for coffee?'
> 'Yes, missis; but never take master's clean e'sock. Master done use, then I take.'

Servants tried their best to pick up useful English. Emily Eden describes a rainy day at home in 1836: two tailors are sitting by the window making a new gown for her; two Dacca embroiders are working at a large frame, a sleepy *bearah* is pulling away at the *punkah*; and five servants are seated in a circle with an English spelling book, learning by rote.

One might surmise that the memsahib would welcome such an evolution, but paradoxically the opposite was true. 'Servants who spoke English were not considered desirable, because they could learn the family secrets,' writes Margaret Macmillan.[39] They also led to situations which seem humorous in retrospect but must have been awkward when they occurred. Macmillan narrates the story of Monica Campbell-Martin who asked a servant about his *sardi* (cold); the latter thought he had been asked about his *shadi* (marriage). When he replied in the affirmative, she advised purgatives and a good rest in bed as the cure. There were graver dangers than a misunderstood prescription. *The Tank Tragedy* in Major Walter Yeldham's *Lays of Ind* is about Mrs White and the *ayah* who 'do whatever Missis please' until she was fined half a month's pay. Then she tattled:

> *Colonel White was over forty;*
> *Jane, his bride, was seventeen;*
> *She was also very naughty,*
> *For she loved a Captain Green.*
> ...

Every evening, at dinner,
Colonel White would tipple deep,
And that pretty little sinner
Let her Johnny fall asleep;
Then, beyond the dark verandah,
In a shady nook unseen,
She would folly and philander
With the wicked Captain Green.
...

Mistress White she had an ayah—
'Do whatever Missis please;
'Missis send her letters by her,
'Missis only give rupees.
'Master Green, he handsome master—
'Plenty fun-fun, plenty spend—
'Never know him when he passed her—
'Always be that master's friend!'
Once that ayah stole a jewel,
And her mistress—'Ayah say
'Missis very very cruel!'—
Fined her half her monthly pay.

The upshot was that the *ayah* told the master about the mistress; the cuckold-colonel confronted the missis and the captain. In the ensuing scuffle, all three slipped on the grassy slope and drowned in a water tank.

Jewel in the Crown

There has been some controversy over who precisely is portrayed in Joshua Reynold's *George Clive and his Family with an Indian Maid*, painted between 1763–1765, but there is no dispute about the maid. She wears bangles on her wrist, rings on three fingers of her right hand and seems far more affectionate towards the child than the parents. She is an *ayah*, the nurse who, as a surrogate mother, got closer to a British family than any other Indian.

The first chapter of Charles Allen's obituary of the Raj, titled *The Shrine of the 'Baba-Log'*, is about the *ayah*. Allen, who did a series of interviews for the BBC with those who had lived in India between 1900 and 1947, quotes Vere Birdwood:

> They had this capacity to completely identify with the children they looked after, and it seemed as if they could switch on love in an extraordinary way. They were so dedicated to their work, in a sense so possessive of their children that it was almost impossible for a good *ayah* to yield up her charge even for a few hours.[40]

Even a dyspeptic like Charles Doyley, who thought his servants were crafty and lazy when they refused to wash his feet in a large brass or copper vessel, grudgingly accepts that the *ayah* was invaluable to the young British bride, particularly if she was a 'Dhood-Dhye', or wet nurse.[41]

Gentle and patient to an extent that would astonish the rough and ready English nursemaids, she lived with the baby, but in her own style. She came from among the poorest of families, and on arrival received three sarees, six blouses, a comb, a mat, a blanket, a tin to drink out of, a cup and dish for her meals and oil for her hair which she washed at least once a week. The 'Lady Resident' paid her *ayah* ten rupees a month, which was topped up occasionally. When the child took its first step, or cut its first tooth, the *ayah* expected a *baksheesh* (tip). These were minimal rewards for a great sacrifice: her own child had been taken away by friends while she was breast-feeding. She would sing a lullaby in her language, and sometimes, when this was inadequate to put the child to sleep and the memsahib was out for dinner, a touch of opium was helpful. That was the Indian way.

The painted wooden toys for the infant in Calcutta came from Benares; clay animals and figures of a 'hat-wearer' (as the English were called) in bright uniform seated on an ungainly horse from Murshidabad. Every evening the *ayah* and the *bearah* took the baby for an airing. 'Ayahs waited up patiently at night to take care of their mistresses when they came home from parties,' writes Margaret MacMillan. 'A good *ayah* became a friend to her mistress and often helped her through difficult times...'[42] She took charge of the memsahib's wardrobe and perhaps even jewellery in addition to taking care of the infant.

Perhaps the most extraordinary expression of Indo-British literature was the brilliant transliteration of English nursery rhymes into Hindi, weaving strands from two cultures into a wonderful knit. In the 1860s, T.F. Bignold, an ICS officer, recorded this sparkle of creative genius:

- Old Mother Hubbard/ Went to the cupboard/ To get her poor dog a bone/ When she got there,/ The cupboard was bare,/ And so the poor dog got none.

  Dharmi Dai/ Handi tak gayi/ Kuttey ko deney hadhi;/ Wahan jab ayi/ To kuchch na payi;/ Rah gaya rozahdar!

- Humpty Dumpty sat on a wall,/ Humpty Dumpty had a great fall./ Not all the Queen's horses, not all the King's men/ Could put Humpty Dumpty together again.

  Hamti Damti charh gaya chhat;/ Hamti Damti gir gaya phat,/ Raja ka paltan, Rani ke ghorey/ Hamti Damti kabhi na jorey.

- Goosey, Goosey, Gander,/ Where shall I wander?/ Upstairs or downstairs,/ Or in my lady's chamber?/ Old Daddy long-legs/ Wouldn't say his prayers;/ Take him by the left leg/ And throw him downstairs!

  Hans, Hans, Raj Hans,/ Kidhar jaana hota?/ Upar jaawen, nichey jaawen,/ Bibi-ji ka kotha?/ Burha behuda/ Chod diya namaaz;/ Gorh dhar key phenk dey,/ Pir paaye-daraz.

- Little Miss Muffet/ Sat on a tuffet,/ Eating her curds and whey,/ When a great ugly spider/ Came and sat down beside her/ And frightened Miss Muffet away.

  Mufiti Mai,/ Dahi malai/ Ghas mein baith key khai,/ Jab bara sa makra/ Uski sari pakra,/ Bhagey Mufiti Mai!

- Higgledy, piggledy, my fat hen!/ She laid eggs for gentlemen,/ Sometimes eight, and sometimes ten,/ Higgledy piggledy, my fat hen!

  Hakali, makali, murghi mera!/ Anda parhey barah terah;/ Parh ke bhej de sahib ka derah;/ Hakali, makali, murghi mera!

- If all the world were apple-pie, and all the seas were ink,/ And all the trees were bread and cheese, what should we do for drink?

  Darya shor siyahi ho, zamin bakir-khani,/ Sara jungal dahi ho, to kaun dega pani?

- Dickory, dickory, dock;/ The mouse ran up the clock,/ The clock struck one,/ And down she run,/ Dickory, dickory, dock.

  Dekho re, dekho re, dekh!/ Ghari bajegi ek!/ Jab ghanta hua,/ To kud gaya chuha,/ Dekho re, dekho re, dekh!

- Mary, Mary, quite contrary, how does your garden grow?/With silver bells and cockle shells, and pretty maids all in a row.

  Miriam meri tirchni terhi phuta gulisatan?/ Chandi ka ghanta wa kauri ka panta wa larki khub jawan.[43]

British mothers understood the emotional bonds and were quietly grateful. As one wrote, a baby has been born

> and in comes the dusky stranger, all pride and expectation, all hope and joy. It is fortunate that there is no difference in young babies—that the one is as ugly a little thing as the other—and so she is not disappointed: on the contrary, she sees with one glance of her glittering eyes, which have their source of sensation in her woman's heart, a thousand charms that distinguish her *baba* from all the other babies in the universe. With something akin to a mother's feelings, she takes the infant in her arms, which seems incontinent to become a part of herself, lying all day on her knees and sleeping all night in her bosom; and from that moment the nurse, the child and the *paun*-box are always together... I still sometimes hear in fancy her cradle-song humming in my own Old Indian ear as I am falling asleep—although many a long year has passed since I heard it in reality...[44]

The lullaby is full of love:

> *Sleep on, sleep on, my baba dear!*
> *Thy faithful slave is watching near,*
> *The cradle wherein my babe I fondle.*

Is made of the rare and bright-red sandal;
And the string with which I am rocking my lord,
Is a gay and silken cord... Sleep on, sleep on, my baba dear!
Sleep on, sleep on, my baba dear!
Thy faithful slave is watching near,
The mother of hearts is the powerful queen,
The loveliest day that ever was seen;
And there ne'er was slave more faithful, I trow,
Than she who is rocking the cradle now.[45]

The cradle and toddler years had to end, generally around the age of seven when children were sent 'home' for a 'proper' education. The separation was as difficult for the mother as for the surrogate mother. Both accepted the inevitable with strained hearts and got on with the rest of their lives as interdependent mistress and servant.

The one great worry of Anglo-Indian society was the extent to which the *ayah* would gossip. Emily Eden was quite convinced that the *ayah* was to blame. In a letter to Mrs Theresa Lister dated 25 January 1837, Eden described Calcutta as

> a gossiping society... they sneer at each other's dress and looks and pick out small stories against each other by means of the *ayahs,* and it is clearly a downright offence to tell one woman that another looks well. It is not easy to commit the crime with any regard to truth, but still there are degrees of yellow, and the deep orange woman who has many fevers does not like the pale primrose creature with the constitution of a horse who had not had more than a couple of agues. The new arrivals we all agree are coarse and vulgar—not fresh and cheerful, as in my secret soul I think them. But that, you see, is the style of gossipry.[46]

The prolific author Maud Driver, in her book, *The Englishwoman in India* published in 1909, has a few stern comments about the *ayah* who judges the Englishwoman's

> conduct by Eastern standards, and communicates those judgements without reserve to an admiring circle of listeners

over her evening hookah. For the *ayah* is a bone-bred gossip; her tongue is a stranger to the golden fetter of truth; and without risk of serious misstatement, it may almost be said that the unscrupulous chattering of her and her kind has done more to darken understanding and confirm countless misconceptions than any of the ways and works of Englishwomen themselves.[47]

Her contemporary J.M. Graham had a more risible experience:

She is an inexhaustible and trustworthy source of much scandal... She is very clean, but performs her ablutions at odd times. I walked into the nursery bathroom at 11 am one day, and found the *ayah's* ample proportions sans raiment squatting on the floor, while she threw cupfulls of water over herself at intervals. She greeted me with a bright and friendly smile—'Little master sleeping "m".' I retired in confusion, which was born either of decent self-respect, or of a false shame generated by civilisation. She left me three times to bury one who had never lived, and each time tucked some of my possessions into her luggage. One, packed insecurely in her draperies, fell out at my feet; neither of us evinced the least surprise, so complete was the understanding between us.[48]

Inevitably, men like the racist Aitken were rancid:

What if the impress of those swarthy lips on that fair [European] cheek are but an outward symbol of impressions on a mind still as fair and pure, impressions which soap and water will not purge away? Yes, it is so. The *Ayah* hangs like a black cloud over and around the infant mind, and its earliest outlooks on the world are tinted by that medium... Under the same guidance it will, as it grows older, tread paths of knowledge which its parents never trod. Whither will they lead it? We know not who never joined in the familiar chart of *Ayahs* and servants, but imagination 'bodies forth the forms of things unseen' and shudders. Let us rejoice that a merciful superstition, which regards the climate of India as deadly to European children, will step in and save the little soul.[49]

What even Aitken understood was that a household full of servants was an option unavailable in Britain. Retirement was a rupture from a lifetime of comfort. Vernende's *A Ballad of the Bawarchikhana*, written when the glory of the Raj had begun to fade into the fog of memory, is nostalgic:

The bandobast has turned to dust, departed are the staff
Who ruled our lives and spoilt our wives,
    but often made us laugh—
A fitting epitaph.
Their presence felt where'er we dwelt:
    the discreet cough and sighs,
The low salaams, the itching palms,
    the shrewd observant eyes,
The loyalty and lies
Were all a part, close to the heart, of India's strange delight,
Which we regret, while we forget the heat, the dust and bite
Of insects in the night.
Old servants true pass in review as we relive those years,
But, best of all, I still recall a prince of profiteers,
A rogue who had no peers.
A man of guile with ready smile, an artist and a crook—
The kind you'll find all over Hind, described in many a book—
A not uncommon cook.
Abdullah Khan, our Khansaman, obeyed the Prophet's charge
To kneel and pray an hour a day, which left him ample marge
To prey upon the Raj.
Who could forget who once had met that mirror of his race—
The grave repose, the spotless clothes,
    the slow unhurried pace,
The strongly bearded face—
The look of grief if called a thief, the air of pained surprise
If someone noted he's promoted all the humble pies
To paise in disguise?
A naukar full of dhoka and exceedingly chalak,

Whose measured seer was nowhere near but
    well below the mark
By more than one chittak.

The elegy ended with the philosophical observation that they could have fired Abdullah but only got someone worse. (A *pie* was the smallest unit of currency, with three to a *paisa*; a *seer* was around two pounds, and a *chittak* about two ounces.) As for the *dhobi* and the *darzee*: it was well observed that the washerman delivered clothes which required a tailor, and the tailor gave them back in a state which needed a washerman.

On Her Majesty's Public Service

The wondrous story of Queen Victoria, first empress of India, and her Indian *khidmutgar* remains a mystery wrapped in official amnesia. Victoria's heir Edward VII found it inexplicable that she could consider a lowly servant her son, banished him from England after her death and ordered the destruction of all the Queen's letters to her Indian child.

In 1887, the 24-year-old Mohammad Abdul Karim, son of a hospital assistant from Jhansi, was sent by the Government of India to join Queen Victoria's retinue to mark her golden jubilee. Karim was educated in a *medressa*, or seminary, but he had the distinction of being a *hafiz*, or someone who could recite the whole Quran from memory. His more relevant skills, as far as the Raj was concerned, were cooking Indian food and waiting at the Queen's table.

To the surprise of the staff, he was soon teaching the formidable Queen Hindustani. His rise in her affections was astonishing. The Queen took him along on all her travels and upgraded the chicken curry, dal and *pilau* that he cooked into her meal rotation. He was promoted to the position of 'Munshi [teacher] and Indian Clerk' at a salary of pounds 12 a month. Abdul Karim was showered with honours like CIE (Commander of the Indian Empire) and CVO (Commander of the Victorian Order). His portrait, painted by Rudolf Swoboda in 1888, makes him look like a deferential intellectual, in a high silk turban, holding a book. The picture is part of the royal collection.

His influence was such that when the Liberal Prime Minister Lord Roseberry offered Lord Cromer the viceroy's position, he also urged him to accept the offer quickly before Abdul Karim persuaded the Queen to reject the nomination.

Courtiers did not know what to make of it, but they tried their best to sabotage the 'preening social climber who had excessive influence over his mistress's Indian views'. The Queen dismissed this as jealousy. Her most trenchant royal put-down came when Karim's enemies accused him of lying

> about his background, claiming his father was a surgeon-general instead of the apothecary at the Agra jail—a discovery that delighted the courtiers but infuriated Victoria who reacted to their snobbery by reminding them she had known one archbishop who had been the son of a butcher and another whose father had been a grocer. No criticism was permitted of a person she seems to have doted on more than any man in her life after Albert, Melbourne and her Highland servant, John Brown, all of whom were dead by the time Abdul Karim appeared at Court. In her letters to him she signed herself, 'Your affectionate Mother, V.R.I.' and, on advising him about his wife's gynaecological problems, wrote, 'There is nothing I would not do to help you both, as you are my dear Indian children...'[50]

David Gilmour believes that this was merely a display of her 'maternal instincts towards her Indian subjects'. The Queen's view was well known; no people were more affectionate if treated with kindness than Indians.[51]

In deference to the Queen's wish, Karim was the last person permitted to see her body in 1901 before the casket was buried. Then came the revenge of the palace. The Queen's letters to her 'son' were destroyed, and Karim was sent back to Agra, where he died at the young age of 48.

Gilmour writes:

> According to her biographer, Elizabeth Longford, she had had romantic feelings for 'brown skins' since childhood. Devoid

of snobbery and racial feeling herself, she would not allow people to disparage other races or refer to them as black: [Prime Minister] Salisbury himself was made to apologize for referring to Indians as 'black men'.[52]

Much had changed during the 63 years of Victoria's reign: the telegraph and steamship brought Britain and India closer; travel took three weeks rather than four months; the newly-built Ganges Canal irrigated thousands of square miles between Hardwar and Kanpur; India's North East was dotted with tea plantations; 25,000 miles of railway tracks reduced an earlier palanquin journey of three weeks to one day; there were gaslights in Calcutta.

But much more remained stagnant. Gilmour writes:

Yet in India, away from the ports and the railways and the irrigation canals, the pace of change was extremely slow... even over so long a reign hundreds of thousands of villages altered little in appearance and not much in material wealth. By 1901 they might have a school and a small dispensary, a few more effective well, some avenues of trees planted by zealous District Officers in an effort to prevent soil erosion. But little else would have changed...[53]

Crowds gathered in Calcutta on the day of Queen Victoria's funeral in January 1901, and shops shut in mourning. The Viceroy, Lord Curzon, attributed this to the Queen's 'overpowering effect on the imagination of the Asiatic', but Bengal was burdened by a more desolate reality.

The people's poets like Kabirdas Gonsai and Baradaprasad Roy asked caustic questions in their rural songs:

Kothai ma Victoria?
Pet bhorey pai na khetey, kaj ki pathey?
Kaler jaley kay ki gasey?
...

Chai na ma tarer khabor
Dudiner parey
Kar khabor key korbey deshey?

Sumanta Banerjee has translated these lines: 'Where are you, mother Victoria? I don't even have two full meals; what's the use of roads? What's the use of tap water and gas light [in Calcutta]? I don't need news through the wire, mother. Who'll hear our news after some time?'[54]

Wealth was the privilege of the British and their handful of Indian collaborators, while the poor died of hunger from the onset to the end of the Raj. When at the height of his wealth and power, Maharaja Nandakumar invited 100,000 Brahmins to fulfil a religious obligation, the poor ridiculed this feast in a couplet: '*Keu khele machher mudo, keu khele bonduker hudo* [Some were treated to the delicacy of fish-heads, others to the thrust of the musket-butt]'. A century later, Dwarkanath Tagore, owner of Carr, Tagore and Company, hosted sumptuous dinner parties for the city's English top brass at his garden house in Belgachia in north Calcutta while the lower orders mocked the ostentation:

Belgachhiar baganey hoy chhuri-kantar jhanjhani,
Khana khaoar kato maja,
Amra tar ki jani?
Janey Thakur Company.

Banerjee translates: 'Knives and forks are clanking in the Belgachhia garden house; what fun with all that food around! But what do we know of it? It's all an affair of Tagore Company.' They taunted the sahib in idioms like *Company's latgiri, parer dhoney poddari*; or, Company servants have become aristocrats by usurping the wealth of others.[55]

Queen Victoria advised Lord Curzon to get a valet like Abdul Karim. He ignored the suggestion and took an 'English body-servant' who had an 'engaging manner, and unlimited effrontery' but was 'a little uncertain about his aspirants'. In plainer words, he spoke cockney. The effrontery extended to impersonating the viceroy. A traditional Kerala boat waited to take Lord and Lady Curzon from ship to shore across the surf while they were on a visit to Cochin and Travancore in 1900. Uncertain about the boat's stability, the viceroy chose to await more steady transport. While waiting, Curzon saw his valet, a lady's maid by his side, step on the beach from the swan-boat to loud cheers of welcome from the Kerala grandees and assembled populace. Lord Curzon thought it was all very jolly; after all, his valet was only taking the maharaja and infantile Indians for a ride.[56]

The Coolie Murder Case

Late on the night of 3 September 1925 in Simla, a rickshaw-puller was kicked to death by a berserk English Army officer, while his dinner party guests waited at the end of the evening to go home. No sahib or memsahib bothered to help the 'coolie'.

Pamela Kanwar narrates the story of 'The Rickshaw Coolie Murder Case':

> Jageshwar, a rickshaw coolie, muffled under a ragged sheet, dozed off on the porch of Yates Place, the home of Mansel-Pleydell, Controller of the Army Canteen Board. Along with several other coolies he was waiting to take his passengers, who were dining at Yates Place, home. Well past midnight, the dinner over, Mansel-Pleydell stamped out to wake up the coolies. Jageshwar sat up and stumbled, as his feet were entangled in the covering sheet. An enraged, swearing Mansel-Pleydell kicked him out, off the porch, and kicking, pushed him about the garden until he collapsed into a flower-bed. Jageshwar died of a ruptured spleen and three broken ribs in the early hours of the morning.[57]

The other Indian rickshaw-pullers, including Bakhia, Jageshwar's cousin, watched tongue-tied as the severely injured Jageshwar moaned helplessly on the ground. The rickshaw-pullers ferried the English guests to their homes and then returned, picked up Jageshwar and carried him to the Chhota Simla Police Station. The constable on duty would not take down Jageshwar's statement, which accused the Englishman of kicking him repeatedly and viciously. The 'coolie' died later that night.

Bakhia contacted Rai Bahadur Mohan Lal, a municipal commissioner, who decided to intervene. Next morning a case was registered at the Sadar Police Station in Lower Bazar. Newspapers picked up the story. Influential Indians took up the cause, and the

Army officer was put on trial. British officials, anxious to protect Mansel-Pleydell, put heavy pressure on the rai bahadur to retract his testimony. Mohan Lal refused. In court, the English officer's lawyers tried to malign the Mohan Lal's integrity by suggesting that his statement was biased in favour of Indians. He was asked in the witness box why the 'coolies' 'salaamed' him. With a touch of pride, Mohan Lal replied, 'Half of Simla *salaams* Mohan Lal.' Mansel-Pleydell was convicted after a six-month trial but sentenced to only 18 months rigorous imprisonment and a fine of ₹4,000. That was the price of an Indian life in British justice.

Mansel-Pleydell did not regret the crime, but he could not face the humiliation. He committed suicide in prison.

India had changed, once again.

9

Justice Pulbandi and the Black Zamindar

Dustoory leapt effortlessly from the Persian of sultans into the English of British rule. It meant the usual, or the customary. *Hobson-Jobson*, always a stickler for detail, calls it:

> that which is customary. That commission or percentage on the money passing any cash transaction which, with or without acknowledgment or permission, sticks to the fingers of the agent of payment. Such 'customary' appropriations are, we believe, very nearly as common in England as in India; a fact of which newspaper correspondence from time to time makes us aware... Ibn Batuta tells us that at the Court of Delhi, in his time (c. 1340), the custom was for the officials to deduct 1/10 of every sum which the Sultan ordered to be paid from the treasury...[1]

The British percentage was flexible. The bribe could be 10 per cent of the contract or more. The dictionary quotes *Hicky's Bengal Gazette* of 29 April 1780: 'It can never be in the power of a superintendent of Police to reform the numberless abuses which servants of every Denomination have introduced, and now support on the Broad Basis of Dustoor.' Indo-British relations prospered best when Company officials, and the new Indian elite they spawned, cooperated in corruption. Anthony Weltden, the governor of Calcutta in 1710, assigned negotiations for graft to his wife and daughter not because he was squeamish, but because they ensured a better bargain.

Gobindaram Mitra, the deputy collector of Calcutta between 1720 and 1726, was anointed the first 'black zamindar' by his British masters. Mitra's official duty was to extract revenue, which he did through inarguably persuasive methods. His cudgel-wielding goons called *paiks, naibs* and *naiks*, were let loose upon the citizenry. This triptych became the template of the future Calcutta police, the equivalent of constables, head constables and investigating officers.

Gobindoramer chhodi, or Gobindaram's stick, entered popular parlance as a metaphor for power. Expanding this clout, Mitra became Calcutta's first godfather of white-collar crime: inflating tenders, fudging accounts, manipulating auctions for public works or land sales which were conducted from his home to emphasize his control over the outcome. He monopolized the best deals, often under fictitious names, inflated contract estimates for repairs or construction and split the excess with the contractor. In a typical instance, he won the auction for 18 bazaars and rented out the property immediately, collecting a 100 per cent advance from the tenants. In other words, he became a commercial landowner without spending a rupee.

Mitra's luck ran out in 1752, when John Zephaniah, the new governor, demanded accounts. However, he retained large reserves of chutzpah. Mitra replied that all records till 1738 were lost in the great storm of that year, and the rest had been eaten by white ants. The zealous Zephaniah prosecuted him, but Mitra escaped with the support of complicit officials. In the proper style of a mafia don, his remit ran to the judiciary.

Sumanta Banerjee writes:

Ironically enough, the trendsetters in the art of crime in the early days of Calcutta were not the poor rogues from the city's underworld, but the British lawmakers and the Bengali privileged classes, who struck deals with each other, and helped themselves to money and property by dispossessing the people and milking resources.[2]

Calcutta was powerful, ambitious, wanton and delinquent. A sharp-eyed observer, Mrs Sherwood, describes how precisely luxurious it was:

...the splendid sloth and the languid debauchery of European society in those days—English gentlemen, overwhelmed with the consequences of extravagance, hampered by Hindoo women and by crowds of olive-coloured children... Great men rode about in State coaches, with a dozen servants running before and behind them to bawl out their titles; and little men lounged in palanquins or drove a chariot for which they never intended to pay, drawn by horses cajoled out of the stables of wealthy Baboos.[3]

Warren Hastings returned to India, sent as a deputy governor in Madras in 1769, after the fortune he had amassed from his first stint was lost by mismanagement. His despair was compounded by the death of his wife and son. On the ship to Madras, he fell in love with Anna Maria Chapuset, wife of the itinerant Baron Imhoff, who nursed him after he fell ill during the journey. He was promoted to governor and reached Calcutta in February 1772. It was not till 1776 that Marian's divorce came through, and Maria became Marian, and then Mrs Hastings. Warren Hastings gave Marian a dower of ₹ 100,000 on their marriage, and she wore a gown trimmed with fine point and a cap full of diamonds and pearls at their first public appearance after the wedding. The man who gave her away was a schoolfriend of Hastings, Sir Elijah Impey, the first chief justice of the Supreme Court of Judicature at Fort William.

Calcutta was in the grip of fortune hunters, gamblers and conspirators. In 1774, three members were appointed to Hastings's Council: Philip Francis, just 33 years old, along with two elder Army officers, General John Clavering, the first member and commander-in-chief, and Colonel George Monson, each on a handsome annual salary of £10,000. The three conspired with such vitriolic intensity against Hastings, 'so sensitive to rebuke and so proud of his character', that he 'could not breathe in this air of unrelenting malice', according to a biographer.[4] Malice, however, had value. Francis was assured, after a year in Calcutta, that Hastings was ready to buy off the three allies for £100,000 apiece. This was equivalent to a British prime minister silencing his Cabinet colleagues with money from a private fortune collected through corruption. Hastings was justifiably anxious. An Indian aristocrat with incriminating documents had joined the power struggle.

Nandakumar, awarded the title of 'Maharaja' by Emperor Shah Alam in 1764, was among the wealthiest and most influential nobles of Bengal. 'In appearance,' writes H.E. Busteed, 'he has been described as tall and majestic in person, robust, yet graceful. When the misfortune which has immortalized his name befell him he was nearly seventy years of age.'[5]

On 11 March 1775, Maharaja Nandakumar wrote to the governing council accusing Hastings of having taken £45,000 as a bribe from him and Mir Jafar's widow Munni Begum through his agent Kanta Babu to make certain appointments. He produced vouchers as evidence. The council ordered a humiliated Hastings to pay the equivalent amount into the treasury.

Nandakumar was neither naïve nor politically innocent—he was party to an attempted coup against Hastings. Nor was his ally Francis a saint, having filled his own pockets whenever he got the opportunity, consoling himself with the specious argument that he was merely bleeding bloodsuckers. What they did not expect was Hastings's counteroffensive through Impey. On 19 April 1775, the government prosecuted Nandakumar for conspiracy. On 6 May he was arrested for forging documents.

The imperious Brahmin maharaja chose a lofty response. He claimed he could not stay or eat in the designated prison as this would defile his caste. A tent was erected for him. He restricted his diet largely to sweets and bathed in the nearby Hooghly, which is a tributary of the holy Ganges.

Impey began the trial on 8 June, at the peak of a boiling summer. Judges rose four times a day to change their robes. The trial ended at midnight of 15 June 1775. Maharaja Nandakumar was found guilty by an all-English jury led by John Robinson, an employee of the East India Company. Impey sentenced him to death. According to Busteed, the prosecuting counsel was so 'unequal to the labour of the prosecution, especially that of cross-examination' that the judges, with the exception of one, Justice Robert Chambers, 'took this duty on themselves, and carried it out in prodigious detail, recalling witnesses over and over again'.[6]

The charge had been fabricated, the trial rigged; the conviction was based on a statute not applicable in Calcutta, according to a ruling by Justice Chambers, a former Vinerian professor at Oxford, in a later case. Deputations for reversal or mercy were summarily rejected.

Calcutta's sheriff Alexander Mackrabie, Francis' brother-in-law, found the maharaja completely composed and resigned to 'God's will' on the eve of his execution. It was Mackrabie who succumbed to emotion: 'I found myself so much second to him in firmness, that I could stay no longer.' The next morning,

> There was no lingering about him, no affected delay. He came cheerfully into the room, made the usual salaam, but would not sit till I took a chair near him. Seeing somebody look at a watch, he got up and said he was ready, and immediately turning to three Brahmins who were to attend and take care of his body, he embraced them all closely, but without the least mark of melancholy or depression on his part, while they were in agonies of grief and despair.[7]

On 5 August 1775, a Saturday, the wail of Indians could be heard across Calcutta as the 'Brahmin of Brahmins' was hanged at eight in the morning at Cooly Bazar near Fort William.

Hastings did not waste time delivering his thank you notes. Impey's frontman Archibald Fraser, who kept the seal of the Supreme Court, was given a contract of ₹420,000 for bridge repairs as against the previous contract of ₹25,000 per year. Calcuttans, lost for all else except words, gave Impey a derisive nickname, 'Justice Pulbandi' (roughly: Justice Bridge-dealer). The irrepressible Hicky used the term gleefully in a poem about a public petition against Impey which was sent to London:

> *Poolbundy once in a high fit of crowing*
> *Exclaimed thus to Archibald Sealer the Knowing!*
> *I told you that those dar'd sign the Petition,*
> *Shou'd all be dispatched with great expedition!*
> *Shall the Company's factors, and even their clerks*
> *Attempt upon us to send home their remarks?*
> *Shall prentices dare to insult thus their better?*
> *Besides that, they robe within my own door*
> *In daily oppressing and squeezing the poor!*[8]

Jibe was supplemented by parody:

> A few days ago was held a Grand Council upon affairs of
> state... it was resolved that Lord Poolbundy should continue
> to hold that title for life and that a *sunnud* [Mughal deed]
> should forthwith be granted to him for another *Jaghire* in
> addition to the three he now enjoys in order to enable him to
> support his honour with beaming dignity and this proceeds
> from the love the Great Mogul bears him for his long, faithful
> and disinterested services.[9]

The new 'Great Mogul' was of course Warren Hastings.

Impey was impeached by the House of Commons in 1788 for
'gross and scandalous partiality' but not convicted. Burke was
convinced that Hastings 'murdered Nuncumar (sic) through the
hands of Sir Elijah Impey' and Macaulay felt that only 'fools and
biographers' could doubt that this was a judicial murder.[10] The title
of Henry Beveridge's account, *The Trial of Maharaja Nanda Kumar:
A Narrative of a Judicial Murder*, was unambiguous. Beveridge
dedicated his book to his wife Annette, 'who has taken so much
interest in the attempt to vindicate the reputation of A PERSECUTED
BENGALI'. He established that the bond was not a forgery, but
the genuine deed of 'Bolaqi Das Seth'; that circumstantial evidence
pointed to Hastings as the real prosecutor; that the principal witness
against Nandakumar, Kamaluddin Khan, was a business associate of
Hastings through his agent Kanta Babu, reputed to be 'the scum of
the earth'; that Impey conducted the trial unfairly; that the jury was
prejudiced and incompetent and that the prosecution entirely failed
to prove that the bond was a forgery.

Beveridge wrote:

> They will remember that Cornwallis, an honourable
> gentleman and no Whig, wrote in 1786, only two years after
> Impey's departure from India, begging that he might not be
> sent out again, and observing that all parties and descriptions
> of them agreed about him. That again, in 1788—the year of
> the impeachment—the same high authority wrote that he was
> very sorry for Hastings, but that if they wanted somebody

to hang, they might 'tuck up' Sir E. Impey without giving anybody the smallest concern. When the dust of controversy has been laid, men will recur to the opinion of Burke, and accept in shame and sadness the verdict which he pronounced in his speech on Fox's East India Bill. 'The Rajah Nuncomar was, by an insult on everything which India holds respectable and sacred, hanged in the face of all his nation, by the Judges you sent to protect that people, hanged for a pretended crime, upon an *ex post facto* Act of Parliament, in the midst of his evidence against Mr Hastings. The accuser they saw hanged. The culprit, without acquittal or inquiry, triumphs on the ground of that murder—a murder not of Nuncomar only, but of all living testimony, and even of evidence yet unborn.'[11]

Hastings and Impey punished Francis too, although this time they did not have to manufacture a case. Francis was quite flagrantly guilty of adultery with the remarkable beauty, Noel Catherine Verlee, wife of a stolid Company official named George Francois Grand. Impey's vengeance took the form of sizeable damages granted to her husband; 50,000 *sicca* rupees, equivalent to 5109 pounds, two shillings and 11 pence sterling. Justice Chambers again dissented. Catherine left India in December 1780, flourished as the mistress of several French aristocrats and in 1802 stunned Paris by becoming the wife of Napoleon's Foreign Minister Charles Maurice de Talleyrand. She was buried in the Montparnasse Cemetery. A portrait of Catherine Noel Grand de Talleyrand-Perigrod, Princess de Benevent, hangs in the Metropolitan Museum of Art in New York.

William Hickey, a successful barrister who earned £80,000 in a good year and travelled in a phaeton with two noble Arabian horses, is objective about the Nandakumar episode:

There is no doubt but that in summing up the evidence and charging the Jury the Chief Justice, Sir Elijah Impey, was as hostile to the prisoner as could be. The Jury, after being shut up many hours, and great difference of opinion prevailing amongst them, at last brought in a verdict of Guilty, but which several of them have since assured me they would sooner have starved than consented to had they entertained the most distant idea of execution following such a verdict, and most indignant were they upon finding the sentence carried into effect. Upon the day of the Rajah's execution every Hindu, high and low, at an early hour in the morning left Calcutta in the utmost despair.[12]

The legal profession did not have a very exalted reputation. Hickey writes that he was known as

the Gentleman Attorney, in contradistinction to the blackguard practitioners, of which description I am sorry to say there were several. In fact, with the exception of Messrs Palfrey and Nail, or, Foxcroft, Johnson, Jarrett [who was solicitor to the Company], and Smoult, I never met any attorneys in the company I kept, which always was the best.[13]

In such a fetid environment, criminal lawyers were seldom short of a brief. A popular doggerel of the time went *Jaal, juochuri, mithye katha/ Ei teen niye Kolikata* (Forgery, swindling and lies/ These three things make up Calcutta). In 1795, the government tried some feeble reform with an order: 'All servants belonging to the Company's Shed had been strictly prohibited from demanding or receiving any fees or *dastoors* on any pretence whatever.' Everyone shrugged off the diktat.

Impey's Bengali *dewan*, Maharaja Sukhomoy Ray, built a huge palace in north Calcutta from the wealth which stuck to his palms on its way to the chief justice. Ray's son Raja Baidyanath Ray became a city celebrity through the familiar method of bribes and parties for the rich and donations to hospitals and schools for the poor. He was a favourite of Governor-general Lord Amherst. It may, or may not, be a coincidence that Ray's troubles began after Lord Amherst's term ended in 1828. On 11 January 1830, the *Calcutta Gazette* broke a sensational story:

A true bill of forgery, we regret to observe, has been found against Rajah Buddinauth Roy. We say so, because it must always be a subject of regret, to see a person who moved in such a sphere as the rajah did and whose character hitherto has, we believe, been unblemished, placed in such a position as he now stands in.[14]

The raja was a partner in the newly founded Bank of India, which flooded the market with fake currency and forged government securities printed at a hideout in a 'native' part of the town, Radhabazar. The courts, however, found him guilty merely of gullibility rather than crime.

Prankrishna Haldar was far more successful as a grand host, generous benefactor and surreptitious crook. Haldar got reams of laudatory attention in newspapers like the *Samachar Darpan* for philanthropy, providing medicines to the poor or building a bridge across the river. He hosted mass meals during the annual Durga Puja festivals, as well as select parties for the well-heeled, where he carried conspicuous consumption to an impressive level by smoking tobacco rolled in 100-rupee notes. Prankrishna Haldar had money to burn.

Never shy of publicity, Haldar placed this advertisement in the *Calcutta Gazette* of 20 September 1827:

> Baboo Prankissen Haldar of Chinsurah begs to inform the Ladies and Gentlemen, and the Public in General, that he has commenced giving a Grand Nauch from this day, that it will continue till the 29th Inst. Those Ladies and Gentlemen who have received Invitation Cards, are respectfully solicited to favour him with their company on the days mentioned above; and those to whom the Invitation Tickets have not been sent (strangers to the Baboo) are also respectfully solicited to favour him with their company. Baboo Pran Kissen Haldar further begs to say, that every attention and respect will be paid to the Ladies and Gentlemen who will favour him with their Company, and that he will be happy to furnish them with tiffin, dinner, Wines, & c., during their stay here.[15]

High-priced singer-dancers like Nikki and Ushuran were hired for such celebrations. Nikki was in such demand that one enamoured Bengali zamindar employed her on a salary of ₹1,000 a month.

Friends who had supped on Haldar's tiffin, dinner and wine were startled when he was arrested in 1829 for forgery of Company promissory notes and securities. Haldar was indicted for cheating over ₹5,000,000, a colossal amount at the time, but the scale of his underhand operations was much larger. He was sentenced to seven years in a penal settlement. His high society friends pressured the Supreme Court to grant mercy, but the judges did not buckle. Haldar's properties in Calcutta, Chandernagore and Chinsurah were seized and auctioned. One of his mansions on the riverbank was converted into the well-respected Hooghly College in 1836.

The story of Prankrishna's brother Nilamani (also spelt 'Nilmunny' or 'Nilmoney') is equally extraordinary, according to the diaries of Richard Blechynden (1759–1822), an architect and surveyor who came to Calcutta at the age of 22 and rose to become the superintendent of roads. He has left a remarkable portrait of public and private life between 1791 and 1822. Blechynden settled down in Calcutta, married an Indian and was devoted to his 'mixed-race' children. Among his enterprises was part ownership of the *Chronicle* newspaper, but his income came from construction, where the politics of commissions and contracts was cut-throat. Men like Belchynden, Raja Nabakrishna ('Knobkissen'), Raja Gourdass and Francis Gladwin, member of the Board of Revenue, skirmished for graft with the help of aides and intermediaries like Petembre Ghose, Rammohan Chatterjee, Gopey Kissen and Titoo Metre. Belchynden remarks that 'Knobkissen' was once unassailable because he was a 'Kayastha ally' of Warren Hastings.

Debt was always a difficulty in business, and punishment for default was harsh. The prevailing wisdom was expressed by William Roper, an officer in the Bombay marine, who said in Belchynden's presence that 'natives only lend to Europeans for the pleasure of putting them into Goal'.[16] Roper might have had a point.

Peter Robb writes:

There were complex issues of reputation and trust, and sometimes permanent breaches in social relations, because of disagreements around work or money… Rich Europeans in Calcutta and indeed Europe often behaved in such fashion towards those who provided them with services. It was the very irregularity of these arrangements that provided a role for influence and representations on a basis of friendship.[17]

Trust and friendship were greater when the skin colour was the same.

In his diaries, Blechynden railed at 'Nilmunny's slipperiness', adding ruefully that 'Babu Nilmunny Haldar, a man who came from a rich family... was *banian* to Sir Henry Russell', a judge. The babu and the knighted judge were partners in sleaze. In 1799, Haldar bought a commercial site for ₹45,000 with the intention of developing a range of shops on either side of the street, after which Sir Henry issued an order 'requiring gold and silver dealers to locate themselves in his bazar'. Full coffers and huge smiles all around. If a judge was on the take, so were officials up and down the line.[18]

There existed an 'undoubted divide between Europeans and Indians', according to Robb, which

> lay between the instrumental friendships of Europeans, from which Indians seemed excluded, and the transactions and relationships that such friendships supported, in which both Indians and Europeans were closely involved...[Indians] might be respected, and were often assisted, but were never treated as social equals; neither English nor Indian society expected it.[19]

And so, Meer Khan, a 'good looking man', might eat everything and drink 'claret like an European' till he became tipsy but could not join the society of equals. Culture, as always, created its own bafflements. The British could never comprehend why 'Nilmunny' spent ₹150,000 on his father's funeral, giving dinner for 6,000 Indians, and a further ₹125,000 on the first anniversary of the death. For the Bengali babu, this was invaluable prestige; for the English, this was silly waste.

Blechynden found the foibles of babus inscrutable. Writes Robb:

> In his private life, too, Nilmunny Haldar resembled his more famous compatriot, Dwarkanath Tagore. He was said to have two Hindu girls in the Mutchua bazar, 'very slim beings... once kept' by a European, and to cohabit and smoke a hookah with them. He had a house at Chinsura where he would spend a week or more at a time, watching and (it was said) enjoying the favours of dancing girls. His wife and mother both objected. His mother wanted to go and live with one of her brothers. Every time they were in dispute, however,

Nilmunny was said to raise the walls of his compound by five or six bricks to intimidate her. Blechynden, despite his many concubines, did not behave like this; but some Europeans did.[20]

The mutual perplexity never disappeared. In 1860, the impeccably honest John Beames was told that it would be an insult to reject wedding presents of a few silver rupees or one or two gold mohurs from the 'chief natives' of his district, Gujrat in Punjab. He spent this money, ₹ 400, on a reciprocal meal. Since Hindus and Sikhs were reluctant to dine in the company of flesh-eaters, they were each sent a tray of fine flour, rice, ghee, sugar and spices along with a live sheep or a goat. Muslims were invited to a feast in a tent. *Pilao* and boiled mutton were prepared in huge cauldrons. Beames writes:

When the natives could eat no more, they sent a message asking to see us. So we all went out, and as we approached the tent were greeted by a thunder of eructations from the assembly. We were rather shocked at this, but it was explained to be a compliment, and was meant to show us that they had thoroughly enjoyed their banquet![21]

Beames does not use too many exclamation marks, but the collective belch was a loud violation of his sensibilities.

Lord Wellesley had formed the first police force in Calcutta, a river unit to check shenanigans on the waterfront. In 1829, Lord Bentinck set up a review committee under Charles Barwell, the chief magistrate of Calcutta. Unsurprisingly, it found the river police corrupt. In 1842, the Calcutta police was divided into Upper, Middle and Lower divisions. The first was deployed in the 'Black Town', which had lodges for 'coloured' sailors in Khalashitala, Chinese opium dens and brothels in Bowbazar. The Middle division dealt with the European civilian section; while the third administered the area between Fort William and Kidderpore, the habitat of British soldiers. While all three had a British superintendent, the last was manned only by white policemen.

By the middle of the 19th century, Calcutta had become the second largest city in the Empire with a population of over 500,000;

London had an estimated 1,000,000 residents. Law was less of a priority for the police than order. Changing names of sites and streets is an incurable Indian itch, but there is still a place in Calcutta called Chorbagan, or the garden of thieves, derived from its reputation as a centre for forgery. Calcutta also became famous for gambling. The most innovative variation was 'rain gambling' in which the punter was offered odds on whether it would rain at a specified time or not. There were mass protests when the authorities banned this climate lottery in 1897. Calcutta's hobgoblin image survived till the 1970s. A popular song from the 1958 hit film *Howrah Bridge* contains these lines: *Eent ki ikki, paan ka dukka/ Kahin joker kahin satta hai/ Suno ji, yeh Kalkatta hai... Sar par paaon rakh kar bhaago, katney wala patta hai/ Suno ji, yeh Kalkatta hai* (Two of diamonds, ace of hearts/ A joker, or perhaps a seven/ Listen: this is Calcutta./ Run away as fast as you can, you are going to lose whatever cards you get/ Listen: this is Calcutta).

Under Company rule, justice was heavily biased in favour of the British. In 1790, Cornwallis abolished the old Nizamat courts and created an English jurisprudence by which Indian judges were relegated to lower courts with lower salaries. A white man could be tried only by a white judge and jury. The reforms initiated in 1859 were more impressive in theory than in practice. Indians had already found ways to subvert the inequity through shady practices like the 'tamarind tree witness'. This witness-for-hire would sit under a tree near a court, waiting for agents who tutored him to give false evidence. Hindus would swear on a bottle of Ganges water, and Muslims on their holy book, and then lie without a qualm from the witness box. Everything was hidden in plain sight. Constables, court officials and His Honour maintained a grave face. A few gave voice to their spleen in doggerel: *Lord! How they lie, unmoved by fear/ Of all their million ugly gods;/ I make out scarcely half I hear, But then it's lies, so what's the odds?*[22]

Proactive judges decided that the best thing to do was disbelieve the police. David Gilmour writes:

> They [the police] had acquired such a reputation for bringing false cases against people they wanted to put in jail that nobody trusted them, least of all the judges. One judge in

Bengal was prone to acquit in cases where police evidence was crucial: if a prisoner confessed, he believed the confession had been extorted by the police; if stolen property was found, he suspected it was a police plant... So distrusted were the police that senior judges were given powers unknown to their colleagues in Britain: they could demand to see the police diary containing all the facts and statements on the inquiry.[23]

Corruption was the reward taken by the Indian police for protecting the British Raj.

Every judge was hardly a paragon of virtue. In *John Barleycorn Bahadur: Old Time Taverns in India*, an oft-quoted book published by Thacker, Spink & Co. in 1944, the raconteur, pianist and author Major Henry Hobbs describes 'The Chief Presidency Magistrate, a stodgy old-timer otherwise a European gentleman who was somewhat notorious for taking bribes, from both sides, and even then giving a wrong decision. This did not prevent him claiming to be always guided by his conscience'.[24] Pramod Nayar reproduces a satirical scene from 1 April 1873:

Mr Moneybag, a civilian judge, was seated in a luxurious easy-chair without his coat, in the lofty enclosed verandah of the second floor of his house (we were going to write palace) in Harrington Street, Chowringhee... Mrs Moneybag, looking fresh and extremely pretty... was reposing her elegant form on a handsome spring couch... Two little Moneybags—earthly cherubim—were seated on an out-spread mat, surrounded by expensive toys...[25]

The well-meaning Lord Ripon attempted judicial reform. In 1883, a bill named after Courtenay Ilbert, legal member in the Viceroy's Council, proposed that Indian judges could henceforth preside over the trial of a European. The consequent uproar was fuelled by a concoction of arguments: investment would dry up if the liberties of British citizens were imperilled; Indians who kept their wives in *purdah* could not be permitted to pass judgment on civilized white women and so on. The planters were most vehement, worried that their harsh treatment of labour might provoke an Indian judge to send them to jail. A 'monster meeting' was held in the Calcutta Town Hall; planters came down from the hills to insult Lord Ripon in public; an Anglo-Indian Defence Association was created and the chief justice indicated what he thought when his wife organized a ladies' petition in protest. *The Englishman* correspondent Britannicus summed up the mood in a sentence: 'The only people who have any right to India are the British; the so-called Indians have no right whatever.' The *Friend of India* exclaimed: 'Would you like to live in a country where at any moment your wife would be liable to be sentenced on a false charge, the Magistrate being a copper-coloured Pagan?' There was even talk of mutiny against the viceroy. *Punch* printed a cartoon of Ripon as a mahout, being attacked by the British from the *howdah*, titled 'The Anglo-Indian Mutiny'.

Lord Ripon compromised. A European could demand a jury in which at least half the members were white.

One mistake made in this process of change was the decision to transfer rural cases to a court in town. According to Vernede, 'Justice administered at a distance became justice removed from reality, justice delayed, expensive and open to manipulation'.[26] Always happy to turn a problem into a poem, Vernede dwells on R.L. Yorke, a sessions judge of Meerut:

> *His judgment had been over-ruled,*
> *Because the man he'd tried*
> *Had been condemned on evidence*
> *Of witnesses who'd lied.*

Yorke had accepted a medical certificate which proved that the accused, brought into court on a *charpoy*, had been ill in bed at the time of the relevant robbery and murder. As soon as judgement was pronounced, the accused picked up his string-bed and walked out.

Crinkles were smoothened out by men like Suleiman Khan, the hero of the aptly titled 'Palm Song':

> *Suleiman Khan was a zubberdust man,*
> > *but fond of the ladies too.*
> *He'd an iron fist and a very long list of all the villains he knew.*
> *They came to no harm if they greased his palm,*
> > *as sensible rascals did;*

But no 'Pro Quo' if a fellow said 'No' and failed to
*   produce his 'Quid'.*
A crock of gold to the daku bold,
*   dug up from the bania's floor;*
A golden fleece for the Chief of Police—
*   for that was the old dastur.*
So all was peace in the land of grease, until, on a fateful day,
A thief, Dharam Jit, decided to cheat by hiding his swag away.
There was no challan by Suleiman Khan,
*   no summons came to obey;*
But a strange disease affected his knees and
*   turned his tegument grey.*
He asked his wife and the light of his life to mix
*   him a strong julep,*
Which gave him a pain that affected his brain so much that
*   he could not sleep.*[27]

The 'helpful' advice that Dharam Jit received was to pass on a fifth of the stolen swag to Suleiman Khan in 'a very secluded spot'. The moral of the story? 'Make sure that your wife and the light of your life is a wholly respectable dame.'

Kind Hearts and Baronets

William James Hershcel's grandfather discovered the planet Uranus, and his father Sir John, a baronet, was a well-known astronomer. William's contribution to science was of more practical use in daily life. He discovered fingerprinting—or, more accurately, palm-printing—in a district of Bengal called Jangipur.

In 1858, the conscientious Herschel was about to sign a contract for road-building material with a contractor called Rajyadhar Konai, when it occurred to him that he could take a precaution. He asked Konai to mark the contract with a print of his right hand. Herschel did not imagine that he was doing anything radical, or that this innovation would revolutionize the criminal-justice system. Bengalis were familiar with *teepshoi*, through which an illiterate woman could attest a document by dipping the tip of her finger in ink and forming a blot on paper. Herschel made the palm-print part of government procedure, arguing that an indent was indisputable evidence of identity. The fingerprint was possibly the proudest invention of the alumni of Haileybury, the college for East India Company's premier civil servants.

Lord Wellesley started the College of Fort William in 1800 to educate Company servants in Indian history, languages, law and religion. The directors, who had not been consulted, reduced it to a school for languages and in 1806 established the East India College in England. Its students were nominees of the directors. Three years later, the site was shifted to Haileybury in Hertfordshire, near the River Lea, 21 miles north of London.

John Beames, from a family with more lineage than money, entered the college in January 1856 after an 'easy' examination on Sophocles's *Antigone*, Horace's *Epistles*, Luke's *Gospel* and school level geometry and algebra. 'Haileybury,' records Beames, 'was a happy place, though rather a farce as far as learning was concerned... while the facilities for not learning were considerable, those for learning were, in practice, somewhat scanty.'[28] It had good rowing, cricket and racquets over four 20-week terms spread across two years. The curriculum extended from natural philosophy, mathematics, law, history, economics to Sanskrit, Arabic and Persian, which were considered the chief reason for the course. Sanskrit was taught by 'Monier Williams, a little, swarthy, peppery Welshman but a renowned scholar'. Reverend Thomas Robert Malthus, author of a worrisome theory on population and survival, was professor for three decades.

It was more of a lark than hard preparation for life in India. At seven, a 'bedmaker' entered the student's small but snug room, lit the fire, and disappeared. A 'scout' filled the bath with cold water, laid the table for breakfast, cleaned boots and tried his best to awaken the sleeping scholar before chapel at eight, which was compulsory for three days a week. Many just made it in slippers and overcoat before the doors were shut. Breakfast in the room consisted of bread, butter, curried sole or mutton chop washed down with tea or coffee. A student giving a breakfast party might serve tankards of beer or claret.

Then came time for a quiet pipe before the daunting business of dealing with tailors and tradesmen. Lectures began at 10. The serious took notes; the rest drew sketches and waited for a lunch of bread, cheese and beer. Afternoons went by in rowing, cricket or billiards. Dinner was at six, after which a studious few retired to read far into the night, and the rest to carouse until later, ignoring the 11 pm bedtime bell. Those who had disappeared to London for the evening would return around two in the morning. Their punishment, if caught, was writing out passages from Greek and Latin. This could be outsourced at a rate of a shilling for a hundred lines.

This convivial nepotism could not last. The British government wanted proconsuls for an Empire rather than mere surplus sons of the gentry. Competition in recruitment was introduced in 1853 in search of a cadre from the best institutions—Oxford, Cambridge, Edinburgh, King's London and Trinity College Dublin—offering a good salary and handsome pension. Haileybury shut down in December 1857. The concept of government as a trust took its first hesitant steps.

Imperialism was not in dispute—they were all committed to the British Empire. The difference lay in the emerging philosophy of sympathetic governance adopted by an altruistic fringe. An early exception from general behaviour was Sir Bartle Frere, who served from 1835, and fought hard to prevent the unjust annexation of the princely state of Satara, ruled by 'Kakaji' (or Uncle) Narsopant Tatia. As an administrator, he organized the first Indian municipalities. When he left Satara, his colleagues were in tears. As commissioner of Sind from 1850, Sir Bartle built canals, roads, railways and bungalows for travellers. When the authorities claimed that Sind was too backward for a postal service, Frere printed his own stamps and set up local mail. His deputy John Jacob is credited with supervising the construction of 2,589 miles of roads and 786 bridges. As governor of Bombay, Frere improved sanitation and health facilities to such an extent that Florence Nightingale sent letters of praise.

The uprising of 1857 did not end British rule, but it certainly shattered complacence. Lord Canning, the governor-general and then viceroy between 1856 and 1862, insisted that the new way forward was reconciliation rather that revenge and earned the nickname 'Clemency Canning'.

Development became a passion, or *shauq*, for those few ICS officers ready to step out of their ivory towers. Supplicants and applicants crowded their verandahs, even on a weekend. Charles

Allen writes about the revival of a Mughal tradition, which was accessibility to the humblest petitioner. There were early morning queues of *mulaquatis*, who came to meet and greet; *salaam-wastis*, who paid their respects, and *feriyaadis*, with a grievance or a plea, all maintaining the formalities of *ijazat-o-barkhast*, or permission and departure. Frontier Pathans used a Pushtu proverb to define their relationship with the more sympathetic British officers: patience is bitter, but the fruit is sweet.[29]

The sahib had his own protocol. He never revealed his personal feelings. His career had begun on a heart-breaking note, for when he bade farewell in England he could not be certain if he would see his parents again. A 'griffin', or fresher, did not get home leave before eight years.

Gilmour tells the moving story of Sir Henry Stokes, whose wife died young in Madras, forcing him to send his infant son to aunts in England. Stokes returned home after retirement, but after three years his son won a place in the ICS. Sir Henry broke down upon bidding goodbye and wrote to the young man:

> You may be sure that all the good wishes that love could dictate follow you from this side. You have never given me any cause for displeasure or anxiety and I have no fear for the credit of the old name in the old service to which I was so long proud to belong. I am glad now that you have gone to Madras. Your poor mother would be proud and happy if she could see you now. Her early death was the greatest misfortune which could have happened to both of us... I am done now and my chief desire is to see you buckle to [work]....[30]

Sentiment was discouraged in Victorian sensibility, so tears remained unshed.

The last words that John Beames heard, as the steamer slipped out of Southampton in 1858, were his father shout, 'God bless you!' Beames did not see his father again. Beames's reputation rests on his willingness to stand up for justice and his splendid work on the *Comparative Grammar of the Modern Aryan Languages of India*. Writing became a hobby—he was a contributor to a sparkling, sarcastic and successful weekly, *Indian Observer*, brought out by a set of brilliant young bureaucrats, teachers and barristers. Its brief existence ended in 1873 after it published scathing criticism of Lord Mayo and his two chief advisers, Sir John Strachey and Sir Richard Temple. Beames was 'cruelly persecuted' for 'a series of articles on the condition of the peasantry of Orissa'.[31]

Beames was appointed collector and magistrate of the coastal district of Balasore in 1869, three years after yet another devastating famine. Salt was a government monopoly, leading to high salaries, heavy tax, smuggling, down-the-line corruption and police oppression against the impoverished when they tried to boil brine for a handful of salt. The salt agent lived in a huge palace at Contai on a salary of nearly ₹ 4,000 per month, or twice that of Beames. Indians in the Salt Police, or Salt Darogas, got around ₹ 50 from the government and many times that from the contractor, enabling them to buy large estates. As Beames put it, each precaution taken by the Board of Revenue was circumvented by the Board of Smugglers.

Beames described the salt tax as oppressive and its implementation as harsh. One day, an old and frightened woman who had been dragged 50 miles from her village was brought before him. All she had done was to make some salt from the sea to mix with her morning rice. Instead of punishing her, Beames rebuked the police. When asked to explain, Beames stood by his decision. The patriarchs of the British government never understood the injustice of this law until in 1930 Gandhi picked up a pinch of salt from the shores of Gujarat and challenged the colonial rulers to do their worst.

The mainstream of Raj administration was in the control of men who did not understand Beames either. They treated Indians with degrees of contempt, evident in their conversation or in that fashionable pursuit of the era, comic poetry. Major Walter Yeldham, who used the pseudonym 'Aliph Cheem', dedicated his work:

To Anglo-Indian folk
Who can relish a little joke,
This book is dedicated.
If haply to rouse a smile,
Or an idle hour beguile,
The modest tome is fated,

Accomplished will be the dream
Of diffident 'Aliph Cheem'.[32]

By Anglo-Indians he meant, as it was then understood, the white British community in India. The joke was not so little when Indians were the target. On issues of colour, the otherwise affable major was routinely offensive, to judge by a poem like *The Rights of Woman*:

On the hills they call Neilgherries,
Where they grow the coffee-berries,
And the climate's something just between the
     torrid and the cold,
There exists a race of n_____,
Of extraordinary figgers,
And of habits so peculiar, that their story must be told.[33]

The major does rouse a smile when writing about the profound Brahmin 'Humptee Dumptee Frumtee Chundrer' and 'Baboo Humbul Bumbul Bender', the 'Brahmin warm' who was a defender of the 'progress of reform'.[34] But the language of most sahibs and memsahibs of his time was vitriolic, as Percival Spear points out:

The conjugal pair become a bundle of English prejudices and hate the country, the natives and everything belonging to them. If the man has, by chance, a share of philosophy and reflection, the woman is sure to have none. The 'odious blacks', the 'nasty heathen wretches', the 'filthy creatures' are the shrill echoes of the 'black brutes', the 'black vermin' of the husband... Not that the English generally behave with cruelty, but they make no scruple of expressing their anger and contempt by the most opprobrious epithets, that the language affords.[35]

Indians reacted with individual bursts of helpless anger. Bengali villagers, liable to confuse Christians with Christianity, called the British maneaters and their faith a 'devil religion'. When a missionary told a girl studying dance that no unholy person could ever enter the kingdom of heaven, she retorted that in which case there would be no Europeans in heaven.

The Anglican church, however, was never seen as a threat by Indians. The early Jesuits of Goa had been dextrous in their conversion schemes. Before it was stopped by a papal bull in 1704, they had incorporated caste in Christianity, keeping Dalits out of 'Brahmin' churches. The East India Company took a mercantile view. It decided that the risks involved in proselytizing were not worth the reward of heavenly blessing. When Anglican missionaries were allowed into India after 1813, initial apprehensions proved ephemeral. Spear narrates a delightful tale: Calcutta's Brahmins, a trifle anxious about the arrival of Bishop Heber, sent one of their own to meet the prelate:

> He reached the Bishop's house, but when he saw the size of the mansion, the number of carriages waiting at the door, and the throng of servants, he laughed, and returned to tell his companions that whatever dangers might threaten Hinduism, the Bishop was not one of them.[36]

If Bishop Heber had been wearing a loincloth and sleeping in a hut, Brahmins might have been less complacent.

The behaviour of individuals was another matter. Even priests were not above casual brutality. In 1860 Beames, then in Jhelum, met a 'doleful procession: the Thanadar, Moharrir and Jamadar with their heads artistically bound up in bloody rags, blood dried in clots on their faces, and their clothes torn and dusty'. An intoxicated padre had beaten them with a thick stick the previous night. Beames thought that the victims were exaggerating but could not deny the violence. He suggested a compromise, a balm from the padre in the form of a present. Instead, in a 40-page letter, the priest accused Beames of spying upon the clergy and instigating anonymous accusers. For good measure, he called Beames an assassin, Pontius Pilate and Judas Iscariot. The matter was finally settled through the intervention of the bishop.[37]

The largest group of Indian Christians were Eurasians, or those of mixed descent. Neither their faith nor their parentage protected them from British racism. This tragedy has never been fully recognized, nor ever adequately compensated. This disgraceful chapter in British history, manipulated out of school texts and public memory, constitutes a blot on Britain that is indelible and indefensible.

'True Caste' and 'Half-Caste': The Lost Children of Anglo-India

Before 1900, the British were Anglo-Indians and British-Indians were called Eurasians. This is the sense in which *Hobson-Jobson* uses Anglo-Indian in its definition of 'Home': 'In Anglo-Indian and colonial speech this means England.' England was home, however, only for the 'pure' whites—there was no space for the 'half-breed'. The switch in 1900 had a reason. Eurasians were renamed Anglo-Indians to stress their Indian blood and distance them further from the 'pure' whites of Britain. This was not an innocent shift; their Indian half denied them the right to claim Britain as 'home'.

The Portuguese called their children from Indian mothers 'Luso-Indian', or 'Mestizos' and gave them the rights of Portuguese citizens. Perhaps the most famous Mestize was Jeanne Albert, also known as Jeanne Begum, from San Thome. Her second husband, Joseph Francois Dupleix, was the most successful French governor in India; they met after Dupleix captured Madras in 1746. The French and Europeans like the Danes, who gave a home and workplace to William Carey, were far less colour conscious than the British. 'There was no colour prejudice among the French... [by] 1790 there were said to be only two families in Pondicherry of pure blood, of whom the sons of one had married women of the country,' writes Spear.[38]

The British began with fewer inhibitions. In 1684, the Company directed its Council in Madras to 'prudently induce' employees 'to marry Gentoos in imitation of ye Dutch politics and raise from them a stock of Protestant Mestizes'. A mixed-race community was considered 'of such consequence to posterity that we shall be content to encourage it with some expense and have been thinking for the future to appoint a pagoda to be paid to the mother of any child who shall thereafter be born of such marriage'. 'East Indians' wore a hat and Western dress and were known as 'Topas' (from *topi*, Hindi for a hat); those who could afford it sent their children to school in England, who then returned to serve the Company.[39]

Attitudes began to change after the Company conquered Bengal by 1765. Between 1786 and 1795, the British took three odious decisions which turned the children of British India into second-class citizens.

The first was a 'Standing Order' that banned an 'East Indian' orphan, or a child who had lost the father, from going to England. The declared reason was unapologetically racist:

> [T]he settlement and education in England of such orphans involved a political inconvenience because the imperfections of the children, whether bodily or mental, would in process of time be communicated by intermarriage to the generality of people in Great Britain, and by these means debase the succeeding generations of Englishmen.[40]

In plain language, half-British children would over time 'infect' and 'debase' pure British blood.

A pernicious theory fostered in the septic environment of white England—that those of mixed descent inherited the most dangerous characteristics of both races—was turned into government policy. The English became convinced that they would be devoured by their own children. Lord Valentia, on an inspection tour between 1802 and 1806, described Eurasians as an evil threat, for they combined the aspirations of 'natives' with the ability of the British:

> The most rapidly accumulating evil in Bengal is the increase of half-caste children… This tribe may hereafter become too powerful for control. With numbers in their favour, with a close relationship to the natives, but without an equal proportion of pusillanimity and indolence which is natural to them, what may not in future be dreaded from them… I have no hesitation in saying that the evil ought to be stopped…[41]

British fathers began to treat their own children as evidence of guilt rather than love. The presence of Indian blood was pollution. Eurasians were smeared with epithets like 'half-caste', 'half-and-half' and 'eight annas' (16 annas made a full rupee), *mustees*, *creoles*. Mixed marriages became taboo. Eurasians were gradually consigned to settlements, and the distance between them and the English became almost as great as between the 19th-century Brahmin and the outcaste, according to Spear.[42]

In 1791, Lord Cornwallis suddenly barred East Indians from government employment. This was followed by the exclusion of all

Indians from senior tiers of governance, on the specious grounds that while every Indian was irredeemably corrupt, British corruption could be contained by better emoluments.

Four years later came the decree that only men of 'pure' European descent on both sides could serve in the marine, judiciary, police or revenue departments and 'half-castes' enter the military merely as 'fifers, drummers, bandsmen and farriers'. The last was a decision which the Company would immediately regret. Never short of hypocrisy, the authorities ordered Eurasians, on pain of death, to enlist in the wars against Tipu Sultan of Mysore. As soon as Mysore was defeated in 1799, they were again forbidden from joining the Company army.[43]

One of the greatest names in India's military history could not join his father's army because his mother, Jeany, was a Rajput. James, son of the Scottish Lt Col Hercules Skinner, was born in Calcutta in 1778, the second of seven siblings, with two sisters and four brothers. He was traumatized at the age of 12 when his mother committed suicide—a traditional woman, she felt that family honour had been compromised by her husband's decision to send their daughters to 'mixed race' school. As he entered his teens, James was determined to emulate his father, but Hercules Skinner saw no future for his son in the Company Army.

Philip Mason, a sympathetic chronicler of the Raj, has written a thinly fictionalized biography of James, *Skinner of Skinner's Horse*, in which Hercules explains, with a breaking heart, to a despondent son why he is being apprenticed to a Scottish printer:

'But, Jamie, can you no' see,' he said, 'that you're neither English nor Rajput and I must do the best I can for you? Can ye no' see? If you were English, I could get you a commission in the Company's service. You might be a country cadet, as I was myself, commissioned out here. But there's a rule against that now; you know it well. Your mother was a native of India and they'll not commission you. It's the law. If you were a Rajput, I could take you as a recruit and you could rise to be a subedar. But you're not a Rajput either. You're country-born. There's no place now in the army for one of your birth. I'm to blame. I know it. I know it well. I blame myself severely.'[44]

James ran away to join General Benoit de Boigne, the commander of Maharaja Daulat Rao Scindia's forces, where his courage and flair attracted immediate attention. But when war broke out between the Marathas and the British, the Marathas would not trust Anglo-Indians in the field.

Skinner's genius forced one British general to recant, at least partially. In February 1803, Lord Lake, the commander-in-chief of the Bengal army since 1801, asked Skinner to raise an irregular cavalry and fight alongside him. The 1st Skinner's Horse, or the Yellow Boys, a unit of light cavalry in yellow uniforms, was born. Later, it was absorbed into British ranks and remains part of the Indian Army. His soldiers called James Skinner 'Sikandar Sahib'; Sikandar is the Indian name of Alexander. It was a rare tribute. Skinner, rewarded with a *jagir* in Hissar with an annual income of ₹20,000, settled down in grand style, building a town house at Kashmiri Gate in Delhi, where he lived with both Hindu and Muslim wives. Every member of the household was free to practise his or her faith. James's portraits, both as a young officer in Delhi and in his more mature years, indicate that his skin was brown rather than fair. In 1828, he was made Companion of the Order of Bath and given the rank his father held, of lieutenant-colonel.

Skinner's memoir, *Tazkirat al-Umara*, is written in Persian. Percival Spear describes the confluence of cultures eloquently: 'He wrote Persian more easily than English; he is perhaps the only Englishman who has written his memoirs in that tongue. His manners were Indian, his hospitality proverbial... Skinner himself was a legend; his family was an abiding wonder'.[45] Skinner built St James Church in Delhi, which was consecrated in 1836, five years before his death.

John Lang met Skinner's eldest son Joseph in Delhi. Traditions set by the father were maintained:

Mr Joseph Skinner's house was, at all times, open to all travellers. He was without exception the most hospitable man that I ever met in any part of the world. At his board were to be met daily, either at luncheon or at dinner, civilians and military men of every rank and grade in the service, as well as native gentlemen of position in India—Hindoos and Mahommedans... the most remarkable native that I ever met at Mr Skinner's hospitable board was the late Maharajah Hindoo-Rao, a little, fat, round Mahratta chieftain, with small twinkling eyes, and a countenance replete with fun and quiet humour.[46]

Hindu Rao was a Scindia.

A partial reversal of institutional discrimination began in 1833. Eurasians were gradually co-opted into the railways, police, customs, public works, postal systems and sections of the military, but not into the top echelons of administration, while bias was harder to correct at the popular level.

Beames, although a liberal, gave vent to prevailing attitudes when describing Mrs Howe, the wife of the master attendant of the Port of Calcutta, whom he had met while staying at 3 Middleton Street in 1858: 'The Calcutta half-castes are for the most part a lazy, immoral, useless set; but there are exceptions to the rule and one does occasionally meet with an honest and industrious half-caste...' Mrs Howe was among the exceptions because she was a 'leading spirit in all the benevolent schemes and spent hours every day driving about in her large shabby old barouche with a pair of jobbed horses carrying help to the poor, begging for them or writing letters on their behalf'. She was particularly industrious in helping those who had survived the fighting in Awadh during the 1857 uprising.[47]

The most unfortunate Eurasians were children of planters in Bengal and Assam. Barring the odd exception, their children from local Nepalis, Lepcha or Assamese mistresses were consigned to miserable poverty when an English bride arrived. Their financial and emotional deprivation touched the heart of a Scottish missionary Rev. Dr John Anderson Graham and his wife Katherine, who came to the beautiful Himalayan region of north Bengal in 1889. Eleven years later, they opened a boarding school, St Andrews Colonial Homes, for six children in a rented cottage. The sympathetic Lieutenant-governor of Bengal, Sir John Woodburn, leased 100 acres on the slopes of the Deolo hills; grants came from the government and donations from Scotland. The children called their benefactor 'Daddy Graham'.

The 1881 census kept Eurasians outside the circle of supremacy. The 145,000 'pure' Europeans were described as a 'ruling race'; everyone else was clubbed within the Indian population of 250,000,000 spread across an area the size of Europe. English newspapers endorsed the calibrated penumbra. The correspondent of the widely read *Pioneer* reported from the Calcutta races in 1881 that 'most of the elite were present. Outside the enclosure the Native and Eurasian public were to be seen in their thousands'.[48] Only 1 per cent of Calcutta was 'pure' British.

Clubs, the white islands of British India, kept out 'natives' and Anglo-Indians till they could. David Gilmour provides interesting details of their tenacity. The very exclusive Bengal Club in Calcutta, founded in 1827 at around the same time as the Athenaeum, Reform and Garrick clubs, had no Indian members and frowned upon white men who married outside their colour. It was forced to make an exception for General Richards, who wed twice, first to a Eurasian and then to an Indian Jat woman, before he died at the age of 83 in 1861. The Planter's Club in Darjeeling shut its doors upon a Scottish tea garden manager, who in his sixties married a tribal tea-picker called Jeti.

The Bengal Club was started, as its first president Colonel John Finch explained, because there was no adequate hotel or coffee shop in Calcutta. Its premises were initially at Tank Square in Dalhousie and later moved to its present location on Chowringhee Street. The most impressive palatial sanctum for the new aristocracy was the Madras Club, which opened in 1831 and became reputed for its hot curries. Two years later came the Byculla Club in Bombay. Sind Club in Karachi was a late entrant since Sind was not conquered by the British till 1843. Officialdom created its own degrees of segregation; juniors were allowed to use only one end of the Madras Club bar, reputed to be the longest in Asia.

Women were confined to a disparaging 'hen-house', or *moorgikhana*. They could play tennis on the lawns and gather on the verandah for their evening gin and tonic, brandy-*pawnee*, or whisky and soda (*bilayati pawnee*, foreign water). The bar was off-limits, except on an occasion like Armistice Day, 1918, when they were permitted the 'high honour' of serving drinks. Alcohol was measured by the peg; club wits explained that this meant a peg in your future coffin.

Just before the First World War, Ernest Hartley was forced to resign from both the Bengal Club and the Saturday Club in Calcutta because he had married a half-Parsi woman. His daughter Vivien left India for the United States and became an international phenomenon as the actress Vivien Leigh. Queenie Thomson, born in Bombay, used to whitewash her skin and pretend she was from Tasmania in her quest for acceptance in snooty British-Indian society. She became Merle Oberon.

White supremacy was the spine of colonialism. Charles Allen interviewed Terence 'Spike' Milligan for his Raj series, broadcast over BBC Radio 4 in 1974. Milligan, who was born in Ahmednagar and spent his childhood in the Poona cantonment, described hockey games with Indian children. He told Allen that he had a fine hockey stick purchased from the upmarket store Timothy Whites, but Indians always won, even when using a stick hewn from a tree. But they remained 'inferior': 'They beat me at everything—yet I never thought of anything else except of Indians being inferior. I was born to believe that we were the top people.'[49]

Allen quotes *The Indian Gentleman's Guide to Etiquette*, published in 1919, which offers a novel justification for segregation in trains:

> The Indian gentleman, with all self-respect to himself, should not enter into a compartment reserved for Europeans, any more than he should enter a carriage set apart for ladies. Although you may have acquired the habits and manners of the European, have the courage to show that you are not ashamed of being an Indian, and in all such cases, identify yourself with the race to which you belong.[50]

A British soldier seen joking or talking to an Indian two or three times was called a 'white n____'.[51] There were a few things the two races could exchange, but laughter was not on that list. Claude Auchinleck, who retired as the last commander-in-chief of the Indian Army, described the demands of 'white superiority':

> Supposing you were on leave in the Himalayas and riding along a mountain track. If an Indian came along the other way riding his mule of his pony, he was supposed to get off. Similarly, an Indian carrying an open umbrella was supposed

to shut it. It sounds ridiculous but that attitude was still being imbued into the newcomer to the Indian services when I first went out.[52]

On the other hand, Indian women could not understand why European women ran around in underpants while playing tennis. The cultural gap never narrowed. Christian evangelists actively blocked attempts by the British to familiarize themselves with Indian art and disparaged Indian ethics even as they proclaimed the virtues of their own social behaviour, then rife with class snobbery.

Charles Allen quotes Frederick Radclyffe Sidebottom's tale about transient love in the time of a class ceiling:

> I can remember the occasion when a governor's daughter happened to be a passenger aboard the ship. The first class was full of very stuffy people and she took a fancy to a very handsome young second class steward and when the fancy-dress ball was being held she danced with him all night, and the next morning—they having parted, perhaps, only half an hour beforehand—he approached her and she froze him absolutely stiff in his tracks and said, 'In the circle in which I move, sleeping with a woman does not constitute an introduction.'[53]

The governor's daughter might constitute a fringe case, but society was in atrophy. Eileen, daughter of the Fourth Earl of Minto, Gilbert John Elliot-Murray-Kynynmound, viceroy between 1905 and 1910, fell in love with one of her father's ADCs. Her marriage was forbidden because the proposed husband was a mere subaltern in the Deccan Horse. The obedient Eileen instead wed another ADC, Lord Francis Scott, the younger son of the Duke of Buccleuch, from the Grenadier Guards.[54]

Eurasians often tried to cosy up to the British by imitating their contempt for Indian n-----s, but this did not win them any greater acceptance. Dennis Kincaid describes the lacerating disdain to which Anglo-Indians were subjected by the 'True Whites', even in church:

> But one part of the congregation—the Eurasians—took little share in this almost family-gathering. Their menfolk would

appear as smart as any, perhaps smarter with their large
signet rings and gold-headed canes. The women's dresses
were, however, rather *outre*. They had started well enough in
the current fashion but their wearers could not resist an extra
rose here, another purple bow there, a love-knot, several
gold chains and two or three huge brooches. But these little
solecisms were not the cause of the constraint which fell on
other members of the congregation when they appeared, of
the almost masochistic obsequiousness of the Eurasian men
or of the nervous giggles and gawky bows of the Eurasian
women. They were as painfully aware of their colour as
of their whiter neighbours' disdain, which they, hating as
they did all even darker than themselves with pathological
ferocity, could not but acknowledge in their heart of hearts
to be justified. They bowed, giggled and grinned their way
past the True Whites and settled themselves in overflowing
numbers in shabby carriages whose coachmen were attired
in compensatory glory and drove off to their house furnished
in unconscious caricature of English taste, with even more
occasional tables, silk cushions, brassware and potted ferns
than in the bungalow of the Collector. In the crowded drawing-
room an occasional blushing subaltern, having met one of
the daughters at a dance, would be entertained with stifling
hospitality, while the rest of the station sneered and quoted
Mr Kipling's apt description of the wiles of such people and
the snares that they set for the young unmarried officer...[55]

Officials were ostracized if they stepped over the white line. In the
1930s, W.H. Pridmore was informed in Agra that he would be
banished to a remote and unpleasant district if he dared marry Sybil,
daughter of an Irish soldier and a half-Indian mother. Gilmour writes:

It was widely agreed that the British-Indian 'mix' tended to
produce attractive girls, but men and women from the British
middle classes looked down on them for both snobbish and
racial reasons, mocking their provincialism, their 'chee-chee'
accents and the way (they said) that they smelled of garlic and
cheap scent. The barrier between 'true caste' and 'half-caste'

had become so rigid since the days of General Innes [James, of Madras, who had six Eurasian daughters in the early 1800s] that Eurasian/Anglo Indian girls went to desperate lengths to pretend that they were not at all Indian...[56]

Anglo-Indians could enter a corporals' or a sergeants' mess, but not an officers' club. They in turn did not allow Indians into their institutes. Railway colonies with large Anglo-Indian populations had two clubs, one for Anglo-Indians and another for Indians.

In 1891, the ICS officer Harcourt Butler, serving in the United Provinces, could not get a notable city Brahmin membership of the Allahabad Club, although the Indian had been accepted as a member of London's Reform Club in Pall Mall. The rigidity began to ease after the end of the First World War, but at an unhurried pace. One Indian officer in Dehradun who had applied for membership was invited to dinner before the ballot. He was very nice but cleared his throat and spat on the floor halfway through the meal. He was blackballed by the Indian members too.[57]

Indians and Anglo-Indians could not become members of the Bengal Club till 1959 or the Madras Club till 1960; Saturday Club in Calcutta had relaxed its rules only a few years earlier. In a very British example of sophistry, segregation was defended as an exercise in democracy. A club was an association whose members were free to exclude those they wished to keep out. How could the pure British let their 'hair down' before a native who might carry tales to a newspaper or, worse, be a closet 'Congresswallah'?

Men like St John Philby, a junior magistrate in Punjab in 1914 and father of a two-year-old son called Kim, were rare. Philby threatened to resign from the Lyallpur Club if an Indian he had proposed for membership got blackballed. He won his point. Philby was one of a kind: he would later serve as advisor to King Ibn Saud of Saudi Arabia and convert to Islam, while his son Kim, a high-ranking intelligence officer, became Britain's most famous traitor, defecting to the Soviet Union in 1963 after three decades of betrayal.

Philby's Lyallpur was far smaller and hence more flexible than centres of power like Calcutta or Madras. But even in the small principality of Balasore, in Orissa, rules could be rigid. The prince of Balasore could hardly be kept out after he had provided the club building rent-free and promised to pay for repairs, but there was no influx of Indians in his wake.[58] When the government recognized that it was time to unbend, it could do little against the hidebound. Told that the Byculla Club and Yacht Club would not alter their rules, Lord Willingdon, the governor of Bombay between 1913 and 1918, sponsored the sprawling Willingdon Sports Club, financed by Indian and British donations. Willingdon opened its doors to all races in November 1917. The Calcutta Club accepted Indians as well, but it was all too little, too late.

India's independence in 1947 saw a large outflow of Anglo-Indians to Commonwealth countries like Australia and Canada. It says something about the deep roots of racism that in the 1950s Australian immigration officers ignored their legitimate visas and turned some of them back. They were not white enough.

10

Charpoy Cobra: Life After War

In September 1864, a bystander at the court of the king of Bhutan spat on the face of the Honourable Ashley Eden, secretary to the government of Bengal, splattering him with betel juice. The British Raj decided that the only way to wipe off the stain was war. A large force in two columns, its supplies loaded on 8,500 cashiered bullock carts, entered Bhutan.

The Army struggled back to India in early 1865, its troops stricken with fever or dysentery; very few had wounds. General Duncombe, who commanded the left wing, returned on a *palki*, a sort of sedan chair, immobile from rheumatism. The king of Bhutan remained on his throne. There are no accounts in the history of the British Empire on this inglorious retreat, but John Beames, who as collector of Purnea found the 8,500 bullocks, has mentioned details in *Memoirs of a Bengal Civilian*. The British never attempted a second invasion of Bhutan.

Eight years before this misadventure, the British faced the very real possibility of losing territory from Allahabad to Peshawar during what they condemned as a 'mutiny' and Indians now describe as the first war of independence. The uprising hit the Company like a thunderbolt from a clear sky.

In February 1856, the Governor-general, Lord Dalhousie, sent a message to his successor Lord Canning saying that India was 'at peace without and within' and he could see 'no quarter from which formidable war could reasonably be expected'. Below the calm surface, anger among the sepoys (English rendering of *sipahis*) had been building up for many reasons, from the arbitrary ouster of the nawab of Awadh in 1856 to a controversy over grease used in new cartridges. The sepoys were convinced that it came from beef and pork, violating the faith of both Hindus and Muslims. They did not believe the British explanation that it was only bees' wax and clarified butter.

There were 2,912 Indians and 1,863 Europeans stationed with the 3rd Light Cavalry at Meerut when, on 9 May 1857, 90 sepoys were sentenced to 10 years of hard labour by court martial. Sepoys passed *chapatis* from unit to unit in a coded signal which defied British comprehension. Colonel A.R.D. Mackenzie wrote:

> Everyone remembers the mysterious *chupattis* or flat wheaten cakes which, shortly before the Mutiny, were circulated from regiment to regiment. The message conveyed by them have never been fathomed by Englishmen; but there can be no doubt that they were in some way a signal, understood by the sepoys, of warning to be in readiness for coming events.[1]

At 5 pm on Sunday, 10 May, a rumble was heard amid preparations for the evening church service. The war against British rule had begun. Col. Alfred Mackenzie, who survived the initial onslaught, says that the main objective of the 'rebels' was to free the colleagues who had been court martialled. But the sepoys were not without a plan—they seized Delhi, which was about 60 miles south.

Britain was stunned. Haileybury mourned, along with the country, this day of 'national humiliation'. Beames, who was preparing for India, recalls the sermon on this day by Rev. Henry Melvill: 'The old grey head bowed in sorrow, the rough but beautifully modulated voice and the majestic eloquence of the preacher who at last in one awful burst of passionate oratory hid his faced in his hands and wept aloud...'[2]

The British response was led by Sir John Lawrence, the chief commissioner of Punjab, who earned the sobriquet 'Saviour of India' by the speed with which he disarmed the 30,000-strong 'Hindustani' regiments stationed in his province, raised infantry and cavalry units and mobilized the heavy artillery at the Ferozepur arsenal for the siege of Delhi which began in the second week of June. Brigadier-general John Nicholson a young veteran of the Afghan wars during which atrocities were committed by both sides, and Nicholson had suffered torture and then killed ruthlessly during the British 'retribution', was given command of the moveable column which fought its way from Peshawar and was instrumental in the recapture of Delhi. Among Nicholson's proposals, made with an easy conscience, was 'a Bill for the flaying alive, impalement, or burning of the murderers of the women and children at Delhi. The idea of simply hanging the perpetrators of such atrocities is maddening'.[3] He did not survive to fulfil such vicious objectives. Nicholson was mortally wounded when storming Delhi on 14 September and died within 10 days. England celebrated the recapture of Delhi with general illumination.

British humiliation abated with victory in Delhi, but the rage spiked into vengeful triumphalism after Kanpur and Lucknow were retaken. More than 800,000 Indians, mostly civilians, are estimated to have been killed in the conflict and its terrifying aftermath. The total number of British dead was estimated at around 6,000, according to Douglas Peers in *India Under Colonial Rule: 1700–1885*; among them were 34 ICS officers.

The revenge was designed as a lesson for generations. For one year, every officer was permitted to summarily shoot, hang or imprison any suspect. Civilians were massacred; cities were devastated. Muslims were forced to lick the blood of the dead and eat pork, Hindus to eat beef. Torture was common. Victims were seared with hot irons, waterboarded and had pepper or hot chillies laced into their eyes or pushed up the anus. Inflammatory stories were spread of 'savages' and 'wretches' killing 'all Christians, without regard to sex or age' and women and children being tracked down and shot dead to the accompaniment of 'fiendish yells'. Col Mackenzie summed up the rationale of revenge: 'Since they had butchered our defenceless women and children, we would have been more than human, we would have been less than men, if we had not exterminated them as men kill snakes wherever they meet them.' Hundreds were blown into the air and 'won the death they deserved'.[4]

The sepoys were guilty of at least one massacre in Kanpur of 120 women and children in June 1857. In the volatile mood of that moment this was spun out into multiple tales of barbarism. 'Remember Cawnpore!' became a war cry. The *Spectator* published a letter 'advocating the exhibition, in perpetuity, of the monster Nana Sahib (if we catch him), as a human specimen of a Bengal tiger, in the

Tower or elsewhere… Such a perpetual exhibition would probably be a torture more refined than any physical torture'.[5] Macaulay noted that England was inflamed to a degree unprecedented in memory.

In his two-volume *History of the Sepoy War* published in 1875, Sir John Kaye challenged the allegation that British women had been dishonoured in the palace of Nana Sahib Dhondu Pant, or Balaji Rao Bhat, the eighth Peshwa, who was anointed leader of the uprising at Kanpur: 'Our women were not dishonoured save that they were made to feel their servitude. They were taken out, two at a time, to grind corn for the Nana's household.' William Muir, an intelligence officer who was on the front lines, also rejected such accusations, as did a special Commission of Enquiry set up in Agra.[6]

Vengeance was uninterested in subtleties. Kaye quoted James Neill:

> Every stain of that innocent [British] blood shall be cleared and wiped out… The task will be made as revolting to… each miscreant's feelings as possible, and the Provost-Marshall will use the lash in forcing anyone objecting to complete his task. After properly cleaning up his portion the culprit is to be immediately hanged, and for this purpose a gallows will be erected close at hand.[7]

Sir William Russell, the great Irish war correspondent of the *Times*, records in his diary for 23 February 1859 that 'the executions of natives in the line of march were indiscriminate to the last degree… In two days forty-two men were hanged on the roadside, and a batch of twelve men were executed because their faces were "turned the wrong way when they were met on the march"'. Villages were set on fire on a whim. That was all you needed for a death sentence—to turn your face the 'wrong way'.

Montgomery Martin wrote to the *Times*, London, on 19 November 1857 that he had given up walking in the backstreets of Delhi after seeing the bodies of 14 women, their throats cut from ear to ear by their husbands for fear of being caught by British soldiers. Their husbands then killed themselves.[8]

Robert Dunlop's eyewitness account of brutality is graphic:

The slightest mawkish mentality [in the treatment of arrested mutineers] would be fatal. All men able to carry arms were shot down or put to the sword and their residences burnt. The only prisoners taken, some fifteen in number, were ordered out of camp, and executed in the evening by order of the Military Commandant. Often and often have I seen natives executed, of all ages, of every caste, and every position in society, yet never have I seen one of them misbehave. They died with a stoicism that in Europe would excite astonishment and admiration...[9]

The sagacious Conservative leader and future prime minister, Benjamin Disraeli, warned, while speaking at Aylesbury on 30 September 1858, that vengeance was not justice:

The horrors of war need no stimulant. The horrors of war, carried on as the war in India at present, especially need no stimulant. I am persuaded that our soldiers and our sailors will exact a retribution which it may, perhaps, be too terrible to pause upon. But I do, without the slightest hesitation, declare my humble disapprobation at persons in high authority announcing that, upon the standard of England, 'vengeance' and not 'justice', should be inscribed... I protest against meeting atrocities with atrocities. I have heard things said, and seen them written of late, which would make me almost suppose that the religious opinions of the people of England had undergone some sudden change; and that instead of bowing before the name of Jesus, we were preparing to revive the worship of Moloch.[10]

Moloch is the fallen angel in *Paradise Lost* who urges other devils in Pandemonium, Satan's palace, to renew the war against God and the angels. The *Times*, London, in its editorial of 10 June 1857, wanted Company civil servants to be put on half-pay for the neglect which had fuelled Indian anger:

There never was a people so easily governed. We should not have acquired the obedience, the confidence, and even the affection of 170,000,000 people, had they not possessed a wonderful pliancy of temper, and had we not also had within ourselves some natural gifts of command... Let the Company be wisely consistent; let it extend the penalty to all who deserve it. Let it put all the European officers on half-pay, seeing that their neglect is the chief cause of their misfortunes.[11]

American journals warned against excess, even while generally accepting British rule as enlightened. Charles Hazewell made the perceptive point in the *Atlantic Monthly* that for 'the first time in the history of the English dominion in India, its power has been shaken from within its own possessions, and by its own subjects...'[12]

The Illustrated London News saw, in its issue of 4 July 1857, a 'foreign hand':

We have the strongest reasons to suspect that Russian emissaries are, and have long been, at work, not only at the outposts and frontiers of our Indian Empire, but in the very heart of the country, in exciting dissatisfaction against British rule, and in stirring up the native population against us...[13]

Russian intrigue, it alleged, was sustained by roubles.

The Anglican Church had its own interpretation: the 'rebellion' was a message from God. The British in India had been ashamed of Christianity, rather than being proud of the God who had given them the land. They had hidden the glory of the Bible from Indians to seek glory for themselves. Christianity was the only guarantee against a second rebellion. This argument remained part of the liturgical narrative through the century. Rev. J.E.C. Welldon, the bishop of Calcutta between 1898 and 1902, could not comprehend why Queen Victoria was more popular than Jesus Christ and dreamt of a modern Constantine who would deliver the Indian Empire to Jesus.[14]

Wisdom, though subdued by the thirst for disproportionate revenge, was not totally lost. The Viceroy Lord Canning ignored Prime Minister Lord Palmerston's desire to raze the great mosque built by Shah Jahan in Delhi, the Jama Masjid, to the ground. It would have been a heinous instance of religious and cultural vandalism.

Queen Victoria praised Lord Canning, but most of her cheerleaders wanted nothing but the noose and lash for Indians. A letter published in *The Englishman*, a Calcutta newspaper, on 11 June 1857 held virtually every Indian to be guilty, if only by association:

Now is the time for the Government to assert its rights. As the conquerors of a country, let no sentimentalism interfere and pamper men who attribute all concessions to fear. This rise has not originated with the Sepoys; doubtless the cowardly prating, cunning Bengalee and Oriah Brahmins have put up men, whom they hate and fear, in order to try and creep, under their defence into the lucrative posts should the Government of India be overthrown... The natives of India are not yet sufficiently civilized, for the liberty which they have been allowed to enjoy...[15]

Intellectual bureaucrats like Alfred Lyall, who had killed a man in battle and hanged sepoys, shared this view. He thought that the British 'imperial tribe' had over-reached in trying to introduce 'European civilization' over a people opposed to such ideas.[16] India, he prophesied, would be free as soon as it found its Napoleon. Gandhi, as it so happened, was born 12 years after 1857.

Indian memories were etched into folk music. In 1911 William Crooke travelled across Awadh to compile *Songs of the Mutiny*. Among them was the lament sung by Ali Sayyid of Faizabad:

The soldiers of the Rana raised trouble in Oudh, my Ram.
The Lord sent a letter: 'Come and join us, Brother Rana.
I will get military honours from London and make you
    governor of Oudh.'
The Rana wrote an answer: 'Don't play with me.
As long as there's life in my body, I will dig you up and
    throw you away.'
All the zamindars met together and joined the English.
So first the Raja's clan was destroyed and secondly his fort
    was dug up.[17]

Saligram Kayasth of Itawa recalled the dire fate of Bahadur Shah Zafar, who was, oddly, convicted of treason against his own government:

O, *for what infidelity to my salt have I now been banished*
    from my country?
O, *the people weep in the streets, the merchants weep in the*
    shops.

Rameshwar Dayal of Itawa extolled the Rani of Jhansi:

Well fought the brave one; O, the Rani of Jhansi.
The guns were placed in the towers, the heavenly (magic)
    balls were fired.
O, the Rani of Jhansi, well fought the brave one.
All the soldiers were fed with sweets; she herself had treacle
    and rice.
O, the Rani of Jhansi, well fought the brave one.[18]

Shital Prasad Shukla of Mirzapur granted the British courage and
skill:

The Hindus cried 'Ram, Ram' and the Musalmans
    'Allah, Allah',
Fearless men fought in the field, and used all the force they
    could.
The (British) braves entered the field like vast elephants.
With no fear of death they set their faces to the front...[19]

The Gujjar women of Saharanpur saw the conflict through the naivete
of their beloved. Each line is followed by a refrain about the first
battlefield, in Meerut:

People got shawls, large and small; my love got a kerchief.
There is a great bazaar at Meerut; my love did not know
    how to plunder.
People got dishes and cups; my love got a glass.
There is a great bazaar...
People got cocoanuts and dates; my love got an almond.
There is a great bazaar...
People got coins of gold; my love got a half-penny.
There is a great bazaar...[20]

Philip Mason writes:

> Bitterness on the Indian side was stronger among some of the
> princes and nobles and the more educated, but it was not
> so much on account of the ruthless oppression of the revolt
> as at subsequent slights and rudeness. G.O. Trevelyan has a
> story almost inconceivable to anyone who knew India in the
> next century of a planter lashing out indiscriminately with a
> hunting-crop at a group of Indians who had paid to come on
> to a race-course and had had the effrontery to stand in a good
> place for the finish.[21]

Not quite inconceivable, Mr Mason. Sir George Otto Trevelyan had
reported a common affliction—the arbitrary violence which many
British men considered a right. Mason admits that Calcutta's traders
and young officers freely indulged in expressions such as 'I hate the
natives' or 'I like to beat a black fellow', an entitlement fortified by
the fact that British rule 'was growing steadily stronger; perhaps
because the English were becoming intoxicated by power'.

Even a lighter note was not always very light. The 'frontispiece'
of Hilton Brown's *The Sahibs* is a caustic précis of the English view
of India in 1859 titled *Curry and Rice*:

What varied opinions we constantly hear
Of our rich, Oriental possessions;
What a jumble of notions, distorted and queer,
Form an Englishman's 'Indian impressions'!
First a sun, fierce and glaring, that scorches and bakes;
Palankeens, perspiration, and worry;
Mosquitoes, thugs, cocoanuts, Brahmins, and snakes,
With elephants, tigers and curry.
Then Juggernaut, punkahs, tanks, buffaloes, forts,
With bangles, mosques, nautches, and dhingees;
A mixture of temples, Mahometans, ghats,
With scorpions, Hindoos, and Feringhees.
Then jungles, fakeers, dancing-girls, prickly heat,
Shawls, idols, durbars, brandy-pawny;
Rupees, clever jugglers, dust-storms, slipper'd feet,

Rainy season, and mulligatawny.
Hot winds, holy monkey, tall minarets, rice
With crocodiles, ryots, or farmers;
Himalayas, fat baboos, with paunches and pice,
So airily clad in pyjamas.
With Rajahs—But stop, I must really desist,
And let each one enjoy his opinions,
Whilst I show in what style Anglo-Indians exist
In Her Majesty's Eastern dominions.[22]

The Rani of Jhansi and Begum Birjis Qadr of Awadh were genuine martyrs in the Indian cause, but the Raj would not have survived without crucial help from most Indian princely states. On 26 October 1857, William Muir, the head of intelligence based in Agra, wrote to J.W. Sherer, who was in 'Cawnpore', that the maharaja of Gwalior had rendered the British 'noble service'.[23] The Rajputana Agency, Patiala, Kapurthala, Rampur, Jodhpur and Nabha sent troops, while Jang Bahadur Rana of Nepal came personally to assist in the siege of Lucknow, which fell to the British in March 1858.

In a curious footnote, the Ottoman sultan of Turkey, Abdulmejid I, Caliph of Muslims, sent £1,000 to London for the succour of the British who had suffered in 1857.[24] As a sum it was petty; as a gesture it was significant.

Veena Talwar Oldenburg estimates that the loot from Lucknow was far more than the authorities admitted. She details the contents of one barrel, from a list of 40, which reached London. The 41 items in 'Barrel No. 12' included a red velvet cap jewelled with diamonds, emeralds and pearls; with a gold laced cap with similar accompanying jewels; richly jewelled sword belt; pearl-and-diamond cup; pearl, diamond and lapis lazuli armlets; golden pestle and mortar; pearly rosaries; the richest necklaces, broaches and bracelets aplenty; '8 Qurans in Gold and 8 in paper' and much more. As Oldenburg notes:

And so this list goes on and on, of fabulous jewels and other valuable objects, in the detailed catalogue of the dozens of barrels—full of jewels seized from the systematic looting of the royal residences in Lucknow. These exquisite trophies were despatched to England to bedeck Queen Victoria and the royal family.[25]

Dennis Kincaid considers 'the strange outburst of racial hatred among the secure civilian population of Calcutta' inexplicable since the English were never threatened in their capital. He attributes the racial hatred to 'atrocity gossips' who 'enjoyed themselves with salacious and untrue details' spread through journals. Kincaid adds:

> But once the rising was over and every 'guilty city' had been visited with fearful vengeance it might have been hoped that the victors would soon abandon an attitude of hostile tension. This did not happen. Long after the last rebel had laid down his arms, been hanged or vanished into the jungles the Calcutta Press continued its ferocious tirades.[26]

Contemplating the war he had just covered, Russell observes that the liquidation of East India Company's rule on 2 August 1858 was not enough to soothe passions:

> The mutinies have produced too much hatred and ill-feeling between the two races to render any mere change of the name of the rulers a remedy for the evils which affect India, of which those angry sentiments are the most serious exposition; and however desirable it might have been to introduce that change, I do not think it was cheaply purchased at the price of much innocent blood, and by the growth of bitter hostility between the natives and the members of the race to which their rulers belong. Many years must elapse ere the evil passions excited by these disturbances expire; *perhaps confidence will never be restored*; and if so, our reign in India will be maintained at the cost of suffering which it is fearful to contemplate.[27]

This was prescient. The price of innocent blood was high.

Russell's analysis is a tribute to the editorial balance of the Empire's most influential newspaper:

> Either it was a military mutiny, or it was a rebellion more or less favoured by the people when once the soldiery broke into insurrection. If it was a pure military insurrection, it is most unjust to punish the country people and citizens by fines and hanging for complicity in acts with which they of their

own accord had nothing to do: it is also impolitic to inflict chastisement upon them for not actively resisting armed men, drilled and disciplined by ourselves, and masters for the time of the whole country. We cannot punish sympathies: the attempt is sure to quicken animosities and provoke national, deep-rooted antipathy.[28]

The Calcutta English press never missed an opportunity to quicken animosities long after the last 'rebel' had been hanged. When in 1865 an English planter called Rudd was convicted for the murder of a local shepherd over a trivial dispute, the *Bengal Hurkaru*, thus far a notable proponent of capital punishment, wrote leaders against the wickedness of the death sentence, organized processions and held mass meetings to save Rudd from the rope.

The *Englishman* printed letters claiming that the only people who had any right to India were the British; the *Friend of India* denounced the induction of Indian magistrates who were 'copper-coloured' pagans and 'secret devotees' of the Goddess Kali who wanted Rudd as a human sacrifice. British justice, commendably, ignored the media. Rudd was hanged.

The Army was remodelled, as it had to be after a mutiny. Before 1857, the Company had 230,000 Indian and 40,000 British troops; the new ratio became closer to 2:1.[29] Recruits now came mainly from communities which had fought alongside the British, the shift justified by the pretentious theory of 'martial' and 'non-martial' races, or 'fighting' and 'sedentary' peoples. Sikhs and Gurkhas were placed in what were called 'Class Regiments'; other Indians went into mixed formations to prevent ethnic unity. Trust disappeared. Indians were barred from artillery units.

Field Marshal Sir Claude Auchinleck, whose father had served in 1857, described the new dispensation to Charles Allen:

> Generally speaking the Gurkhas were very, very fine mountain soldiers. The Sikhs were very tenacious, very brave, and would carry out orders to the letter. The Punjabi Mohammedan troops, who formed something like fifty per cent of the Indian Army, were very biddable, very leadable and easily trained but never quite up to the standard of the Sikh or the Gurkha.

Then came the Indian troops from further south; the Jat, very heavy, solid and wonderful in defence, very similar in outlook, speech and everything else to the Norfolk man. Then came the soldiers from the foothills, the Dogras, the Garhwalis and after them a big belt of soldiers from much further south based on and around Poona; the Mahrattas, very brave and to be reckoned with but quite at home in the hills as the troops from further north. Then you got the Sappers and Miners, the Engineers, some from the Punjab, some from the UP and some from Madras, like the Madras Sappers and Miners who were descendants of our old Madras Army—all of them excellent troops.[30]

British officers came from the upper classes. Spike Milligan told Charles Allen:

I really thought they [officers] were the gods and never got very close to them without being terrified out of my life. They had very loud voices, very proper, were very well turned out and always on horses, always taller than me, doing things with tremendous panache. If you heard the click of heels you knew the officer was somewhere near and somebody was standing to attention. They used to stand to attention like ramrods. I watched my father salute and I thought his arm would drop off with the ferocity of his salute.[31]

The Army, steel fist of authority, evolved into a vibrant institution of cooperation but not of equality. The generals, having learnt from 1857, took care not to impose British morals upon troops, who were permitted the flexibility of cultural idiosyncrasy. The least raunchy line of a famous Pathan marching song called *Zakhmi Dil*, or Wounded Heart, was: 'There is a boy across the river with a ____ like a peach—but, alas, I cannot swim.' Kincaid has used a blank instead of the original word, which remains a good idea.[32]

There was a revealing difference in the send-off for troops headed overseas. The British marched out to 'Oh! It is grand to be a soldier!' or 'When the boys come marching home again'. Indians heard a more realistic 'We don't want to fight but, by Jingo, if we do!'. If the Indian soldier was bewildered by the prospect of fighting on the sands of Egypt or in the ports of China, he never let doubt compromise loyalty. He remained 'true to his salt', or *namak-halal*.

There was no discrimination in the rulebook, but as the number of Indian officers grew, ways were devised to prevent British officers from serving under them. Auchinleck recalls one young Indian officer telling him, 'You British officers of the Indian Army don't know India. All you know are your servants and your *sepoys*.'[33]

The incessant casualties of the First World War and the urgent need for replenishment made nonsense of the martial races theory. The Army recruited anyone willing and able to meet its requirements. Around 1,300,000 Indians served during the Great War; more than 74,000 lost their lives. Such extraordinary sacrifice did not alleviate ingrained bias against brown and black recruits, which has now been documented by a special committee of the Commonwealth War Graves Commission. It found that at least 116,000, and perhaps up to 350,000 war casualties had not been commemorated because of entrenched racism in the army. On 22 April 2021, British Prime Minister Boris Johnson apologized and promised to build new memorials to the forgotten.

The martial races theory was formally abandoned by the Indian Army only in February 1949.

The Purity Crusaders

Queen Victoria's civilian establishment, unlike her Army, seemed more determined to upgrade Bengali morals than to improve the Empire's economic well-being.

From the 1830s, printing presses at Calcutta locations such as Chitpore Road, Sobhabazar, Ahiritola and Goranhata, collectively dubbed the Battala press, began to churn out risqué literature. Attempts to curb unregistered printing in 1835 and pornographic material in 1852 were ineffective against popular demand. The conscientious Reverend James Long wrote to the lieutenant-governor of Bengal on 1 July 1855 that 'obscene pictures... are exposed to sale and hawked about in the public streets and villages and that there exists no law by which the publishers or vendors of these pictures can be punished'. He gathered a list of 500 Bengali titles designed to 'suit the depraved taste of the country and accumulate the libidinous passions'. His fulminations contributed to a law against the sale of obscenity without doing much to hurt the trade.[34]

In 1874, the government proscribed 15 Battala books and arrested hawkers on Strand Road for selling titles like *Russick Turunginee* (Luscious Girl), *Nobo Roso Sagur* (A Sea of New Juice), *Ki Bhoyanak Bessya Suktee* (How Powerful is a Prostitute's Strength), *Adi Ros* (Original Juice), *Prem Natuck* (Love Drama, in two editions) and *Narir Solo Kala* (Sixteen Arts of a Woman). A prim official recorded on file that he had the books translated into English to

> determine whether their contents are calculated to pollute the mind or to excite corrupt passion of the reader. For the purpose of discovering the truth as to this matter, one has to read at least some portions of the book; this is no enviable task, though in the interests of humanity, it may be regarded as a duty...[35]

Victorian bureaucrats read pornography only out of a deep sense of duty.

Two decades later, in 1893, the secretary to the government of North-Western Provinces and Oudh (roughly equivalent to modern Uttar Pradesh) wrote to the chief secretary of Bengal protesting against an advertisement placed by Calcutta businessmen in *Bharat Jiwan*, a Hindi newspaper from Benaras, on 31 July which offered *Kamoddipan*, or 'lust-stirring oil'. The aphrodisiac was not cheap:

> This oil enables the old to enjoy the pleasures of youth. If the *nas* [which means a sinew or nerve and is a slang term for the organ of generation] has been weakened by excessive sexual intercourse, onanism or some other cause, it is set right and restored to its original vigour by the application of this oil. To see the bracelet on your arm needs no looking glass. Use and see its effects. Price per *tola* ₹5.[36]

The chief secretary of Bengal replied that four years earlier the viceroy had, upon receiving a petition from the Calcutta Missionary Conference, ordered an enquiry led by Sir Steuart Bayley, lieutenant-governor of Bengal. It concluded that such advertisements were not punishable under Sections 292 and 293 of the Indian Penal Code. The Battala press marched on.

Christian missionaries, in alliance with Bengali moralists, sought to arouse the public's conscience against such sin. Keshub Chandra Sen, president of the Brahmo Samaj, spoke at the Town Hall during the opening session of the Society for the Suppression of Public Obscenity, which appointed Raja Kali Krishna Deb president and the Rev. Soorya Coomar Ghose secretary. 'Christians and Brahmos, Mahomedans and Hindoos, united on the ground of a common moral principle to declare that the nascent literature of the country should no longer be allowed to run the risk of becoming polluted and polluting,' commented the Baptist paper *Friend of India*.

The eminent writer Bankim Chandra Chattopadhyay went a bit over the top when he claimed that it 'would not be an exaggeration to say that obscenity is the national vice of the Bengalis. Those who may consider this an exaggeration, should merely think of Bengali jokes, Bengali abuses, the wranglings among Bengali women of the lower orders, and Bengali *jatra, kobi* contests, *panchalis…*'.[37]

The Battala press was more than a few shades of ribaldry for the 'lower orders'. Its inexpensive booklets challenged the oppressive impositions of religious orthodoxy. Poems in sing-song couplets known as *dobashi* used references from mythology deemed 'unIslamic' by the Wahabi clergy or narrated a history of the world from Adam to the Prophet Mohammad in which legend was woven into fact. Other tracts promoted a subaltern view of controversies like dowry, widow remarriage, alcoholism or prostitution, written in a breezy style refreshingly different from the hectoring tone of crusaders.

Battala flourished in the shadows, a walk away from the limelight, taunting establishment hypocrisy. The poor gathered in its dens to gossip, smoke, drink and laud with poetic aplomb the pleasures they could afford:

Baghbajarey ganjar adela, guli Konnagarey.
Battalae mader adda, chondur Bowbajarey.
Ei shab mahatirtha jey na chokhey herey,
Tar mato maha papi nai trisangsarey.

Or: Baghbazar is best for hemp, Konnagar for opium pills, Battala for gossip over a drink, Bowbazar for a puff of opium. There is no sinner bigger than one who does not visit these mighty places of pilgrimage.[38]

The government used the limited consensus on risqué booklets to restrict anything that was 'scandalous, defamatory, seditious, obscene or otherwise prejudicial to the public interest', as wide a cover for censorship as it was possible to fashion. The playwright-actor Amritlal Basu and director Upendranath Das were sentenced to a month's imprisonment for producing *The Police of Pig and Sheep*, a thinly veiled lampoon of the police commissioner Sir Stuart Hogg and his superintendent, Lamb.[39] As one wise person commented when London's Society for the Suppression of Vice was established in 1809, it was a society for the suppression of vice among those who earned less than £500 a year. This was equally true of Calcutta in the 1880s.

The British were less puritan than their homilies suggested. In 1862, during the summer of the Victorian era, the lieutenant-governor of Bengal, Sir John Grant, decided upon retirement that he could not continue living with a wife who had borne eight children, two of whom were regrettably not his. Grant was persuaded to change his mind by his eldest daughter. Simla, in full bloom during the 1860s and 1870s, was nicknamed 'Capua', the Roman Empire town known for perfumes and fornication. Lt Herbert Du Cane wrote to his father in 1885 that while he had applied for three months' leave to visit Simla, the prospect did not please him since the hill station was famous for gambling, drinking and breaking the seventh commandment. Young Herbert could hardly have told his father that he was heading for three months of cards, alcohol and adultery. Rudyard Kipling, who based the fictional Mrs Hauksbee on his friend Isabella Burton, wrote of Lady Edge, the wife of the chief justice of Allahabad High Court, that she was inclined to be naughty though much over forty, and gave herself away in 'double handfuls'. The very naughty had nicknames: Passionate Haystack, Charpoy Cobra, Bed-and-Breakfast, Lilo, or the comparatively prosaic Vice Queen, who notched up conquests on her bedstead. The cuckolds bore this with fortitude, until they couldn't.[40] For the very prudent, the safest place for an escapade was a coupe on a night train, away from the keen glances of servants.

It mattered less to a race-driven sensibility if white men had dark-skinned mistresses. While this became less prevalent in India after the 1830s, it remained common practice in Burma. Burmese women were among the most liberated in the world—they had neither caste nor veil and married or divorced as they pleased.

David Gilmour writes that 90 per cent of British officers in Burma had mistresses. The viceroy chose to ignore what he could not change, but the bishop of Calcutta, Rev. Welldon, was more militant. Mrs Ada Castle, the wife of a police officer, who had become a terror in Rangoon because of her 'purity crusade', complained about the acting deputy commissioner of police Walter Minns, who lived quite openly with two Burmese ladies and took one of them on tours. Curzon, worried about the impact of scandal on British prestige, wrote to Sir Frederick Fryer, the Lieutenant-governor of Burma. Minns responded, doubtless with a stiff upper lip, that his travelling companion was a nurse. Fryer promoted him to deputy commissioner.

In 1903, 25 British officials married their Burmese mistresses, but Minns's name was not among them, possibly because marriage would have made him guilty of bigamy.

The British Bubble

In 1880, Prime Minister William Gladstone, conscious of the need for reform, sent George Frederick Samuel Robinson, First Marquess of Ripon, as viceroy. Within two years, Ripon eased restrictions on Indian publications, prohibited child labour before the age of seven, introduced a weekly holiday for Indian workers, lowered the salt tax, encouraged local education and tried to end discrimination in the courts. He also got on well with Indian princes. In 1883, his shooting party, as guests of the maharaja of Darbhanga, bagged four tigers, 47 buffaloes, 280 boar and 467 deer. It would not have required much marksmanship to shoot buffaloes. But such convivial bonhomie was not the norm.

Val Prinsep, the visiting portrait artist, records 'the discontent and dissatisfaction of the European community' when some Indian princes sat down while the Viceroy was still standing at Lord Lytton's reception on 1 January 1877. Prinsep heard British hotheads declare that they should have forced the Indians to prostrate in a *salaam* to the British flag and cut off their ears. They were angry at 'talk of the "Black Raj", where everything is sacrificed to the native. There have been no balls for the ladies, no parties without dark gentlemen'.[41]

Prinsep was sympathetic towards Indian sentiment:

I myself do not see much harm in all this attempt to civilize the native, but I fear it does not always succeed. To see the great rajahs at a party is pitiable. Their dignity is offended, and they sit and sulk in corners... There is no denying the fact that lately the distance between the races has been much increased, especially on the English side... I hear all kinds of stories about the British subalterns. I myself was witness to their behaviour at the Viceroy's levee. They made loud remarks about the rajahs present, and expressed a wish to cut their ears off to get their jewels, or bonnet them, &c—quite forgetting that many of the rajahs understand English... One cannot be surprised if they, like the worm, wish sometimes to turn.[42]

Officials insisted on deference and even servility from 'natives'. They had been pampered from the beginning of the Raj: a painting dated to 1810 by Sir Charles D'Oyly, a baronet who served in Bengal for more than three decades, shows a young cadet on a chair in the centre of the hall watching nautch during Durga Puja celebrations while fat and fawning Indians surround him.

After 1857 the gulf became impassable, writes Margaret MacMillan:

British society was turning in on itself. The opening of the Suez Canal in 1869, together with faster and safer communications between Britain and India, meant that the exiles could keep closer ties with Home... The exiles took to referring to themselves as 'white Brahmins', at the pinnacle of the caste system. Mrs Leopold Paget, who came to India in the 1860s with her husband's regiment, remarked that the British treated Indians with a 'pride and contempt, as of a lower order of beings'. One of the more awkward discoveries of the 19th century was that Indians were largely Aryan, part therefore of that great human family which had also populated northern Europe.[43]

But instead of the Aryan tag being an upgrade, it became evidence of how far Indians had drifted from the European ideal. MacMillan quotes Curzon, a great enthusiast of the mission to 'civilize' the subjects, telling a British audience at Bombay's Byculla Club:

...the Almighty has placed your hand on the greatest of His ploughs, in whose furrows the nations of the future are germinating and taking shape, to drive the blade a little forward in your time, and to feel that somewhere among these millions you have left a little justice or happiness or prosperity, a sense of manliness or moral dignity, a spring of patriotism, a dawn of intellectual enlightenment or a stirring of duty where it did not exist before—that is enough, that is the Englishman's justification in India.[44]

By patriotism, Curzon meant loyalty to the Raj, in his view the best thing ever to happen to India. Curzon was certain that God had sent the British to India for the lasting benefit of humanity. As for India's national pride, that was an oxymoron since India had never been a nation. Some enterprising imperialists described India as a continent of foreigners, arguing that there were no Marathas apart from the ruling clan in states like Gwalior, Indore and Baroda and the Hindu population of Hyderabad was ruled by a Muslim Nizam. Ergo: if the British left, India would disintegrate. Such thinking was accepted as gospel truth till the end of the Raj.

Those liberal administrators who reached out to Indians through 'mixed' or 'international' parties could end up with strained nerves. Henry and Annette Beveridge divided their garden into enclosures for mingling and separate dining for Hindus, Muslims and the British. Indian hosts reserved chairs for European guests, which undermined the possibility of conversation. Both sides seemed more comfortable in their own space.

The Madras correspondent of the *Pioneer* reported in 1881 that Indians were no longer invited to the Queen's birthday ball, as used to be the case. Conversely, Harcourt Butler, as a young ICS officer in the United Provinces, was shocked when a Brahmin washed his hands after the handshake in a basin of water carried by a servant.[45] Till the 1920s, the Maharaja of Chhatarpur would avoid shaking hands with Europeans because they ate meat. Indians greeted one another with either namaste or salaam, so the question of touching did not arise in Indian courtesies.

The insular Raj society was rife with angularities that had ancestry but no explanation. In some places, a new arrival waited for residents to invite him; in others, he was required to make the first move by leaving his card. For some eccentric reason this had to be done at noon, when the Indian sun was at its fiercest. Calcutta was more sensible. You could drop your card after morning service on Sunday. The hostess would, of course, never be 'at home', but the newcomer could expect an invitation to tea or dinner. Tea was an entry point for introductions. British India was a dinner society.

Pedigree, the class differentiator in London, was comparatively passé in India. Post and pay determined status. John Thompson observed when he came to India in 1897 that life was bound to be uniform because no one in the civil service was rich, no one was poor, no one was too old and no one was too young. Perhaps that was why snobbery was fierce, whether at the rarefied levels of the viceroy's council or the humbler railway service, where a dispute over precedence was adjudicated by whether you were station master on a main line or a subsidiary line. The subsidiary line deferred to the main artery. The educational service was lower in ranking than the railways. Lockwood Kipling, the author Rudyard's father, who was in the education department, was often bumped up in the seating arrangements at Simla by Lord Dufferin because he had better conversation. In contrast, Curzon was as stiff as his collar at the obligatory Simla garden party. Dressed in frock coat and top hat, he would honour the anthem leaning on a stout stick, sit in his appointed chair under the shamiana with the allotted guest and depart precisely at the predesignated minute.

Mary Curzon, his rich American wife, tried her best to make amends. Vicereine at the age of 28, she mingled with Indians, wore a maternity frock made from sari material and used Indian fabrics and design for her evening dresses. Curzon hated going to functions, so Lady Curzon did all the heavy lifting—parties, races, weddings, polo matches, et al. However, according to that fine-tuned charter of snobbery, the Warrant of Precedence, which had become an obese 15 pages, her first dance at a state ball was with the lieutenant-governor of Bengal, who ranked just below the viceroy in his province, followed by the commander-in-chief of the Army. Bishop Welldon grumbled that he got bored sitting with the same people at every dinner.

Indians were kept outside this intricately woven web of dancing, cocktails, coffee, tennis, lunch, picnics, moonlit evenings and sunny winter garden parties. The best fun was in fancy dress, not least because it meant an evening without a white tie. Calcutta, as the guardian of manners, took a much harder line on etiquette than Madras or Bombay.

E.M. Forster's friend Goldsworthy Dickinson, who travelled on the same boat to India, mocked memsahibs with 'empty minds and hearts, trying to fill them by despising the natives'. Most memsahibs put on the grand airs of a higher class because they had servants in India; the true daughters of earls thought they were 'under-bred and over-dressed'. All memsahibs were not alike, but enough existed to create a stereotype.

The British took modest pride in their high percentage of cranks. Harry Hobbs, the avuncular author of *Our Grief Champion*, *Indian Dust Devils* and *John Barleycorn Bahadur: Old Time Taverns in India*, started work in Calcutta as a piano-tuner at the age of 19, opened a famous music shop and died in his adopted city in 1956. Calcutta, he says, was permeated with a 'disgusting odour' when he arrived in 1883; the water was unpleasant; the side streets were 'sodden with the filth of generations'. But Calcuttans had fun. 'Few will deny that in an international contest for cranks and eccentrics, drunk or sober, British Indians, if placed second, would be justified in lodging a protest. But how they add to the fun of life!'[46] He had enjoyed better food and whisky than he would have in England, along with cheap tobacco and servants. The local caviar, roe of the *rohu* or *katla* fish, was tasty but came with a health warning:

You're all right inside the bar,
But Khubburdar the caviar.

The extravagance of the old days had been tamed, but life was still good in the British bubble. English newspapers leavened their sanitized information with the variable wit of officials protected by an alias. Momos penned this lampoon for the *Times of India*:

The Ladies of Mahabaleshwar
In wraps and furs delight,
And often get pneumonia
'Neath blankets two at night;
But Poona! Oh, in Poona,
The gauziest wisps appal,
And ladies sleep (they tell me)
With nothing on at all.
The Ladies of Mahabaleshwar
In such sweet charms abound
That doctors say their livers
Are marvellously sound;
But Poona! Oh, in Poona,
They scold and nag all day,
And contradict their husbands
Until they fade away.[47]

The White Baboo

As Empress of India after 1877, Queen Victoria changed her signature to *Victoria Regina et Imperatrix*. India was, in a well-known phrase, the jewel of her crown. She could be sentimental about Indians in an era when men like Curzon believed sentiment was a physical illness. Her prime ministers tended to be wary of the sovereign's well-meaning suggestions as, within the limitations of imperial culture, the Queen tried to reinvent her image from distant empress to a maternal guardian.

She met reformers like Keshub Chandra Sen, who came to the palace on 13 August 1870. On this visit to England, Sen appealed to Victorian ladies to help millions of their Indian sisters suffering from the ills of regressive Indian religious practices. His audience was much moved by sentences like 'Shall we hear those cries and lamentations with hearts of steel? Shall we not weep over this scene of spiritual and intellectual desolation that spreads far and wide over that once glorious country?' A few, like Annette Beveridge, did

> go across the ocean and scale hills and mountains, to surmount difficulties and to risk health, in order to wipe the tears from the eyes of weeping Indian sisters, to rescue them from widowhood, from the evil customs of premature marriage, and to induce them to feel that there is something higher and nobler for them to aspire to, but most of London's high society went back to their mansions after a few rousing cheers for Sen.[48]

A few Victorian 'Civilians', short for ICS officers, began to introspect. Was British rule proof of an 'Imperial Destiny' or a historical interregnum in which India had been given in trust to a distant race? Were they Plato's 'guardians' or colonial despots? Were they bearing the White Man's Burden (a phrase used by Kipling for America's presence in the Philippines) or leading their wards towards modern horizons? Was liberty a British principle or a universal right? What should be their response when Indians became so 'improved' as to demand self-rule?

Many thought, like Macaulay but without his vituperative certainties, that education was the answer to aspiration. This had consequences. Philip Mason writes:

> Attitudes, however, were changing... by the 1880s, when the 'educated Indian' was a reality, he became a rival and it was easy to be irritated by his airs of adult independence. At the same time, far from meekly accepting all that Western education offered, Hinduism had turned back to its own traditions... and more educated Indians were in varying degrees nationalist at heart.[49]

There was increasing pressure to address a structural flaw; there were no Indians at the highest tiers of governance in a vast land of some

250 districts with an average size of 4,430 square miles. There had never been an Indian at Haileybury. The first hint of change came in 1853 when the civil service was opened to all 'natural-born subjects' of Queen Victoria.

Macaulay took the high ground in oratory and shifted to lower levels in practice:

> I allude to that wise, that benevolent, that noble clause which enacts that no native of our Indian Empire shall, by reason of his colour, his descent, or his religion, be incapable of holding high office... I shall be proud of having been one of those who assisted in the framing of the Bill which contains that clause. We are told that the time can never come when the natives of India can be admitted to high civil and military office. We are told that this is the condition on which we hold our power... Against that proposition I solemnly protest, as inconsistent alike with sound policy and sound morality.[50]

Then, with a sleight of rhetoric, Macaulay entered a caveat: 'I feel that, for the good of India itself, the admission of Natives to high offices must be effected by slow degrees.'[51] The slow degrees were so hesitant that no Indian was admitted into the ICS till Satyendranath Tagore, the elder brother of Rabindranath Tagore, joined in 1864. In 1869, four more passed the test, three of whom rose to eminence: Surendranath Banerjea, the nationalist leader; Romesh Chandra Dutt, the economic historian, and Behari Lal Gupta, a judge. The pace remained a crawl; in 1910 only 6 per cent of the ICS was Indian.

Allan Octavian Hume, considered cantankerous and contrarian by his seniors, helped inspire the formation of the Indian National Congress in 1885 with the objective of increasing the presence of Indians in the administration. Born in 1829, Allan was promoted to secretary for revenue, agriculture and commerce in 1871. Eight years later, he was removed for the unpardonable sin of criticizing Lord Lytton. He retired to Simla, where he concentrated on his passion, ornithology: his collection of specimens remains the largest single portfolio of Indian bird skins in the Natural History Museum at London. By the time he left for England in 1894, the stir for a different India had started where change always begins, in the mind.

Its advocates paid a limited price. Gilmour writes:

> The only group of Civilians who may have had a legitimate
> grievance was that small band regarded as 'unsound' on
> account of their support for Indian nationalism. Henry
> Beveridge probably missed his promotion to the Calcutta
> High Court for this reason. Yet it would be illogical to expect
> an empire to promote employees, however talented, who in
> effect advocated its liquidation. In any case the supporters
> of the Indian National Congress did not do too badly.
> Neither Allan Hume nor William Wedderburn nor Henry
> Cotton mouldered in a 'penal station'; all of them achieved
> senior positions in the secretariat at least. Cotton, who was
> sometimes referred to as a 'white baboo', may have been
> passed over once or twice in his career, but in the end spent
> six years as head of a province before retiring and becoming
> President of the Congress.[52]

Beveridge recounts his brush with Judge Norris of the High Court,
who 'hated Indian life' and wanted to punish an officer whose
sympathies lay with Bengalis. Norris censured Beveridge for decisions
the latter had taken while posted in Patna. Beveridge also mentions a
letter of protest he wrote to the *Englishman* when he saw the police
excluding Indians from an area in Calcutta's Eden Gardens to which
Europeans were being admitted.[53]

The first entrance test for ICS in India was held at Allahabad in
1922, the year in which Prime Minister Lloyd George praised the
ICS as the 'steel frame of the whole structure'. The frame got a slight
twist; minorities were given weightage to increase their numbers in
the service. Between 1925 and 1935, 311 Indians were taken into
the ICS as compared to 255 Europeans. These select Indians were
sent for a two-year course in either Oxford or Cambridge to become
proper Brown Sahibs.

They were vetted for loyalty. With Gandhi's movement gaining
momentum, each Indian candidate was screened to ensure that he
was on the right side of the Raj.

> Considerable care was exercised in this secret operation, which
> involved both a security clearance and a character reference.

In 1923–4, when the criteria employed in this process were again discussed in the Home Department (particularly the question of whether or not ICS candidates whose near relatives were 'undesirable' should be refused permission to sit the entrance examination), it appears that the security clearance was chiefly concerned with assessing whether or not the candidate could be trusted politically.[54]

One candidate was dismissed as unsuitable because his elder brother had joined Gandhi's ashram and taken on the responsibilities of a 'master tailor'. The term seems ambiguous; stitching handspun khadi could not have required much mastery.

There was a clear duality in Indian aspirations—the desire for freedom could not obviate the parallel desire for achievement, often reflected in a hybrid imagination. Sumanta Banerjee quotes a 19th-century Bengali poem urging Kartika, son of Goddess Durga and brother of Ganesha, Saraswati and Lakshmi, to learn 'Western' fashions and style his hair like Prince Albert, Victoria's consort:

> *Phul pukurey pheley diye parho ohey boot*
> *Sherry, champagne khao ruti bishkut.*
> *Bauri kheuri hoye kato Albert-sinthi,*
> *Shikho ohey hab-bhab adhunik reeti.*

Banerjee translates: 'Throw away your flowers into the tank, and put on a pair of boots. Drink sherry, champagne and eat bread and biscuit. Shave off the hanging curls and part the hair in the Albert-fashion. Learn the manners of the modern times.'[55]

Along with bread and biscuit, Shakespeare travelled, if a bit unsteadily, into the dust and flair of Bengal, creating a resplendent patois in which it was impossible to tell whether *Hamlet* had found a new audience or Shakespeare had become half-Bengali. In *An Ignorant in India*, published in 1911, Raymond Vernede describes a country fair in north Bengal with evident sympathy and charming humour.[56] Both sides laughed to see such fun as the Bengali dish ran away with the English spoon.

The highlight was a performance of *Hamlet* in Bengali, which began at 8 pm and continued beyond midnight. The collector was the chief guest; Vernede came along for the experience. They travelled 40 miles over two days on one *tonga* (open horse carriage), four ponies and two elephants and shot a leopard en route before it could hurt Clothilde, Vernede's wife.

At the fair, a policeman sighted the sahibs and immediately took charge to ensure that the privileges of the ruling class were secure:

> Authority in this country—where, according to the babu, liberty calls loudly to the soul of every man—is not regarded as a means to an end. It is an end in itself and a veritable passion. If a Bengali sees a chance of bullying, he will take it, and his fellows will accept the part of victims with almost equal ardour... To left or to right he would dart, shoving some poor unfortunate who might conceivably have been in our way had we been going that way. The person shoved would seek credit by shoving the man nearest to him, who would shove the next, who would shove a boy, who would shove a smaller boy. Nobody seemed to mind.[57]

The band struck up *God save the King*, into which a few other tunes had crept in, as the sahibs were escorted to a suite by a middle-aged barrister, Mr Chundar, dressed in a *sola topi*, frock coat, trousers and unlaced canvas shoes. There were two musicians on stage, a harmonium maestro to the left, in coat, *dhoti*, patent-leather shoes and a brown polo cap and a *tabla* drummer on the right. The maestro played

> with one hand daringly, as a novice rides a bicycle to show off to a friend, while with the other he fetched betel from his waistband and transferred it to his mouth; or he would, in an ecstasy of abandonment, crash both fists on to the harmonium, crossing the keyboard and coming back again before one could stiffen one's muscles to bear it...[58]

The *tabla*, to mix metaphors, was a poor second fiddle. The music was invaluable. Whenever action palled, an actor would break into song, and the musicians would leap to the fore.

The Bengali *Hamlet* was a Muslim prince. This was perfectly logical, for the plot revolved around his mother's remarriage. A

Hindu widow could not remarry, but a Muslim queen could. The Hamlet of Bengal was, therefore, Jahangir.

In the opening scene, Hamlet-Jahangir's mother kills the king by pouring poison in his ear with the help of her brother-in-law and lover Farrukh. Feigning anguish, the queen claims tearfully that the king has died of snake bite. That is a death rural Bengal can relate to.

Jahangir wears Hamlet's famous black cloak, along with rowing shorts and football boots. He carries a highwayman's pistol in his girdle and a gunmetal watch on a chain over his breast. The watch is not ornamental. Visibly faithful to the text, Hamlet-Jahangir checks the time to ensure that it is truly past twelve, the 'witching time of night,/ When churchyards yawn and hell itself breathes out/ Contagion to this world...' before he sips hot blood.

Horatio has become Akhtar; the lord chamberlain is Humayun. Ophelia has mutated into Meherbano. Mansoor, son of the vizier, is madly in love with her, but her heart belongs to Hamlet-Jahangir. Meherbano wears a cherry-coloured knee-length satin dress and black stockings, without shoes. The clown-cum-gravedigger is Suleiman, who walks on and off the stage whenever he feels the audience needs a laugh; his jokes get resounding endorsement from the harmonium and the drum.

The big scene is a ten-minute sword dance by Hamlet-Jahangir vowing vengeance after a chat with his father's ghost, accompanied by a competitive musical combat between Jahangir and the harmonium player, won with ease by the latter. In the final act, Hamlet-Jahangir shoots Mansoor with a rook rifle. Everyone dies in turn. Ophelia stabs herself with a large dagger covered in silver paper, staggers and is about to complete her dramatic fall when she realizes that the stage is packed with bodies. With a smart professional touch, Ophelia kicks a corpse in the ribs, jerking it out of the way in convulsive spasms. She now has the space needed for tragedy. There is wild applause.

The ghost is the only character in the Bengali Hamlet which looks fully English.

Bengal had not recovered from Curzon's traumatic partition in 1905 when Vernede went to the country fair. The reunification of the state in 1911 was some balm; but the accompanying transfer of British India's capital from Calcutta to placid Delhi was a second body blow. On 23 December 1912, Bepin Behari Bose, scion of Bengal gentry and leader of the Indian Independence League, threw a homemade bomb at Lord Hardinge as the viceroy proceeded through Chandni Chowk on an elephant. Hardinge escaped with a flesh wound, but his attendant, seated behind, was killed. Bose escaped to Japan. During the Second World War he helped raise the Indian National Army from PoWs who surrendered to Japan in Singapore. The INA, under the command of Subhas Chandra Bose, fought against the British.

The British Raj, invincible in its prime, lingered uneasily during decline. The nostalgia of the last generation of British civil servants, men who once had to but whisper *Koi hai?* (Anyone there?) for an Indian servant to materialize, was infused with lament. Vernede recalls the pathos of a sahib whose every wish was once an Indian's command:

> *An antique air surrounds his chair in drawing room and club,*
> *An old Koi-Hai, left high and dry, a faraway look in his eye,*
> *And dreaming of the days gone by, the good old days in 'Jub'.*
> *The leather tan proclaims a man whose world has lost its hub:*
> *No ready thralls to answer calls, no boy brings whisky when*
>   *he bawls,*
> *Stretched out at ease in marble halls, as once in good old*
>   *'Jub'.*
> *No butler staid in gold brocade to serve him with his grub;*
> *No khidmatgar to bring cigar, or fill the brown tobacco jar,*
> *No chauffeur now to wash his car, no sweeperess to scrub.*
> *No bhishti thin with glistening skin to fill his morning tub;*
> *No dhobi foots to iron his suits, no beaters to attend his*
>   *shoots,*
> *No bearer to remove his boots, or give his back a rub.*
> *No fellow bore to share the floor, no crony at the pub;*
> *No boy around to feed the hound, no syce to bring the pony*
>   *round;*
> *No-one to meet on common ground and no-one left to snub.*
> *When all is said—he's not yet dead, he goes on paying his*
>   *'sub';*
> *So please be kind and do not mind if he continues to remind*
> *Us of the days he's left behind—the good old days in 'Jub'.*[59]

Charles Allen writes:

> While the expression *Koi-Hai* was used principally to call
> for servants, it had another meaning; the *Koi-Hai* was the
> old India hand, the 'character' to be found on every station,
> like the man who 'kept a tame cobra on his office table to
> discourage thieves and whose wife left him because he used
> to go to bed in his boots', or the Chief Medical Officer who
> 'fired all six rounds of his revolver into the bonnet of his car
> when it broke down a lonely road', or even the sugar planter
> who 'used to turn out every morning with a hunting horn,
> immaculately dressed in a well-cut riding coat and a cravat
> and a riding whip, and go off to inspect the cane on his horse
> blowing his hunting horn and shouting "Yoiks, Tally Ho!".' If
> British India abounded in—and made much of—its characters
> there were good reasons for it. Eccentricity frequently grew
> out of isolation, from loneliness of the kind that forced a
> colourful character of Percival Griffiths' acquaintance—later
> shot by Bengali terrorists—to 'play bridge with cook'.[60]

The colourful character played bridge with his cook and worked for
a lifetime in India, but he never once called it home.

11

The Englishman in India Has No Home and Leaves No Memory

It was nightfall at Simla Club in 1857. The lamps were gleaming along the long row of windows. Waiters hurried towards the dining room. It was whispered that old Major Stager had won ₹700 in the card room from a young officer, while his boyish whist partner, 'well known as a cool hand', pocketed nearly twice as much from an elderly civilian with a large liver and a fat purse.

Dinner was announced. The food was good, the wine plentiful, the conversation animated. The last jelly finished, cheroots and brandy-*pawnee* came out. Some returned to cards; others took to song; no one pulled rank. A group of 'Bacchanalians' seized 'Ginger Tubbs' still seated in his chair and carried him around to proclamations of 'hip-hip-hurrah' in praise of his skill at singing a comic ballad. Nothing was more remarkable, noted Russell, than the behaviour of Indian servants, who stood 'in perfect apathy and quiescence, with folded arms, and eyes gazing on vacancy as if in deep abstraction, and at all events feigning complete ignorance' of what was going on around them.[1]

No Indian could be a member of this club, of course. Russell asked a member 'who knew something of the natives' what Indians thought of such discrimination. '*They?* Why, they don't think about us at all. They look upon us as out-of-the-way, inscrutable beings, whom it would be quite useless to perplex their heads about, and they're too well accustomed to this sort of thing to wonder at it,' he replied. Later, Russell sought a second opinion, from an Indian. He asked 'a native gentleman one day if he ever heard that our servants complained of us, or laughed at us, or tried to enter into the spirit of our revelries'.

The answer was conditional: 'I will speak the truth, if the Sahib will not be displeased at it.' The Indian continued:

> Does the Sahib see those monkeys? They are playing very pleasantly. But the Sahib cannot say why they play, nor what they are going to do next. Well, then, our poor people look upon you very much as they would on those monkeys, but that they know you are very fierce and strong, and would be angry if you were laughed at. They are afraid to laugh. But they do regard you as some great powerful creatures sent to plague them, of whose motives and actions they can comprehend nothing whatever.[2]

The power was indisputable—the British had lost just one out of 18 wars between 1757 and 1857. Indians might not laugh at the British in public, but privately they disparaged British rule as an incomprehensible plague sent by malign destiny.

The comparison with monkeys came instinctively to those who witnessed colonial parties from the silence of sidelines. Russell read in a 'native' journal an Indian's description of a British dinner. A large assemblage sat down at table. Sahibs and memsahibs devoured chunks of pig and swallowed a great deal of wine, after which the ladies went upstairs to recover. The gentlemen drank till restraint evaporated and shouted out each other's names until

> the man whose name was called stood up, and then putting their feet on the tables, and waving their glasses till they could scarcely stand, whereupon they went to the room where the ladies were, and caught them round the waists and began to haul them about as they were nautch girls...[3]

Russell called this 'Mohawkery', after high-class ruffians on London streets.

Russell learnt a little more about Indian angst when laid-up in his rooms. Word spread among hill chiefs that the 'Queen's news-writer', or 'Malakaukbaree', was in Simla. They rushed to Russell in the hope that he would convey their grievances to the mighty Queen. The analogy was not totally miscued. Queen Victoria did read *The Times*.

As Russell travelled, his empathy for India grew. The moon had just risen on the night of 14 October 1857 as he headed to the Artillery Headquarters in Agra, when his eyes fell on a dazzling white dome surrounded by four glittering pinnacles. It was the Taj Mahal. 'It is wrong to call it a dream in marble,' he wrote, 'it is a thought— an idea—a conception of tenderness—a sigh, as it were, of eternal devotion and heroic love, caught and imbued with such immortality as the earth can give.'[4]

Russell's travelling companion made an incisive comment: 'If the people of this land really built the Taj, the sooner we English leave the country the better. We have no business to live here and claim to be their masters.' The hawks, and Mohawks, insisted that the Taj must have been designed by Europeans, since Italians like Niccolao Manucci were in India when it was built.

Only one category of Indians was offered marginal space in the charmed colonial social circles: princes who had burnished their loyalty with fluent English and European mores in a significant leap westwards from the culture of their ancestors, the Brindians. In the 1840s, the nawab of Awadh was convinced that the European women he saw dancing at a ball were poorly trained nautch girls and not particularly good ones either. He exclaimed after a short while that enough was enough.[5] The children and grandchildren of these nawabs and maharajas learnt to party in London and Paris and dance a mean foxtrot.

Queen Victoria was indulgent towards rajas, to the irritation of a stickler like Curzon who refused to equate men in funny headgear and necklaces with true-blue aristocracy. David Gilmour writes:

> Curzon complained that its members were all invested with a kind of halo in her eyes and were treated indiscriminately as if they were important royalty. A turban with jewels was so alluring to her that she seemed not to care what sort of character it embellished. She liked the psychotic and irascible Maharaja of Holkar because he sent her a telegram on her birthday. She expressed such concern about the treatment

of the Gaekwar of Baroda, who was deposed in 1875, that she had to be reminded by the Viceroy, Lord Northbrook, that the prince's character and behaviour were 'so bad as to render him entirely unworthy of sympathy...' In spite of her Viceroys' protests, the Queen encouraged the princes to visit her at Windsor, where they were so petted by the Court and London society that they were reluctant to return to India and govern their states.[6]

The more confident rajas simply sidestepped Calcutta. The maharaja of Cooch Behar, a friend of the Prince of Wales, preferred Windsor and Sandringham to Calcutta's haunts, where he was in ever-present danger from creditors. The raja of Kapurthala was so flattered when Queen Victoria allowed him to talk on equal terms with her relatives, the Tsar of Russia and the Kaiser of Germany, that he promptly upgraded himself to maharaja on his return to India. Sir Pratap Singh, Maharaja of Idar and inventor of the *jodhpur* riding breeches, had a burning if unfulfilled desire to lead a charge of the Jodhpur Lancers in the service of the Empress.

Their progeny became tabloid fodder as they swanned around Europe. 'They danced on floors of long seasoned Balkan oak to the music of Jack Hylton and Vincent Lopez,' writes Ann Morrow, of the years after the First World War.

> Geraldo and his Gauchos introduced them to the tango and the rumba, and in Deauville Monsieur Max was the master of the complicated Scissor steps. Laughing girls wearing gardenias jived with the Princes till dawn to 'Alexander's Ragtime Band' and 'Everybody's Doin' It'. They loved night clubs like Les Ambassadeurs, The Embassy and the Kit Kat and the jazz of the Californian Ramblers. It was thought important for the young maharajas to dance well. But first the Turkey Trot, then the giddy abandon of the Charleston and the Black Bottom.[7]

There was money to waste, and they knew how to waste it: on wine from Montrachet and Chateau Latour, diamond bracelets from Asprey and gifts for instant admirers among telephone operators, beauticians, singers, nurses and indeed trapeze artists. Their whims could be ingenious. Even a rupee-pincher like the last Nizam of Hyderabad Mir Osman Ali Khan, richest of the potentates, once bought the whole shop at Spencer's in Madras so that he could choose a pair of shoes at home. A maharaja of Scindia offered wine and cigars to dinner guests on a specially built toy train which he could apparently rush past a guest he did not like. The Maharaja of Kashmir Hari Singh walked to the wicket in his huge turban whenever he wanted to bat irrespective of who was at the crease. He was given out, preferably leg before, only when he signalled that he was tired, after 15 or 20 minutes at the crease. The maharaja of Darbhanga tried to buy every winner of the Crufts dog show in Britain.[8] The princes made no distinction between the state exchequer and personal funds.

The straitlaced Curzon, contemptuous of the 'half-Anglicized, half-denationalised, European women-hunting, pseudo-sporting, and very often in the end spirit-drinking young native chiefs' tried to contain such habitual indulgence and blamed his predecessors for winking at vice and encouraging extravagance.[9] He soon learnt the limits of power.

His attempts to sober up the Rana of Dholpur, who had become an 'inebriate', failed. In 1900, Maharaja Gaikwad of Baroda sent word that he was going to England for his wife's medical treatment. Curzon, convinced that this was an excuse to enjoy the fleshpots of Europe which brought 'shame' on India, refused. Gaikwad bought a passage and left for England. Curzon initiated a campaign accusing the maharaja of being rude and treacherous. Gaikwad retaliated by passing orders that Europeans in his state would henceforth be subject to his civil and criminal laws, imposed restrictions on trains and appointed a critic of British rule, Romesh Chandra Dutt, to his court.[10]

Curzon was, however, delighted when the maharaja of Jaipur constructed a temple on the ship taking him to England for Edward VII's coronation, with enough holy water from the Ganges to last four months. When the Raj began to wind down in 1946, its civil servants had an unusual problem: thousands of files detailing the extravagant peccadillos of princes which they were reluctant to bequeath to the republican government of free India. Sir Conrad Corfield, the ICS stalwart in charge of princely states, burnt the files.

Lesser Indians got the attention of a patron. Curzon professed that the millions he had to tend were schoolchildren, in need of a ward, education, discipline and an occasional touch of the cane. Like a very superior headmaster, he sent instructions; he did not speak to his schoolchildren.

The Punch and Curzon Joust

The English language could have been an effective bridge between the British and an influential middle class, but the two never conversed. Sahibs interacted with servants at home and subordinates at work. They spoke out of need or necessity, not out of choice. Servants had a smattering of half-pronounced English words, while their memsahibs obliged with similar hotchpotch in native lingo. A thin sliver of aspirational Indians started to use English for supplication, couched in the extravagant praise of one seeking favours.

Indian English began as an imagined language.

The correspondent of the *Hindoo Patriot* wrote in 1857 about the classic Sanskrit play written by Kalidas, *Shakuntala*:

> Foreigners contemplate with ecstasy the genius of our poets. The universities of Europe are not tired of pouring over the musty tomes of ancient Sanskrit literature. The Sacoontollah of Kallidas has undergone the most finished translations in Germany and in England. But amongst the people for whose forefathers the immortal bard taxed his genius, his admirable work is a sealed book almost.[11]

Syntax sank into bathos when Indian versifiers sought the soaring heights of romantic poetry: *Soft summer hours/ Freshening April showers/ Joyance rains upon me/ Weaving the chaplets you have yet to gain.*[12]

Lord Curzon preserved a letter from an unnamed heir to a 'Native State', who was trying to explain why he had been unable to call upon the viceroy:

> I wrote to Mr A—to procure me interview with your Sublime Lordship. Although he is very aptitude, theological, polite,

susceptible, and temporising, yet he did not fulfil the desire
of the Royal blood. When your susceptible Lordship was at
the Judge's Bungalow, I wrote again. What I heard of your
superfine Lordship's conduct, the same I have seen from
the balcony of my liberal Highness father. Your inimitable
Lordship returned the complements of thousands of people
that were standing on the street, but my fortune was such
that I could not play before sumptuous Lordship upon my
invaluable lute, which will be very relicious to the ear to
hear... I hope that your transident lordship will keep your
benevolent golden view on the forlorn royal blood to ennoble
and preserve the dignity of His Highness father in sending the
blessing letter of the golden hands.[13]

His Transident Lordship was so amused that he wrote in his notebook:

I find that in addition to the adjectives already quoted,
he described me at one time or another as parental,
compassionate, orpulent, predominant, surmountable,
merciful, refulgent, alert, sapient, notorious, meritorious,
transitory, intrepid, esteemable, prominent, discretional,
magnanimous, mellifluous, temperate, abstemious,
sagacious, free-willed, intellectual, inimitable, commendable,
all-accomplished, delicious-hearted, superfine, ameliorative,
impartial, benevolent, complaisant, efficient, progressive,
spiritual, prudent, philanthropic, equitable.[14]

Some of the epithets might even have been correct, like notorious or
transitory, but not quite in the way that the correspondent intended.

From the 1890s, a small but effective group of well-educated
professionals shed linguistic and political diffidence to challenge the
Raj in confident English. Gandhi, Dadabhai Naoroji, Aurobindo
Ghose, Badruddin Tyabji, Motilal Nehru, Chittaranjan Das, C.
Rajagopalachari and a host of lawyers and editors turned English
into a vehicle for Indian protest.

Chittaranjan Das went to London to take the ICS examination
after graduating from Presidency College; he failed and used his
considerable talent towards advocacy of Indian nationalism. He

canvassed in the 1892 election for Dadabhai Naoroji, the Liberal candidate from Finsbury Central who became the first Indian to be elected to the House of Commons. Naoroji, who had been professor of Gujarati at University College London a quarter century before, took his oath on Khordeh Avesta, the Parsi holy book.

Naoroji's epic dissection of the Raj was published in 1901 and framed the nationalist discourse by arguing, with meticulous evidence in a book of over 600 pages, that colonial rule was little more than brutal economic exploitation. Naoroji condemned a government that had been 'destructive and despotic to the Indians' since its inception.[15]

Naoroji quoted a letter, dated 17 May 1766, in which East India Company directors admitted that every Englishman was 'exercising his power to the oppression of the helpless Natives... We have the strongest sense of the deplorable state... from the corruption and rapacity of our servants... by a scene of the most tyrannic and oppressive conduct that ever was known in any age or country'. Naoroji commented that 'the same has remained in subtle and ingenious forms and subterfuges up to the present day with every increasing impoverishment'. He calculated that the financial drain upon the Indian people had grown to a humungous £30,000,000 a year.[16]

Naoroji cited Lord Salisbury, Secretary of State for India in 1884: 'As India must be bled the lancet should be directed to the parts where the blood is congested or at least sufficient, not to those which are already feeble from the want of it.' Naoroji's forensic analysis went further:

> But the drain is not all. All the wars by which the British Indian Empire is built up have not only been fought mainly with Indian blood, but every farthing of expenditure (with insignificant exceptions) incurred in all wars and proceedings within and beyond the frontiers of India by which the Empire has been built up and maintained up to the present day has been exacted from the Indian people. Britain has spent nothing.[17]

The sword having failed, the pen became the scalpel of resistance. Romesh Chandra Dutt's *Economic History of India Under British*

Rule, published in 1902, was as influential as Naoroji's magisterial declamation. Simultaneously, journalism expanded the space for complaint and protest. Between 1868 and 1896, more than 120 Indian newspapers and magazines were registered with the authorities in Punjab, Agra, Awadh, Rajputana and the Central Provinces. In Madras, the *Hindu* began to get published from 1878.

The *Poornachandrodaya* of 3 November 1863 gave credit to the government for appointing three Indians to the newly formed Indian Legislative Council: Maharaja Narindra Singh Bahadur, ruler of Patiala; Raja Deo Narain Bahadur, a zamindar, and Raja Dinkar Rao Raghunath Bahadur, a former minister of Gwalior State. It also pointed out the obvious, that the number was too small to have any effective say in legislation. *Som Prakash* was much sharper on 16 November 1863: 'All classes affirm that the present Legislative Council is a mere farce, where the members have no authority, how can they secure the confidence of the people?' On 10 September 1870 the *Oordu Guide* published an article objecting to the presence of only the wealthy in the Council, without any reference to their administrative capacities. The *Bharat Bhartiya* of 1 March 1873 remarked that the good expected of the Council had not materialized because it was a body of high government officers, rich European gentlemen and Indian rajas. W.C. Bonnerjee, who would later become president of the Indian National Congress, said at an 1888 public meeting in Croydon, England, while referring to an Indian who always voted after a hint from the viceroy: 'Gentlemen, I make bold to say that the presence of Indian gentlemen in the Legislative Councils is mere make-believe.' C.Y. Chintamani dismissed the Indians in Council as 'silent figureheads' and 'magnificent non-entities'. Just as a Muslim had to leave his shoes outside a mosque, he said, an Indian had to leave his conscience and principles outside the Legislative Council.

The *Amrita Bazar Patrika*, which started as a Bengali weekly from Jessore in 1868 and turned bilingual in 1871, was the standard-bearer of Bengali disaffection. It wrote in 1868:

We have been pained to see that some of our contemporaries object to a representative government in India, on the plea that the time has not come for the measure. Well, when will it come? Their arguments that a little freedom gives a zest for more, that the natives must never touch the forbidden fruit lest they be too knowing, are founded upon the most unchristian principle that 'might is right'.[18]

Insurrection spread to popular theatre. The government was worried enough to legislate against an increasingly aggressive Bengali press and stage:

> both of which were being used by the nationalistic bhadralok to hit out at the colonial administration. The Dramatic Performances Act of 1876 was introduced in retaliation against political plays like *Chakar Darpan* (about the brutal treatment of the Assam tea plantation workers by the English planters), *Gaekwad Darpan* (about the victimization of the Maharaja of Baroda by the English Resident), and Bengali farces that lampooned Prince Edward—Queen Victoria's son—who visited Calcutta in 1875.[19]

Magazines modelled on London's *Punch* found their niche after a hesitant start. Their early cartoons tended to be sentimental rather than witty. The *Oudh Punch*, founded by Munshi Sajjad Husain and published between 1877 and 1937, was perhaps the best of a motley lot. Among its contributors were the poet Akbar Allahabadi and the novelist Ratan Nath Dhar Sarshar; its criticism was so acerbic that the government forced its closure in 1912, but it was revived in 1916.

The duel between scribe and imperialist sharpened with the arrival of 41-year-old George Nathaniel Curzon as viceroy from 1899 to 1905. Queen Victoria worried, before his appointment, that he might be too 'narrow-minded' for India. She wrote to Lord Salisbury, now in his third spell as prime minister, in 1898:

> The future Viceroy must really shake himself more and more free from his red-tapist, narrow-minded council and entourage. He must be more independent, must hear for himself what the feelings of the natives really are and do what he thinks right and not be guided by the snobbish and vulgar overbearing and offensive behaviour of many of our civil and political agents, if we are to go on peacefully and happily in

India and to be liked and beloved by high and low, as well as respected as we ought to be, and not trying to trample on the people and continually remind them and making them feel that they are a conquered people. They must of course feel that we are the masters, but it should be done kindly and not offensively, which alas, is so often the case. Would Mr Curzon feel and do this?.[20]

Snobbish. Vulgar. Overbearing. Offensive. These were adjectives used by Queen Victoria about her own civil servants in India.

Curzon believed, not without justification, that the loss of India would mean the decline of Britain into a third-rate power. His tenure started amid yet another calamity, famine compounded by plague. The initial Indian reaction was hopeful. The *Hindi Punch* of December 1898 announced Curzon's appointment with an illustration of a beautiful sari-clad lady, a pen in hand, asking Curzon when kind words would translate into deeds. In September 1899, *Maratha Punch* depicted Curzon as Lord Krishna intent upon destroying the serpent Kalia; while *Hindi Punch* showed two Brahmins propitiating Lord Ganesh. The elephant god had the face of Curzon, while the mouse at his feet was captioned 'Loyalty'.[21]

Curzon gladdened Indian hearts when he went to see famine conditions and set up a relief fund in India and England. He pointed out, with characteristic acerbity, that Maharaja Scindia of Gwalior had donated a hospital ship worth ₹ 2,000,000 for the British war effort but contributed only the interest on a fixed deposit of ₹ 1,500,000 for starving Indians. Ironically, Emperor Wilhelm II of Germany, upon hearing of the 'fearful distress' in India, was able 'to realise a sum of over half a million in a very short time' from the German public. In a letter dated 7 March 1900, Queen Victoria thanked him on behalf of her subjects. The *Gadgadat* in May that year showed Curzon showering coins on desperate Indians, and in November depicted Curzon's round face as a full moon journeying across the Bombay Presidency.

The mood began to sour when Curzon announced a 6,110-mile railway line at a cost of ₹ 600,000,000 in the middle of mass deaths. Curzon's interest in the railways was strategic rather than economic. He proposed extending tracks along with a wireless connection to Afghanistan. Abdur Rahim, the amir, rejected the offer as encroachment on his independence. Curzon responded that railways would enable the British to send forces in an emergency. The amir answered, coolly, that this was precisely what he feared.

Famine was synonymous with British rule. 'In 1769,' writes Banerjee, 'rigorous enforcement of the land tax by the Company's agents, despite scarcities in the rural areas, led to the famine of 1770, which wiped out one-third of the population of Bengal—about 10 million people. In Calcutta itself, 76,000 people died.'[22] Rev. James Long saw children die on their mother's breasts and the Ganges become 'corrupt' from corpses. Indian zamindars like Shitab Ray and Najabat Ali Khan organized free food for the starving, but the Company was fixated on raising taxes to record levels. The worst casualties were in towns with the strongest British presence, like Calcutta, Hooghly and Murshidabad.[23]

An unnamed conscience-stricken Company employee who had just joined service wrote of Calcutta:

Still fresh in memory's eye the scene I view,
The shrivelled limbs, sunk eyes, and lifeless hue,
Still hear the mother's shrieks and infants' moans,
Cries of despair and agonizing moans,
In wild confusion dead and dying lie;—
Hark to the jackal's yell and vulture's cry,
The dogs' fell howl, as midst the glare of day
They riot unmolested on their prey!
Dire scenes of horror, which no pen can trace,
Nor rolling years from memory's page efface.[24]

The technological breakthrough achieved by the camera recorded the terrifying pain of starvation more graphically than words. Photographs from the great famine of 1876–78 in the Madras Presidency show skeletal figures of adults and babies dying as they stare at the lens, their faces slumped towards oblivion. Eminent Victorians like Florence Nightingale spoke up. She insisted that the problem was not shortage of food but the government's unwillingness to transport it to the dying, even as it diverted resources to the impending invasion of Afghanistan. But honourable prime ministers, viceroys and high officials buried their heads, collected the cash and let Indians perish in millions.

Annie Besant listed, in the introduction of *How India Wrought Her Freedom*, published in 1915, 22 major famines under British rule: Bengal in 1770; Madras in 1783; Awadh in 1784; Bombay and Madras in 1792; Bombay in 1803; north India in 1804; Madras in 1807; Bombay in 1813; Madras in 1823 and 1833, 1854; Orissa and Madras in 1866; Bengal in 1874; Madras in 1877; Madras and Orissa in 1889; Madras, Bengal and Rajputana in 1892 and across nearly half of British India between 1896 and 1899.

When in 1865 the monsoons failed in Orissa, those British officials with a conscience asked the Bengal government to import rice, only to be blandly told that the administration could not interfere with the laws of supply and demand. Around 1,000,000 died of starvation and disease in Orissa. The secretary of state for India, Lord Cranborne, criticized the Bengal government's policy as a 'fetish'. He was in the India Office (now as Marquess of Salisbury) when famine returned to Bengal and Bihar in 1874 and ensured some alleviation through food distribution and crisis employment on road and railway construction. But the next Viceroy, Lord Lytton, thought too much money had been 'wasted' in 1874 and reduced the relief budget during the Madras famine two years later. Lytton accused the governor of Madras, the duke of Buckingham, of 'extravagance', ordered restriction of rations and could see nothing but relief camps 'swarming with fat, idle, able-bodied paupers' when he deigned to visit. As Gilmour points out, he 'managed to miss the millions who were dead or dying'.[25]

That catastrophe provoked the government into setting up the first Famine Commission, chaired by Sir Richard Strachey. It established the Indian Famine Code of 1883 while noting that 'scarcity' and 'near scarcity' could not be classified as famine. At the beginning of the drought in the 1890s, Indians got sermons instead of succour. Curzon, determined to be ruthlessly correct when he suspected waste or worse, stiffened relief eligibility and pronounced that 'alms' from the government would weaken the fibre of self-reliance and hence amount to a public crime.

But as corpses began to pile up, and the toll once again crossed 1,000,000 dead, relief expenditure went up to £8,500,000. Curzon's substantive contribution was to set up an Irrigation Commission as a long-term solution. There was more good news when the Punjab Land Alienation Act prevented moneylenders and merchants from seizing land from farmers in lieu of debt. The *Hindi Punch* in November 1901 praised Curzon as a David killing the Philistine Goliath.

The good that Curzon did was oft interred in the bones of autocracy. He dismissed eminent Indian intellectuals like Naoroji, Gopal Krishna Gokhale, Surendra Nath Banerjee and Pherozeshah Mehta, who blamed the plight of India on colonial exploitation, as a handful of rich zamindars. The East, he pontificated, was a hotbed of deceit, and the concept of honesty was a gift from the West, inducing a sharp response from Calcutta newspapers like *Bengali, Bharat Mitra* and *Amrita Bazar Patrika. Hindi Punch* now printed a cartoon of Naoroji blowing a large trumpet into the deaf ear of 'The Sleeping Beauty', or the British Raj.

Princes were the only true 'native' enthusiasts at the 10-day Imperial Durbar for Edward VII in Delhi from 29 December 1902. Indian papers published unflattering cartoons of highnesses like the nizam of Hyderabad and the maharaja of Patiala at this 'day-dream' event. The Durbar ended with a speech in which Curzon pronounced that Indian peace and prosperity could only be ensured by the British Crown. This was followed by a 101-gun salute. Gandhi castigated the feudatories for wearing trousers befitting cooks (*khansamas*) and shining boots as they bowed before the British.

No Indian leader understood the virulence of racism better than Gandhi. On 26 October 1896, he told an audience in Madras about his experiences in South Africa:

We are the 'Asian dirt' to be 'heartily cursed', we are 'chockful of vice' and we 'live upon rice', we are 'stinking coolie' living on 'the smell of oiled rag', we are 'the black vermin'... We 'breed like rabbits' and a gentleman at a meeting lately held in Durban said he was sorry we could not be shot like them.

Free India's first Prime Minister Jawaharlal Nehru, alumnus of Harrow and Trinity, Cambridge, reveals how contemptuous the British were even of their allies. When Nehru went to see his university play a visiting Indian side in June 1911, he heard how the chancellor of

Cambridge had refused to stand up when awarding honorary degrees at a convocation to the maharaja of Bikaner and the Aga Khan.[26]

Curzon was more polite, but he never disguised his belief in white superiority. As he explained in his 1904 budget speech, birth, breeding, character, education and administrative skill gave the British natural rights to the Indian Civil Service. It was perhaps fated that Curzon would be responsible for the decision that tipped Indian sentiment from demand to defiance.

In 1903 the government announced the partition of Bengal, ostensibly for administrative reasons but in fact to divide a culturally homogenous province along Hindu-Muslim lines. Bengal was cut in half on 16 October 1905. The people protested, through demonstrations, denunciatory articles, speeches and angry posters such as the one showing Curzon draped in a butcher's wrap, his right hand on the handle of a huge axe, while a supine Mother Bengal lay at his feet, her body cut at the waist and knees into parts labelled 'East Bengal' and 'Assam'. The poster was captioned '*Vandalism*: Partition, 1905'.[27]

The poet Bal Mukund Gupta, editor of the Urdu weekly *Kohinoor*, wrote: *Who has broken Bengal into two pieces?/ Who has ruthlessly separated brother from brother?/ Said Curzon—I am alone the propagator of this/ My hands are of iron, my heart a lump of stone.* Surendranath Banerjee described the decision as a lethal bomb which had shattered harmony. The radical sage Aurobindo Ghosh expressed his outrage in a letter to his wife: his country was not geography, but a mother whom he worshipped. Could he continue living complacently while a demon sat on her chest, trying to suck her blood?

Censorship restricted coverage but could not erase criticism entirely. An Indian Mr Punch looked on woefully as Curzon, carrying a heavy lock in his left hand and key on his right, flaunted the Press Telegrams Copyright Bill while Mother India, bound in rope, was on her knees.

With conscious insensitivity, Curzon restored the memorial to the 'Black Hole' demolished more than eight decades earlier and banned *Vande Mataram*, an ode to the motherland which had become a national song. Indians, unwilling to forgive pepper-shot insults, cheered when 'Jungi Laat' (War Lord) Herbert Kitchener, the commander-in-chief of the Indian Army in 1902, won his administrative duel with the

'Mulki Laat' (Country Lord) Curzon over the status of the military member in the Viceroy's Council. Kitchener wanted sole control of the army. Curzon, never one to soften a phrase if a hard one would serve, described this as 'military despotism' and used this defeat as the ostensible reason for his resignation.

Papers which had been enthusiastic about his arrival were relieved at Curzon's departure. *Vaishyoparak*, a monthly magazine from Calcutta, summed up popular feeling:

> *O Laat! What are you waiting for*
> *The boat waits for you, jump into it*
> *What shall we say*
> *As you sow, shall you reap*
> *Here, goodbye, Ram salaam,*
> *Let the boat move.*
> *Oh Lord, we had sung praises of you*
> *Now leave us Lord,*
> *You have troubled us enough.*[28]

In its issue of 28 March 1925, *Matwala* published a caustic obituary of Curzon:

> On the 20th the former Viceroy of India, Lord Curzon, died in England. Alas! the passionate politician who sowed the seeds of India's awakening is no more! The Partitioner of Bengal, the obstacle to the spreading British sultanate, the wise one has been taken from this earth. The man who had the potential of being even Lord Lytton's master in the art of suppression, has gone to the other world... Grief! Now who will worry about the welfare of India while sitting in the British parliament? Who will deliver long addresses on the problems of India in the House of Commons? Who will pay the debt he owes India from across the seven seas? O God! Grant our late Lat Sahib's soul strength, since it was due to him that so many Indian souls are at peace.[29]

The fad of mimicking Western manners waned, and leaders of the Bengali *bhadralok* began to stress their Indian identity in dress, rituals and lifestyle. Nabinchandra Sen, a Bengali poet, describes the novelist Bankimchandra Chatterjee's drawing room (*baithak khana*) in his house at Naihati in 1877:

> It was a hall adjacent to a small Shiva temple room, and on the far side, there were two rooms. All around the hall, near the walls, there were two or three couches and cushioned chairs. The walls had a few paintings hanging on them, and in one corner, there was a harmonium.

Rosinka Chaudhuri contrasts this with Bankim's satirical essay on Hindu College radicalism, where the Anglophile babu's drawing room had

> Chairs, table, punkahs (fans)—seldom meant to be pulled, American clocks, glassware of variegated hues, pictures for which the *Illustrated London News* is liberally laid under contribution, kerosene lamps, book-shelves filled with Reynolds' *Mysteries*, Tom Paine's *Age of Reason* and the *Complete Poetical Works* of Lord Byron, English music-boxes...[30]

Satirists like the Urdu poet Akbar Allahabadi were forthright:

> *Hindu-Muslim hain hairan dono gharb-e-daur mein*
> *Shokhi-e-atfal khud sar qabil-e-izhar neest.*

> (Hindus, Muslims are amazed in this era of the West,
> These children of arrogance are beyond description.)

Allahabadi taunted attitudes spawned by the Raj:

> *Nai tehzeeb mein dikkat zyada toh nahin hoti*
> *Mazahib rahtey hain qayam, faqat imaan jaata hai.*

> (There isn't too much difficulty in a new culture,
> Religions remain in place, only faith disappears.)

The self-deprecatory Allahabadi, who died in 1921 at the age of 76, survived long enough to witness the astonishing surge of Gandhi's mass movement from 1920:

Buddhu Mian bhi Hazrat-e-Gandhi ke saath hain
Go khaaq-e-raah hain, magar aandhi ke saath hain.

(Even Mr Stupid is with Mahatma Gandhi,
He may be just a speck on the way, but he is with a storm.)

Gandhi could have learnt to ride a horse and joined the ICS after he was called to the bar in 1891 at the age of 22. Instead, he chose a loincloth and *lathi* (long walking stick) to lead a powerful resistance against the mightiest Empire in history. Gandhi ensured that the British Empire died exactly where it was born, in India.

The Naked Fakirs of the East

One of Gandhi's less-known talents was an ability to use laughter as a piquant missile in the armoury of non-violence. During his visit to England in 1931 for the second Round Table Conference, Gandhi was asked by journalists what he thought of Western civilization. It would be a good idea, the Mahatma replied.

The quip must have been especially pungent for Winston Churchill, still an intermittently successful provocateur rather than the icon he would become. Churchill, the eternal imperialist, had famously dismissed Gandhi as a 'malignant subversive fanatic' and seditious lawyer 'now posing as a *fakir* of a type well-known in the East, striding half-naked up the steps of the Viceregal Palace', after Gandhi's pact with the Viceroy Lord Irwin in March 1931.

Churchill's contradictions have been well-documented. He described Hindus as a 'beastly people with a beastly religion' because they had the temerity to challenge his beloved British Empire. Churchill got along quite well with Indians who supported the Empire. According to Josh Ireland, Churchill nicknamed his son Randolph 'Chumbolly' after the flower called *chameli* in Hindi. Randolph, it must be added, reacted sharply against racism. When immigration officers at Johannesburg once asked about his race, Randolph Churchill replied, 'Human'.[31]

Churchill's reference to the 'well-known type' of fakir echoed three centuries of misunderstanding over this strange Indian phenomenon. Rationalists attributed a fakir's inexplicable feats to deceptive chicanery rather than superhuman ability. Churchill, unable to decipher how anyone could survive without food, stood in a long queue of sceptics when he accused Gandhi of faking three-week fasts.

More than six centuries before Churchill, Marco Polo was taken aback by the sight of a naked yogi (an ascetic):

> Amongst the natives of this region there is a class peculiarly devoted to religious life, who are named Chughi [Jogi], and who in honour to their divinities lead most austere lives. They go perfectly naked, not concealing any part of their bodies, and say there can be no shame in that state of nudity in which they came into the world. With respect to what are called the parts of shame, they observe that, not being conscious of the sins of the flesh, they have no reason to blush at their exposure.[32]

In 1674, Dr John Fryer witnessed fakirs in Surat who:

> by continual Abstinence bring themselves into a strange Emaciated habit of Body, that they seem only walking Skelitons... At another time a Gentu Fakier was enjoined for Forty days to endure the Purgatory of five Fires; there being a great resort by reason of a Festivity solemnized all that while; when I came early in the Morning (invited by the novelty and incredibility of the thing) he was Seated on a four-square Stage or Altar, with three Ascents, some Two Feet high, and as many Feet square, ready to shew...[33]

This ascetic now moved into spectacular high gear:

> ...and in this Interim four Fires being kindled (any of them able to roast an ox) at each Corner of the upper and least Square, he having finished some Fopperies with his Pot, Scoevola-like with his own hands he increased the Flames by adding combustible Stuff as Incense to it; when removing from his Neck a Collar of great Wooden Beads, he made a Coronet of them for his Head; then bowing his Head in the middle of the Flames, as it were to worship, holding the other Beads in his

hands, with his Head encircled between his Arms, his Face opposite to the Sun, which is the fifth Fire, he mounted his Body with his Feet bolt upright, and so continued standing on his Head the space of three hours very steddily, that is, from Nine till Twelve...[34]

Fryer acknowledges that his account would be dismissed as imposture by English readers 'but if it be, it would make a Man disbelieve his own Eyes'. He could not deny what he had seen:

I saw a Fakier of the Gentus, whose Nails by neglect were grown as long as my Fingers, some piercing though [sic] the Flesh... Others with their Arms Dislocated so, that the ... head of the Bone lies in the pit or valley of the Arm; in which Case they are defrauded of their Nourishment, and hang as useless Appendices to the Body; that unless relieved by Charity, they are helpless in all Offices to themselves. Others Fixing their Eyes upon Heaven, their Heads hanging over their Shoulders, are uncapable of removing it from the Posture they are in, being accustomed to that uninterrupted Rest, having contracted and stiffned the Tendons of the Muscles and Ligaments of the Neck, that both those belonging to the Gullet, or the motion of the Head, are unserviceable; insomuch that no Aliment, not Liquid, can pass, and that too with much difficulty...[35]

He continues:

Another devotee had made a Vow not to lye down in Sixteen Years, but to keep on his Feet all that while; this came accompanied with two others under the same Oath, the one had passed Five, the other Three Years; all Three of them had their Legs swoln as big as their Bodies... The Eldest having undergone the compleat Term, to crown all, was intombed in the same standing Posture Nine Days without any sort of Food; and lest any Pretext of that kind might lessen his Undertaking, he caused a Bank of Earth to be heaped on the Mouth of his Cave...I saw him presently after his Resurrection, in great State raised on a Throne under a Canopy, before which was

Fire made in the Pit he had been, where he put his Hands, being anointed with Oyl, untouch'd by the Flames... the Banyans gave him Divine Honours, and saluted him prostrate, offering before him Rice, and throwing Incense into the Fire: He had a Red Trident in his hand, and is enrolled one of the Heroes or Demi-Gods in their Superstitious Kalender.[36]

The British were bewildered by the ease with which Indians took the incredible in their stride. Indian magic was quite evidently far beyond known human capacity, while the fakir and the mantra seemed to derive power from the divine.

Francois Bernier, in India between 1656 and 1668, and the gem merchant Jean-Baptiste Tavernier, who visited six times between 1630 and 1668, record such standard tricks as making an egg hatch in less than five minutes or creating a mango tree from a dry piece of wood. Niccolao Manucci's experience was of a different order. A servant's hand got stuck in the soil when he tried to pluck a radish from a field. The farmer, after being placated with some money, gave the servant a beating, and then recited a *mantra* which released the hand. Manucci adds:

I could never sufficiently state to what an extent the Hindus and Mahomedans in India are in the habit of practising witchcraft. I quite well know that if I were to recount that they can even make a cock crow in the belly of the man who stole and ate it, no credit would be given to me. Nevertheless, the truth is that many a time I heard the crowing in different cases, and of such instances I was told over and over again.[37]

Manucci records numerous 'diabolic' cases such as this:

A woman wished to become with child, and not succeeding with drugs, had recourse to a magician. His orders were that at midnight she should go and stand below a large forest tree which in India is called *badd* [a fig tree]. It produces a small red fruit. Here she was to perform the sacrifices to which he had instructed her. She then became pregnant, and the tree referred to became sterile, and never yielded fruit so long as it lived.[38]

There are stories of a Portuguese friar in Sao Thome who was bewitched by a 'negro woman', by which Manucci meant a dark-coloured lady; of Thome Borges de Villalobo, who saw a conjuror perform such a fearful dance that he nearly died before he was revived by a magic potion; of a rich widow who saw the face of a future husband in the yolk of eggs poured in a glass phial. Manucci became a friend of this husband. There are any number of tales about 'superstitions and sorceries' collated from the Italian's personal experiences.[39]

The chaplain John Ovington accused sadhus, or Hindu 'ashmen', of committing a 'thousand villanies', but conceded that they had the capacity of distorting their limbs without any mask or appearance of deceit. Some could keep their arms permanently raised; others gazed fixedly at the sky and stars; still others were able to dislocate their arms forming unique patterns.[40]

An incredulous British Parliament passed a resolution in 1793 that India had to be rescued from useless superstition through useful knowledge and moral improvement. Some Europeans, however, found traditional Indian knowledge miraculously helpful.

Half a century after the Parliament resolution, the Australian John Lang was in Bijnore when he succumbed to tic-douloureux, a painful disorder of the cranial nerve which causes sudden stabs of agony. His host's servants brought a local healer.

The native doctor was a tall, thin Mussulman, with a lofty forehead, small black eyes, long aquiline nose, and finely chiselled mouth and chin... He put several questions to me, but I was in too great pain to give him any replies. He begged of me to sit down. I obeyed him, mechanically. Seating himself in a chair immediately opposite to me, he looked very intently into my eyes. After a little while, his gaze became disagreeable, and I endeavoured to turn my head aside, but I was unable to do so. I now felt that I was being mesmerized. Observing, I suppose, an expression of anxiety, if not of fear, on my features, he bade me not to be alarmed. I longed to order him to cease; but, as the pain was becoming less and less acute, and as I retained my consciousness intact, I suffered him to proceed. To tell the truth, I doubt whether I could have uttered a sound. At all events, I did not make the attempt.

Presently, that is to say, after two or three minutes, the pain had entirely left me, and I felt what is commonly called, all in a glow. The native doctor now removed his eyes from off mine, and inquired if I were better. My reply, which I had no difficulty in giving at once, was in the affirmative; in short, that I was completely cured.[41]

The 'native doctor' noted cheerfully that only one person had gone to sleep or become unconscious during his treatment. His best patients, he added, were alcoholics. He could cure 'drinking madness' by locking up a patient's eyes. A grateful John Lang gave the doctor a cheque for ₹100, equivalent to what he would earn perhaps in half a year, only to discover that the cheque was never cashed. The doctor explained disingenuously that no one would believe he had been paid so much if he did not show them the cheque.

Most Europeans found the behaviour and 'squalor' of street-side fakirs and *byragis* trying. Fanny Parkes dismissed most of them as rascals and libertines. She could not, however, hide her awe at a mendicant she saw during the sacred Kumbh Mela in Prayaag in January 1833.

One man whom I saw this day at the *mela* was remarkably picturesque, and attracted my admiration. He was a religious mendicant, a disciple of Shiva. In stature he was short and dreadfully lean, almost a skeleton... His left arm he had held erect so long that the skin and flesh had withered, and clung round the bones most frightfully; the nails of the hand, which had been kept immovably clenched, had pierced through the palm and grew out at the back of the hand like the long claws of a bird of prey. His horrible and skeleton-like arm was encircled by a twisted stick, the head of the *cobra de capello*, with its hood displayed, and the twisted withy looked like the body of the reptile wreathed around his horrible arm. His only garment the skin of a tiger thrown over shoulders, and a bit of rag and rope at his waist... Acts of severity towards the body, practised by religious mendicants, are not done as penances for sin but as works of extraordinary merit, promising large rewards in a future state. The Byragee is not a penitent, but a proud ascetic.[42]

Such yogis were the stars of festivals at which hundreds of thousands gathered. The early 19th-century text, *Hindoostan*, edited by Frederic Shoberi, reproduces portraits, 'drawing from life', of two mendicants in Benaras in 1792. Holy men did sleep on a bed of nails.

A Brahmin *brahmachari* named 'Perkhasanund' (Prakashanand) left home at 20 and spent 12 years in a cave in Tibet, an ordeal during which his skin was nearly devoured by vermin. Upon emerging, he began to 'lie on a bedstead, the bottom of which is stuck full of iron spikes... He never afterwards slept on any other bed. To render this penance the more meritorious, he had logs of wood burned round his bed during the intense heat of summer: and in winter he had a pot perforated with small holes hung up over him, from which water kept continually dropping on his head'. A report on this bed of nails was published in *Asian Researches*, authored by 'Mr Duncan', a former governor of Bombay.

A second yogi, the 'Fakir Praoun Poury' (Fakir Pranpuri) is seen sitting on a bed upon a tiger skin, arms crossed over his head, a posture he adopted for four decades. Born in Kanauj, he had run away from his Rajput family at the age of nine, begun his penance at the age of 18 during the Kumbh Mela at Allahabad and wandered through Nepal, Persia and Central Asia. In their portraits, both the fakirs have a slight smile, which might or might not be condescending. All they wear is a minimal loincloth.

Shoberi quotes an eyewitness who saw a mango seed being buried in the ground while strange incantations were uttered, after which a slender tree rose from the spot. Within an hour it had reached a height of over four feet. In a fine coup d'état, the magician plucked green mangoes from this tree and offered it to a sahib to taste. 'The process was certainly most adroitly managed,' writes Shoberi, 'and excited proportionate pleasure and surprise'.[43]

Real-time action was more blood-curdling. Peter Lamont describes the horror of Reverend Hobart Caunter at the Madras barracks in 1834 upon seeing a conjuror thrust a sword several times into a closed wicker basket which contained a cherubic eight-year-old girl. Blood began to stream out. Moments later the basket was lifted. There was no one there. The girl was seen nearby. A guard had to be placed to prevent the audience from attacking the conjuror.

In 1837 Sir Claude Martin Wade saw a fakir buried alive without food, water or air in the court of Maharaja Ranjit Singh at Lahore. The fakir survived. 'There was, to say the least, a great deal of confusion among the Victorians about how to explain all this. Some felt that these seemingly inexplicable feats suggested powers unknown in the West,' writes Lamont.[44]

Any special evening of entertainment for British soldiers included dancing girls, contortionists, jugglers, fortune-tellers and snake charmers, some of whom could pull a pencil-thin snake through a nostril and take it out through the mouth. For awed Europeans, this was beyond human.[45]

Churchill belonged to the school of hard-boiled imperialists who scorned 'Indian tricks' and the religious baggage trundling in its wake. He was determined never to be outwitted by a toothless Mahatma without an appetite who had adopted the garb of a fakir. What Churchill did not appreciate was that Indians had always understood the difference between the artifice of a conjuror and the power of a man of God. Churchill might have understood India better if he had read his fellow European, Manucci. The Italian records a remarkable incident during the reign of the despotic Mughal rulers, Aurangzeb:

> A curious thing happened to Aurangzeb. Going through the street which goes straight from the mosque [Jama Masjid] to the fort [Lal Qila, or Red Fort], he passed close to a shop where a *faqir* was seated who had formerly been a disciple of the same teacher, Mulla Salih. On seeing the king pass, the *faqir* discharged at him a potful of human excrement, which defiled his throne and his body. At the same time the *faqir* uttered a cry. Let not the reader be amazed at such boldness, for it is quite impossible to set forth completely the irreverence of these *faqirs*, of whom I have already spoken in my First Part. They act thus in full confidence that no one will dare to ill-treat them....[46]

The all-powerful Aurangzeb did not dare ill-treat the fakir who threw a pot of excrement at him in full public view. The emperor summoned him but only to understand the reason for his rage. Any other subject would have been beheaded.

Aurangzeb also knew the difference between a true devotee and a religious plutocrat. His chief enforcer, Qazi Abdul Wahab, was an ideological ally in charge of imposing religious law and thus among the most powerful men in court. A portrait of the qazi in the third volume of Manucci's travelogue shows him reading, sitting cross-legged against a large cushion, fanned by servants, while students, seated and standing, listen to his discourse. There are three women in the mostly male group, their heads covered but faces unveiled.

Qazi Abdul Wahab was reluctant to arrange the marriage of his daughter since she was an efficient manager and guardian of the money he took in bribes. She fell in love with a young man from the neighbourhood, who would visit her at home when the qazi was out. They knew that Abdul Wahab would never agree to their marriage. The daughter thought up a brilliant ruse. We can take the story forward in Manucci's words:

> Next she decided to leave the house one day in a covered palanquin, having first sent all the property [money stashed at home] to a place of security. Then she went in the youth's company to the *qazi's* public audience. On arriving there, the youth said to Abd-ul-wahhab that he and the woman in the palanquin had made a vow to be married by him. The *qazi*, not recognising the woman to be his daughter, asked her if she consented to marriage with the youth. Disguising her voice, she answered 'Yes'. The *qazi* performed the ceremony and dismissed them.[47]

The young couple, rightly fearful of the father's wrath once he discovered he had been duped, hastened to the captain of the guard at the palace, who was a friend of the husband, and begged for an audience with Aurangzeb to:

> get His Majesty to act the godfather in the matter. Aurangzeb laughed over the story, and at once gave an order to bring the *qazi* to him, before he had gone home and found out that his daughter was not in the house; they were to tell him that what he had done was well done, but not a word was to be breathed about the marriage or anything else. Rendered

anxious by such a message, Abd-ul-wahhab started for his house, and found that his daughter was not in her apartments. Searching, and again searching, he discovered a small opening made in the wall, and by this time realized that the marriage he had just performed had been the marriage of his daughter. He was much cast down, but his sadness was doubled when, on opening his boxes, he found that all that he had gathered together by impostures had been carried off by his daughter with a liberal hand. From his contretemps, aggravated by heart complaint, he fell ill and died in great pain, a terrible death.[48]

The date of Abdul Wahab's death has been recorded as the 18th of Ramzan 1086, or 10 December 1675.

Churchill would have benefited equally from the ICS mandarin Sir William Hunter's moving eulogy to a true Christian fakir, *The Old Missionary*, published in 1895 by Oxford. Hunter was among the finest civil servants of the Raj, a superb administrator and prolific author whose scholarly studies ranged from *The Indian Musalmans*, a monograph on the validity of Jihad in India, to *Annals of Rural Bengal* and *A Brief History of the Indian Peoples*. Hunter also wrote for the *Times*, London on Indian affairs.

The old Scottish missionary lived in India for but one reason, to serve Jesus through complete dedication to the poor. He had studied medicine, learnt Sanskrit and the local dialect to help the villagers of southern Bengal. He lived alone with an adopted daughter whose natural parents had died. Her love, his mission, his faith and his books were the fulcrum of his life.

His small library contained a

rather tattered collection of grammars and lexicons of the Indian vernaculars, a few Sanskrit texts, translations of the Testament in various Indian dialects, medical works, and a dusty shelf of treatises of the Irvingite sect. The inner end of the room was lined with a bookcase partitioned into pigeon-holes, for the manuscript slips of the dictionary of the hill-language on which the old man had long been at work. In earlier life he compiled a grammar of that hitherto unwritten speech. The dictionary was the labour of his age, and as its progress became slower with advancing years, the venerable scholar had grown almost querulously anxious about its completion...[49]

In a corner of the room 'stood a redwood press filled with books of a very different sort—voyages and naval biographies of the last century, with bundles of faded letters and papers sent out to the missionary from his deserted Scottish home, on his father's death'.

The villagers came to him for justice, 'with salutations of "O Incarnation of Justice," "O Refuge of the Poor," each bringing a boundary dispute, or a feud about the water courses, or some knotty question of inheritance, which must otherwise be determined by blows'. The Old Missionary would settle all quarrels on Sunday evenings at a camp in the neighbouring hamlets, so that 'the sun should go down on no man's wrath'. His methods were simple.

After hearing both sides the Old Missionary delivered judgement, that the man was to give a feast, that he was to get back a fair share of the watered lands with the grazing right for his buffaloes in the jungle, and that, to make his name great, he should enlarge the village tank which no longer sufficed to irrigate the surrounding cultivation.[50]

The elders would signify approval, to chants saying that his name would live for ever. The reconciled parties would then have a friendly wrangle over how much should be spent on goat-flesh and rice-beer at the feast. The Old Missionary was a philosopher, writes Hunter, reflecting on the riverbank and watching with calm but friendly eyes as the stream of ancient races and religions flowed past.

Inevitably, one day, those eyes had to close. The Old Missionary was buried in his church. No European could have served Indians with greater passion and compassion. But his obituary was no different from those of his countrymen, writes Hunter: 'The Englishman in India has no home and leaves no memory.'

Dadabhai Naoroji, while praising honourable exceptions, found the reason for this isolation in the colonial mind:

Every European is isolated from the people around him. He is not their mental, moral, or social leader or companion. For any mental or moral influence or guidance or sympathy with the people he might just as well be living in the moon. The people know not him, and he knows not, nor cares for, the people. Some honourable exceptions do, now and then, make an effort to do some good if they can, but in the very nature of things these efforts are always feeble, exotic, and of little permanent effect... They [Europeans] do not belong to the people; they cannot enter their thoughts and feelings; they cannot join or sympathise with their joys or griefs. On the contrary, every day the estrangement is increasing. Europeans deliberately and openly widen it more and more...[51]

Indians knew that this distance was a measure of racism. They found ways to deal with or circumvent rulers who never became one of them. A handful joined the masters and were rewarded. Others made a virtue of necessity. Those who tried violence failed. But India understood that the man and the moment had come when its semi-naked fakir, Gandhi, began his long and non-violent march in 1920.

The last word on imperialism is best left to an imperialist who understood India. Rudyard Kipling's *The Ladies*, much recited on the ships between India and the Englishman's home, is about the women he loved and left behind:

> *I've taken my fun where I've found it;*
> *I've rouged an' I've ranged in my time;*
> *I've 'ad my pickin' of sweethearts,*
> *An' four o' the lot was prime.*
> *One was a 'arf-caste widow,*
> *One was a woman at Prome,*
> *One was the wife of a jemedar-sais*
> *An' one is a girl at 'ome.*
> *...Then I was ordered to Burma,*
> *Actin' in charge o' Bazar,*
> *An' I got me a tiddy live 'eathen*
> *Through buying supplies off 'er pa.*
> *Funny an' yellow an' faithful—*

> *Doll in a teacup she were—*
> *But we lived on the square, like a true-married pair,*
> *An' I learned about women from 'er!*
> *...Then we was shifted to Neemuch*
> *(Or I might ha' been keepin' 'er now),*
> *An' I took with a shiny she-devil,*
> *The wife of a n....r at Mhow;*
> *Taught me the gipsy-folks' bolee;*
> *Kind o' volcano she were,*
> *For she knifed me one night 'cause I wished she was white,*
> *And I learned about women from 'er!*

The volcanic dark lady of Neemuch lived with her English lover and taught him her *bolee* (language) but knifed him one night because he wished she was white. Even those who came close to the British were repelled by white racism.

Notes

Chapter 1

1. C.M. Naim, 'Popular Jokes and Political History: The Case of Akbar, Birbal and Mulla Do-Piyaza', *Economic and Political Weekly* 30, no. 24 (17 June 1995).
2. Mohammad Mujeeb, *The Indian Muslims* (Munshiram Manoharlal, 2003), 360.
3. Ibid., 262–63.
4. Ibid.
5. Ibid., 166–67.
6. Ibid., 363.
7. Niccolao Manucci, *Travels in the Mogul Empire AD 1656-1668* (Asian Educational Services, 1996), 165.
8. David Dean Shulman, *The King and the Clown in South Indian Myth and Poetry* (Princeton Legacy Library, 1985), 181–82.
9. Ibid., 200.
10. Roy Moxham, *The Theft of India* (HarperCollins, 2016), 96.
11. John Fryer, *Travels in India in the Seventeenth Century: by Sir Thomas Roe and Dr John Fryer* (Trubner & Co, 1873) British Library History of Travel edition, 307–08.
12. Ibid.
13. Niccolao Manucci, *Storia do Mogor, Or, Mogul India 1653–1708*, Vol. II (Alpha Editions, 2020), 5.
14. Ibid., 150.
15. Ibid.
16. Ibid., 107–08.
17. Ibid.
18. Ibid., 6.
19. Ibid., 7.
20. Ibid., 159–60.
21. Ibid., 154.
22. Ibid., 7–8.

23. Ibid., 8.
24. Abdullah Yusuf Ali, *The Meaning of the Holy Quran* (Amana Publications, 1989).
25. Abhishek Kaicker, *The King and the People: Sovereignty and Popular Politics in Mughal Delhi* (Oxford University Press, 2020), 99.
26. P.J. Marshall, in *The Eighteenth Century in Indian History*, ed. P.J. Marshall (Oxford University Press, 2003), 4.
27. Val C. Prinsep, *Glimpses of Imperial India* (Mittal Publications, 1979).
28. David Gilmour, *The British in India: Three Centuries of Ambition and Experience* (Allen Lane, 2018), 407.
29. *Eating God: A Book of Bhakti Poetry*, ed. Arundhati Subramaniam (Penguin, 2014). Includes some of Rahim's poetry, translated by Mustansir Dalvi.
30. Mohammad Mujeeb, *The Indian Muslims* (Munshiram Manoharlal, 2003), 363.
31. *Ghalib: The Poet and His Age,* ed. Ralph Russell (Oxford India Paperbacks, 1997), 55.
32. Ibid.
33. Ibid., 18–19.
34. Ibid., 27. His translation is lyrical.
35. Ibid., 23, 29.
36. Ibid., 20.

Chapter 2

1. Robert Ivermee, *Hooghly: The Global History of a River* (HarperCollins India, 2021), 23.
2. Francois Bernier, *Travels in the Mogul Empire 1656–1668*, (Archibald Constable and Company, 1891; republished by Asian Educational Services, 2010), 439–40.
3. Edward Terry, *A Voyage to East-India wherein some things are taken notice of in our passage thither, but many more in our abode there, within that rich and spacious empire of the Great Mogul, mixt with some Parallel Observations and Inferences upon the Story, to profit as well as delight the Reader* (T. Martin and T. Allestrye, 1655).
4. Ibid., 78–86.
5. Ibid.
6. Ibid. Section II, 87–88.
7. Ibid., 91–93.
8. Ibid., 99.
9. Ibid., 232.
10. Ibid., 239.
11. Sir Jadunath Sarkar, *A History of Jaipur* (Orient Longman, 1984), 16.
12. Marco Polo, *The Travels of Marco Polo*, trans. William Marsden, ed. Manuel Komroff (The Modern Library, 2001), 217–18.

13. Niccolao Manucci, *Storia do Mogor, Or, Mogul India 1653–1708*, Vol. II (Alpha Editions, 2020), 46–47.

14. Ibid.

15. Robert Ivermee, *Hooghly: The Global History of a River* (HarperCollins India, 2021), 65.

16. Ibid., 312.

17. Ibid., 266.

18. Ibid.

19. John Fryer, *Travels in India in the Seventeenth Century: by Sir Thomas Roe and Dr John Fryer* (Trubner & Co, 1873) British Library History of Travel edition, 320.

20. Ibid., 184.

21. Travels of Fray Sebastien Maurique, Routledge, 2016, 47.

22. John Fryer, Travels in India in the Seventeenth Century: by Sir Thomas Roe and Dr John Fryer (Trubner & Co, 1873) British Library History of Travel edition, 306.

23. Ibid., 309.

24. John Fryer, *Travels in India in the Seventeenth Century: by Sir Thomas Roe and Dr John Fryer* (Trubner & Co, 1873) British Library History of Travel edition, 185.

25. R.V. Vernede, ed., *British Life in India: An Anthology of Humorous and Other Writings Perpetrated by the British in India 1750–1947, With Some Latitude for Works Completed after Independence* (Oxford University Press, 1995), 87–88.

26. Ibid., 181–82.

27. Ibid.

28. Ibid., 316.

29. Ibid., 326.

30. Ibid., 352–53.

31. Ibid., 271.

32. Ibid., 179–80.

33. Ibid.

34. Ibid., 280.

35. From the *Consultation Book* of Fort St George, quoted in Hilton Brown ed., *The Sahibs: The Life and Ways of the British in India as Recorded by Themselves* (William Hodge & Company, 1948), 153.

36. John Ovington, *A Voyage to Suratt, In the Year, 1689* (Jacob Tonson, 1696).

37. William Hickey, *Memoirs of William Hickey*, Vol. II, 1775–1782, ed. Alfred Spencer (Hurst and Blackett, 1918).

38. Ibid.

39. Fanny Parkes, *Begums, Thugs & Englishmen: The Journals of Fanny Parkes*, ed. William Dalrymple (Penguin, 2002), 80–81. Original published in 1850.

40. Hilton Brown ed., *The Sahibs: The Life and Ways of the British in India as Recorded by Themselves* (William Hodge & Company, 1948), 100.

41. Ibid., 15–16.

42. *British Social Life in India 1608–1937,* edited by Dennis Kincaid, an Indian Civil Service officer who died young in 1937; reprinted by Rupa in 2015, page 26.

43. John Fryer, *Travels in India in the Seventeenth Century: by Sir Thomas Roe and Dr John Fryer* (Trubner & Co, 1873), British Library History of Travel edition, 326.

44. Ibid., 277.

45. Romila Thapar, *Early India: From the Origins to AD 1300* (Penguin Books, 2002).

46. Edward Terry, *A Voyage to East-India* (T. Martin and T. Allestrye, 1655), 373.

47. Marco Polo, *The Travels of Marco Polo*, trans. William Marsden, ed. Manuel Komroff (The Modern Library, 2001), 249.

48. *A Journal of the First Voyage of Vasco da Gama 1497–1499*, trans. E.G. Ravenstein (Asian Educational Services, 1995); published in London for Hakluyt Society in 1898 with notes, an introduction and appendices by E.G. Ravenstein.

49. *Coromandel: A Personal History of South India*, by Charles Allen, Little, Brown, 2017, 231–232.

50. Ibid., 49–50.

51. Marco Polo, *The Travels of Marco Polo*, trans. William Marsden, ed. Manuel Komroff (The Modern Library, 2001), 238.

52. *A Journal of the First Voyage of Vasco da Gama 1497–1499*, trans. E.G. Ravenstein (Asian Educational Services, 1995), 60.

53. Ibid., 67.

54. Ibid., 77.

55. Richard Eaton, *A Social History of the Deccan 1300–1761: Eight Indian Lives* (Cambridge University Press, 2005), 79.

56. Ibid., 156–57.

57. Robert Ivermee, *Hooghly: The Global History of a River* (HarperCollins India, 2021), 219.

58. Niccolao Manucci, *Storia do Mogor, Or, Mogul India 1653–1708*, Vol. II (Alpha Editions, 2020), 145.

59. Francois Bernier, *Travels in the Mogul Empire 1656–1668* (Archibald Constable and Company, 1891); republished by Asian Educational Services, 2010.

60. Roy Moxham, *The Theft of India: The European Conquests of India 1498–1765* (HarperCollins, 2016), 126–27.

61. Alan Machado Prabhu, *Slaves of Sultans* (ATC Publications, 2015), 64–65.

62. John Fryer, *Travels in India in the Seventeenth Century: by Sir Thomas Roe and Dr John Fryer* (Trubner & Co, 1873) British Library History of Travel edition, 382.

63. Elizabeth M. Collingham, *Curry: A Tale of Cooks and Conquerors* (Vintage Books, 2006).

64. Ibid.

65. Elizabeth M. Collingham, *Curry: A Biography* (Chatto & Windus), 169–70.

66. Alan Machado Prabhu, *Slaves of Sultans* (ATC Publications, 2015), 82.

Chapter 3

1. John Fryer, *Travels in India in the Seventeenth Century: by Sir Thomas Roe and Dr John Fryer* (Trubner & Co, 1873), British Library History of Travel edition, 242.

2. Ibid., 270.

3. *Travels of J. Albert de Mandelslo in 1638 and 1639,* trans. John Davies (J. Starkey & T. Basset, 1669).

4. Pramod K. Nayar ed., *Days of the Raj* (Penguin, 2009), 169–70.

5. John Ovington, *A Voyage to Suratt, In the Year, 1689* (Jacob Tonson, 1696).

6. Ibid.

7. Roy Moxham, *The Theft of India: The European Conquests of India 1498–1765* (HarperCollins, 2016), 84–85.

8. J. Talboys Wheeler, *Early Records of British India: A History of the British Settlements in India, as told in the Government records, the works of old travellers, and other contemporary documents, from the earliest period down to the rise of British power in India* (Trubner and Company, 1878).

9. Nick Robbins, *The Corporation that Changed the World: How the East India Company Shaped the Modern Multinational* (Orient Longman, 2006).

10. Nicholas Dirks, *The Scandal of Empire: India and the Creation of Imperial Britain* (Permanent Black, 2009), 11.

11. Ibid., 39.

12. Jesse Norman, *Edmund Burke: Philosopher, Politician, Prophet* (William Collins, 2013), 106.

13. Ibid., 107.

14. Thomas George Percival Spear, *Master of Bengal: Clive and His India* (Purnell Book Services, 1975), 159–60.

15. Nicholas Dirks, *The Scandal of Empire: India and the Creation of Imperial Britain* (Permanent Black, 2009), 54–56.

16. Ibid.

17. Ibid.

18. John Keay, *The Honourable Company: A History of the English East India Company* (Harper Collins, 1993), 383.
19. Ibid.
20. For more details see Sumanta Banerjee, *Crime and Urbanization: Calcutta in the Nineteenth Century* (Tulika Books, 2006), 25.
21. Geoffrey Moorhouse, *Calcutta: The City Revealed* (Penguin Books, 1974), 48.
22. Sumanta Banerjee, *Crime and Urbanization: Calcutta in the Nineteenth Century* (Tulika Books, 2006), 3.
23. David Gilmour, *The British in India: Three Centuries of Ambition and Experience* (Allen Lane, 2018), 77.
24. Thomas Duer Broughton, *Letters Written in A Mahratta Camp During the Year 1809, Descriptive of the Character Manners Domestic Habits and Religious Ceremonies of the Mahratta* (Archibald Constable and Company, 1892), reissued by Asian Educational Services, 1995, 2, 25–26. Broughton was formerly commander of the Resident's escort at the court of Scindia.
25. Ibid.
26. Ibid.
27. Ibid.
28. *The Tuzuk-i-Jahangiri or Memoirs of Jahangir, From the First to the Twelfth Year of His Reign*, Vol. 1 (Munshiram Manoharlal, 1968), 354.
29. Ibid., 179–80.
30. Thomas Duer Broughton, *Letters Written in A Mahratta Camp During the Year 1809, Descriptive of the Character Manners Domestic Habits and Religious Ceremonies of the Mahratta* (Archibald Constable and Company, 1892), reissued by Asian Educational Services, 1995.
31. Ibid.
32. Ibid.
33. Ibid.
34. Ibid., 130.
35. Ibid.
36. Ibid.
37. Ibid.
38. Ibid.
39. Ibid., 139.
40. Peter Lamont, *The Rise of the Indian Rope Trick: How a Spectacular Hoax Became History* (Abacus, 2004), 12, 18.

Chapter 4

1. David Gilmour, *The Ruling Caste* (John Murray, 2005), 12–13.
2. Tarun Mukhopadhyay, *Hicky's Bengal Gazette* (Subarnarekha, 1988), 25–26.

3. Ibid., 26–27.
4. Elizabeth M. Collingham, *Curry: A Tale of Cooks and Conquerors* (Vintage Books, 2006), 174.
5. Percival Spear, *Twilight of the Mughals* (Oxford University Press, 1973), 63–65.
6. Rosinka Chaudhuri, *Freedom and Beef Steaks* (Orient BlackSwan, 2012), 18–19.
7. Robert Ivermee, *Hooghly: The Global History of a River* (HarperCollins India, 2021), 40.
8. *Early Records of British India*, 164
9. Robert Ivermee, *Hooghly: The Global History of a River* (HarperCollins India, 2021), 47–48.
10. Ibid., 77–78.
11. Ibid., 62.
12. Elliot Madge, *Henry Derozio: The Eurasian Poet and Reformer* (Naya Prokash, 1982).
13. Percival Spear, *The Nabobs: A Study of the Social Life of the English in Eighteenth Century India* (Oxford University Press, 1963), 131–132.
14. Rosinka Chaudhuri, *Freedom and Beef Steaks* (Orient BlackSwan, 2012), 46.
15. Translated by Rosinka Chaudhuri.
16. Tapan Raychaudhuri, *Europe Reconsidered: Perceptions of the West in Nineteenth Century Bengal* (Oxford University Press, 2000).
17. Elizabeth M. Collingham, *Curry: A Tale of Cooks and Conquerors* (Vintage Books, 2006), 177.
18. Thomas Babington Macaulay, *Minute on Education*, presented on 2 February 1835.
19. Ibid.
20. Ibid.
21. David Gilmour, *The British in India: Three Centuries of Ambition and Experience* (Allen Lane, 2018), 404.
22. Henry Yule, A. C. Burnell, *Hobson-Jobson: A Glossary of Colloquial Ando-Indian Words and Phrases, and of Kindred Terms, Etymological, Historical, Geographical and Discursive* (Asian Educational Services, 2006).
23. Ibid.
24. Narasingha P. Sil, *Problem Child of Renascent Bengal: The Babu of Colonial Calcutta* (K.P. Bagchi & Company, 2017), 5.
25. Ibid., 10–12.
26. David Gilmour, *The Ruling Caste* (Pimlico, 2007), 258.
27. Elizabeth M. Collingham, *Curry: A Tale of Cooks and Conquerors* (Vintage Books, 2006), 145.
28. Ibid., 140.
29. Ibid., 146.

30. Percival Spear, *The Nabobs: A Study of the Social Life of the English in Eighteenth Century India* (Oxford University Press, 1963), 67.
31. Hilton Brown ed., *The Sahibs: The Life and Ways of the British in India as Recorded by Themselves* (William Hodge & Company, 1948), 50–51.
32. Henry Hobbs, *John Barleycorn Bahadur: Old Time Taverns in India* (Thacker, Spink, 1943); also quoted by Vernede, 168.
33. Elizabeth M. Collingham, *Curry: A Tale of Cooks and Conquerors* (Vintage Books, 2006), 112–13.
34. *British Social Life in India 1608–1937*, ed. Dennis Kincaid (Rupa, 2015), 119–20, 125.
35. Christopher Hibbert, *Wellington: A Personal History* (HarperCollins, 1998), 20.
36. 'Indian Cookery', in *The Englishwoman in India*, by a Lady Resident (Pantianos Classics, 1864).
37. *Calcutta Gazette*, 4 April 1816.
38. *Soldier Sahibs: The Men Who Made the North-West Frontier*, Abacus, 2001, 34.
39. Henry Fane, *Five Years in India* (Henry Colburn, 1842).
40. Aliph Cheem, *Lays of Ind* (Thacker, Wining & Company, 1871).
41. Margaret MacMillan, *Women of the Raj: The Mothers, Wives and Daughters of the British Empire in India* (Thames & Hudson, 2018), 202.
42. Percival Spear, *The Nabobs: A Study of the Social Life of the English in Eighteenth Century India* (Oxford University Press, 1963), 34.

Chapter 5

1. Victor Jacquemont, *Letters from India: Describing a Journey in the British Dominions of India, Tibet, Lahore, and Cashmere During the Years 1828, 1829, 1830, 1831*, Vol. II (Gyan Publishing House, 2020), 209–10.
2. Ibid.
3. Edward Terry, *A Voyage to East India* (Hardpress, 2019), 87, 119, 178, 210, 285.
4. Niccolao Manucci, *Travels in the Mogul Empire AD 1656–1668* (New Delhi: Asian Educational Services, 1996), 273–74.
5. John Fryer, *Travels in India in the Seventeenth Century: by Sir Thomas Roe and Dr John Fryer* (Trubner & Co, 1873), British Library History of Travel edition.
6. J. Talboys Wheeler, *Early Records of British India: A History of the British Settlements in India, as told in the Government records, the works of old travellers, and other contemporary documents, from the earliest period down to the rise of British power in India* (Trubner and Company, 1878).

7. J. Nource, *Letters from the Island of Teneriffe, Brazil, the Cape of Good Hope, and the East Indies* (Gale Ecco, 2010), quoted in Pramod Nayar, Pramod K. Nayar ed., *Days of the Raj* (Penguin, 2009), 161.

8. *Narrative of a Journey Through the Upper Provinces of India from Calcutta to Bombay, 1824–1825;* Bishop Heber, 66–67.

9. Pramod K. Nayar ed., *Days of the Raj* (Penguin, 2009), 160–61.

10. Percival Spear, *The Nabobs: A Study of the Social Life of the English in Eighteenth Century India* (Oxford University Press, 1963), 131–32.

11. Victor Jacquemont, *Letters from India*, Vol. II (Gyan Publishing House, 2020), 214.

12. James Forbes, *Oriental Memoirs: Selected and Abridged from a Series of Familiar Letters Written during Seventeen Years Residence in India* (White, Cochrane, and Co., 1813), quoted in Pramod K. Nayar ed., *Days of the Raj* (Penguin, 2009), 164.

13. Pran Nevile, *Sahibs' India: Vignettes from the Raj* (Penguin, 2010), 22.

14. Henry Yule, A. C. Burnell, *Hobson-Jobson: A Glossary of Colloquial Ando-Indian Words and Phrases, and of Kindred Terms, Etymological, Historical, Geographical and Discursive* (Asian Educational Services, 2006), 620.

15. Aliph Cheem, *Lays of Ind* (Thacker, Wining & Company, 1871).

16. Ibid.

17. Percival Spear, *The Nabobs: A Study of the Social Life of the English in Eighteenth Century India* (Oxford University Press, 1963), 131–32.

18. Dennis Kincaid, ed. *British Social Life in India 1608–1937* (Rupa, 2015), 143–44.

19. Ibid., 146–47.

20. Sumanta Banerjee, *Dangerous Outcast: The Prostitute in Nineteenth-Century Bengal* (Seagull Books, 2019), 219.

21. Charles Allen, *Plain Tales from the Raj: Images of British India in the Twentieth Century* (Abacus, 1994), 196.

22. Pramod K. Nayar ed., *Days of the Raj* (Penguin, 2009), 126.

23. David Gilmour, *The Ruling Caste* (John Murray, 2005), 152.

24. Sumanta Banerjee, *Dangerous Outcast: The Prostitute in Nineteenth-Century Bengal* (Seagull Books, 2019), 158, 160–61.

25. Ibid., 79–80.

26. Ibid., 170.

27. Ibid., 90.

28. David Gilmour, *The British in India: Three Centuries of Ambition and Experience* (Allen Lane, 2018), 71.

29. Sumanta Banerjee, *Dangerous Outcast: The Prostitute in Nineteenth-Century Bengal* (Seagull Books, 2019), 42.

30. Victor Jacquemont, *Letters from India*, Vol. II (Gyan Publishing House, 2020), 240–41, 244.

31. Percival Spear, *Twilight of the Mughals* (Oxford University Press, 1973), 164.
32. Victor Jacquemont, *Letters from India*, Vol. II (Gyan Publishing House, 2020), 253–54.
33. Ibid., 244.
34. William Hickey, *Memoirs of William Hickey*, Vol. II, 1775–1782, ed. Alfred Spencer (Hurst and Blackett, 1918).
35. William Hickey, *Memoirs of William Hickey*, Vol. III and IV, 1775–1782, ed. Alfred Spencer (Hurst and Blackett, 1918).
36. Percival Spear, *The Nabobs: A Study of the Social Life of the English in Eighteenth Century India* (Oxford University Press, 1963), 65.
37. David Gilmour, *The British in India: Three Centuries of Ambition and Experience* (Allen Lane, 2018), 328.
38. Percival Spear, *Twilight of the Mughals* (Oxford University Press, 1973).
39. David Gilmour, *The British in India: Three Centuries of Ambition and Experience* (Allen Lane, 2018), 288–90.
40. Emily Eden, *Up the Country: Letters written to her Sister from the Upper Provinces of India* (Curzon Press, 1978), 373.
41. Heber, 453.
42. Victor Jacquemont, *Letters from India*, Vol. II (Gyan Publishing House, 2020), 247.
43. Fanny Parkes, *Begums, Thugs & Englishmen: The Journals of Fanny Parkes*, ed. William Dalrymple (Penguin, 2002), Chapter 32. Mrs Parkes's original work was published in 1850 as *Wanderings of a Pilgrim in Search of the Picturesque*.
44. Ibid.
45. He also became the third prime minister to marry while in office, after Robert Walpole, who wed Maria Skerret in 1738 and the Duke of Grafton, who married Elizabeth Wrottlesley in 1769. Lord Liverpool wed Mary Chester, a friend of his recently deceased wife, in 1822.
46. H.G. Keene, *Sketches in Indian Ink* (Oxford University, 1891), quoted in R.V. Vernede, ed., *British Life in India: An Anthology of Humorous and Other Writings Perpetrated by the British in India 1750–1947, With Some Latitude for Works Completed after Independence* (Oxford University Press, 1995), 35.
47. Ibid.
48. R.V. Vernede, ed., *British Life in India: An Anthology of Humorous and Other Writings Perpetrated by the British in India 1750-1947, With Some Latitude for Works Completed after Independence* (Oxford University Press, 1995), 35.
49. Charles Allen, *Plain Tales from the Raj: Images of British India in the Twentieth Century* (Abacus, 1994), 38.

50. Ben Macintyre, 'Joe Biden's roots are in the British Empire', *The Times*, 16 January 2021, https://www.thetimes.co.uk/article/joe-bidens-roots-are-in-the-british-empire-dpfgpmrch.

51. Ibid.

52. David Gilmour, *The British in India: Three Centuries of Ambition and Experience* (Allen Lane, 2018), 402–03.

Chapter 6

1. Niccolao Manucci, *Storia do Mogor, Or, Mogul India 1653-1708*, Vol. II (Alpha Editions, 2020), 43–49.

2. Ibid.

3. Francois Bernier, *Travels in the Mogul Empire 1656–1668* (Archibald Constable and Company, 1891; republished by Asian Educational Services, 2010), 263–64.

4. Robert Ivermee, *Hooghly: The Global History of a River* (HarperCollins India, 2021), 73.

5. Niccolao Manucci, *Storia do Mogor, Or, Mogul India 1653–1708*, Vol. III (Alpha Editions, 2020), 366–68.

6. Ibid., 370.

7. Ibid.

8. Ibid., 378.

9. Ibid., 378–79.

10. *Early Record of British India*, 106–07.

11. Percival Spear, *The Nabobs: A Study of the Social Life of the English in Eighteenth Century India* (Oxford University Press, 1963), 39.

12. Ibid., 130, 131.

13. Nicholas Dirks, *The Scandal of Empire: India and the Creation of Imperial Britain* (Permanent Black, 2009), 75.

14. Maya Jasanoff, *Edge of Empire: Lives, Culture, and Conquest in the East 1750-1850* (Vintage, 2006).

15. Pramod K. Nayar ed., *Days of the Raj* (Penguin, 2009), 230–32.

16. Ibid.

17. John Keay, *The Honourable Company: A History of the English East India Company* (Harper Collins, 1993), 304–05.

18. Henry Elmsley Busteed, *Echoes from Old Calcutta: Reminiscences of the days of Warren Hastings, Francis, and Impey* (Rupa, 2000), 569.

19. J. Talboys Wheeler, *Early Records of British India: A History of the British Settlements in India, as told in the Government records, the works of old travellers, and other contemporary documents, from the earliest period down to the rise of British power in India* (Trubner and Company, 1878), 251–52.

20. David Gilmour, *The British in India: Three Centuries of Ambition and Experience* (Allen Lane, 2018), 36.

21. Nicholas Dirks, *The Scandal of Empire: India and the Creation of Imperial Britain* (Permanent Black, 2009), 12.
22. Jesse Norman, *Edmund Burke: Philosopher, Politician, Prophet* (William Collins, 2013), 128–29.
23. Henry Elmsley Busteed, *Echoes from Old Calcutta: Reminiscences of the days of Warren Hastings, Francis, and Impey* (Rupa, 2000), 216–17.
24. Ibid., 219, 221.
25. Ibid.
26. William Hickey, *Memoirs of William Hickey*, Vol. II, 1775–1782, ed. Alfred Spencer (Hurst and Blackett, 1918), Chapter XXI.
27. Percival Spear, *The Nabobs: A Study of the Social Life of the English in Eighteenth Century India* (Oxford University Press, 1963), 65.
28. Henry Yule, A. C. Burnell, *Hobson-Jobson: A Glossary of Colloquial Ando-Indian Words and Phrases, and of Kindred Terms, Etymological, Historical, Geographical and Discursive* (Asian Educational Services, 2006).
29. Ibid., 705.
30. Frank Perlin, in *The Eighteenth Century in Indian History*, ed. P.J. Marshall (Oxford University Press, 2003), 56.
31. Reginald Heber, *Narrative of a Journey Through the Upper Provinces of India from Calcutta to Bombay, 1824–1825* (Philadelphia, 1829), 464–65.
32. Heber, 464–65.
33. Ibid., 33.
34. Percival Spear, *Twilight of the Mughals* (Oxford University Press, 1973), 77.
35. Heber, 475.
36. Emily Eden, *Up the Country: Letters written to her Sister from the Upper Provinces of India* (Curzon Press, 1978), 367–68, 371, 375.
37. Ibid.
38. Ibid.
39. William Howard Russell, *My Diary in India, in the Year 1858–59*, Vol. 2 (Routledge, Warne, and Routledge, 1860).
40. David Gilmour, *The British in India: Three Centuries of Ambition and Experience* (Allen Lane, 2018), 322–23.
41. David Gilmour, *The Ruling Caste* (John Murray, 2005), 153.
42. Ibid., 135–36.
43. Charles Allen, *Plain Tales from the Raj: Images of British India in the Twentieth Century* (Abacus, 1994), 227–28.
44. Alen McMillan, *Divers Ditties: Chiefly Written in India* (Constable, 1895).
45. William Wilson Hunter, *The Indian Musulmans* (HardPress, 2018).

46. Charles Allen, *Plain Tales from the Raj: Images of British India in the Twentieth Century* (Abacus, 1994), 225–26.
47. David Gilmour, *The Ruling Caste* (John Murray, 2005), 256.
48. Ibid., 19.
49. R.V. Vernede, ed., *British Life in India: An Anthology of Humorous and Other Writings Perpetrated by the British in India 1750–1947, With Some Latitude for Works Completed after Independence* (Oxford University Press, 1995), 250–51.
50. Ibid.

Chapter 7

1. Henry Yule, A. C. Burnell, *Hobson-Jobson: A Glossary of Colloquial Ando-Indian Words and Phrases, and of Kindred Terms, Etymological, Historical, Geographical and Discursive* (Asian Educational Services, 2006), 419.
2. Ibid., 293.
3. Tom Stoppard, *Indian Ink* (Faber, 1995), 19.
4. G.V. Desani, *All About H. Hatterr* (Aleph Classics, reprinted in 2018), 119.
5. Henry Yule, A. C. Burnell, *Hobson-Jobson: A Glossary of Colloquial Ando-Indian Words and Phrases, and of Kindred Terms, Etymological, Historical, Geographical and Discursive* (Asian Educational Services, 2006), 570.
6. John Beames, *Memoirs of a Bengal Civilian* (Eland, 1984), 87.
7. Percival Spear, *The Nabobs: A Study of the Social Life of the English in Eighteenth Century India* (Oxford University Press, 1963), 58–59.
8. John Lang, *Wanderings in India and Other Sketches of Life in Hindostan* (Rupa, 2015), 86–99.
9. Ibid.
10. Ibid., 246.
11. Ibid., 247–48.
12. Ibid., 249–50.
13. Ibid., 251.
14. William Hickey, *Memoirs of William Hickey*, Vol. II, 1775–1782, ed. Alfred Spencer (Hurst and Blackett, 1918), Chapter XIV.
15. Tarun Mukhopadhyay, *Hicky's Bengal Gazette* (Subarnarekha, 1988), 11–12.
16. *Hicky's Bengal Gazette*, quoted in Dennis Kincaid, ed. *British Social Life in India 1608–1937* (Rupa, 2015), 128–29.
17. Tarun Mukhopadhyay, *Hicky's Bengal Gazette* (Subarnarekha, 1988), 17–18.
18. Henry Elmsley Busteed, *Echoes from Old Calcutta: Reminiscences of the days of Warren Hastings, Francis, and Impey* (Rupa, 2000), 299–300.

19. Victor Jacquemont, *Letters from India: Describing a Journey in the British Dominions of India, Tibet, Lahore, and Cashmere During the Years 1828, 1829, 1830, 1831*, Vol. II (Gyan Publishing House, 2020), 243.
20. Hugh David Sandeman, *Selections from Calcutta Gazette*, Vol. VII, 1806 to 1815 (Bibhash Gupta, Microform Publication Division, n.d.).
21. William Hickey, *Memoirs of William Hickey*, Vol. II, 1775–1782, ed. Alfred Spencer (Hurst and Blackett, 1918), Chapter X.
22. Ibid.
23. Pran Nevile, *Sahibs' India: Vignettes from the Raj* (Penguin, 2010), 85.
24. *Soldier Sahibs: The Men Who Made the North-West Frontier*, Charles Allen, Abacus, 34.
25. Pramod K. Nayar ed., *Days of the Raj* (Penguin, 2009), 54.
26. David Gilmour, *The British in India: Three Centuries of Ambition and Experience* (Allen Lane, 2018), 484–85.
27. William Hickey, *Memoirs of William Hickey*, Vol. II, 1775–1782, ed. Alfred Spencer (Hurst and Blackett, 1918), Chapter XV.
28. Maya Jasanoff, *Edge of Empire: Lives, Culture, and Conquest in the East 1750-1850* (Vintage, 2006), 82–83.
29. Henry Elmsley Busteed, *Echoes from Old Calcutta: Reminiscences of the days of Warren Hastings, Francis, and Impey* (Rupa, 2000), 222–23.
30. David Gilmour, *The Ruling Caste* (John Murray, 2005), 307–309.
31. Ibid., 238.
32. Ibid., 240.
33. Henry Elmsley Busteed, *Echoes from Old Calcutta: Reminiscences of the days of Warren Hastings, Francis, and Impey* (Rupa, 2000), 244–45.
34. Ibid., 249.
35. Hilton Brown ed., *The Sahibs: The Life and Ways of the British in India as Recorded by Themselves* (William Hodge & Company, 1948), 48.
36. Emily Eden, *Letters from India (1836-1840)* (Richard Bentley & Son, 1872).
37. Lord Beveridge, *India Called Them* (George Allen & Unwin, 1947), 200, 394.
38. *The Collected Poems of Rudyard Kipling*, Wordsworth Poetry Library, 46–47.
39. Charles Allen, *Plain Tales from the Raj: Images of British India in the Twentieth Century* (Abacus, 1994), 156–57.
40. 'A letter from a lady in Calcutta to her Friend in England', *Calcutta Gazette*, 12 August 1784.
41. Hilton Brown ed., *The Sahibs: The Life and Ways of the British in India as Recorded by Themselves* (William Hodge & Company, 1948), 115–16.

42. Charles Allen, *Plain Tales from the Raj: Images of British India in the Twentieth Century* (Abacus, 1994), 159.

43. R.V. Vernede, ed., *British Life in India: An Anthology of Humorous and Other Writings Perpetrated by the British in India 1750–1947, With Some Latitude for Works Completed after Independence* (Oxford University Press, 1995), 92.

44. Rudyard Kipling, *Lessons for Mrs Hauksbee: Tales of Passion, Intrigue and Scandal* (Speaking Tiger, 2017), 42.

45. Rudyard Kipling, 'Thrown Away', in *Plain Tales from the Hills* (Thacker, Spink and Co., 1888).

46. Rudyard Kipling, 'Georgie-Porgie', in *Lessons for Mrs Hanksbee: Tales of Passion, Intrique and Scandal* (Speaking Tiger, 2017), 1–10.

47. Rudyard Kipling, 'Without Benefit of Clergy', in *Macmillan's Magazine*, 1890.

Chapter 8

1. Roy Moxham, *The Theft of India* (HarperCollins, 2016), 91.

2. Roy Moxham, *The Theft of India: The European Conquests of India 1498–1765* (HarperCollins, 2016), 91–92.

3. Percival Spear, *The Nabobs: A Study of the Social Life of the English in Eighteenth Century India* (Oxford University Press, 1963), 128–29.

4. John Fryer, *Travels in India in the Seventeenth Century: by Sir Thomas Roe and Dr John Fryer* (Trubner & Co, 1873), 450.

5. Percival Spear, *The Nabobs: A Study of the Social Life of the English in Eighteenth Century India* (Oxford University Press, 1963), 128–29.

6. Ibid.

7. R.V. Vernede, ed., *British Life in India: An Anthology of Humorous and Other Writings Perpetrated by the British in India 1750–1947, With Some Latitude for Works Completed after Independence*, (Oxford University Press, 1995), 169–70.

   We owe such knowledge to a favourite pastime of bureaucrats; memoirs or anthologies of anecdotes in prose and verse. Raymond Vernede, who followed his father into the Indian Civil Service in 1928, compiled an excellent anecdotal social history with thoughtful commentary. Vernede was Raj blue blood. His wife Nancy was the daughter of Sir Charles Kendall, ICS, a judge of the Allahabad High Court. Raymond and Nancy married in 1937 and left India only after 1947.

8. Ibid., 748.

9. Percival Spear, *The Nabobs: A Study of the Social Life of the English in Eighteenth Century India* (Oxford University Press, 1963), 109.

10. Sumanta Banerjee, *Crime and Urbanization: Calcutta in the Nineteenth Century* (Tulika Books, 2006), 15.

11. Ibid., 15–17.
12. Ibid.
13. Thomas Duer Broughton, *Letters Written in A Mahratta Camp During the Year 1809, Descriptive of the Character Manners Domestic Habits and Religious Ceremonies of the Mahratta* (Archibald Constable and Company, 1892), reissued by Asian Educational Services, 1995, 114.
14. Hilton Brown ed., *The Sahibs: The Life and Ways of the British in India as Recorded by Themselves* (William Hodge & Company, 1948), 225–26.
15. John Murray, *Travels in Europe, Asia and Africa*, quoted by Pramod K. Nayar ed., *Days of the Raj* (Penguin, 2009), 57–58.
16. William Hickey, *Memoirs of William Hickey*, Vol. II, 1775–1782, ed. Alfred Spencer (Hurst and Blackett, 1918), Chapter X.
17. Lord Beveridge, *India Called Them* (George Allen & Unwin, 1947), 202–03.
18. David Gilmour, *The British in India: Three Centuries of Ambition and Experience* (Allen Lane, 2018), 347.
19. Tarun Mukhopadhyay, *Hicky's Bengal Gazette* (Subarnarekha, 1988), 20.
20. David Gilmour, *The British in India: Three Centuries of Ambition and Experience* (Allen Lane, 2018), 345.
21. Pran Nevile, *Sahibs' India: Vignettes from the Raj* (Penguin, 2010), 4, 6.
22. R.V. Vernede, ed., *British Life in India: An Anthology of Humorous and Other Writings Perpetrated by the British in India 1750–1947, With Some Latitude for Works Completed after Independence* (Oxford University Press, 1995), 171.
23. Sir William Russell, *My Diary in India, in the Year 1858–59*, Vol. 2 (Routledge, Warne, and Routledge, 1860), 407–08.
24. Ibid., 264.
25. Ibid., 272–73.
26. Hilton Brown ed., *The Sahibs: The Life and Ways of the British in India as Recorded by Themselves* (William Hodge & Company, 1948), 222, 225.
27. Sir William Russell, *My Diary in India, in the Year 1858–59*, Vol. 2 (Routledge, Warne, and Routledge, 1860), 272–73.
28. John Beames, *Memoirs of a Bengal Civilian* (Eland, 1984), 102.
29. Dennis Kincaid, ed. *British Social Life in India 1608–1937* (Rupa, 2015), 224–25.
30. Lord Beveridge, *India Called Them* (George Allen & Unwin, 1947), 206.
31. R.V. Vernede, ed., *British Life in India: An Anthology of Humorous and Other Writings Perpetrated by the British in India 1750–1947, With Some Latitude for Works Completed after Independence* (Oxford University Press, 1995), 118–20, 125–26.

32. Ibid.

33. Ibid.

34. Ibid.

35. Pramod K. Nayar ed., *Days of the Raj* (Penguin, 2009), 97.

36. Ibid., 98–100, 111.

37. Ibid.

38. *The Englishwoman in India: For ladies proceeding to, or living in, the East Indies; information on Outfit, Furniture, Housekeeping, Rearing of Children, Duties, Servants, Stable Keeping and Travel,* by A Lady Resident (Pantianos Classics, 1864), Chapter 5.

39. Margaret MacMillan, *Women of the Raj: The Mothers, Wives and Daughters of the British Empire in India* (Thames & Hudson, 2018), 173.

40. Charles Allen, *Plain Tales from the Raj: Images of British India in the Twentieth Century* (Abacus, 1994), 22.

41. Pramod K. Nayar ed., *Days of the Raj* (Penguin, 2009), quoting *The European in India*, 87, 89.

42. Margaret MacMillan, *Women of the Raj: The Mothers, Wives and Daughters of the British Empire in India* (Thames & Hudson, 2018), 187.

43. R.V. Vernede, ed., *British Life in India: An Anthology of Humorous and Other Writings Perpetrated by the British in India 1750–1947, With Some Latitude for Works Completed after Independence* (Oxford University Press, 1995), 214–15.

44. *Chambers's Edinburgh Journal, New Series, 1852*, quoted by Pramod K. Nayar ed., *Days of the Raj* (Penguin, 2009), 245–46.

45. Pramod K. Nayar ed., *Days of the Raj* (Penguin, 2009), 247.

46. R.V. Vernede, ed., *British Life in India: An Anthology of Humorous and Other Writings Perpetrated by the British in India 1750–1947, With Some Latitude for Works Completed after Independence* (Oxford University Press, 1995), 24–25.

47. Hilton Brown ed., *The Sahibs: The Life and Ways of the British in India as Recorded by Themselves* (William Hodge & Company, 1948), 219.

48. Ibid., 218; from *The Land of the Lotus*.

49. Ibid., 219, 220, from *Behind the Bungalow*, 1889.

50. David Gilmour, *The Ruling Caste* (John Murray, 2005), 6–7.

51. Ibid.

52. Ibid., 5.

53. Ibid., 9–10.

54. Sumanta Banerjee, *The Parlour and the Streets: Elite and Popular Culture in Nineteenth-Century Bengal* (Seagull Books, 2019), 128.

55. Ibid., 97–98.

56. Lord Curzon, *A Viceroy's India: Leaves from Lord Curzon's Notebook* (Sidgwick & Jackson, 1984), 45, 51.

57. Pamela Kanwar, *Imperial Simla: The Political Culture of the Raj* (Oxford India Paperbacks, 1990).

Chapter 9

1. Henry Yule, A. C. Burnell, *Hobson-Jobson: A Glossary of Colloquial Ando-Indian Words and Phrases, and of Kindred Terms, Etymological, Historical, Geographical and Discursive* (Asian Educational Services, 2006), 333.
2. Sumanta Banerjee, *Crime and Urbanization: Calcutta in the Nineteenth Century* (Tulika Books, 2006), 1.
3. Dennis Kincaid, ed. *British Social Life in India 1608–1937* (Rupa, 2015), 110.
4. Keith Feiling, *Warren Hastings* (Macmillan, 1954), 188.
5. Henry Elmsley Busteed, *Echoes from Old Calcutta: Reminiscences of the days of Warren Hastings, Francis, and Impey* (Rupa, 2000), 105.
6. Ibid., 118–19.
7. Ibid., 135.
8. Tarun Mukhopadhyay, *Hicky's Bengal Gazette* (Subarnarekha, 1988), 93.
9. Ibid., 90.
10. Keith Feiling, *Warren Hastings* (Macmillan, 1954), 137.
11. Henry Beveridge, *The Trial of Maharaja Nanda Kumar: A Narrative of a Judicial Murder* (Thacker, Spink and Co., 1886), 7.
12. William Hickey, *Memoirs of William Hickey*, Vol. II, 1775–1782, ed. Alfred Spencer (Hurst and Blackett, 1918), Chapter XI.
13. Ibid.
14. Sumanta Banerjee, *Crime and Urbanization: Calcutta in the Nineteenth Century* (Tulika Books, 2006), 98.
15. Ibid., 109.
16. Peter Robb, *Useful Friendships: Europeans and Indians in Early Calcutta* (Oxford University Press, 2014), 153, 158, 160, 164, 170.
17. Ibid.
18. Ibid.
19. Ibid., 159, 171, 176.
20. Ibid., 171.
21. John Beames, *Memoirs of a Bengal Civilian* (Eland, 1984), 113.
22. Alen McMillan, *Divers Ditties: Chiefly Written in India* (Constable, 1895). David Gilmour, *The Ruling Caste* (John Murray, 2005), 82.
23. David Gilmour, *The Ruling Caste* (John Murray, 2005), 127.
24. Henry Hobbs, *John Barleycorn Bahadur: Old Time Taverns in India* (Thacker, Spink, 1943), 61.
25. Pramod K. Nayar ed., *Days of the Raj* (Penguin, 2009), 137–38.
26. R.V. Vernede, ed., *British Life in India: An Anthology of Humorous and Other Writings Perpetrated by the British in India 1750–1947,*

With Some Latitude for Works Completed after Independence (Oxford University Press, 1995), 58.

27. Ibid., 65.
28. John Beames, *Memoirs of a Bengal Civilian* (Eland, 1984), 63.
29. Charles Allen, *Plain Tales from the Raj: Images of British India in the Twentieth Century* (Abacus, 1994), 221.
30. David Gilmour, *The Ruling Caste* (John Murray, 2005), 71.
31. John Beames, *Memoirs of a Bengal Civilian* (Eland, 1984), 203.
32. Aliph Cheem, *Lays of Ind* (Thacker, Wining & Company, 1871).
33. Ibid.
34. Ibid.
35. Percival Spear, *The Nabobs: A Study of the Social Life of the English in Eighteenth Century India* (Oxford University Press, 1963), 141.
36. Ibid., 105.
37. John Beames, *Memoirs of a Bengal Civilian* (Eland, 1984), 117–18.
38. Percival Spear, *The Nabobs: A Study of the Social Life of the English in Eighteenth Century India* (Oxford University Press, 1963), 62.
39. S. Muthiah and Harry MacLure, *The Anglo-Indians: A 500-Year History* (Niyogi Books, 2013), 20–21.
40. Ibid.
41. Ibid., 25.
42. Percival Spear, *The Nabobs: A Study of the Social Life of the English in Eighteenth Century India* (Oxford University Press, 1963), 61–64, 136–38.
43. S. Muthiah and Harry MacLure, *The Anglo-Indians: A 500-Year History* (Niyogi Books, 2013), 25–26.
44. Philip Mason, *Skinner of Skinner's Horse* (Andre Deutsch, 1979).
45. Percival Spear, *Twilight of the Mughals* (Oxford University Press, 1973), 164–65.
46. John Lang, *Wanderings in India and Other Sketches of Life in Hindostan* (Rupa, 2015), 236–37.
47. John Beames, *Memoirs of a Bengal Civilian* (Eland, 1984), 85.
48. Margaret MacMillan, *Women of the Raj: The Mothers, Wives and Daughters of the British Empire in India* (Thames & Hudson, 2018), 52.
49. Charles Allen, *Plain Tales from the Raj: Images of British India in the Twentieth Century* (Abacus, 1994), 26.
50. Ibid., 231.
51. Ibid., 232.
52. Ibid., 232.
53. Ibid., 49.
54. David Gilmour, *The British in India: Three Centuries of Ambition and Experience* (Allen Lane, 2018), 298.
55. Dennis Kincaid, ed. *British Social Life in India 1608–1937* (Rupa, 2015), 302–03.

56. David Gilmour, *The British in India: Three Centuries of Ambition and Experience* (Allen Lane, 2018), 312.
57. Charles Allen, *Plain Tales from the Raj: Images of British India in the Twentieth Century* (Abacus, 1994), 122.
58. David Gilmour, *The British in India: Three Centuries of Ambition and Experience* (Allen Lane, 2018), 400–01.

Chapter 10

1. Alfred Robert Davidson MacKenzie, *Mutiny Memoirs: Being Personal Reminiscences of the Great Sepoy Revolt of 1857*, edited by Mushirul Hasan, (Niyogi Books, 2008), 82–83.
2. John Beames, *Memoirs of a Bengal Civilian* (Eland, 1984), 74.
3. Pramod K. Nayar, *The Penguin 1857 Reader* (Penguin, 2007), 156.
4. Alfred Robert Davidson MacKenzie, *Mutiny Memoirs: Being Personal Reminiscences of the Great Sepoy Revolt of 1857*, edited by Mushirul Hasan (Niyogi Books, 2008), 39–40.
5. Pramod K. Nayar, *The Penguin 1857 Reader* (Penguin, 2007), 200–01.
6. Alfred Robert Davidson MacKenzie, *Mutiny Memoirs: Being Personal Reminiscences of the Great Sepoy Revolt of 1857*, edited by Mushirul Hasan (Niyogi Books, 2008), 44.
7. Pramod K. Nayar, *The Penguin 1857 Reader* (Penguin, 2007), 144.
8. Ibid., 143.
9. R. Bentley, *Service and Adventure with the Khakee Resslah or Meerut Volunteer Force During the Mutinies of 1857–58* (1858), quoted in Pramod K. Nayar, *The Penguin 1857 Reader* (Penguin, 2007), 140.
10. Pramod K. Nayar, *The Penguin 1857 Reader* (Penguin, 2007), 168–169.
11. Ibid., 207–208.
12. Ibid., 250–255.
13. Ibid., 201.
14. David Gilmour, *The Ruling Caste* (John Murray, 2005), 18.
15. Pramod K. Nayar, *The Penguin 1857 Reader* (Penguin, 2007), 196.
16. David Gilmour, *The Ruling Caste* (John Murray, 2005), 17.
17. Pramod K. Nayar, *The Penguin 1857 Reader* (Penguin, 2007), 307–09. Also see P.C. Joshi ed., *Folk Songs in Rebellion, 1857: A Symposium* (Delhi People's Publishing House, 1957).
18. Ibid.
19. Ibid.
20. Ibid.
21. Philip Mason, *The Men Who Ruled India* (W.W. Norton, 1953), 185.
22. Hilton Brown ed., *The Sahibs: The Life and Ways of the British in India as Recorded by Themselves* (William Hodge & Company, 1948).
23. Alfred Robert Davidson MacKenzie, *Mutiny Memoirs: Being Personal Reminiscences of the Great Sepoy Revolt of 1857*, edited by Mushirul Hasan (Niyogi Books, 2008), 69.

24. Pramod K. Nayar, *The Penguin 1857 Reader* (Penguin, 2007), 255.
25. Veena Talwar Oldenburg ed., *Shaam-e-Awadh: Writings on Lucknow* (Penguin Books, 2007).
26. Dennis Kincaid, ed. *British Social Life in India 1608–1937* (Rupa, 2015), 266–67.
27. William Howard Russell, *My Diary in India, in the Year 1858–59*, Vol. 2 (Routledge, Warne, and Routledge, 1860), 258.
28. Ibid., 258–59.
29. David Gilmour, *The Ruling Caste* (John Murray, 2005), 11.
30. Charles Allen, *Plain Tales from the Raj: Images of British India in the Twentieth Century* (Abacus, 1994), 240–41.
31. Ibid., 190.
32. Dennis Kincaid, ed. *British Social Life in India 1608–1937* (Rupa, 2015).
33. Charles Allen, *Plain Tales from the Raj: Images of British India in the Twentieth Century* (Abacus, 1994), 236.
34. Bidisha Chakraborty and Sarmistha De, *Calcutta in the Nineteenth Century: An Archival Exploration* (Niyogi Books, 2013), 158–62.
35. Ibid.
36. Ibid.
37. Sumanta Banerjee, *The Parlour and the Streets: Elite and Popular Culture in Nineteenth-Century Bengal* (Seagull Books, 2019), 204.
38. Ibid., 96–97.
39. Ibid., 209.
40. David Gilmour, *The British in India: Three Centuries of Ambition and Experience* (Allen Lane, 2018), 314–20.
41. Val C. Prinsep, *Glimpses of Imperial India* (Mittal Publications, 1979), *Glimpses of Imperial India,* by Val C. Prinsep, Mittal Publications, Delhi; first printed in 1878, pages 38–39.
42. Ibid.
43. Margaret MacMillan, *Women of the Raj: The Mothers, Wives and Daughters of the British Empire in India* (Thames & Hudson, 2018), 79–80.
44. Ibid.
45. David Gilmour, *The British in India: Three Centuries of Ambition and Experience* (Allen Lane, 2018), 408.
46. R.V. Vernede, ed., *British Life in India: An Anthology of Humorous and Other Writings Perpetrated by the British in India 1750–1947, With Some Latitude for Works Completed after Independence* (Oxford University Press, 1995), 167.
47. Dennis Kincaid, ed. *British Social Life in India 1608–1937* (Rupa, 2015), 355.
48. Lord Beveridge, *India Called Them* (George Allen & Unwin, 1947), 84.
49. Philip Mason, *The Men Who Ruled India* (W.W. Norton, 1953), Chapter 11.

50. Thomas Babington Macaulay, quoted in Dadabhai Naoroji, *Poverty and Un-British Rule in India* (Swan Sonnenschein, 1901), 91.
51. Ibid.
52. David Gilmour, *The Ruling Caste* (John Murray, 2005), 219–20.
53. Lord Beveridge, *India Called Them* (George Allen & Unwin, 1947), 259–60.
54. David C. Potter, *India's Political Administrators: From ICS to IAS* (Oxford University Press, 1996), 113.
55. Sumanta Banerjee, *The Parlour and the Streets: Elite and Popular Culture in Nineteenth-Century Bengal* (Seagull Books, 2019), 143.
56. R.V. Vernede, ed., *British Life in India: An Anthology of Humorous and Other Writings Perpetrated by the British in India 1750–1947, With Some Latitude for Works Completed after Independence* (Oxford University Press, 1995), 229–41.
57. Ibid.
58. Ibid.
59. Ibid., 261–62.
60. Charles Allen, *Plain Tales from the Raj: Images of British India in the Twentieth Century* (Abacus, 1994), 125.

Chapter 11

1. William Howard Russell, *My Diary in India, in the Year 1858–59*, Vol. 2 (Routledge, Warne, and Routledge, 1860), 146–50.
2. Ibid.
3. Ibid.
4. Ibid.
5. Margaret MacMillan, *Women of the Raj: The Mothers, Wives and Daughters of the British Empire in India* (Thames & Hudson, 2018), 84.
6. David Gilmour, *The Ruling Caste* (John Murray, 2005), 4.
7. Ann Morrow, *Highness: The Maharajahs of India* (Grafton Books, 1986), 93.
8. Charles Allen, *Plain Tales from the Raj: Images of British India in the Twentieth Century* (Abacus, 1994), 237.
9. David Gilmour, *The Ruling Caste* (John Murray, 2005), 189.
10. Pramila Sharma, *Curzon-Nama: Autocrat Curzon Unconquerable India* (Eshwar, 1999), 151–52.
11. N. Krishnaswamy and Archana S. Burde, *Linguistic Colonialism and the Expanding English Empire: The Politics of Indians' English* (Oxford University Press, 1998), 95, 98.
12. Ibid.
13. Lord Curzon, *A Viceroy's India: Leaves from Lord Curzon's Notebook*, introduced by Elizabeth Longford (Sidgwick & Jackson, 1984), 57–58.

14. Ibid.
15. Dadabhai Naoroji, *Poverty and Un-British Rule in India* (Swan Sonnenschein, 1901), viii–x.
16. Ibid.
17. Ibid.
18. Parmatma Sharan, *The Imperial Legislative Council of India* (S. Chand & Co., 1961), 91–93.
19. Sumanta Banerjee, *Dangerous Outcast: The Prostitute in Nineteenth-Century Bengal* (Seagull Books, 2019), 187.
20. Pramila Sharma, *Curzon-Nama: Autocrat Curzon Unconquerable India* (Eshwar, 1999), 13, quoting from *Letters of Queen Victoria*, Vol. III, Series III.
21. Ibid., 146.
22. Sumanta Banerjee, *Crime and Urbanization: Calcutta in the Nineteenth Century* (Tulika Books, 2006), 71.
23. Robert Ivermee, *Hooghly: The Global History of a River* (HarperCollins India, 2021), 91.
24. Quoted by Hunter, *The Annals of Rural Bengal* (1868); reproduced in Sumanta Banerjee, *Crime and Urbanization: Calcutta in the Nineteenth Century* (Tulika Books, 2006), 71.
25. David Gilmour, *The Ruling Caste* (John Murray, 2005), 114–15.
26. M.J. Akbar, *Nehru: The Making of India* (Penguin, 1988), 73.
27. Pramila Sharma, *Curzon-Nama: Autocrat Curzon Unconquerable India* (Eshwar, 1999), 132.
28. Ibid., 140.
29. Ibid., 9.
30. Rosinka Chaudhuri, *Freedom and Beef Steaks* (Orient BlackSwan, 2012), 122–23.
31. Josh Ireland, *Churchill & Son* (John Murray, 2021).
32. Marco Polo, *The Travels of Marco Polo*, trans. William Marsden, ed. Manuel Komroff (The Modern Library, 2001), 248.
33. John Fryer, *Travels in India in the Seventeenth Century: by Sir Thomas Roe and Dr John Fryer* (Trubner & Co, 1873), 294–98.
34. Ibid.
35. Ibid.
36. Ibid.
37. Niccolao Manucci, *Storia do Mogor, Or, Mogul India 1653–1708*, Vol. II (Alpha Editions, 2020), 134.
38. Niccolao Manucci, *Storia do Mogor, Or, Mogul India 1653–1708*, Vol. III (Alpha Editions, 2020), 189–215.
39. Ibid.
40. John Ovington, *A Voyage to Suratt, In the Year, 1689* (Jacob Tonson, 1696).

41. John Lang, *Wanderings in India and Other Sketches of Life in Hindostan* (Rupa, 2015), 361–62.

42. Fanny Parkes, *Begums, Thugs & Englishmen: The Journals of Fanny Parkes*, ed. William Dalrymple (Penguin, 2002), Chapter 23.

43. Frederic Shoberi, ed., *Hindoostan* (Rupa, 2006), 142–44, 475.

44. Peter Lamont, *The Rise of the Indian Rope Trick: How a Spectacular Hoax Became History* (Abacus, 2004).

45. Charles Allen, *Plain Tales from the Raj: Images of British India in the Twentieth Century* (Abacus, 1994), 193.

46. Niccolao Manucci, *Storia do Mogor, Or, Mogul India 1653–1708*, Vol. II (Alpha Editions, 2020), 192.

47. Ibid., 188–89.

48. Ibid.

49. William Wilson Hunter, *The Old Missionary* (H. Frowde, 1897).

50. Ibid.

51. Dadabhai Naoroji, *Poverty and Un-British Rule in India* (Swan Sonnenschein, 1901), 204.

Index

A Ballad of the Bawarchikhana, 227

A Brief History of the Indian Peoples, 324

A Defence of Hindu Idolatry, 101

Adventures of Qui Hi, 121

A History of Jaipur, 34

Ain-i-Akbari, 30, 171

Akbar, Jalaluddin, 2–7, 9
    Akbar, 2–7, 19, 30–31, 92
    Emperor, 16, 18, 21, 29

Alaler Gharey Dulal, 104

Alam, Shah, 133, 138, 148–49

Album, Fraser, 132

Allahabadi, Akbar, 307, 314

Allen, Charles, 47, 113, 144, 170, 197, 221, 262–63, 278–79, 297

Altman, James, 142

Amrita Bazar Patrika, 306, 311

Ananga Ranga, 172

Anglo-Indian Defence Association, 248

Anglo-Indian Mutiny, The, 248

Anglo-Indian, xv, 59, 106, 118, 127, 175, 178, 189, 216, 225, 248, 253, 256, 265

Anglo-Indians, xv, 106, 192, 254, 256, 259, 261, 263, 265–66, 276

Annals and Antiquities of Rajasthan, 76

Annals of Rural Bengal, 324

Annual Register, 120

Arab-Moor Muslims, 59

Asian Researches, 321

Asiatic Journal of Bengal, 158

Atharva Veda, 5

Atlantic Monthly, 272

Auckland, Lord, 74, 137, 167

Auliya, Shaikh Nizamuddin, 6, 29

Aurangzeb, 8, 11–19, 22, 36, 38, 44, 46, 59, 66, 91, 119, 147–53, 322–23

A Vocabulary in Two Parts, 99

Bahmani Sultanate, 50

Bandel, 30

Bandopadhyay
    Bhavanicharan, 129
    Krishnamohan, 94

Banerjee, Sumanta, 74, 128, 208, 231, 235, 293

'Bapoo Sahib,' 82

Barwell, Richard, 74

Battle of Buxar, 70

Bay of Bengal, 51

Beames, John, 172, 178, 215, 245

Bebinca cake, 59

Begum, Mulka, 140, 142

Begum, Roshan Ara, 59–60

Bengal Army, 113, 138, 189–90, 259

Bengal Club, 261, 265

Bengal Gazette, 185–86
Bengali, 311
Bernier, Francois, 318
Besant, Annie, 310
Beveridge, Henry, 102
Bhar, Gopal, 8–9, 11
Bharat Jiwan, 281
Bharat Mitra, 311
Bhonsales of Nagpur, 75
Biden, George, 145
Biden, Joe, 145
Biden, Joseph Robinette, 145
Birbal, 2–4, 9
Bishop of Oxford, 73
Black Hole, 68, 123, 157–58, 312
Board of Revenue, 243, 253
Bombay Duck, 108
Bombay establishment, 130
Bombay Natural History Society,
    217
Bonaparte, Napoleon, 75
Boyd, Hugh, 206
Brahmo Samaj, 101, 282
British
    dispensation, 73
    empire, 105, 267
    Foreign Bible Society, 135
    India, 87
    library, 132
    officer, 25
    parliament, 319
    policy, 79
    Raj, 19, 267, 296
    rule, 1, 27, 71, 90, 95, 100,
        106, 161, 171, 184, 234,
        251, 299
    traders, 129
    victory, 165, 215
British Life in India, 198
British Magazine and Review, 126
Budaq Beg, 147
Burke, Edmund, 134, 156, 160, 185
Burnell, Arthur, 118, 175
Byculla Club, 261, 266

Calcutta
    authorities, 130
    culture, 128
    female school, 103
    Missionary Conference, 281
Calcutta Gazette, 112, 187, 193,
    197, 208, 241–42
Carey, William, 99, 101
Chakar Darpan, 307
Chambers's Edinburgh Journal, 63
Charnock, Job, 66, 131
Charter Act, 86
Chattopadhyay, Bankim Chandra,
    106, 282
Chaudhuri, Rosinka, 90, 93,
    95–96, 104, 314
Chawri Bazar, 139
Christie, Agatha, 176
Church Missionary Society, 130
'City of Dreadful Night,' 103
Clive, Robert, 70
Collingham, Lizzie, 57, 59, 89,
    109, 113
Commonwealth War Graves
    Commission, 280
Company rule, 98, 246
*Comparative Grammar of the
    Modern Aryan Languages of
    India,* 172, 252
Contagious Diseases Act of 1868,
    127
Coote, Eyre, 99
Croke, Frances, 142
Crooke, William, 273
Curry and Rice, 275
Curzon, Lord, 130, 232, 303, 313
Curzon's Council, 126

Dacres Lane, 130
Dahlawi, Amir Khusrau, 19
Damarla Venkatadri Nayaka, 149
Das, Anish, 176
Das, Kabir, 20
Das, Mahesh, 2

Dastanubuy, 25
David Drummond Dharamtala
    Academy, 93
Dawe's, W.H., 114
Day, Francis, 149
*Decline and Fall of the Roman
    Empire,* 93
Dharma Pustaka, 100
Dilkhoosha, 136
Dirks, Nicholas, 71, 155
Diwan-i-Aam, 89
Diwan of Khwaja Hafiz, 78
Doolaly Syndrome, 125–31
Doyley, Charles, 222
Driver, Maud, 197, 225
Dubois, J.H. Valentin, 208
Duke of Goa, 51
Duke of Wellington, 74, 165, 176

East India Company, 12, 31, 34,
    36, 40, 43, 59–60, 65–66, 69,
    71, 74–75, 86, 92, 99, 112–13,
    138, 142, 145, 149, 158, 164,
    186, 190, 204–05, 237, 250,
    305
Eaton, Richard, 50
Echoes from Old Calcutta, 211
*Economic History of India Under
    British Rule,* 305–06
Eczema, 195
Eden, Emily, 137, 168, 212
Edinburgh Review, 93
Elliot, H.M., 103
English Education Act, 98

Fatehpur Sikri, 4, 30
Fay, Eliza, 108, 212
Fazl, Abul, 2, 4, 5
First World War, 191, 261, 265, 280
Forbes, James, 121
Forster, H.P., 99, 100
Fragments of the Mughal Empire,
    92
Francis, Philip, 161

Freedom and Beefsteaks, 104
French Revolution, 63, 160
Friend of India, 101, 248, 278, 282
Fryer, John, 12, 36–39, 41–42, 44,
    56–57, 61–62, 64, 119, 205,
    316–17

Gaekwad Darpan, 307
Gandhi, Mohandas Karamchand,
    27, 97
Gardner, James, 140
Gazette, 183, 185
Geeta, 99
Ghalib and the British, 23
Gilmour, David, 86, 102, 130, 136,
    146, 192, 229, 246, 261, 284,
    300
Gladstone, William, 169, 284
God save the King, 294
Graham, J.M., 226, 260
Great War, 280
Grierson, George, 172
Gupta, Bal Mukund, 312
Guzishta Lucknow, 118
Gwalior, 76

Hakeems, 136
Haldar, Rakhal, 107
Hastings, Warren, 18, 72–73,
    88, 123, 160–61, 163, 183,
    185–86, 236, 239, 243
Hawkins, Francis, 167
Hawkins, John, 60
Heber, Amelia, xi, xvii, xix–xx, 87,
    120
Heber, Bishop, xi–xxii, 23, 83, 87,
    89, 120–21, 138, 166, 255
Heber, Emily, xi, xiii, 87
Hedges, William, 131
Hibbert, Christopher, 111
Hickey, William, 111, 134, 187, 240
Hicky, James Augustus, 88, 182
Hicky's Bengal Gazette, 88, 183, 234
Hijli island, 69

Hindi Punch, 308, 311
Hindoo Patriot, 303
Hindu, 306
Hindu rule, 95
History of the Sepoy War, 270
Hitopadesha, 99–100
*Hobson-Johnson: A Glossary of
    Colloquial Anglo-Indian Words
    and Phrases*, 118
Hohlee songs, 80
Hooghly river, 18, 149
How India Wrought Her Freedom,
    310
Howrah Bridge, 246
Hughes, Robert, 36, 197
Hunter, William, 72, 324
Hussain, Imam, 175

Ibbetson, Denzil, 126
Illustrated London News, 85, 272,
    314
Imperial Gazetteer of India, 171
India Gazette, 185
Indian Army, 50
Indian Civil Service, 18, 169
Indian Cookery, 106, 114
Indian culture, 98
Indian Ink, 176
Indian National Congress, 105,
    292, 306
Indian Observer, 171, 252
Indian Penal Code, 127, 282
Ispahani, Haji, 90
Itihasamala, 100
Ivermee, Robert, 30, 53, 91

Jacquemont, Victor, 117, 131
Jadoo-ka-chukkur, 81
Jafar, Nawab Mir, 69
Jahan, Shah, 6–8, 12, 18–19, 54,
    62, 78, 118–19, 148–49, 272
Jahangir, 6, 12, 18–19, 29, 31,
    33–34, 41, 54, 74, 78, 84–85,
    172

Jahangir, Mirza, 89
Jain temples, 12, 92
Jam-i-Jumsheed, 180–81
Jamuna river, 3, 165
Jasanoff, Maya, 156, 191
Jawami al-Kalim, 6
Jenkinson, Charles, 143
Jenkinson, Robert, 143
Johnson, Begum, 142–43
Johnson, Samuel, 160, 284
*Journal of Travels to Arabia and
    the East*, 108
'Juggut Gooroo', 18

Kalima, 4, 20
Kalinga Bazar, 130
Kama Sutra, 172
Kanwar, Pamela, 232
Keay, John, 72, 158
Keene, H.G., 144
Khan, Alivardi, 68, 92
Khan, Daud, 152
Khan, Fazil, 77
Khan, Jafar, 15, 35
Khan, Murshid Quli, 91–92
Khan, Saadat Ali, 88
Kincaid, Dennis, 123, 216
*Kindred Terms, Etymological,
    Historical, Geographical and
    Discursive*, 118, 175
King George III, 143
Kipling, Rudyard, 103, 194–95,
    200, 283, 326
Kistna river, 164
Kohinoor, 312
Kollur mines, 63, 151
Kulliyat-i-Mir, 100
Kuveers, 80

Lays of Ind, 122, 220
Lear, Edward, 115
Lipimala, 100
Lisbon's Targus river, 49
Lodi, Sikandar, 29

London *Times*, 145
Lyall, Alfred, 171, 173
Lyallpur Club, 265

Macaulay, Thomas Babington, 97
Mackintosh, William, 209
Mackrabie, Alexander, 109, 158
MacMillan, Margaret, 115, 220,
    222, 285
Mahmud, Nasiruddin, 6
Manohar Kahaniyan, 27
Manucci, Niccolao, 8, 147
Maratha
    camp, 208
    force, 165
    leaders, 17
    Punch, 308
    ruler, 75
Marshall, P.J., 17
Mason, Philip, 258, 275, 290
Matwala, 313
Memoirs of a Bengal Civilian, 267
Mill, James, 85
Minute on Education, 98
Mishra, Surya Narayan, 90
Mitra, Gobindaram, 234
Monson, George, 192, 236
Moxham, Roy, 55, 65, 204
Mughal
    authority, 17, 44
    court, 134
    dress, 138
    empire, 29, 32, 34, 52–53, 66,
        75, 99, 138, 156
    mission, 150
    protocol, 148
    rule, 11, 22, 24, 59
    ruler, 138
    succession politics, 136
Muharram processions, 38
Muir, William, 172, 270
Mukhopadhyay, Bhudev, 96–97
Munro, Thomas, 86
Muntakhabut Tawarikh, 2

Naga hills, 172
Nair, P. Thankappan, 136
Naoroji, Dadabhai, 325
Narayan, Udai, 91
National Gallery of Ireland, 135
Naval Kishore Press, 27
Neill, James, 270
Niebuhr, C., 108
Norman, Jesse, 68–69

Ochterlony Monument, 133
Oriental Club, 106
Oriental Fabulist, 100
Orme, Robert, 92, 119
Oudh Punch, 307
Ovington, John, 42, 59, 62, 64, 96
Ovington, Thomas, 189
*Oxford Dictionary of National
    Biography*, 137

'Palm Song', 248
Paradise Lost, 271
Paramahansa, Ramakrishna, 96
Parker, Henry Meredith, 96
Parker, John, 36
Peninsular wars, 143
Perlin, Frank, 164
Peshwas of Pune, 75
Pioneer, 287
Polo, Marco, 35, 46, 48, 84, 316
*Popular Jokes and Political
    History: The Case of Akbar,
    Birbal and Mulla Do-Piyaza*, 3
Portuguese rule, 51, 55–56
Pott, Robert, 134
Prem Sagar, 100
Pukka Sahib, 136
Purusha Pariksha, 100
Pythagorean theory of
    transmigration of souls, 37

Qutub al-Aqtab Shah Daulat, 4

Rabb-ul aal-ameen, 6

Raja Protapaditya Charita, 100
Rama, Tenali, 8–11
Ramayan, 100
Ramlochan, Raja, 88
Rani of Jhansi, 179, 274, 276
Rao, Daulat, 79, 81
Rao, Surjee, 82–83
Ray, Kishen, 92
Raychaudhuri, Tapan, 97
Reinhardt, Joseph, 138
Richard Temple, 19
Ripon's Council, 105
Robb, Peter, 243
Robbins, Nick, 66
Rohilla war, 185
Rolling home to dear old Blighty, 125
Roy, Raja Rammohun, 100–101
Royal Asiatic Society, 76, 172
Russell, Ralph, 24

Sahib, Chanda, 69
Sakuntala, 99
Samachar Darpan, 125, 242
Samajik Prabhanda, 96
Samru, Walter, 138
'Samru ki Begum', 138
Sastri, Sibnath, 95
Saturday Magazine, 85
Scindia, Daulat Rao, 23, 75
Scindia camp, 76
Sen, Ballal, 128
Sen, Keshub Chandra, 122, 282, 289
Seven Grammars of the Dialects and Subdialects of the Bihari Language, 172
Shah, Alam, 138
Shah, Bahadur, 17
Shah, Ibrahim, 51
Shah, Nadir, 17, 67–68, 137
Shah, Yusuf Adil, 50
Shakuntala, 303
Shamsud-Daula of Dhaka, 87

Shikoh, Dara, 6–7, 11, 147
Shore, F.J., 123
Simla Club, 298
Sind Club, 261
Sind desert, 5
Singh, Man, 4
Siyar al-Awliya, 6
Skinner of Skinner's Horse, 258
Spanish Empire, 73
Star Theatre, 129
Suez Canal, 125, 130
Sultan, Tipu, 76
Suri, Sher Shah, 5, 29, 52

Tagore, Debendranath, 101
Taimur, Amir, 29
Tanjore royal family, 175
Tavares, Pedro, 30
Taylor, William, 212
Tazkirat al-Umara, 259
Telegu folk literature, 8–9
Terry, Edward, 117
Terry, Richard, 106
Thapar, Romila, 45
'The Anglo-Indian Mutiny', 248
The Ballad of East and West, 202
The British Conquest and Dominion of India, 173
The East India Vade Mecum, 136
The Enchantress of the Cave, 93
The Englishman, 248, 273, 278
The Englishwoman in India, 197, 225
The History of British India, 85, 93
The Illustrated London News, 272, 314
The Indian Gentleman's Guide to Etiquette, 262
The Ladies, 326
The Land of Regrets, 171, 173
The Nabob, 160
The Naughty Nautch, 122
The Old Pindaree, 102
The Police of Pig and Sheep, 283

The Rights of Woman 254
The Sahibs, 275
The Shrine of the 'Baba-Log', 221
The Spectator, 269
The Times, 300
*The Trial of Maharaja Nanda
    Kumar: A Narrative of a
    Judicial Murder,* 172, 239
The Tutor, 99
The Weatherbys, 182
The Wife's Help to Indian Cookery,
    114
Third battle of Panipat, 68
Times, 66, 145, 168, 270–71, 324
Times of India, 289
Tirumala temple, 86
Tommkyns, Madeline, 144
*Translation of an Abridgement of
    the Vedanta,* 101
*Travels in India in the Seventeenth
    Century,* 36
Travels of Fray Sebastien Manrique,
    52
Tughlaq, Feroze Shah, 6
Tughlaq, Muhammad bin, 84
Tuhfat-ul-Muwahhdin, 100
Turkish baths, 126
Tuzuk-i-Jahangiri, 172

Upanishads, 7, 100

Vaishyoparak, 313
Vakil-ul-Mutlaq, 75

Vanity Fair, 19, 112
Vedanta Chandrika, 101
Vedanta Grantha, 101
Vedantasar, 101
Vernede, R.V., 38
Vidyakalpadrum, 94
Vidyalankar, Mrityunjoy, 101
Vijayanagara Empire, 46
Vikata Kavi, 9

Wahab, Qazi Abdul, 13, 323–24
Wahdah al-wajud, 6
War of Spanish Succession, 73
Watts, William, 142
Wavell, Lord, 170
Wellesley, Richard, 74, 135
Willingdon Sports Club, 266

Xavier, Francis, 55–56

Yacht Club, 266
Yale, Elihu, 150
Yeldham, Walter, 114, 122
Young Bengal movement, 103
Yule, George, 192
Yule, Henry, 118, 175
Yusufzai tribes, 4

Zafar, Bahadur Shah, 22, 24, 136,
    273
Zakhmi Dil, 279
Zephaniah, John, 157–58, 235